THE MATERIAL OF INVENTION

Originally published under the title:
LA MATERIA DELL'INVENZIONE

Mauro Panzeri: Art Director
Marcella Cannalire: Graphics
Dario Moretti: Re-writer
Doretta Cecchi: Editorial Assistant

© Copyright 1986 Arcadia srl, Milano
© Copyright 1986 Progetto Cultura Montedison, Milano

First MIT Press edition, 1989

First English edition
1986, Arcadia srl, Milano

Antony Shugaar: Translator
Raffaella Mortara: Editorial Coordinator
Charles-Henri Pesso Besson: Editorial Advisor

Printed and bound in Italy

ISBN 0- 262-13242-7

Library of Congress Catalog Card Number 88-063574

THE MATERIAL
OF INVENTION

by   Ezio   Manzini

with a Preface by **François Dagognet**

with the contribution of

Pasquale Cau, Leonardo Fiore, Giuseppe Gianotti
Materials and Technology
Alberto Meda, Denis Santachiara
Design Aspects

The MIT Press
Cambridge, Massachusetts

9113

MIT   BE/PP.

Translations, Benedetto Croce once coyly put it, are like women – if they are beautiful, they are not faithful, and vice versa.

Perhaps this translation of *The Material of Invention* is neither. Certainly its virtue has been severely tested by the strange hybrid nature of the original language. The Italian does not belong to any specific technical area; nor does it follow the style typical of scientific or engineering texts.

Given the anomalous quality of the language, the English translation inevitably hovers in a strange limbo between standard usage and attempts at parallel invention.

Moreover, there are some difficulties in rendering certain Italian design terms – such as *progetto*, a lovely portmanteau word that means both "design" and "engineering." The English word "design," in turn, is used in Italian to mean something akin to industrial design. Italian blithely refers to design and technical "cultures," "themes," and "areas" with greater ease than English. Some of the oddness – such as the perhaps excessive use of "resistant" and "resistance," where "strong" or "strength" would have been preferable in English – correspond to a decision to emphasize the active nature of the qualities in question.

I hope, at any rate, that the translation is at least serviceable, and that it does not interfere with the comprehension of this remarkably – and typically Italian – examination of the rapid and radical metamorphosis of a familiar world.

Thanks are due to my co-translator, **Mary Scipione**, who rendered with grace the *Exercises of Invention*.

I would have been lost in a sea of technical perplexities without the advice of **Silvia Silvers**, **Charles-Henri Pesso Besson**, and **Francesco Di Renzo**.

Raffaella Mortara and **Anna Bruno Ventre** have patiently suffered my errors, delays, and bad jokes.

Jeanne Chapman turned an Italian bibliography into an English one, which sounds far easier than it is.

One last notation – I have intentionally translated the recurrent Italian phrase "vice versa," as "contrariwise," rather than using its English synonym. The term is clearly outdated, but it is an offhand reference to two literary figures from the last century – Tweedledee and Tweedledum. For this book, in its way, takes us on a voyage through a (polymethylmethacrylate) looking glass.

Antony Shugaar

To write a book is not only a long and complex matter, it is also emotionally involving. The commitment required is such that it exceeeds any purely professional attitude and invades a few months of one's life so as to follow its moments of enthusiasm but also its moments of depression and exasperation.

Never, I believe, would the task have been completed without the friendship of those who worked with me. But apart from the friends, mentioned by right for their contributions, I want to thank all of those who, with different roles helped make this volume possible and have been able to solve both small and big problems with good humour.

In particular: **Dario Moretti**, who has maintained his wits after spending weeks and months in front of the word processor revising the rather approximate texts which I gave him; **Marcella Cannalire**, who has maintained her capacity to smile in spite of the exasperating graphic difficulties of this volume; and **Mauro Panzeri**, who has given an image to the product, and helped me understand, through his witty and cunning remarks, that a book is not just an aggregate of texts and figures.

Particular thanks are due to **Roberto Coizet** who, beyond his role of publisher, has probably been my main advisor, to the point of becoming an ally or a friend, as the need arose.

Lastly, thanks go to **Antony Shugaar**, who struggled manfully to give meaning – in his own language – to the thoughts I have attempted to express.

It should be added that the volume would not exist if **Patrizia Scarzella** had not taken the first step which set into motion the complex machine that eventually produced this work. To her, therefore, I express my thanks.

Finally, it is customary for an author, with something like a family, to thank those who are dearest to him for their understanding, as they let him work without creating too many problems. I always thought of this as being a ritual. I changed my mind: those who are closest to me demonstrated an exceptional capacity to endure my work neurosis of the past months. For this I thank them with all my heart.

E.M.

"The material of invention" stems from a research project which has involved a consistent number of people and institutions.

Progetto Cultura Montedison was the catalyzing element throughout the research project, and provided the material for this volume.

Montedipe's "*Centro Sviluppo Settori Impiego*" (C.S.I.) provided its long-term experience on plastics and composite materials, and the background of technical information.

Pasquale Alferj and *Roberto Coizet* together with the author, made the feasibility study of the project and established the broad lines of the resulting editorial venture.

Pasquale Cau (director of C.S.I.), *Alberto Meda* (designer and member of the teaching staff of the Domus Academy), *Denis Santachiara* (designer), formed the team that developed the research and contributed with their individual experiences to the editing of the volume.

Leonardo Fiore and *Giuseppe Gianotti* (respectively in charge of and assistant for the Material Science sector of the Istituto G. Donegani, Novara) have contributed as scientific advisors. They also wrote: "Designing Matter. Polimers and Composites".

Maarten Kusters and *Marco Susani* (research staff of the Domus Academy, designers) have contributed to the research, to the evaluation and organization of the documentation. Work was done in the ambient of *Domus Academy*, and was partly based on observation developed there about the relationship between technical evolution and design culture.

Apart from those, mentioned above, who contributed to the whole of the volume, a number of experts have provided important contributions on specific topics.

In particular:
Diana Castiglione (director of Plastic Consult, Milan) has repeatedly provided precious advice and indications on many of the topics dealt with.

Renzo Marchelli (director of *Materie Plastiche ed Elastomeri*) participated in a number of meetings, lending his vast experience as a publicist of technical matters.

Significant and specific contributions were provided by:

Giuseppe Airoldi Montefluos
Marco Binaghi Vedril
Roberta Braglia Istituto Donegani
Benedetto Calcagno Pirelli
Sauro Casadei Tecnomax
Giulio Castelli Kartell
Alberto Cazzaniga Raychem
Remo Cervi C.S.I., Montedipe
Marc Ciget Euroconsult
Ivano Colpani Bayer
Luigi Corbelli Dutral
Claudio Cremaschi Monfrini
Arturo Fiocca
General Electric Plastics Italia
Mauro Fregola Bayer
Natale Macchi B Ticino
Bernardo Maggi Mazzucchelli
Massimo Majowiecki
Università di Bologna
Liberto Massarelli SIV
Stefano Napoli C.S.I., Montedipe
Angelo Pellissero C.S.I., Montedipe
Marco Piana C.S.I., Montedipe
Piero Roccaro Alfa Romeo
Tullo Ronchetti Vedril
Ermanno Rotondi Agusta
Elio A. Savi Sinel
Fulvio Scaglioti Dutral
Fabio Scamoni C.S.I., Montedipe
Carlo Sempio Vedril
Camillo Tosi Istituto Donegani
Giorgio Vittadini C.S.I., Montedipe
Claudio Zarotti Sonda

Numerous designers contributed by developing design-sketches purposely for this volume. They are:

Nicholas Bewick
Sergio Calatroni
Anna Castelli Ferrieri
Clino Castelli
Piero Castiglioni
Piero Gatti
Perry King and Santiago Miranda
Alberto Meda/Denis Santachiara
Davide Mercatali
Richard Montoro
Massimo Morozzi
Francesco Murano
Nautilus
Franco Raggi
Cinzia Ruggeri
Hagai Shvadron
Studio De Pas D'Urbino Lomazzi
Marco Susani

TABLE OF CONTENTS

9

Preface

by François Dagognet

Reading The Material of Invention *is like being invited to a celebration of technology and science. Perhaps it would have been more appropriate to ask a poet to accept the honor of writing this introduction. It would have been easy enough to find him, if one had gone looking, but what a mountain of difficulties he would have had to overcome!*

If we stop to think, European literature has been too preoccupied with confessions, sociology, or fanciful narration to pay any attention to things, materials, and their richness. It has been swallowed up in the abysses of subjectivity. And since one must continually replenish oneself, European literature has continued down that slope that leads to delirium, to the purely imaginary, and extravagance of all sorts.

Few writers, over the ages and recently, have found it seemly to speak about wood, earth, leather, or stone. Similarly, the structures of metal, or rubber, or fibers, have been overlooked. Materials were useful, at the outside, as elements of scenery in which to portray other events. We should assuredly not make blanket statements. At least one contemporary author should be quoted and examined in this context – Francis Ponge.
*Ponge rejected ordinary lyricism and "has allied himself with objects." He has reminded man of the ties that bind him to the Cosmos. He has rehabilitated the objective (pebbles, loaves, oysters, and so on). A remarkable and memorable exception? Alain Robbe-Grillet (*Pour un nouveau roman, *series "Idées," Gallimard) still accuses him of anthropomorphism, saying that Ponge "thinks more with objects than about them."*

And so man began with himself. He has shut himself up in his own prison. Let us appeal without delay, therefore, to materialogical books (such as The Material of Invention*), to free us from ourselves and to acquaint us with the heart of metals, ceramics, and glass. It*

amazes one to see that so many skillful writers have forgotten or obscured even the tools with which they write – smooth white paper, the ink that they set on that paper, the delicate pens with which they labor. Each of these three tools (medium, trace, utensil) have undergone important changes, an evolution that will eventually eliminate them, and for now tends to whittle away at their substance, but the general fascination with the ego reaches such extremes that a writer fails to take into consideration the very things that allow him to write. The tools of production do not enter the act of production. In this exclusion, we see the sign of a tendency to scorn ways and means, marching onward toward immateriality, drawing a line between thinkers and the real laborers.

We shall be promptly informed that poets or novelists have paid scanty attention to their tools because they were taken with the pursuit of a grander and more noble aim, such as the life and conflicts of society, the condition and tragedies of man. How could we be bothered with parchment and quills?

It is here, however, that we went wrong, that we mystified the situation (typical error of the idealist). Man cannot free himself alone. He must turn to "objects" for assistance, even if they are "miserable objects." Humanitarian struggles are never as successful as technological innovations, even though those innovations have been overlooked or underestimated. It is these innovations that change our lives, the work we do, the cities we live in, our vehicles or actions. We see little more than the foam on the surface.

We admit that a few writers escape our embittered reproach. Artists – painters, potters, sculptors – have instead generally managed to sidestep the impasse. They have celebrated, after their fashion, the ingredients, new textures, arrangements, or impasto. Nevertheless, much like a craftsman, they have chosen to devote themselves to creating, rather than to commentary through the word. Once again, materiality has been left without an interlocutor.

Worse yet – not only has the new received scanty notice or celebration, it has often been outright denigrated. Thus, in order to provide an instance of this contempt, suffice it to open to a passage in which the late and brilliant Roland Barthes lambasts plastics: "Despite names that would suit a Greek shepherd (polystyrene, phenoplast, polyvinyl, polyethylene)... this is a graceless material, lost between the exuberance of rubber and the flat hardness of metal... And what betrays it still more is the sound it emits, at once empty and flat; its noise undoes it as do its colors, for it seems capable of acquiring only the most chemical colors; it retains only the most aggressive forms of yellow, red, and green" ("Le Plastique", in Mythologies, 1957). And the "j'accuse" does not end here.

In the past, wood was held up as an example, "a familiar and poetic substance that maintains a continuous link with the tree... Wood does not break, it wears." Plastic cracks or shatters. It communicates a chilly sensation. Inalterable, insensible, and sleek (it could never acquire a patina), plastic remains aloof and extraneous.

Other examples? We have yet to drink from plastic goblets, easy to deform and murky as they are. We still prefer luminous, transparent, solid glass. Plastics could not usurp the domain of glass over precious flagons containing liqueurs, scents, or perfumes. Indeed, plastics are used to package only common and cheap merchandise. At least this is the recurring theme in the cries of essayists taking part in a sort of hunting party. It goes without saying that The Material of Invention takes quite the opposite tack. This is why we consider it such an original and refreshing book.

To be fair, let us add that the biting criticism we cite above was an assault on the first halting efforts of a newborn material, still maladroit and rude. This material, however, far more vital and adaptable than anyone supposed, has developed greatly and now throws its critics into confusion. Let us therefore desist from these futile remarks.

The Material of Invention does more than to reverse – at last! – a cultural approach, and to endow matter with speech (logos), as it

were. It also helps us to redefine matter. Matter has always been thought of in a unilateral and negative fashion. In what way? Matter is depicted through its heaviness, its inevitable thickness, its hardness, in other words, its inertia. Recently, it has been described as black, filthy, and sticky, since the underlying chemistry is closely linked with carbon (hence, coal and hydrocarbons). Let us point out at once that, luckily, silicone was about to play an increasingly important role, as was gallium arsenide and – through them – electronics, information processing, solar energy, telecommunications, fiber optics, semiconductors, generating in turn a metamorphosis of industry, factories, and society. Indeed, it is now impossible to refer to one of these areas without involving the others.

As an immediate and parallel result, The Material of Invention revises our vocabulary. Thus, matter itself loses what most typified it. Unleashing a true conceptual and semantic revolution, the book illustrates and singles out this matter, through inconfutable demonstrations, in all its lightness, subtlety, and "sensitivity," but also in its incorruptibility and solidity – despite and amidst its tenuousness.

The unitary formula begins to lose ground, now that matter manages to fuse the "almost imponderable" with toughness. (The thinnest sail in the world will weigh a mere 2.75 kilograms for an area of 250 sq.m. This sail will be used to power trimarans in competitions such as the America's Cup. Moreover, it will not deform, and it withstands the assaults of wind or bursts of water like sheet metal. It is frail but, at the same time, hard.)

Not only has matter acquired the opposite characteristics to those it had just yesterday, but it associates the most contradictory qualities. Matter loses its old heaviness, its bulky volume, while increasing its resistance and force. Or, in another instance of an unthinkable marriage, matter combines weldability in objects with total impermeability or else slight pliability with an ability to absorb extremely violent shocks (in shields) with total resistance to distortion and a capacity to regain its original state. In short, unions of that which had always been considered incompatible (the coincidentia oppositorum).

Our imaginary adversary, beating us to the punch, will certainly find ways of dampening the enthusiasm that The Material of Invention has generated. He may point out that metals have already enjoyed success in this area. Aluminum, for instance, married lightness to strength, he may say. The fact is that our adversaries are attempting to discount the importance of the revolution, which is to deny its existence. Much trouble for nothing – the materials of today outpace, from all points of view, those of yesterday. Carbon-fiber epoxy-resin composites are at least 50 percent lighter than corresponding aluminum-based materials, leaving aside questions of cost, or – above all – the corrosion resistance with respect to all sorts of agents, or product life span, or resistance, or the economic freedom that is created. Must we then give up metals and metallurgy for "dead?" Not at all – and we shall soon see why.

Change flies so fast, however, that the resistance now comes from society, from our habits, and our excessively repetitious manufacturing structures. Matter outstrips the spirit! Who would have predicted this? What a turning of tables! And so cultural theorists and essayists must help us to give up our attachments and enter the modern world (hindered as we are by the delay of our mentalities). What fate – without their assistance – awaits creators, designers, and architects? The fate of working with intermediate forms and limiting their daring. Our imagination deserves to be freed of its stereotypes, so that materiality can take free flight.

As a last resource, our adversary may retort with what he considers a cutting objection – perhaps the ingredients have changed, but certainly the object is the same. A lamp is still a lamp, and a vacuum cleaner is still a vacuum cleaner. Nothing could be further from the truth.

First off, one cannot separate an object from its constituent parts so easily, that is, one cannot easily separate significance from signifier, to use the terms of The Material of Invention, which could just as well have been entitled The Invention of Material. Secondly, one must admit and think in terms of a "unitary system," because the modification of one provokes the modification of the other. Thus, when the vacuum cleaner in question was made of wood or tin or metal, it required a fairly powerful engine to operate. Hence, a heavy, bulky, cumbersome piece of equipment. The same would be true of a hair-dryer or a coffee grinder! Synthetic materials, however, have transformed and rendered dynamic the electro-household, making it easier to manage, more powerful, and less costly – while the "form"

better weds itself to the "function," because the malleable and even moldable constituent parts lend themselves to the imagination of the designer. A lighter, subtler material tends to be slightly eclipsed, absorbed by the task to be performed. Hence we find a simplified product with flowing, direct lines. This is the birth of industrial esthetics, an art of creating frameworks and bodies for familiar objects. This use of new methods turned factories and merchandising upside down, and saved them from ugliness and bombast. The objection, cited above, to the degree of importance of the constituent parts no long holds, since everything is altered at the same time. The steam iron with the domineering appearance, which overwhelms with its steam even the most rebellious linen, a simple square or round wash basin made of polyethylene that eliminates the weight and the noise that once accompanied each minor impact – both confer upon the kitchen the look of a laboratory and at the same time a sense of ease. We should not be hoodwinked by nostalgia for the good old days and envy for our grandparents, who actually lived badly and amidst fatigue.

In passing, let us essay a hypothesis. Ornamentation, which cheers a piece of furniture or a utensil, could take on a compensatory role. Wood or stone or metal are all bound to non-miniaturization, to large size, and at times to immobility, and a certain static quality. One could eliminate this excess of presence and bulk by means of decoration, sleek lines that run across the surface, lightening it. Modern appliances, to come back to them, possess a striking degree of sobriety, morphological economy (design), and strict composition – an architecture of lightness, another paradox to add to the series!

Let us speak of another innovation that helps us to grasp the importance of "with what," which determines, in reality, "what." Let us not reduce this to the level of a simple system or a variable! The gas tank in new cars is made of high-density extruded blown polyethylene; hence it lends itself to a vast range of forms and can fit into the tightest corners, alongside the engine or other accessories. The gas tank is no longer made of tin plate, which had to be welded at a high cost. It used to take up a great deal of space, contributed to the weight of the vehicle; now, every increase in volume or density corresponds – as the logic of the whole requires – to higher fuel consumption and a reduction in the car's aerodynamic qualities. We could go on practically without end in listing the disadvantages of an autonomous component that does not fit in entirely with the others. A supple material, which slinks in among its neighbors and incorporates itself with them, permits unity, hence speed and even harmony. So let's not have any more down-playing! We tend to disassociate too much the duo of significance/signifier, form/ingredient, when the former is made possible by the latter. Matter is the true "soul" of the vehicle. The body rues all (performance and allure). Let us learn to think in terms of this symbiosis.

This is difficult and will continue to be, because our entire culture leads us in the opposite direction, and has done so ever since the Greeks first formulated their physics and philosophy, since Plato and above all Aristotle. They worked on examples such as a statue or an amphora or a goblet, whether made of alabaster, stone, wood, stucco, or even gold. The only thing that counted was appearance, the figure, or the "form." As for the component parts, they could vary according to circumstances, availability, or commissions. The idea existed – invariable – outside and beyond what incarnated it. The modern world of manufacturing, however, the world revealed to us by The Material of Invention, leads us far from the ancient situation of craftsmen (sculptors, potters, ceramists) and, as we have seen, now imposes total manufacturing unity: "of material, process, product, and engine."

We have touched on the most important themes of The Material of Invention, in our manner. Enthralled by the volume, we feel that we must accord current materiality, so well recognized and celebrated, three characteristics that render it original.

1) First of all, it incessantly recreates itself before our eyes. It emancipates itself by joining the qualities of this or that component – nearby or distant – in order to create blends that at times are, strangely, superior in quality to their constituent parts.

Under these conditions, the belief in a material that is always the same, always imprisoned in its own limited substantiality, as it were, begins to disappear. After all, how we reproached it for its inertia and sameness!

What the proofs, the illustrations, the victories? Our universe hands them out generously. So that glass can be joined to plastic in the windshield of a car. There it stands, transparent, but it can no longer cut when it breaks. This paste glass shatters into a thousand bits or, at the worst, collapses in powder. It has been possible to preserve the translucence of silicate while depriving it of its thorn (injuries). It was simply associated to a soft tissue.

Likewise, one can inject air bubbles or gas bubbles into a polyester bath. The bath emerges clearly lightened, more "swollen," and above all with better thermal insulation. We can decide freely to thicken or flatten it, to undulate it or foam it. We can give it new properties, including "sensory" properties (soft to the touch, no longer rough).

It is possible to assemble not only what is different, but also what is similar, such as in ABS (this abbreviation indicates the combination of acrylonitrile, butadiene, and styrene). Generally, the properties of these blends vary according to proportions, as does the type of bond. Molecules can be united by chance or in a regular sequence (polymer sequences). Thus the demiurge of these alliances (the celebrated composites) can freely use three parameters, which allow him to modulate the nature of the units, their quantity, and their associations.

One of the most frequent and the happiest of marriages is that between the old and the new: cotton or wool or silk with a synthetic (viscose or nylon, for instance). One (natural) is costly, wears out rapidly, dries slowly, can be attacked by parasites, and frays. The other, which costs little to manufacture, basically eliminates these inconveniences. Let's weave them, knit them, unite them!

At an ordinary and everyday level, let us take a look at the wood that they sell us in the stores: chipboard, plywood, fillet. We exult. What is this stuff? Here we are talking about a mix of glue or adhesive with sawdust (chipboard) or else with very light laths of wood (arranged herring-bone in one version, aligned parallel in another). The old material has not been shown the door, but reorganized, if not actually corrected. It used to bend easily, it endured fatigue and bent; it was sensitive to humidity; it flaked terribly. Now it does not expand or contract, it has shed all unevenness, grains, caverns, knots; it has become isotropic. Let's not waste time consoling the nostalgic weeping over the past; let us certainly point out that wood has not been banished or rejected, just transformed. We have kept the texture, the very smell and color; it has just been made stronger, it doesn't warp and it doesn't scale. We can sing victory. The grumblers are only asking for wood to accompany them, aging along with them, or like them, but isn't this just a way of returning to one's self (the ego cult that mirrors itself and has too heavily monopolized literature, if not philosophy)? At any rate, let us meditate on this concept suggested by The Material of Invention: matter that can be modulated in numerous ways, that composes itself — more morphogenesis than morphology — thanks to the interplay of its elementary units, both one with another and with others (composites), whence new glass springs (polymethylmethacrylate), mixed fabrics, and neo-wood.

2) Second aspect: not only does the new cover the old, but it even rejuvenates it. This is what has kept us from talking of a "death of metals and of metallurgy" when, in fact, we are witnessing their rebirth. They too, it is true, went through their "alloys" period, and were modified by the experience, but now we are seeing a far vaster metamorphosis.

First off, the microelectronics of structures and semiconductors has taught us the importance of molecular compositions and of the role of impurities in their circuits (we are capable of controlling the size and shape of these microscropic inclusions). Moreover, it seems that iron and cast iron have been caught up in the whirlwind of the industry of synthetic materials. A distinction was recently made between calm and effervescent metals — the former differ from the latter by avoiding aging and the consequent loss of their mechanical properties. To be more precise, steel, manufactured in continuous casting with the addition of aluminum, which fixes nitrogen, no longer experiences wear. We are increasingly skilled at controlling the properties of elements — they were once manufactured and processed; today they are created at will, at a structural level.

Certain alloys, if cooled very rapidly from a molten state, maintain their liquid state — although they are solids — that is, in a disorderly state (the so-called "amorphous metals").

There is another process that makes metal similar to plastic — magnetoforming. A rapid and intense electrical impulse in the block of an alloy creates, for a thousandth of a second, a violent repulsion between the magnetic field of the coil and the induced current in the metal near it, which is thrust away at over 700 km/h, hitting a matrix with which it merges. At that speed, the metal becomes slightly viscose, and hence "plastic": hence it becomes possible to set aluminum on fragile ceramics without risking breakage.

Whether taking on characteristics of liquids or becoming amorphous like glass, metal has become far more modern; it has lost all of its inferiority. It has lost all rigidity. The success of elastomers and polymers has affected what we thought of as immutable, or unmodifiable. A fountain of youth for the oldest of materials — iron, coal, glass!

3) Last but not least: today we are filling the ancient gap (widened by philosophers of the pure spirit) that separated the psyche from its antagonist or even enemy — externality; to the point that (reciprocal causality) if one produces the other, the other can in turn replace the first, freeing it of its most pressing tasks. Hence the path is open to the true liberation of man.

Material is being "intellectualized" — this is the amazing new development at the end of the twentieth century; the terms "material" and "invention" are beginning to coincide.

The medium can become a "warehouse," thanks to possible ferromagnetism: the impulse received is registered and stored. It will be sufficient to code the messages in a binary system for the magnetized substrate to take on the role of unlimited and untiring "memory." If man forgets rapidly and deforms, the "conductor" preserves all that it is given. Ingenious assemblies connect the individual units. One can then draw inductions and consequences sums, implications, exclusions, differences), the premises of artificial intelligence.

Without having to go that far, the technology of the camera obscura and the daguerreotype (end of the last century) was based on differential light sensitivity — the photosensitivity of silver salts or special thin emulsion that makes it possible to fix events and thus preserve them (graphic memory).
Beginning from the negative (where light appears black and shadows white) it is possible to obtain positive prints at will (Talbot). And what copies: from the most precise (which register tiny details, where one can "count the

hairs in a beard") to the most subjective (the silvery tenderness, the tones and atmosphere of old calotypes). It is as if the eye has been replaced by the machine, but above all the universe is inscribed in the film, where it is perpetuated and "reflected" in representation (image).

The almost mystical act of duplication, from a manual operation becomes a mechanical-chemical operation, unquestionably faster, cheaper, more detailed. Photography, one may say, cannot be compared to an artist's portrait, which unveils the soul, or spirit, of the model: but who would dare to pull out this old argument? The eye and talent of a simple "reporter" are enough to capture in film demeanor, the fleeting moment, the flou.

This example, though old, opens the way to the modern and also confirms the replacement of skill with a simple light emotional mechanism. Certainly, we must learn to use and manipulate it, but here we prefer to note the victory of plastics (nitrocellulose or humid collodion, later gelatin that contains silver salts in suspension, celluloid, which at a certain point replaces glass or metal, stronger than paper but capable of bending, being rolled and unrolled without damage). In conclusion, these new materials make a mental operation (perception and recording) possible, while – at the same time – causing a social revolution and creating a new art – that of the creator of images.

The Material of Invention, a learned and well-documented work, has added iconography to the text, with illustrations and trophies.

We philosophers were especially interested in joining the celebration – a celebration of the liberation of matter from a millennial curse and the freeing of man because, through the new materials and the processes they imply, man is no longer a slave.

Plastics and composites offer him other "merchandise" that is less vile and less overloaded: works of art, instruments, and even another world. This other world, in truth, will make way only slowly and with difficulty. Thus man is uneasy about living in lightness because he has lived for so long amidst heaviness and horizontality. The architect is therefore forced to feign heavy pillars or load-bearing surfaces in order to reassure man. The imagination lags behind and resists the transition.

That is why we rely on The Material of Invention: this book introduces us to our own universe, and indirectly combats the ideology of complaining.
It has two other merits:

1) That of having understood the importance of structures. Philosophers, said Marx, have thought the world, now we have to change the world. Not through "direct action," but through fundamental and material innovations. The spirit, per se, can do nothing – its value lies in the mediations it generates and through which it passes.

On the other hand politicians have not been fooled – everywhere the Ministries of Scientific Research and Industry have created commissions whose task is to promote the transformation or spread of new materials, without which neither missiles nor telecommunications could be conceived, nor synthetic images, nor vehicles, and so on.

2) We know therefore where the real forces lie; it is necessary to temper every superfluous humanitarian position. Forms draw as much strength from this rising tide. Ideas once manifested themselves in what made them concrete or manifested them – this fall was considered indispensable, inevitable though degrading. Today the medium has undergone such a metamorphosis that they require new, increasingly coherent, light, simple, and lively formal structures. They reject the monumental, the overloaded, all that is shiny and plated. The idea springs from matter itself, instead of being imposed on matter. This almost floral or efflorescent conception of a form of beauty that rises, a pure symbiosis of container and contents, the end of dissociations and flaking.

Industry, culture, and art: the forces and forms that surround us and involve us have been explored and surveyed as best possible. It is the reader's task to join this growing movement without delay.

16

Introduction

by the author

To André Leroi - Gourhan

Every object made by man is the embodiment of what is at once thinkable and possible. Something that someone was able to both think of it and physically create. Every object made by man is situated at an intersection of lines of development of thought (models, cultural structures, forms of knowledge) with lines of technological development (availability of materials, transformation techniques, forecasting and control systems).

This interaction between what is thinkable and what is possible, which we refer to as design, is neither simple nor straightforward. There is no broad, free-ranging Thinkable that has only to squeeze into the boundaries of the Possible, because the very awareness of those boundaries is a basic element of what can be thought of.

On the other hand, thought is not merely the acceptance of known limits. The activities of creation and invention are expressed in the ability to relocate the bounds imposed in other systems of reference, thus creating the new, that which until now has not been thought of and indeed seemed unthinkable.

The model one creates of the possible thus becomes a constituent part of creativity.

Ilya Prigogine and Isabelle Stengers write, "The concept of bounds (...) does not only limit what is possible; it can also offer opportunities. This concept is not merely imposed from without upon a real, previously existing situation; it contributes to the construction of an integrated structure and triggers a broad range of understandable, positive consequences."

The Possible with which we must interact no longer presents itself in the form of performances frozen into a few, tangible materials.

Facing the designer is a system of potentiality that cannot easily be referred to a working model.

The Material of Invention is based on the presupposition that if we succeed in creating such a model, it can serve as the key to the enormous hoard of possibilities that technical-scientific development has accumulated too fast for cultural structures to keep up.

The principal aim of this book, therefore, is to supply cognitive tools and cultural reference that may help to make the new fields of the Possible more easily Thinkable for a designer.

A BOOK ON MATTER

The Material of Invention examines the way in which matter becomes material, i.e., how matter becomes capable of being integrated into design, and in the end becomes part of a product. It looks with special interest at the form that this transition — ancient as the history of man — assumes in a technical and cultural phase in which the traditional and intuitive idea of matter appears to wobble dangerously, when the overriding imperative that guides all possible choices can be summed up in the expression: "Less matter, more information."

17

In this context, the central theme of the book lies in the analysis of the possibilities, limits, and design implications of new materials.

The term "new materials" does not merely mean a limited number of sophisticated materials developed in a few advanced applicative areas. We are talking about the entire set of qualities that, to varying degrees, are appearing throughout the landscape of materials – including the most traditional and venerable of them – shifting them with respect to manufacturing processes. The term, in short, expresses a new technical and cultural atmosphere, within which the transformation of matter is taking place.

LEVELS OF DISCUSSION

This book can be looked upon as an integration of two instruments – a macroscope and a microscope. Both assist in seeing things that escape the glance – some because they are too large and complex, and others because they are too small and specific.

We believe that the reader may find both these instruments useful. The macroscope is especially useful in understanding the behavior of transformations that are taking place and their underlying ideas. The microscope helps to form an intuitive idea from specific examples, to understand the profundity of the change, the concrete quality of the newly possible.

Our decision to have "macro" aspects coexist with "micro", may complicate things for the reader.

We ask him to accept these difficulties, and to try to wend his way among the various levels of discussion.

Perhaps he will see that this exercise of being referred from the general to the specific and contrariwise is not – after all – very different from the mental activity and procedures of a designer.

LANGUAGE

The language of this book belongs to no particular discipline. On the contrary, it is an assemblage of linguistic terms and forms drawn from a vast panorama of specialized languages and jargons that are in some way involved in the problem at hand.

We have tried, by following this avenue, to avoid the risk of banalizing, so common in simplified texts.

All things considered, *The Material of Invention* is not meant to be a simplified text. It is meant as a instrument with which to form a transverse knowledge that can span different terrains without losing track of the fundamental nature of the problems on which it is working.

The potential Tower of Babel that looms at the end of this avenue has – we hope – been partially reduced by the editorial effort to lead the reader along step by step, explaining things thoroughly, in a tour of new linguistic areas.

Again, we ask the reader to accept another set of difficulties. We believe that every new word acquired is a new glimpse of the possible.

POSSIBLE APPROACHES

This book is intended as a bridge spanning different cultural areas. Like all bridges – which can be used in both directions – this book would like to provide a great number of entryways and passages. Therefore, in writing and editing it, we have tried to ensure that anyone can find a path through it that corresponds to their own baggage of experiences and interests. The arc from the first page to the last page is one of the possible trajectories, but certainly not the only one. One can, for the most part, read sections and chapters separately, in any order desired. Thereafter, one can look for connecting references, and establishing one's own path.

The first section (*Matter and Ideas*) offers an examination of our current relationship with matter, following three different itineraries: that of a generic observer (*Paths of Experience*), that of someone who works with materials (*Paths of Matter*), and that of someone who designs with materials (*Paths of Design*).

The second section (*Portraits of Families in Motion*) is a succinct overview of materials as they are now and as they are transforming.

The third section (*Playing with the Possible*) organizes reflections and information of a technical and cultural nature in five chapters. Here we delineate a few significant fields of the possible and indicate the range of connections with design culture and the new quality of the artificial.

The five chapters refer to an equal number of "metafunctions" which the designer may have to work with (*Creating the Light and Resistant*, *Creating the Heat Resistant*, *Creating the Elastic and Pliable*, *Creating the Transparent*, *Providing Surface Quality*).

Lastly, there is a section that presents contributions of various sorts.

Exercises in Invention assembles a series of design ideas created for this book by a number of designers, who had to work within the "game rules" 1. Choose a theme having to do with the chapters of the third section; 2. Think of a solution that provides added performance, made possible by new materials , each designer has imagined and depicted, in his own expressive language, something that has been made thinkable by the newly possible.

Designing Matter – Polymers and Composites is a contribution from the heart of the world of polymers and composites. It offers an in-depth examination of matters inherent in the design of synthetic materials endowed with specific properties. Its role in the book is to provide the reader with an organic description of the technical and scientific information that serves as a medium for considerations that are stated in a fragmentary fashion in the text.

THE ORIGINS OF THIS VOLUME

The point of departure, as is true so often, was a network of relations. In the specific case, these relations involved researchers, technicians, and designers, whose experiences showed them every day the potential of new materials, on the one hand, and the difficulties involved in talking about them and making new design solutions practical.

Amidst this atmosphere, the element that triggered this work was a research project sponsored by Montedison's "Progetto Cultura."

The aim of this project was to find a way of making the qualities and potential of new materials subject to communication.

In practical terms, this meant creating connections between various cultural ambients, test the ideas and information that emerged, and find a way of organizing the resulting concepts, information, and examples.

The book is the result of this research project, and bears traces within it of its origins.

Therefore, fully aware that the point we have reached is not the end of a voyage, we hope that it can serve as a beginning. A single, tentative step in the little-visited terrain of transverse knowledge.

MATTER AND IDEAS

"Voyage Room", Occhiomagico, 1982.

Paths of Experience

Matter meets information

A child is playing with a ball – he tosses it against a wall, the ball executes a trajectory, bounces back, and the child catches it with a sudden lunge.

A succession of ordinary actions that nevertheless presuppose – each time they occur – a remarkable heritage of experience, both personal and collective: experience of the qualities of material, of the laws of motion, of the transformations of energy, of the effects of fields of force.

Instinctive movement and automatic reactions reflect great familiarity with "normal" physical reality – in other words, the physical reality normally experienced by bodies possessing mass, in motion in a dense atmosphere within a uniform gravitational field.

Furthermore, a child at play accumulates another form of knowledge that has to do with the appearance of the ball, its lively colors, its springy texture, its smell: all these properties overlap and interweave with the range of properties of the ball; the result is impressed on the memory of the child as deep knowledge, a single image in which odor, color, elasticity, and childhood are linked.

The biological and cultural history of man is based on elementary experiences of this sort, upon which various images, various forms of knowledge, various ways of perceiving the "sense of reality" are progressively accumulated.

Culture is a sediment of shared characteristics formed through a relationship with existence that, in the course of time, is accumulated on these foundations. Although this relationship does not allow one to develop a full-fledged definition of matter, it has nevertheless been sufficient to allow man to work with matter, to produce a prodigious quantity of transformations and, in turn, to interact with the results of this widespread productive activity.

Nevertheless scientific and technical development – from its beginning as a simple idea of reality made up of existing and objective material, passive matter awaiting activity – has today attained such complexity and depth in its capacity to manipulate what exists that it offers a vision of matter (and of our relations with matter) that contradicts all our initial views. And the inadequacy of those initial views has become evident even in everyday life.

Simulated matter

A child is playing with a ball – he tosses it against a wall, the ball executes a trajectory, bounces back, and the child catches it with a sudden lunge.

The cycle is repeated several times, then the screen goes blank and two words appear – "GAME OVER" – the child has finished and exits from the immaterial environment of the videogame in which he was playing.

In the course of our everyday experience nowadays, we also encounter environments of this sort, where "matter" – or perhaps we should say, what we perceive to all intents and purposes as matter – is pure information, astute simulation that plays on our senses and our memory.

There are certainly considerable perceptual differences between playing with the real ball and the simulated ball (in terms of smell, sight, muscle activity); there are however also profound similarities, related to perspectival and stereoscopic perception of one's surroundings, the reactions provoked by the stimuli, creating a considerable sense of psychological involvement. The ease with which we shift from one to another of these fields of experience cannot help but undermine, in the final analysis, the solidity of our convictions about reality.

The old expression "I must be dreaming" expresses what has long been the only possible alternative before a given image: is this an autonomous and subjective creation of my own mind, or am I looking at something

real, possessed of materiality, and therefore possessed of its own objective existence? Today there are three possibilities: either I am dreaming, or I am awake in a physical real environment, or else I am awake in a simulated environment.

The emergence of this third possible pole of experience should be considered carefully, since it opens to discussion the foundations of our relationship with reality in a more immediate and concrete fashion than the most elaborate philosophical discussion.

A simulated environment has the remarkable characteristic of possessing all the properties of the real world, except for the most fundamental property – it lacks physical presence, it has no palpable material existence. The objects of a simulated world can be broken down, split in half, observed from all sides, modified, adjusted. Intersubjective experiences are possible – anyone, under the same conditions, obtains the same results. But these simulated objects cannot be touched because – though they do exist objectively – they do not lie in the material world.

Of course, there is a material basis: the computer with its remarkable calculating ability. One cannot say, however, that a simulated object or environment lie within the computer any more than a dream or an idea lie within the brain. And yet, even if the simulation is technically "made up" of calculations, its final result is truly a new, third dimension of existence.

Here everything is presented as if the image derived from a true material model – objects seem to have been photographed or filmed; nevertheless decisions about the framing of the image are made by the observer, an operation analogous to what we normally do with our eyes before a real object. The computer and its programs thus become an extension of our nervous and sensory systems, a prosthesis that puts us in touch with a world

that does not exist, but which may possess all the characteristics of the material world, and many others besides (for example we can penetrate the objects of that world and examine them from within, we can assemble them and break them down at our leisure, or again we can alter their size and properties continuously or in steps).

Matter made relative

The man moves haltingly, with a sort of awkwardness, and smiles at the television camera while he reaches out to seize a pencil floating in the air. This is happening at a great distance, somewhere in space, but millions of people experience, vicariously, the feeling of mass devoid of weight.

It is common knowledge that mass and weight are different measurements; but the screen shows us a man who is experiencing at first hand a condition that goes against the knowledge of everyone and always. We see and we know that this is *really* happening.

Then the television camera pivots and points at the earth: an earth unlike anything that we have ever seen. Mountains, valleys, everything that makes up the geometry of our planet flatten out; the dimensional scale in which our everyday physical experience takes place is reduced to a slightly corrugated surface, while a new dimension opens to our eyes.

Or let's say we are examining a series of photographs: here is a photo of a compact, solid, shiny, mirrored surface; there, alongside it, is an image enlarged many times of the same surface – what was previously smooth and shiny has become a landscape of mountains and valleys, an orography of fantastic shapes.

The camera's eye goes on with its enlargement – the landscape changes even more, and the mountains are transformed into ordi-

nary blocks of crystals. Still further along, more sophisicated methods of photography allow us to glimpse the atoms and the mysterious void that surrounds them.

The loss of credibility of the intuitive idea of matter has entered into operation here too: through the most spectacular achievements of techno-science and, above all, (as a mass phenomenon) through the circulation of the images of those achievements.

Unlike the experience of the past, we are no longer faced with abstract explanations and models, but with the widespread availability of a new sensory channel: a superview, a remarkable new eye that reaches much further and deeper than the usual range of our experience.

The spread of this superview leads to an important consequence; our experiences become relative. Every day unquestionable facts bring home to us that what was traditionally considered the materiality of existence is, in the final analysis, nothing more than the organization of our particular point of view, of the way in which our senses evolved biologically, of the way in which our cerebral structure has learned to order the information supplied by our environment.

At this point, therefore, even when talking about existing matter, the focal point is no longer on the question "What is matter?" but "How do we see matter?"

The first consequence of this shift in focus is that the distance between real and simulated is far narrower than it seemed at first. In both cases, in fact, our experience is really nothing more than the decodification of a flow of information. The only difference is that, in the second case, this information was originally stored in digital form in the memory of a computer, while in the first case the information was stored in analog form in the matter with which we come into contact.

Matter deferred

The skyscrapers of New York and the Roman Forum; the Space Shuttle and the *Mona Lisa*; Woody Allen's eyeglasses and the President's tie — I can experience all these things, and plenty more, without moving from my easy chair.

The proportion between what we know as a deferred image and what we know by direct experience is shifting more and more in favor of the deferred image. This is a fairly new development, and we can rest assured that its effects — on our way of conceiving know-

ledge and the sense of our relations with objects — have not yet found full expression. Nowadays, travelling to new places is more a process of verifying their correspondence with images seen previously than an encounter with the truly new and unknown.

Today, much of what is manufactured and built is conceived principally as something to photograph or film rather than something to be used, tested, and experienced in its physical reality. Even today's "monumental" architecture (skyscrapers built as the headquarters of large corporations, for instance) is conceived with special attention to the conscious image of the weight and importance that will be acquired when amplified by the mass media.

The quality of being photo and tele-genic has thus become a decisive variable in the organization of the universe of environments and objects with which we enter into con-

tact. A universe that was originally material: an observer now perceives only a limited materiality, however, related to the two dimensions of a screen or a page, a materiality experienced only through what is still visible after that reduction.

Matter and "intelligent objects"

There are (and always will be) objects made of granite, bronze, oak: mute objects that speak only with their existence over time, silent companions of memory. Unlike in the past, however, this static and material fashion of contributing to our space-time environment is only one of the possible states of existence of objects. It has become one component of a far wider and more variegated system.

Within this system, other objects emerge and

nents that confer upon the object its new qualification of "intelligent" occupy dimensions that escape our perception.

Thus all references to form disappear, as it becomes a marginal question: what we consider as being the "form" of a personal computer with a sophisticated inferface, is more a system of relations than the quality of its body. This is a border-line example. But we carefully analize the objects of the new generation, and the role played by artificial intelligence as a component we can appreciate the value of the above statement in an ever-increasing number of cases.

In these new objects, game and function intermingle in ways never experienced before; and – more interesting still – their true form, that is the image that they impress in our minds, does not correspond to their actual physical form, but rather to the form of the system of relations which they imply. On this basis we must conclude that we are not facing a general "crisis of form" but since physical form is undergoing a crisis, a new domain of systems of relations – of forms which vary in time – now exists and needs studying.

Artificial meets natural

A pyramid and a sand dune. A hut and a bird's nest. Order – that is, the improbable – appears in various forms. We refer to some of these forms as artificial, we refer to others as natural.

An ancient linguistic convention establishes as artificial any local order deriving from man's technical and cultural activity. In the final analysis, however, there is only one significant difference between artificial and natural. This difference lies in the periods of time required to develop the rules according to which this local order is produced. If we look at a sand dune, for instance, we see that these rules are represented by the physical laws underlying the history of our planet. If we examine a bird's nest, instead, we see that the rules here are represented by biological laws linked to the genetic evolution of the species. The hut and the pyramid are governed by the collective memory of an ethnic group, tied to cultural and technical transformations.

Three different sorts of time, three different scales that cannot be compared: the artificial is a type of order the laws of which develop more rapidly, so rapidly that from our point of view (that of an observer immerged in this pattern of rapid change) all else seems

tend to prevail whose qualities cannot be defined only in spatial and temporal terms. We may call them a new generation of objects that – rather than being solidly located in space – tend to flow through time. These are objects that interact, communicate, and are endowed with forms of "intelligence" and "sensitivity": we can converse with a computer, but we can converse with an automatic bank teller, and even with a washing machine; we can request information from a machine by pointing to what we want, and we can turn on a lamp with a caress; we can take our temperature by placing a very thin strip of plastic on our forehead, or we can wear an outfit that changes color according to our body temperature... These are objects that techno-science – working with the infinitely small, the incredibly fast, and linguistic structures – pours into our daily lives.

One should note that as new technical developments alter the object and make it "intelligent," they also set the object on a plane with no prior cultural references. This demolishes all critical instruments based on traditional esthetics (based on physical forms), because the physical aspects of the compo-

to be standing still. The artificial is recognized by its "difference," by the way in which its specific order separates it from the natural.

This difference, nevertheless, is not always the same over time. It is a result of the level of technology that went into its creation. The image of the artificial, and the criteria that help us to recognize it, are – in the final analysis – the way a social group internalizes the shared features of what a technical system is capable of doing: a row of poplars, which we perceive as a natural component of the landscape, would be viewed as an unlikely and artificial element by a nomad society that grazes sheep.

If a technical system undergoes a period of rapid change, the need arises to modify the criteria by which one recognizes the artificial. This is the phase we are now experiencing. The transformation of materials, manu-

facturing processes, and technological knowledge has brought about a new artificial that calls into question the traditional recognizability of the artificial, as well as the entire system of space-time relationships that we base on that artificial.

These difficulties depend not so much on the great complexity of this new artificial which we can define as "hyper-artificial," as much as on the speed of the transformations and the way it is placed in time. Our biological rhythms are in fact, the duration of individual cycles of learning and response, the time periods required by society to form models of thought and language all encounter and clash with the accelerating pace of technical transformation, thus producing a sort of crisis in our ability to know and recognize the surrownding environment.

Therefore, any analysis of the recognition of the artificial and of the new paths of experi-

ence necessarily starts with the placement of experience in time, its link to duration, and the way in which experience establishes a relationship with memory.

Planes, spheres, fractal surfaces

The opening scene of Stanley Kubrick's *2001, A Space Odyssey* shows a group of anthropoids sunk in the farthest reaches of prehistory. Before them appears an extremely upsetting and confusing object: a prism of homogeneous material, with straight edges and smooth surfaces. Total panic ensues: the form that the anthropoids sees has no relationship whatsoever with what experience has shown them until then. Nature, in fact, does not produce that sort of order.

Cut to the Industrial Revolution – a rolling-mill produces an unending stream of sheet steel. The material is homogeneous and closely monitored, the surface is flat, the edges are sharp. The machine produces exclusively that very order that is so improbable in nature. The smooth and homogeneous prism is the stereotype of order in the first phase of the Machine Age.

An automated workshop of today: a randomizing program is entered into a numerical control machine; the machine tools work away, producing forms that vary in a haphazard fashion. This is disorder generated by super-control, a new form of the artificial.

For thousands of years, and with innumerable cultural variations, the defined object, regular form, materials that are precious because they are rare – all this has expressed the highest essence of human activity: to make possible what is impossible in nature (or, as we prefer to say nowadays, what is highly unlikely). Drawing a straight line means producing a type of order that nature very seldom produces.

The attainment of this order has been difficult (that is, costly) because it was always necessary to employ natural materials that were ill adapted to the purpose. The intensity of the artificialization of the environment, i.e., of the formation of this sort of order, has always been proportional to the availability of technology, that is, to the possibility of performing transformations that, starting with matter as it is furnished by the natural environment, turn that matter into material that lends itself to the achievement of this other, human order.

A pyramid, a palace, a cathedral, or a medieval sword are all more intensely artificial

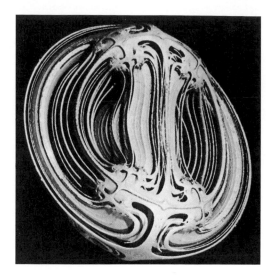

Computer-designed "fractal object" -
artificially producing
a natural geometric form.

than a hut, a wooden chair, or a simple tool. Indeed, in the former objects to a greater degree than in the latter, the need for symbolic representation has led the craftsmen or builders to concentrate the best technical capacity available in the execution, along with the highest possible levels of energy and care, in order to elevate the material employed to forms that are as far as possible from the original, "natural" forms.

In this context, the joint and synergistic triumph of mechanical thought and industrial production constitutes an enormous leap forward without, however, bringing about a break in the continuity of those presuppositions. It is far easier to conceive and execute a straight line by adopting a model of mechanical thought, by organizing production in industrial fashion, and by employing materials that spring from a more sophisticated manipulation of matter.

The materials in this phase become homogeneous and standardized, and their properties are closely controlled. The machine has absorbed many of the technical capacities of the craftsman, but not his attention to detail, to the singular qualities of the item on which he is working. To a craftsman, a knot in the wood or the grain of the stone are obstacles, but they also prompt variations. To a machine they are merely defects. To a craftsman, in other words, material is not an abstract category. Material is this particular piece before him. To a machine, and to the designer that established its operation, material is only a set of controlled properties.

Today one might refer to this sort of relationship with design and production as being out-dated — the tendency to design regular surfaces merely reflected greater ease in terms of calculation and manufacturing, and sprang from the rudimentary technology that was available.

Technical refinement, increasingly refined methods of calculation, the ability to manage complex systems now permit us to operate with non-homogenous materials when needed and to produce objects whose form is quite distant from what the technology of the recent past would have suggested. The technology of the Industrial Age has made straight lines and smooth surfaces a dime a dozen — the same straight lines and smooth surfaces that the craftsman strove to attain with such patience and effort. Neo-technics and new science offer the possibility of producing forms that seem to return to a natural image.

An emblematic case might be that of the "fractal objects" of Benoît Mandelbrot: these are not physical objects, but models that derive from a new computing capacity. These models delineate forms that were never developed by mathematics but that nature produces constantly. Mathematics generated straight lines, circles, ellipses, curves that have derivative. Nature generates the outlines of clouds, the profiles of mountains, forms that no mathematical model was capable of representing. "Fractal objects" reproduce these forms of nature. What has proved however to be the most likely result for nature is here the fruit of an extremely complex algebra, the invention of a brand new space, somewhere between one-dimensional line-space and two-dimensional plane-space.

It therefore requires great intellectual sophistication to simulate nature. The principle can be extended from "fractal objects" to physical objects, to the current generation of

products of technology. The more the image of the new artificial approaches that of nature, the more it is a product of the hyper-control over design and the manufacturing process. The quasi-natural image emerges from an ultra-artificial context.

Simple, complex, almost organic

In Ridley Scott's *Blade Runner*, one of the most serious and intriguing problems that faces the protagonist (and the spectator) is to recognize replicants. These are such perfect bionic robots that only an extremely sophisticated instrument can distinguish them from real humans. Developing technology produces an artificial that can no longer be told from the natural.

Let us take as an example a connecting rod made of carbon composite: the external appearance leads us to intuit an inner cylinder that works under pressure, and bundles of fibers, stretched and oriented according to the direction of the stresses, which hold together the two ends (that is, the head and the foot of the connecting rod) and give the surface a complex and corrugated appearance. The whole reminds one of a bone with its bundles of tendons.

The instrument panel of an automobile, the arm of an easychair, the sole of a running shoe — objects from our everyday environment that are made of a composite "material," in which the various parts are specialized (an extremely resistent "bone," "flesh" to fill or cushion, and a "skin" to provide protection and esthetic qualities...). Though the parts are specialized, they are not separate: they remain a profoundly integrated unit, both in terms of the manufacturing process and in terms of final appearance. The complexity typical of this final image reminds us of the most complex systems that our traditional experience has led us to encounter: living organisms. Obviously, there remains an enormous gulf between the artificial and the organic, in terms of complexity. Nevertheless, the new image of the artificial already appears distant from the stereotype consolidated by paleo-technics.

The "material" of which objects are made therefore appears increasingly difficult to define in simple categories that we can say have been acquired once and for all. The only way to describe the material is to consider it as a system capable of performance: thus we shall speak of a "material," not by defining "what it is," but describing "what it

The almost organic image of an artificial object - connecting rod made of a composite material with oriented fibers. (Doct. Vetrotex)

does."

In this context, the functions that identify "materials" tend to become more and more complex and integrated one with another. The dynamics of this integration began with mechanical functions (reinforcements, housings, joints, hinges), then moved on to those having to do with comfort (the integration of soft parts) and surface quality (ornamentation and texture), all the way — through miniaturization and the production of materials equipped with special electric properties — to the possibility of integrating properties of sensitivity and information capacity into final composite "material." In fact, there are objects that integrate into the "material" of which they are made information input and output systems (membrane keyboards, touch screens, displays), sensors (sheets of piezo-electric material), luminous systems (electro-luminescent plates)...

The list could go on, indicative of one of the most significant trends in the current phase of technical development: the tendency to turn mechanisms and operating systems that previously had to be manufactured as separate objects (formed in turn by clearly defined sub-components) into something that is made of the "material" itself, by reducing the operating "mechanisms" of a macroscopic system to those of a material or a composition of materials. Thus we pass from the mechanical assembly to the integrated joint, from packing to the integration of soft expanded material, from the mechanical keyboard to the membrane keyboard, from the lightbulb to the electro-luminescent surface.

The term "miniaturization," in the current phase, no longer means the production of smaller components: it often signifies the elimination of components as such, attained through the appropriate and in-depth manipulation of the very qualities of matter.

The depth of the artificial

The pair of opposites, artificial/natural, is not – if one is to use the terms strictly – applicable to materials used by man. The wood in a table, inasmuch as it is a processed material, forms part of the artificial just as much as the plastic in a chair. Or, vice versa, the plastic in a chair has the same right to be considered part of the natural since its properties are based on natural laws, as are those of wood. What changes, and what makes the two materials so different, is the level which the technical interference attains, that is, what we would like to refer to here as the "depth" of the artificial.

Erecting a pyramid and building a macromolecule means, in either case, constructing something. One establishes relationships between several elements that are improbable in nature. In the first case, however, the order is on a macroscopic level. A pyramid organizes materials spatially, and modifies only their geometry, without interfering with their intrinsic qualities. When observed in detail, the unchanged structure of the stone can be detected. In the second case, the order is microscopic. Atoms are organized, their arrangement is altered. The level of manipulation is far deeper, though still based on natural laws, on the intrinsic properties of matter. Throughout pre-industrial production, and prior to the triumph of techno-science, the artificial appears as a relatively light layer. With varying degrees of visibility, the natural substrate shows through in all crafts production, such as in the grain in a piece of wooden furniture. A craftsman's knowledge and skill lie in his ability to integrate a natural component in the artifice he has mastered. He does this, not out of an ethical choice due to his respect for nature, but out of pure practical need. This stage of technical development may be defined as that of materials with "enforced" complexity. This definition clearly applies to wood and stone. It applies as well to the first metals and alloys, processed with such crude treatments that they contained great quantities of inclusions and impurities.

Later on, after science became a factor in production around 1850, the use of in-depth methods of analysis and the developing familiarity – on a theoretical level, as well – with the chemical and physical behavior of matter led to the phase of "controlled" complexity, that is, to the progressive fine tuning of processes capable of producing the homogeneous and isotropic materials endowed with definite and constant properties needed by industry.

The current phase, on the other hand, may be defined as that of materials of "managed" complexity. Now anisotropies and impurities can be sought and produced intentionally with an eye to specific results and performances.

In this management of complexity, the capacity for design and manipulation pushes much deeper into the structure of matter: from molecular engineering to the production of specific crystals, all the way to "doping" procedures, the depth of the artificial is increasing. The natural foundation is thrust much further down. In its place remain images and properties that have lost all reference to what preceding experience and the recollection of nature had impressed in our memory.

Micrograph of polyethylene terephthalate (PET).
(Doct. Istituto G. Donegani-Montedison)

Material meets material

Our gaze runs over the objects of our every-day existence. They are forms endowed with qualities; the qualities are the product of the materials. Memory, experience, and intuition attempt to extract names from a mental catalogue: "wood," "iron," "plastic." Our relationship with the real is also filtered through this ability to give names: to see, touch, sample, and, in the end, recognize, that is, attribute on the basis of the subjective local experience wider meanings, that are in turn synthesized in a name.

The collective memory is populated by stone walls, wooden furniture, wool mattresses, iron swords, golden crowns. In these stereotypes, the names of the materials seem to be charged with broader meanings. These names give the object cultural weight and solidity. Stone is durability, wood symbolizes the passage of time, wool is the warmth of intimacy, steel is cold force. Every culture has encountered similar signifiers and meanings in the language of things.

It seems that today however the thread of continuity has been interrupted. Memory, experience, and intuition no longer help. Objects of the most recent generation appear ever more frequently in a guise that allows us to say what they seem to be made of, but we cannot say what they really are made of.

This is not merely a result of our ignorance before new products. Our perplexity has far deeper roots. In a period in which techno-science manipulates the extremely small and manages the enormously complex, matter no longer appears to the scale of our perceptions as a series of given materials, but rather as a continuum of possibilities. Performance and quality of image seem to merge in the in the most disparate ways, generating solutions that defy classification. There derives an inevitable tendency to distinguish between what a material is (in chemical and physical terms) and what a material seems to be.

A world of nameless materials is taking shape. These materials create a crisis in the traditional relationship that we once had with materials, and they prevent us from attributing to them meanings that once endowed them with cultural and physical depth. In this new world, we seem to perceive only surfaces, only local and momentary relationships. In a word, we perceive only appearances.

In a few cases we still guess at the material: that looks like a wooden table, I think the lamp is made of metal. But what are the frame of the computer, the car bumper, the tip of the ballpoint pen made of? There is a growing tendency not even to ask the question anymore. An object is now made of what it seems to be, and of the performances which it offers. This relative autonomy of the image from its material state is not that surprising, after all. Appearance, in the current technical and cultural phase, has in general become the only reality to which we can refer. There is indeed a crisis in one of the prime certainties upon which modern thought was founded — the certainty that there existed an authentic image of materials. Today we can see that this is no longer true, and we are conscious that the crisis of this idea is not only the consequence of a cultural choice which — for the sake of polemics — favors the ambiguity of "counterfeiting" over the "sincerity" of materials. The crisis goes much deeper. It derives from the very properties of new materials that, since they can be treated in a vast range of forms, are capable of offering more than a single "sincere" image of themselves.

And so a new way of viewing things is being formed. A new form of knowledge of the real is developing, whose code of reference is no longer that of the classification of materials according to their properties and intrinsic cultural meanings. Instead, the reference has become a recognition of the level of per formances and of the evocative images generated as integrating parts of a manufactured product.

The recognition of materials

Wood, over the course of its long history, has been treated in many ways. It has been touched, smelled, torn, bent, cut into a thousand different shapes, strained by mechanical stresses for long and brief periods, in dry environments and in humid ones. Wood has been burned, carbonized, distilled, and someone at some time must have tried to eat wood... In each individual cultural area and for each individual type of wood someone gained experience from these tests (whether or not they were intentional), someone observed and registered the behavior, the performance. Through this slow accumulation, the field of possibilities of this material was defined, man internalized wood's characteristics into group culture. Wood (that is, the

31

trees growing in a given climatic area) has thus become a familiar material, endowed with a recognizable identity.

The same is true of all materials employed traditionally. In this process of collective learning, a reply was advanced to the question, "What is a material?" The response took the form of an operative definition, implicit but quite effective: a material is something that, under given conditions (a system of loads, environmental conditions, an observation period) behaves in a given fashion (that is, supplies certain performances). Repeated testing and the context of a lengthy history conferred a special depth to this response. Over time, the identities of materials were consolidated, and these identities were given names.

Traditional procedures, in other words, empirical observation of the relations between conditions of use and performance allowed man to identify materials and consider them, from that moment on, as "known" materials. Contrariwise, once a material was considered to be "known," reference to that material became a handy abbreviation for the set of relations between conditions of use and performance that typified that material. The value of this synthetic form of expression, that is, its socially accepted and unmistakable meaning, was based on two conditions:
— there were few materials and they were quite distinct one from another, so that each corresponded to a well-defined field of relations;
— materials remained constant over time in terms of qualities and properties, and their variations (or the introduction of new materials) were slow enough to allow the adaptation of the system of meanings.

Given these premises, both designer/manufacturers and consumers could refer – rather than to the relations between conditions of use and performance – to the material as an entity that was capable of specific behavior that remained constant over time. Man was sure that he could learn about and recognize the physical world because he could attribute to the elements that made up the material environment names drawn from a lexicon of materials.

In attributing these names, man also assigned to the element in question not only a set of properties that could be empirically tested, but also all that which had been determined by prior experience and all that which was suggested by the name itself. And so, if one were to recognize the surface of a table as being made of "wood," it meant

that one could also predict its behavior, its rate of aging, its reaction to fire, the maximum acceptable load, and so on.

A material's identity was constructed on the basis of knowledge taken as predictable behavior. This prediction was reinforced through conditions of use repeated over time. Thus memory deposited upon the material itself a sediment of cultural values, which in turn became part of conventional communication – qualities such as "precious," "warm," and "homelike."

The very formation of these conventional meanings obviously presupposed the limitation of those meanings (materials in their physical capacity to have properties) and the relative stability of their meaning (just as with words in a living language, the meaning could change but only at a speed that would not interfere with comprehension).

The loss of recognition

The mechanism that produces identity was recently blocked and then definitively put out of operation by the acceleration of technological progress and by the introduction of new materials. Among these new materials, plastics have played a fundamental role in triggering the technical, economic, and cultural dynamics that led to the current new scenario of materials. The history of the image of plastics is the history of a transition from traditional recognizability of materials to their current unrecognizability. By appearing on the stage of the possible and exhibiting their high level of artificiality and their lack of history, plastics provided a decisive contribution to the demolition of the entire system of images and hierarchies of values founded on natural qualities, and the qualities consolidated by perceptual and symbolic tradition.

The history of plastics is not linear. The name itself has drifted slightly in meaning so that today the term "plastic" is undergoing an identity crisis. From an exotic product to a consumer product, from an element of progress to an environmental villain, from a grocery bag to aerospace components, from kitsch to design – all of these connotations have alternated, overlapping without hiding each other from view. When we say "plastic" today, it evokes contradictory impressions. Ambiguity annihilates the evocative qualities of the term.

When plastics entered into industrial production, their plasticity was used not only to conform to various geometric forms, but above all to fit different images. The simplest solution, at the outset, could hardly have been any other that that of appearing as an imitation of other, more noble materials. The Modern Movement at this point criticized this use, calling for the placement of plastics on the same level as other traditional materials. In the final analysis, this criticism was contradictory. Malleability of image is one of plastic's prerogatives. And so, paradoxically, the capacity for imitation of plastic was a "sincere" expression. Nonetheless, the Modern Movement was so powerful that, in order to be admitted to the halls of high culture – and the realms of mass production – plastics had to develop an autonomous image that could be proffered as a "sincere image."

After World War Two, plastic finally found this image when the term "manufacturing" was joined to the term "culture." Several designers and several companies took this difficult step with courage and decision. Plastic thus won a place for itself in the catalogue of accredited materials. Distinguishing features: clear and, appropriately enough, plastic forms, rounded joints, primary colors, generally shiny surfaces, just one material for the entire product. With this *identikit*, plastics have entered into the collective memory alongside the other existing materials. Then, however, this positive atmosphere was spoiled. In the late Seventies the energy crunch and ecological concern cast a negative light upon plastics and began to create problems for this material. Moreover, evolving taste took some of the sheen off the new image that had been created for plastic with such effort. Fantasies about worlds of plastic, naive repetitions *ad infinitum* of a system of simplified forms, were set aside. The central points of the debate, nowadays, have ceased to refer to the materials themselves and now aim chiefly at communications and linguistics.

A careful analysis of recent products shows us however that such design themes as complexity, fragmentation, the use of quotations, and hybridization can be turned into finished products only because the material in which they take shape offers a degree of adaptability that knows no precedents in the history of design. The emphasis on the way objects communicate is made possible by the availability of materials that can be easily adapted to the syntax of design in the same way that the words of a language can be incorporated into the syntax of a text. Plastics filter in

through a thousand different pores inside this new universe of images, producing every sort of form, bearing a fantastic range of meanings. If it is no longer possible to offer a precise image of plastics in the Eighties and Nineties, this is a result – not of their scanty presence – but of the excessive visibility of plastics.

As their number multiplies enormously, as the properties of plastics expand well beyond expectations, and as they are integrated with the most disparate materials, for the most part unbound from ideological and cultural ties, plastic materials are fully developing their qualities of adaptability and mimicry, thus pervading the system of objects. Paradoxically, due to this very excess of qualities, this exuberant and kaleidoscopic presence, plastics are losing their specific identity.

Toward partial recognition

Plastics have not attained this loss of recognition alone. Their entry into the field of engineering possibilities is in fact merely the first signal of a much deeper modification of the entire landscape of materials. In a sort of competition or race towards performances that are aimed at specific uses, the multiplication of materials and processes is causing a general crisis in the prerequisites, at all levels, for the traditional form of knowledge of materials and the makeup of cultural and functional identity. When one is dealing with a material that lends itself so readily to transformation (and so lends itself to successive recognition) in this way, it is no longer possible to classify experiences using names that are endowed with socially recognized meanings.

In this new situation, the observer/user, faced with any material integrated into a component, must necessarily test personally and locally that material's properties (that is, the relationship between conditions of use and performance), and cannot predict *a priori* any properties aside from those detected, nor will he be able to attribute cultural signif-

icance to those properties.

Thus, for instance, a table top made of one of these "unrecognizable materials" displays several of its mechanical capacities, but it is impossible to foresee – except through direct testing – how much weight it will support before collapsing. The table top may possess its own specific image, but until I touch it, I cannot predict its thermal behavior. I can see the table at a given moment, but I cannot foresee its behavior over time or in other settings. Moreover, this is taking place in a context that is well beyond the pure and simple opposition between "true" materials and imitation materials. Midway between real wood and imitation wood today there is real wood that does not look like wood (treated so as to have no link with the traditional image of wood) or even fake wood made of wood (in which a type of wood that in itself boasts only a weak image is treated so as to yield a strong image of wood: knots, grain, etc.).

The most common reaction to these new conditions is to continue to utilize a cognitive method that is analogous to the traditional method, though modified by a filter of doubt. Traditional identities of materials can be used with a degree of approximation ("This material, at least from certain points of view, resembles...") or to construct definitions based on contradictions ("It looks like marble, but it is warm to the touch and far lighter...").

This way of dealing with the image of materials is nonetheless inadequate and makeshift. This approach is insufficient, on the one hand, because the attribution of traditional identities, drawn from one's memory, to new materials cannot help but be approximate, and so frustrating. On the other hand, it is an approach that cannot be used for long because the recollection of archaic identities must necessarily be diluted with the passage of time, proving less and less adequate to the emergence of new systems of perform-

ance and/or image.

What is more, there are already combinations of materials and processes that can produce objects and components that completely lack references – even vague resemblences – with which to connect. For these objects, instead of saying what they are made of, since a repertory of names is lacking, one tends to list the performances of which they are capable. For instance, one refers to a high-touch material, that is, a material endowed with special softness and surface quality. Again, one might speak of a material that "gives light," that is, a material with an electroluminescent or photoluminescent surface. Or else one may refer to materials that change form, that is, plastics or metals with a "memory of form." The question, "What is it?" disappears before the question "What does it do?"

What has been irreversibly eliminated is the possibility of intrinsically endowing the material itself with qualities of image and identity. This is no longer possible for plastics, nor for other materials. The "real wood" that looks like "real wood" is only one possibility among many, a specific image-related performance of wood. On the other hand, it is possible that the identity crisis of materials as such could generate "performance-related identities," and among a material's performances there might be that of producing an image, developed by the designer and decoded by the observer/user.

In this case the new identities of image and/or performance, springing from various materials and various combinations of materials, would become the new words in a language of objects. They would lose, however, the "weight" of meaning that words such as "marble," "wood," and "steel" once had. The new recognizability of materials is destined to be a "light recognition."

"Untitled", Man Ray, 1931

Paths of matter

The hyper-selection of materials

The artificial, in our experience, is similar to a theatrical performance. The audience sits viewing the stage and is absorbed in the fiction. If one looks backstage, however, one sees the machinery that moves the backdrops. The new materials are stage machinery in the great spectacle of communications, computerized imagination, artificial imagination. There is no information without a medium, there is no information processing without single crystal silicon (or, in the future, other materials). Highly complex and highly integrated objects could not exist without materials that provide equally intense performances. If materials, according to our scale of perceptions, become less obtrusive and even seem to disappear from sight, this does not mean that they are playing a less important role. They develop such high levels of performance that we perceive their effects almost without noting the source.

On the other hand, new materials, prior to taking form in the products that are responsible for the remarkable and at times disturbing experience of reality that we are now undergoing, play an equally remarkable and disturbing role with respect to the manufacturing system of which they are becoming an integral part. Designers and manufacturers are faced with an enormous and expanding field of possibilities, where the selection of materials and the selection of transformation process can be combined into one selection that we have defined as a "hyper-selection." For a given product, there is no longer a single material that presents itself as the obvious choice, almost as the only real candidate. Now there are different materials that compete one against another. Only an in-depth and wide-ranging analysis of the entire manufacturing process and – in some cases – of the successive life of the product itself, can lead to the selection of the most satisfactory solution.

The multiplication of materials and the competition that is unleashed between them are in turn both the cause and the effect of much deeper modifications in their very nature. Multiplication signifies specialization in given fields of application. In turn, specialization, in this case, means the production of a set of performances. The final result of this search for complex performances that are increasingly close to a specific field of application is "made-to-order material," or material developed especially for a given use. Once we have reached that goal, even the term "hyper-selection" is outmoded. This is no longer selection, this is design.

Competition among materials

For the first million years or so after his appearance, man used essentially five materials to make tools and objects: wood, rock, bone, horn, and leather. At the beginning of the Neolithic, a complex set of radical transformations took place (the "Neolithic revolution") that also led to a significant enrichment in the range of materials utilized: clay, wool, plant fibers, and – in relatively recent times – the first metals all appeared. For the entire period following, along a 9,000-year span of history, these were the materials used by mankind to construct its artificial environment. Then, the Industrial Revolution, with its profound cultural, social, and economic transformations, led to the sudden and accelerating multiplication of materials available for production. One material – steel – even became the symbol of the first wave of the Industrial Revolution.

Today at the center of attention and the subject of cultural debates are other aspects of technological innovations, and the age in which we now live may not take its name from a material. Perhaps this is the "Information Age."

This age, nevertheless, has a close dialectical relationship with a certain "new matter," whose qualities can be discerned in the light of the intense competition among materials triggered at a certain point in history.

The phenomenon began with the introduction of plastic materials (that is, organic synthetic materials) and their competition with other existing materials. These materials reacted by evolving, by developing a certain resistance, and even launching a counter-attack against the tribe of synthetics. This reaction of "natural" materials was countered by further development of the qualities of plastic materials. A "performance race" ensued, which seems to be accelerating constantly.

Naturally, competition among materials is not in itself a phenomenon that belongs exclusively to our time. In the history of technology, every new material has always been put to uses that were previously the consolidated domain of other materials while, simultaneously, opening the path to new possibilities and new applications that previously had been unthinkable. This is what happened with the metallurgy of copper and

bronze, then with iron, later with steel, and lately with plastics. The difference is in the speed, the increasingly frenetic pace with which the new is introduced.

In particular, this acceleration has developed in the context of the introduction of plastics. Materials have entered an area in which innovation no longer requires the relatively long periods of time of empirical research. Now there is considerable integration of science with technology. The ferment has spread across the landscape of materials, from the emblematic sector of plastics all the way round to traditional materials. Traditional materials have benefited from the integration of science as a factor in production, starting up processes of development that tend to extend the range of their qualities. The development of materials as a whole thus becomes, in a certain sense, coherent and convergent.

Materials made to order

At the turn of the century the manufacture of an automobile involved less than a hundred different materials. Today the same process requires more than four thousand materials, and this diversification is destined to increase. The trend is general – since 1900 the number of materials has leapt several hundred-fold. Attempts have been made to count the new materials, resulting in a number somewhere between fifty and seventy thousand. This figure, however, (given by Henry R. Clauser, in *Industrial and Engineering Materials*) is open to discussion, because it refers solely to standard formulations that appear in manufacturer's catalogues, and does not take into account special formulations. In reality, it is impossible to count the number of materials in existence because they are limitless – as are the possibilities of combining composites with a view to various properties and performances.

From this possibility of combining materials springs the newest and most intriguing aspect of the way in which matter presents itself today to users. Matter is no longer a system of classification of given and well-defined materials, but a continuum of possibilities – based upon which, it is possible to design new materials as they are needed, with desired properties.

This structure gives rise to materials "made to order," with properties that are determined by altering their microstructures (by selecting one or more polymers and appropriate fillers and additives) or macrostructure (by creating composite materials). With respect to the traditional definition, materials "made to order" are quite special – the material does not exist prior to the object in which it is to be integrated. The material exists only after the manufacturing process, as a component of the finished product.

The resulting transformation lends itself to description in visual terms – every material can be compared to a point that exists in a space whose dimensions represent various properties (mechanical, thermal, chemical, electrical, and so on). The coordinates of a point therefore constitute the characteristic properties of the material in question.

Until recently, every family of materials occupied a fairly limited and well-defined zone in this "space of properties." Each zone was separate and distinct from the other zones occupied by other families of materials. Furthermore, the number of families was fairly limited. A designer or engineer would learn –

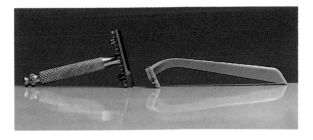

in theory and by practice – the qualities and limits of each family, qualities and limits that consituted a reference point to reality. These were the materials that design had to take into account.

Today things are different – competition between families of materials has led each family to extend its characteristics and broaden its jurisdiction in space, invading fields that were traditionally occupied by other families. Generally speaking, in the "space of properties" every point – that is, every possible combination of properties – is now occupied by one or more materials.

Certainly, the landscape of materials is not made up exclusively of materials made to order – there still are and always will be cases in which it is most appropriate to use standard materials exactly as the manufacturers offer them. The fact remains, nevertheless, that one category is joined to the other and that even the number of standard materials is vastly greater than before, a situation that calls for a total reversal of the old logic of design and manufacturing which tended to consider materials as pre-established givens. Nowadays we must assume that, in principle, materials research is itself a field involving design.

Quantity versus quality

During the first Industrial Revolution, cast iron and steel found their correspondences in a world of machines, bridges, and railroads – all waiting to be manufactured and constucted. The first plastics could count on a bottomless potential of mass consumption waiting to be satisfied. Today, instead, the competition among materials takes as its reference a manufacturing area whose quantitative growth cannot keep pace with the growth – in terms of number and potential – of the materials themselves. The clash is becoming more intense, and the pressure is on to do research on new possibilities. Competition is moving from the terrain of quantity to that of quality.

This trend, together with a growing technical and scientific capacity to perform deep-lying modifications in the structure of matter, is producing materials that, more and more, are designed for specific uses. These new materials are leading to solutions with greater intensity of performances. The new qualities available in turn prompt product redesign, with a view to lighter and better integrated objects. And so a new technical and cultural atmosphere is being generated, that might bear the motto: "Less matter, less energy, more information."

In new materials, just as in traditional materials, this phenomenon is occurring at all levels, from molecular engineering to transformation techniques, right down to design choices. The very structure of a material can provide a greater number of performances with smaller quantities of matter (new alloys, polymers with elevated mechanical properties). The greater formability of a material allows the integration of several operating parts into a single item. It is now possible to process various materials – each with a specific function – in a single operation. There are special finishing operations that can add other qualities to the object.

This situation is giving rise to a generation of dense objects, made of materials with high information content or – in other words – with a high concentration of performances. This transformation leads to a profound change in the relationship between a material and an object.

Traditionally, a material was thought of as an elementary system whose task was to

**Valves for an automobile engine.
The valve stem is made of polyamide imide
and possesses great mechanic and thermal resistance.
(Doct. Amoco Chemicals Corporation)**

"give structure" to a more complex system. Only design could then put together various appropriate materials, formed according to different geometries, so as to produce objects capable of performing complex functions (machinery, equipment, plants, etc.). In the new state of things, the material itself may possess such intrinsic complexity (designed and managed by the "material designer" and then "frozen" into the material) that performs functions. The material provides, in solid state, performances that otherwise would require macroscopic equipment. This second image of materials of course does not eliminate the first image, which still applies in most cases. Nonetheless, the second image of materials constitutes the conclusion of a piece of history that began with the integration of the simplest mechanical functions, made possible by the introduction of plastic materials with their great formability.

Integrating functions

Let us open the back panel of a pocket camera. A glance inside tells us that the camera is made of a single plastic component that, simultaneously, gives the camera structural resistance while linking and protecting all the moving parts and the optical system. A great many problems have been solved through a single molding operation. Another example can be seen in the rear hatch of the Citroën BX. This door is made up of three parts of polyester reinforced with fiber glass. In another model Citroën, the corresponding component, made of metal, is manufactured by assembling twenty-seven separate parts. Yet another case: the use of composite materials in the production of a helicopter rotor and the rotor's successive redesign reduced the number of componenents from the original two hundred ninety-three parts to just ninety-two parts. At the same time, it became possible to eliminate all thirty-two ball bearings and eight lubrication points. All of this reduced the rotor's weight by 50 percent and its cost by 65 percent.

The number of parts that go into an object (and hence the number of steps required in manufacturing it) tends to diminish, while the number of functions performed by each part tends to increase. The force driving this change is the economic cost of assembly operations and the resulting savings of manufacturing, in a single operation, items that integrate various functional subcomponents.

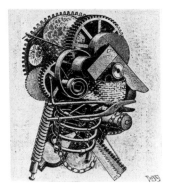

To do so, it is necessary to have materials and processes available that allow one to manufacture components with complex forms as well as to integrate different materials. The path was blazed by plastic materials. Their formability was the first and primary reason for their success in technical applications. The change triggered by plastics, however, soon involved other materials, especially metals. Numerous processes have been developed to increase greatly the formability of metals.

This integration of relatively simple functions (the conferring of structural or esthetic or functional qualities to an object's surface) is just one aspect of a complex phenomenon, linked to the greater capacity to modify materials provided by the techno-science of materials. For instance, a window with a roller-blind is an object made up of different parts assembled with the objective of modulating the flow of incident light. An electrochromic or photochromic plate performs the same function, and it is made of a single material capable of modifying its color and transparency. The material itself integrates the performances that previously were the product of a number of components and materials. In the same way, a lightbulb is the product of the assembly of several parts in order to create a light source, while an electroluminescent system is a film that, excited by a variable electrical impulse, emits light. Here again, the performances of a system composed of macroscopic parts are transferred to a single material (in this case, a stratified composition of several materials, which however produces a single "solid" sheet) capable of analogous performances.

Less and less are materials "something to do something else" (glass to make a lightbulb, wood to make a roller-blind...), and increasingly materials are themselves "something that does something." Indeed, they are what they do – an electroluminescent material is a lightbulb, a piezoelectric film is a sensor.

Material-process-product

The tip of a ball-point pen is made of three different plastics and two metals. The whole is treated with an extremely integrated process that permits very fast manufacturing. The "material" here is the inseparable whole of the specific properties of each component, but also the properties of the process through which the tip is manufactured. Indeed, it is the process, and not so much the material, the decisive element that makes a ball-point pen what it is: a fairly complex product for vast consumption at an extremely low price. In other words, when we speak of materials and the competition between them, we are really always talking about the material-process system.

What we ask of the sole of a running shoe is resistance, flexibility in a few points and stiffness in others, a certain inner softness and a porosity that allows transpiration. The material (or rather the stratification of materials) that provides this set of performances exists only in that there exists a process which makes it possible to manufacture the shoe economically. Vice versa, a touring bicycle, which requires (as would an aeronautics structure) great lightness and mechanical resistance, cannot currently be manufactured with an advanced composite because the processes now available are too complex and costly for this sort of application. Processes and materials are not separable; indeed, for "made-to-order materials" they cannot even be separated from the finished object. The material does not exist independently of the object and the manufacturing process.

The materials of a design in this context are something that, prior to the design, exists only as a set of technical and organizational potentials and methods of computing. These elements at the right moment can be combined as needed, in order to attain a result with specific qualities. The final material bears within it, as if through genetic heredity, the signs of every step in the process that determined its microscopic structure, its macrostructure (if it is a composite material), and its final form.

This characteristic is particularly evident in the case of an advanced oriented-fiber composite whose material macrostructure is established at the moment in which the finished product is manufactured, through the appropriate arrangement of the fibers or reinforcing tissues, differentiated according to the strains predicted in each point. The same characteristic can be detected however in less obvious cases, such as when searching for and promoting preferential orientation of molecules though an injection molding process or by "stretching" a film to increase its mechanical properties. In both cases the finished product is made of a material whose structure has qualities that largely derive from the process and that are dictated by the object's final form.

The inseparability of the set of material process-product is by no means a new develop-

This camera body integrates all its functions in a single item. (Doct. Bayer)

ment. In a wooden table, an iron bridge, or a cement wall, the final result is marked by all three factors. In the past, however, less was done to the microstructure or macrostructure of the material (that is, the artificialization was slight), and, most importantly, the material and the object were two separate steps. Nowadays, the process tends to become a unitary system, which can control the product on all dimensional levels, from the microscopic (or even submicroscopic) right up to the macroscopic.

Materials and the system
1.2.2

Never before as today has it been possible to consider technology as a system of interactions, in turn part of a larger cultural and social system. The great intensity of the information flows in which we are immersed and the planetary diffusion of those flows make the whole of these relations much more closely integrated than in social and cultural environments in the past. If the technical system that emerged from the Neolithic revolution took eight or nine thousand years to spread from the Middle East to the rest of the planet, and if the Industrial Revolution began in England and spread across the world (though certainly not in a uniform fashion) in about two centuries, the transformation prompted by information processing and by new materials has always, from its very beginnings, developed in areas that are geographically distant one from another, but which are in contact and in competition one with another. The system of reference for new developments in technology is by now the entire planet. New materials appear as a pervasive innovation, similar to that of information processing, which penetrates transversally and in a capillary fashion the cultural, social, and technical system, operating on different planes: from organization of production to the structures (and therefore formation) of knowledge, in areas ranging from employment to ecology. Incentives and hindrances to transformation are a reflection of the complex relations that link each indi-

41

vidual element of the system to another element. Today, as always, the new must face the existing as well as the inertia of the complex system represented by the existing. Before we examine this topic, however, we must analyze in greater depth the meaning of the expression "new materials."

The paths of innovation

What is "new" for an end user may not be at all new to a research laboratory. Plastics, for instance, are still a "new" material to many designers. The concept of "new" depends on the target in question, and the very expression "new materials" may be taken in a narrow sense or it may spread to a meaning that is richer in implications.

In a narrow sense, we may define as "new" a certain number of materials that entered recently into the realm of availability, in experimental or manufacturing terms. On the whole, including organic, metallic, and ceramic materials, they do not now exceed 5 percent of the total market, but their growth rate is far greater than that predicted by experts for the set of all materials from now until 1990 (1 percent). We can gain a general idea of the importance that they will take on in the future thanks to a classification based on their stage of development, according to the indications contained in a report *(Genie des materiaux et transformation des processes de production)* published in France in 1985 for the Commissariat General du Plan and for the CNRS. The report proposes four main groupings:
- Materials in a recent phase of industrialization (such as high diffusion reinforced plastics and titanium).
- Materials in a pre-industrial phase (such as advanced composites and high performance ceramics).
- Materials in a phase of development (such as aluminum-lithium alloys).
- Materials that are still being researched (such as amorphous metals).

It is quite difficult to predict which of these materials will have an effective practical development, and how many of them will spread outside the fields of specific and narrow applications for which they were developed.
Nevertheless, although these areas of research and experimentation may generate extremely interesting new develoments, the expression "new materials" may be given a broader meaning, to indicate a far more

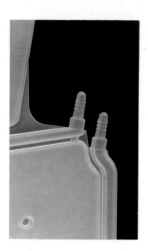

Detail of a blown polypropylene (PP) washing-machine component (mfg. Artesopla). (Doct. Montedison-Himont)

common transformation of what materials have meant traditionally to designers and manufacturers.
In this context, the "new materials" are not only the new polymers, new alloys, new ceramics, or new advanced composites, that is, the cutting-edge materials that are emerging from the most advanced research centers. We may define as "new" even materials that are the result of creative combination of familiar materials. This combination, thanks to a more sophisticated management of matter and energy, leads to greater information content and a higher density of performances.
These new materials are not necessarily the product of large research laboratories. They may spring from any point in the design and manufacturing system in which the new culture of materials is interwoven with creative capacities. Therefore, although it is quite interesting to observe this process of "percolation" which leads certain sophisticated materials to spread from the highest levels of cutting-edge technology toward less limited applications, one must not lose sight of the diffuse innovation that starts from the widest base of the pyramid of mass consumption. The field of packaging (from bottles to containers for frozen foods) has produced new solutions that are no less significant than the advances in the aerospace industry.
This is quite simply a new cultural and manufacturing atmosphere, which in turn does not appear to be uniformly distributed – from the more dynamic centers it tends to extend to other sectors, and in this spread it encounters areas of resistance that are represented by cultural inertia and engineering and economic difficulties. On this terrain as well, the technological *transference* proceeds by steps, amid successes and interruptions.

Here again, perhaps to a greater degree than in high technology, a decisive element is the capacity for diffusion that the new culture of materials will succeed in displaying.

From product to service

If I go to the butcher's and I buy a steak, the butcher is only selling me a product. If I ask the butcher to give me everything I need to make a complicated meat pastiche, he is also supplying me with a service. In the first of the two cases, the purchaser must translate his performance-related needs into product-related terms (that is, he must have singled out the product that provides those performances); in the second case he simply communicates his needs and leaves it up to the shopkeeper to find or assemble the product. In this case as well, in the end, there is a transaction of a material merchandise (the meat), but it is integrated with, and a consequence of that special immaterial merchandise, that is information.

Cross-sections of electric cables. (Doct. B Ticino)

The multiplication of materials and the hyper-selection that derives from that multiplication tend to shift the relationship between manufacturer and user out of the first case and into the second case described above. If the user encounters growing problems in orientation among the many possibilities, of which he has not yet succeeded in amassing a complete experience, he will choose to communicate his needs and to request a solution from a supplier. The manufacturer, for his part, will become more and more accustomed to acting as a service company. Manufacturing will remain his chief activity, but it will fit into the framework of his capacity to meet the various needs of his customers.

The consequences of this trend – consonant with the general development of the entire manufacturing system – are many. The importance and role of many departments of a company will change (customer assistance will become more important and will be integrated with the sales branch). Alongside the huge manufacturers, small and more flexible companies will spring up to meet the needs of smaller customers and to formulate, based on the raw materials, the most appropriate product.

Furthermore, the need for greater flexibility in manufacturing will become clear, dictated by the tendency to produce "made-to-order materials." Even if we keep in mind that standard products will continue to exist for the needs with the greatest volume, the importance that quality and information are taking on today make it such that special products, aimed at specific needs, despite their limited incidence on the total sales volume, will represent the most dynamic and interesting sector of the market that is now forming.

The reorganization of manufacturing and research

Competition among materials is, in concrete terms, competition among social entities. Manufacturers, research centers, university organizations have traditionally constituted lines of privileged relationships, manufacturing sectors, with special outlets: anyone who worked on metals research or manufacturing could look to the automobile industry; anyone who worked on cement and bricks could look to the building industry.

Today, instead, we are witnessing a clash between different "worlds," between different manufacturing sectors. What we are seeing, amidst a thousand obstacles and difficulties, is the emergence of new phenomena that point to a structural transformation of the system in line with the new reality of materials. We see, for instance, metals manufacturers who are trying to integrate with plastics, glass, and wood manufacturers. The boundaries between privileged sectors tend to break down. What comes into being is the formative nucleus of a situation in which the vertical model is replaced by a model in which relations are established, as they are needed between manufacturers in the various fields with a view to a specific objective – to develop and market a new, partially processed composite, or else to manufacture a finished object, created with multimaterial components.

Likewise, traditionally sectorial manufacturers are widening their range of interests. Steel companies are purchasing shares in the composites and ceramics fields, chemical companies are looking into semiconductors or fiber optics. Even automobile manufacturers are trying to adjust to the new possible choices by opening breaches in the steel monoculture on which they are based.

Even materials science and research (traditionally sector-oriented) have begun to re-orient by creating intersectorial centers that do not much work on the study of individual families of materials, concentrating their attention instead on areas of functions that may correspond to various materials. It is this aim that prompted the foundation of the Materials Systems Laboratory at the Massachusetts Institute of Technology. Similar initiatives are taking place in Japan and other countries.

An electronic component with a board made of a ceramic material. (Doct. Hoechst)

And so the traditional division between metals, ceramics, plastics and other research and manufacturing is being broken down. Different areas of competence are being clustered around design themes, in-depth study is being devoted to the entire range of possible solutions.

Materials and information

If we enter a list of properties (mechanical, thermal, electric, optical...) into a computer, and specify the conditions and setting in which they must be achieved, the computer — operating with these inputs, an expert system, and with access to the necessary data banks — will select from the set of materials available those that come closest to satisfying our needs. A more advanced system could even indicate the necessary transformations and combinations of materials that would lead to the optimal "made-to-order" solution, with pointers on the appropriate engineering and the costs.

Computer-assisted materials design is not yet a concrete reality, but it is a goal upon which various partial projects are converging. Today the selection or "made-to-order" formulation of materials are the task of ex-

perts who combine theoretical knowledge with great practical sensitivity. Often only experience can foretell the result of a new combination of polymers, reinforcements, fillers, and additives. In the future, however, the accumulation of experience and the development of materials science will allow the creation of expert systems through which it will be possible to attain, through theoretical channels, if not the final result, at least a narrow range of probable solutions, upon which the successive practical testing can be concentrated. The savings in terms of time and expensive testing will be considerable.

Already materials scientists are urging that all available information be gathered in easily accessible data banks, organized according to criteria useful to the various types of users. The greatest difficulty to be overcome is — here again — that of making information coherent that is traditionally confined to fields of reseach and applications sectors that tend not to communicate. Efforts are already being made in this direction in the United States, with the foundation of the National Materials Properties Data Network, as well as in Japan.

Materials and energy

The interest of the public and of manufacturers in energy problems is directly proportional to the price of a barrel of petroleum. Aside from price fluctuations, however, ever since the first energy crunch the problem has been kept in mind constantly.

The links between materials and energy are numerous and close. They range from the energy cost of the material itself (how much energy is required to obtain a unit of product) to the more interesting energy cost per service yielded (how much energy is required to obtain a given performance). A material may also offer the possibility of exploiting hitherto unusable energy sources.

Within the context of more sophisticated manipulation of matter and of the shrewder use of energy, the new materials occupy a central position, not so much in terms of their energy cost per unit of weight, as much as in terms of overall energy cost (that is, of the material, of the transformation process, and of consumption during the product's lifespan). The attainment of this overall energy objective is the goal set itself by energy analysis, a young discipline that, if correctly applied, helps one to make sensible choices.

In the case of vehicles, for instance, each reduction in weight made possible by the materials can be evaluated in terms of savings of fuel during the vehicle's lifespan. If one reduces the weight of a mid-sized vehicle by 100 kilograms, one obtains, according to current estimates, a savings of half a liter of gasoline per 100 kilometers. A more complex case is that of the choice between plastic and glass bottles. Once we have considered the energy costs of manufacturing and transport, evaluation is made particularly sticky by social and cultural factors such as the willingness of consumers to return "empties" and the political and organizational capacities of the institutions whose task it is to gather and recycle them.

The energy problem is also closely interwoven with the problems of new materials because they can widen the field of available resources. In a few particularly significant cases, new energy possibilities are the direct result of the existence of new materials. The entire field of photovoltaic energy, for instance, depends on silicon. The area of energy savings depends greatly on insulating materials. There are also less obvious examples. The current production of off-shore petroleum, which uses steel, can exploit reserves down to 2,000 meters depth. The adoption of the appropriate high-performance composites could make it possible to exploit reserves at much greater depths, thus greatly increasing the available resources.

Materials and the environment

The increase in intensity of the information contained in matter changes the way in which we produce the artificial environment, and how it encounters (or clashes with) the environmental equilibrium. Indeed, the increasingly refined manipulation of matter should, in principle, reduce consumption and waste per unit of performance provided. And yet we should be aware that the materials produced, because they derive from a deeper artificialization of matter, are far harder to reintegrate into natural cycles, once the object's useful life is over. Furthermore, composite materials are, almost by definition, difficult to recycle because they contain various materials, bonded in an almost inseparable fashion. Recycling in fact is based on obtaining parts made of a homogeneous material from old objects. This is quite difficult, or completely impossible, to do when different materials occur in a profoundly integrated form. The problem arises, for instance, in view of the massive advance of composites in the manufacturing of automobiles. Metal com-

ponents will be replaced with parts that will be far more difficult to recover or recycle.

In the end, the environmental repercussions of a trend that we can sum up as "less matter, less energy, more information" profoundly modify the framework of references. We can finally begin to solve, in principle, old problems generated by the ham-handed operation of paleo-technics. Less obvious and much more serious problems appear, however, generated by neo-technics and by the hyper-artificiality that it produces.

It took nearly two centuries to create a culture of ecology capable of distinguishing the terms of the environmental problem posed by the first phase of industrial history. Let us hope that today we shall succeed more rapidly in identifying the new terms of the problem, and the avenue toward a possible solution. Faced with the performance density of neo-technical objects, and faced with their unsettling "quasi-organicity," which actually corresponds to a great dissimilarity from all "natural" bases, we must develop an ecological culture that can deal with the more obvious problems of quantity as well as the subtler dilemmas posed by quality.

This is imperative – not because of any futile opposition to the transformation in progress, but because a cultural component is needed that can help guide new developments toward an acceptable equilibrium with the laws of nature, to which we are bound by our biological origin.

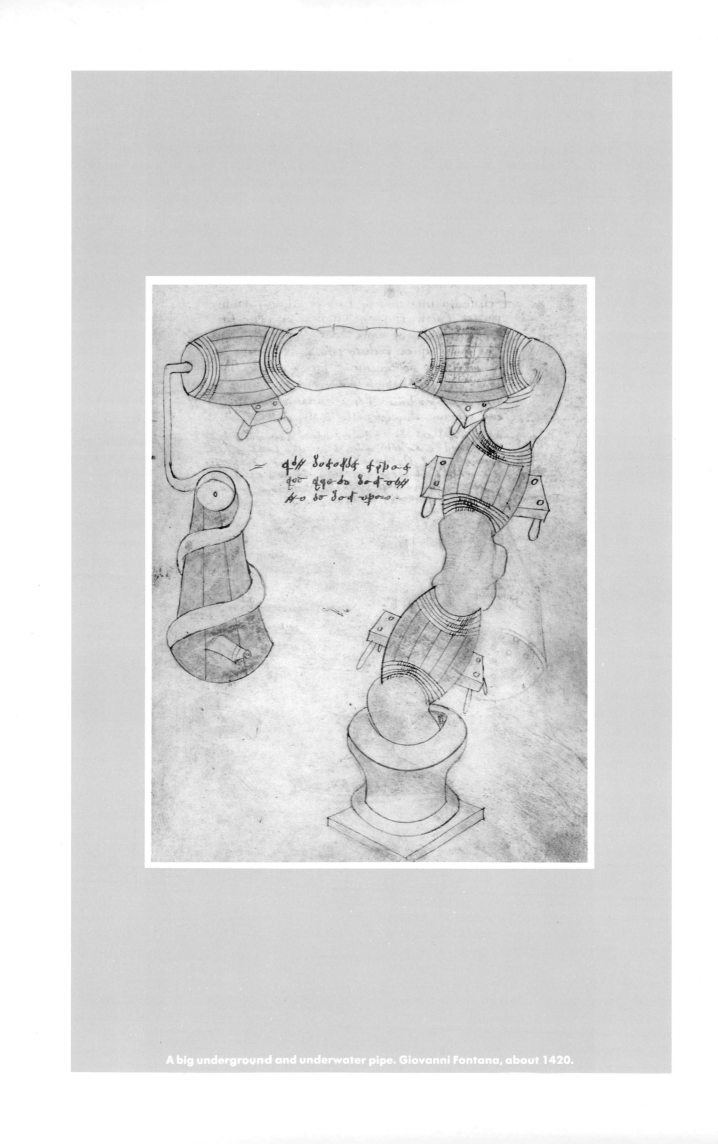

A big underground and underwater pipe. Giovanni Fontana, about 1420.

The paths of design

Thinkable and possible

Beavers construct dams that are perfect pieces of hydraulic engineering; bee hives are physical habitats constructed according to a specific social organization. The capacity to transform the matter of one's environment, adapting it to specific needs – that is, engineering – is not the exclusive domain of humans. Indeed, for over a million years man worked on a fundamentally zoological type of engineering. He manipulated rocks, sticks, and bones in a fashion that has more to do with the way beavers use wood than with the way a modern engineer uses various materials. The difference does not lie in the refinement of the technology itself – beavers and bees are quite the equals of engineers here. The central point is the distance between the individual and the matter in use. A thinking individual can see himself as separate from the environment in which he moves. Of course, this separation did not come about overnight. According to Andre Leroi-Gourhan the flint chipped by the hand of an ancient anthropoid must not (could not) have been clearly distinct to him from, say, his own thumbnail. Nevertheless, it was flint and not a thumbnail. The fact that it existed separately and outside of the body and its immediate appurtenances called for ways to conceive and speak of it. The resulting form of thought and language were certainly just a rudimentary as were the technical qualities of the object in question. Already, however, something radically different from animal engineering and communication was taking shape. It was still a quasi-zoological form of engineering, but the prefix "quasi" contains all of the future potential of man. The history of *homo sapiens* emerges from the long period of quasi-identity between the individual and the environment, between the individual and matter. If we follow the thread of the relationship between technology and culture, it is as though we are watching a gradual process of separation of the self that thinks and the matter upon which that self operates. The paths of design criss-cross an inclined plane that stretches from quasi-zoological engineering to a relationship with matter that is marked by a system of codes, languages, and models. Upon this plane, the paths of design intersect with numerous other complex paths. Design also means to plan and to choose, that is, to receive and process stimuli, select among models of thought and systems of values.

This has always been true, but today the growing gap between the individual and matter makes the cultural component of design – responsible for creating a link between the former and the latter – more evident. The importance of this component is clear in both directions. Technical knowledge and language are the well from which design and invention draw stimuli for planning. And they are also the basis of the organization of means that constitute the practice of design.

There have been, on the other hand, periods of history during which the development of the technical component and its impact on reality have made it difficult to adapt language and models of thought, systems of values, forms of knowledge. We are certainly living through one of these periods: the paths of experience and those of matter force design to deal with a "newness" that is present at all levels – from the meaning of one's actions to the words with which one expresses that meaning, from the selection of the terrain on which one works to the channels of communication of knowledge and of stimuli. To redefine the meaning and practice of design within this new framework implies a demanding cultural excursion. We can however, take one element for granted – the human value of creative, inventive, design-oriented thought, and the need to stimulate that thought. Our attempt to clarify the current relationship between individual and technology is an effort in that direction.

47

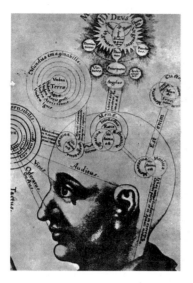

Design and invention

It is possible to imagine an elephant flying, flopping its ears as wings; it is possible to imagine a spaceship that travels faster than light. The human mind is capable of imagining anything, of "seeing" what does not exist. A little over thirty thousand years ago, the last major genetic mutation took place in the human species, generating modern man and freeing the prefrontal area of the brain where associations occur. This alteration enormously increased man's ability to project, to picture mentally things that do not exist. Since then, without any significant changes, down to the present day, man has imagined – he has dreamed of flying like birds, of sinking into the sea like the fish, of running fast as a gazelle...

Man however already possessed hands with which he had manipulated matter for more than a million years, turning rocks and clubs into tools and weapons. Hands accustomed to transforming existing matter through new techniques together with a brain capable of performing every sort of association generated the history of man as we know him. The history of design began with the history of man. Indeed, this was the origin of a special category of the imaginable – the feasible imaginable, the thinkable that is anchored to a knowledge of the technical means available, through which the thinkable can become possible.

Conceiving the possible is the basis of every design activity. The thinkable/possible is based on an integration of the capacity to imagine – peculiar to man, and as such outside of history (human history, not biological history of course) – with an historic component: the development of technical means available at a given moment, systems of depiction and the references of significance

with which they connect at a given moment and in a given cultural setting. From these historically determined data, the thinkable/possible can produce the new, can take a leap from what exists and can even deny what exists. It cannot ignore what exists – what exists is the bed in which creative thought is formed and from which it draws stimulus. It is the ground against which the leaper thrusts.

The thinkable/possible can reach its objective through well-known and much-used paths, or it can uncover new paths. From the general background of design activity stands out the special case of invention. Design and invention both integrate thought with practice and are both based on a combination of intuition and strategy. While in design, however, the accent falls on the aim (in terms of wider social and cultural values or in terms of narrower manufacturing needs), the dominant nature of invention is the novelty of the technique uncovered, and the underlying motivation may be a pure attribution of worth to the new, seen as the opening of another game of the possible.

Design and invention therefore have different histories, and the interweaving of technical development with social and cultural transformation have varying resonance. The meeting ground of development and transformation constitutes an atmosphere, an environmental condition where design and invention can find more or less room to move.

Invention and repetition

The lightbulb that suddenly flashes over the heads of comic-book characters is one of the most immediate ways of depicting the birth of an idea. The emergence of the new is a sudden light that reveals something in the mind that was not there before and that appears as if by enchantment.

In the formation of an idea, there is an element of chance. The appearance of ideas can be predicted in terms of probability (given certain conditions, that idea had to occur to somebody; for that matter, history shows many cases of independent simultaneous inventions), and not in deterministic terms (ideas cannot be produced on command). With respect to this component of chance, invention – or the new produced by man – has something in common with the new produced by nature. Just as in biological evolution the new is the product of an error of transcription of the genetic code, that is, an error of information, the basis of invention is an improper use of information, an improper mental connection with respect to what was accepted and known up to that point. The metaphoric and daring use of mental images and models that are transferred from one field to another, creates new hypotheses and new untested possibilities.

In the case of biological evolution, the new — i.e., the haphazard genetic mutation — may or may not be accepted (that is, has greater or lesser possibilities of seeing its genetic "baggage" reproduced and consolidated) depending on how it corresponds with the physical environment. The idea may also gather strength if from the original dare other ideas are created and these lead to the emergence of a new thinkable/possible. In this case, the role that is played by the natural environment for genetic mutation is taken on by the cultural, technical, and economic environment in which the new idea falls.

The two poles of newness and repetition coexist in the systems of society and production. There is an alternation between periods in which continuity predominates and phases

J.S. Bach, "The well-tempered clavier", Prelude no.1.

that seem to favor breaks with the past. This is a feature that seems to be common to all complex systems: thermodynamic systems that are far from equilibrium, biological systems, social organizations, the structures of scientific knowledge, manufacturing systems, and systems of objects.

The history of the latter, in particular, may be depicted as a bundle of threads, each of which represents the genealogical line of a specific object. To adopt the terminology of George Kubler, we could define these lines as formal sequences, that is, series of solutions linked by ties of tradition and influence. Within each sequence the redesign of new objects takes the form of a series of refinements that do not vary in terms of the engineering strategy with which the specific problem was approached and resolved, nor the formal structure. Each of these formal sequences begins with an invention and ends only when the time is ripe for a new invention to propose radically different approaches.

Furthermore the history of an object and its development over time is not independent from the history and development of other objects — the formal sequence of each evolves within a social, cultural, and manufacturing system whose transformations prepare for the phases of breaks with the past, the foundations of great renovations, the periods of inventions. Thus an important variation in a given sequence, or the beginning of a new sequence, require that there first be a significant accumulation of micro-transformations, of progressive shifts either in the area of symbolic meanings or in that of techniques, or in both. This accumulation can take place in various ways and over various lengths of time.

On the more technical side, for instance, innovation penetrates into the system of objects in two phases. First, the new makes its way along secondary routes, modifying as little as possible the existing manufacturing systems and organizational models. This is the phase in which, for instance, new materials are employed as imitations, that is, as pure subsitutes of a material used previously. In the second phase, instead, the entire system is redefined as a function of the innovation available. For this to happen, however, it is necessary that the ripening of economic opportunity for change should coincide with the cultural maturity of the various social entities involved, as well as coincide with the inventive and design capacity to overcome the traditional reference model, so as to exploit all the possibilities of the new.

As far as the symbolic meaning and formal references of objects are concerned, breaks with the past can take place in an even more explosive fashion. Here again, they are the product of a previous phase of accumulation. Kubler cites as an example the sudden transformation of art and architecture that took place during the first two decades of this century, showing how the technical transformation had taken place previously

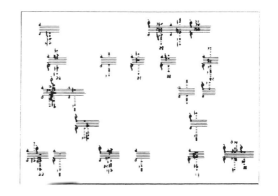

J. Cage, "Winter music"

49

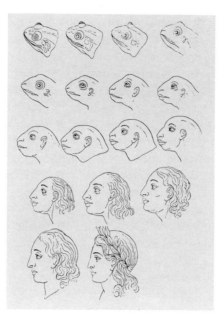

and with a certain continuity over time, and how, on this foundation, the sudden eruption of the Modern Movement seemed as if "a great number of men had suddenly realized that the repertory of forms that they inherited no longer corresponded to the meaning of existence" (*The Shape of Time*). One might say the same of what is occurring today, especially concerning the relationship between invention, linguistic renovation of design, and engineering and manufacturing development.

The twentieth century has witnessed enormous changes in scientific paradigms, in technical potential, in social structures, and in the very perception of reality. These changes have yet to find corresponding changes in models of thought, design practice, and appropriate cultural references. Even in the area of technical solutions, the presence of the new takes place most often in the context of traditional manufacturing models (the first phase, mentioned above) rather than in the context of a radical redefinition of the problem.

Without doubt, the ferment is widespread — mechanical/reductive technical thought is shifting toward systemic and synergetic approaches, the formal culture of the Modern Movement is swept away by new worlds of images, and a new culture of complexity is beginning to appear. Invention still commands an open space before it, however. The new generated by techno-science is still largely potential in the field of technical transformation of products, and above all defies any cultural classification: "The repertory of forms (...) no longer corresponds to the meaning of existence." Designing today means beginning new formal sequences. Design and invention can finally interweave.

Local and global

A man drives a nail with a hammer — free subjective action modifies what exists with a specific aim, and by means of a technical tool. This simple relationship between individual, matter, and technique, became a more generalized model in the thought underlying design linked to the historic phase of modernity, capable of spreading to all levels until it included the entire social and manufacturing system. Technology in its entirety was like an enormous hammer, with which the individual could decide what to do.

Today this approach seems inadequate to us. The interaction of many individuals and many hammers produces a system that functions according to a logic that cannot be confined to the rationality of single persons. Technology is not an easy tool to use, indeed, it assumes the appearance of a sort of organism whose development escapes all attempts at subjective control.

The history of design, of man's relationship with matter, is therefore the history of a special life form — genetically endowed with the possibility of making choices — which produces and sustains an artificial world where, in the final analysis, no subjective idea, either individual or collective, can determine the direction or outcome. It is the history of the relationship between the intentions of social entities endowed with local capacities to choose and control, and the operation of a complex system of which they form part.

As soon as the first stone was withdrawn from the world of things and made into a tool, that is, an "object," there was established an embryonic form of that relationship between aims and means that we call "design." In this first event, the control was merely local — the stone was used to break a shell. The fact that the act in question was the beginning of man's history is not related to design but merely to the haphazard emer-

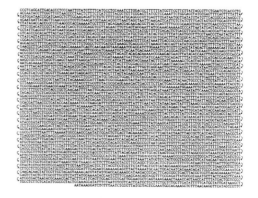

Brief tract of the sequence of the DNA bases of an Escherichia Coli cell.

gence of an improbable event.

English entrepreneurs in the mid-eighteenth century designed locally for their own profit. No one decided to create the imposing transformation of the environment, and of society generated by the Industrial Revolution. Today, the huge corporations working in information science are designing new forms of artificial intelligence. Their motivations are to beat their competition and to remain competitive on the market. Has anyone, however, really sat down to predict the influence of these innovations?

The only real novelty nowadays is that our history allows us to turn and look at past events, and that the speed of the change underway helps us to perceive, in our direct experience, the signals of a change whose dimensions we can hazard a guess, but the results of which we neither know nor control.

This diffuse sensation of transformation constitutes the basic tissue of the new culture emerging from the crisis of the modern. In particular, what has collapsed is the myth of the demiurge, that dream of power in which practically everything could be designed so as to be globally consistent, ranging from the smallest object to broader social organisms. Today we are learning that there is not just a single rational system that may prevail. We are learning that each objective has relative validity and that no outcome is permanent. Furthermore, we are beginning to see that everything that happens takes place on the crest of a wave of transformations that all have worked to generate, but that no single individual can control.

In this atmosphere, design has lost a measure of self-confidence, and experiences the individual's loss of power as if it were a defeat of reason. This self-awareness, however, may well be interpreted differently. We may suppose that from the crisis of demiurgic design a more mature form of design may emerge, expressed by a subjectivity that feels itself to be part of a broader system in which human choices, historical dynamics, and natural laws are integrated toward a future which, as it were, is anybody's bet. From this point of view, if no individual is capable of deciding on the "big picture" for the future, all however are players in a game the outcome of which will emerge fom the conflicting integration of a number of individual options.

The idea of design that takes shape here is certainly less monolithic than we had believed in the past. The great overall game indeed is articulated as a number of different games, each with its own rules and players, who in turn offer various settings in which design can make its choices. These choices range from driving a nail all the way up to programming a corporate strategy or establishing a territorial policy – these forms of planning and design require one to move through subsystems with different histories, various levels of complexity and different operating models. Design implies the capacity to move through this network of overlapping and connected models, negotiating convergences between social entities, discussing and determining in each instance the aims and meanings.

Creativity and knowledge

The wave of transformations of technoscience can be experienced as an oppres-

sive and uncontrollable force, or it can be approached from the surfer's point of view. A very high wave also provides an excellent opportunity for those who have the capacity and courage to ride it correctly.

If and how one can influence the wave, how one can affect the its overall direction, remain unanswered questions. The image of the surfer, nevertheless, has the advantage of describing a positive attitude toward the objective impossibility of individual control over the huge transformations now in progress. Not only is the surfer/designer not tumbled head over heels by the wave – he manages to use his knowledge and experience to choose and act, thus ensuring his prerogative to be creative in a way that is appropriate to the new situation.

On the other hand, moving on the wave by simultaneously following and dominating it, by controlling the unforeseen factors and even playing with them, implies a thorough familiarity with waves. Knowledge of the development of technology, of its dynamics, of its internal currents therefore constitutes the basis of any form of creativity that is not to be thrust to the sidelines nor swept away.

Out of this knowledge, and out of the relationship that one succeeds in establishing between ideas and matter, design takes shape, both in practical terms (that is, moving from the idea to matter) and in the opposite direction (that is to say, from matter to the idea).

Traditionally, for craftsmen and artists, matter – observed and known through direct experience – has represented not only a concrete limitation to work against, but also an enormous source of creative stimuli. Today, matter tends to be increasingly artificial and decreasingly material, thus changing the quality of this framework of references and the way in which one approaches it. The new matter from which stimuli are now drawn no longer provides the physicality of a given material as much as it provides a set of possibilities and performances, a "possible" that emerges from what can be manufactured through an engineering system capable of performing ever more subtle manipulations.

The "matter" of design and invention can therefore take the form of a process which allows one to produce, variously, a given composite, a computing method leading to a new approach to a structural problem, a flexible automated manufacturing process that imposes a new set of limitations while simultaneously creating new possibilities. Another possible result (and this is by far the richest vein of stimuli and references) is that what has already been accomplished in other fields and which can be transferred to a new application – transferring images and ideas even prior to transferring technology – can become a source of generative metaphors.

The field of the possible thus spreads enormously both vertically – toward in-depth specialization – and horizontally, toward what has been accomplished in other sectors. This sets up not only the problem of quantitative knowledge but also that of qualitative knowledge – conceiving the possible by referring to this new matter that is richer in forms, more abstract, more fluid in some ways and more rigid in others.

Modes of knowledge

1.3.2

In the history of *homo sapiens*, magic, religious, and philosophical thought, that is, those forms of thought that are linked to the ability to use language to produce symbols, rapidly attained a level of complexity comparable to today's. Technical thought, on the other hand, has followed a different path. The relationship between matter and those who work with it evolves over longer periods of time. The tendency toward abstraction encounters, in the physical quality of materials, a lasting tie with the more practical and immediate aspects of our experience. From cave culture onward, the craftsman was a figure whose "knowledge" followed rules dictated by matter – his actions, his thought were always linked and subalternate to the requirements of the material with which he worked. The craftsman's technical knowledge consisted in a profound familiarity – in physical terms and in terms of perception – with materials. The observation and practical manipulation of these materials often was the best technical school available. In every one of a craftsman's technical operations, there was the accumulation of historical experience that has filtered out the most profitable techniques, eliminating all others. This development is so profoundly determined by the qualities and requirements of materials, that the relationship between craftsman and matter seems practically unchanging over time. The knowledge of a craftsman is that of one who can do something, and do it well, but who does not know why he does it in that way. Innovation, when it arises, is the result of a fortuitous piece of happenstance – often the product of an error that has yielded positive results, rather that of a deliberate design choice in the modern sense of the word.

Magicians, philosophers, and priests, instead, operate directly in the realm of thought, images, abstract connections, and languages. They do not feel the require-

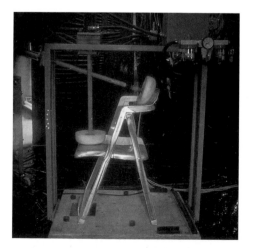

**Load testing a plastic chair.
By using reflection polariscopy,
it is possible to observe the effects
of stress on the product.
(Doct. Montedison-CSI)**

ments of matter, do not have to provide perceptible results. Their mental model is synthetic, rather than analytic.

At a certain point in history there emerged a new strategy of thought, which tended to merge these two different models of thought: modern science. Science is bound by matter, that is, results, but its initial hypothesis is based on thought, that is, imagining a result.

Craftsmen and engineers

Science did not immediately become a factor in manufacturing. For a certain period of time it moved parallel to manufacturing, more profoundly affecting models of thought than practical activities. With the coming of the Industrial Revolution, however, science was integrated with engineering, while the criterion of cost-efficiency became a powerful force for innovation, further enhanced by the growing competition between manufacturers and manufacturing sectors. In the new technical and cultural setting, the available materials multiplied and their development accelerated.

All previous models of behavior and technical knowledge were now useless. The practical knowledge and the initiatory education of craftsmen was deprived of a fundamental element necessary to their reproduction — time. With the restriction of available time but with the possibility of theoretical foreshadowing, a new figure is created: that of the engineer, who does, not what he has seen others do, but that which he knows how to compute.

Unlike craftsmen, engineers use a precise and referential language to describe themselves and their procedures. They know what they are doing and why they are doing it. They do not see the new as a leap into the void, because their calculations allow them to foresee the results. Matter is no longer a specific piece of wood or stone to which he must turn his hand, but an abstract model characterized by parameters (properties) and by relationships between those parameters. To an engineer, a material is known when its properties are known, which is to say, codified in numerical form.

The passage to an abstract and codified relationship with matter certainly did not come about overnight. For about two centuries theoretical knowledge and practical experience coexisted. The number of materials and the pace of their development were such that designers could work on a given material long enough to be able to integrate their

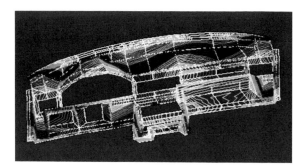

Computer simulation of the behavior of material flows within the mold - it becomes possible to improve the mold while reducing the amount of empirical testing required. (Doct. Montedison-CSI)

familiarity with its properties, expressed in numerical parameters, with empirical testing of its qualities. Designers learned from books, but they had time and the possibility to pick up the tricks of the trade in the field, as it were. This hybrid knowledge typifies the image of the modern designer, and it is still the most common image.

Today, the situation has changed. An abstract and theoretical knowledge of materials is no longer just one of the possible approaches, but the only feasible approach.

There is still room for knowledge and practices similar to the crafts tradition, thanks to the multiplicity of current manufacturing and marketing options, but design must take into account the dominant trend — the number of materials available prevents a designer from acquiring experience on each of them. The appearance of "made-to-order" materials, which do not exist before the design, make that a conceptual impossibility.

Extending the knowable

Today, a designer who intends to work in the field of possibilities made available by technical innovation not only must find an orientation among numerous options, but must especially adapt his intuitive capacity, creativity, and work method to the general trend toward abstraction, immateriality, and multiplicity of the parameters with which he must deal in order to work with matter.

Traditional, "non-specialized" material set limits that had repercussions on the final image of the object and that profoundly typified that object. At the same time, the oversizing that non-specialized material forced designers to adopt not only offered freedom to maneuver in formal and functional terms, but left a certain margin for excess and even error. The designer, furthermore, once he had internalized his familiarity of certain properties through practice, could concentrate on a few design parameters, taking the others for granted.

Everything changes when one encounters new – or even custom-designed – materials, having a specialized set of properties, which are used ever closer to their limit conditions. Precisely because each feature is optimized, if any parameter is not taken into consideration, or if any variation in the conditions of use is neglected, can the product collapse.

Thus, while technical and scientific development expands the field of the possible, it requires on the other hand a more-than-proportional expansion of what must be known and controlled. The mass of knowledge called for is such that design is increasingly becoming a collective activity practiced by a growing number of actors, each of whom makes a specific contribution, each with a different body of knowledge and awareness.

This multiplication of partial technical knowledge constitutes a further distancing of the individual from matter. Between matter and an engineer during the first industrial phase there stood only engineer's calculations and models. Today, between each individual and matter there stands not only his portion of knowledge, but the knowledge of all the other actors in the process. The possible that each individual can conceive thus largely depends on an exchange of information, a capacity to establish contact with those who know how to perform certain other processes.

The possible therefore takes on two aspects. The first is purely theoretical and is the limitless set of manipulations of matter, made up of all that techno-science has developed and produced. The other is feasible. This is the possible that springs from communication between different areas of knowledge.

On the other hand, even the new thinkable/possible has two aspects. The first is the growing possibility of manipulation in very specific areas of expertise that springs from specialized knowledge (the invention of a new polymer, the perfection of a new algorithm). The second derives from the opening of new channels of communication between different areas – a thinkable/possible based on a transverse knowledge capable of establishing contact with different technical worlds, languages, and dialects. Techno-science has consolidated on the first of these two levels, while the second level – though it has always existed – has been neglected by recent technical tradition.

The proliferation of languages

The specialization of technical knowledge is a direct consequence of the priority given to one of the goals of modern thought – the most refined and in-depth manipulation of what exists. The languages in which technical knowledge speaks are a concise way of overcoming what is well known and moving directly to the battlefront of the new. Marking off the field of combat, as it were, is the only way to avoid wasting the intellectual energy of researchers. The formation of a group practice and culture (and a related world-view) is the natural response to the search for meaning and the motivations of those who form part of that group.

The advent and consolidation of this trend has resulted in the explosion of the technical and scientific potential. The results have been remarkable. As with any great success, however, this too has led to unforeseen results.

The first is the trend that has led us to observe that specialization seems to be endless. In fact, all specialized knowledge uncovers an array of new problems that generate new specializations. Until recently this was not taken into consideration, and the model common in technical and scientific spheres held that the knowable was a finite quantity of information. The set of all knowledge could be imagined as a pyramid based on specialization.

This image is thrown into crisis when faced with the impossibility of establishing a foundation for the entire structure. The deeper science penetrates into the phenomena that rule nature, the more questions are raised. The narrower the field of interest of technical specializations, and the more new problems and new uncertainties arise outside of that field of interest.

And so specialized knowledge appears, rather than as a solid stone at the base of a pyramid, as a point in which a bundle of straight lines – of problems – meets, opening fan-like above and below the limited area taken into consideration. For instance, one may concentrate exclusively on improving screws. When one's attention is focused on this aspect, however, an enormous range of problems is raised in the fields of materials science, process technologies, computing methods...

The second unexpected result brings to mind the Tower of Babel. At a certain point during the construction of the tower, the multitude of workers suddenly realized that it had become impossible to communicate – all spoke different languages. Every specialized field of knowledge shares problems, expertise, and language with the fields of knowledge that lie immediately upstream or downstream from it, but the great difficulties arise when one attempts to move horizontally.

The multiplication of expertise, language, channels of communication restricts understanding and even awareness of new possibilities, making it increasingly difficult to reproduce the transverse technical knowledge that a designer needs in order to evaluate options. That knowledge was traditionally assembled by stitching together elements of specialized knowledge.

Transverse knowledge

We have spoken of the designer in general terms, as an individual who makes choices, who decides among a range of options based on a hierarchy of values. In reality, designers are quite different one from another, both in terms of the background with which they work and of the system of meanings to which they make reference. Tradition has consolidated two stereotypes – that of the engineer, and that of the architect/designer. The former has been largely identified with the development of modern technology. The latter has an older tradition and a more complex intersection of technical problems not strictly related to manufacturing.

The histories of these two stereotypes are quite different. Engineers have progressively specialized, adopting value systems that exist within the area of their activity: to improve design in technical and economic terms, by confronting specific problems. Architects, on the other hand, have continued to face the entire range of technical possibilities, with reference to a value system that includes social attitudes, linguistic expressions, aesthetic considerations.

This difference in attitudes has generally led architects to have less and less mastery over the body of technical areas, while engineers – thanks to the progressive restriction of their fields of interest, have been able to master a few aspects of new technologies.

The current growing knowledge gap, however, has even hit those engineers who – until yesterday – were considered specialists. In the chapter devoted to the "Paths of Matter," we noted in passing that certain manufacturing sectors – traditionally tied to one material and to its processes of transformation – are now tending to move away from

their specialized production cultures. Therefore new design alternatives in these sectors should be evaluated on the basis of a horizontal awareness which is not part of specialized knowledge. Furthermore, if the development of the manufacturing system tends to emphasize the functions of "service" and "communications," at every level of design, technical aspects must intersect with other complex problems. In the end, the need for a non-specialized knowledge seems not only to survive, but to be destined to remain one of the basic prerequisites of knowledge – in technical terms as well.

The fact that the figure of the individual designer should be replaced by a design team modifies and complicates the landscape without eliminating its general significance – if the collective is made up of different figures, each of which supplies different bodies of knowledge, it is at any rate necessary that they establish a form of communication, a reciprocal awareness of each other's field of expertise – of just what each member knows and what he can do.

Therefore, even though the practical and ideal differences among designers of different origins and interests are considerable and run deep, in the area of matter – or, to be more specific, in the area of the techniques with which one can alter matter – the separation no longer exists between one historic stereotype and the other, between the engineer and the architect-designer. The boundary now separates those who work with the question, "What is this?" (for whom specialized and vertical knowledge is still useful) and those who work on the question "What do I need, and why do I need it?" (for whom new bases in the relationship with the possible must established). The second question, in fact, implies a knowledge and awareness that are not organized around the physical entities of materials but around certain functions and a variety of options.

This technical awareness resembles an operating approach more than a system of classification. Indeed, a complete classification of possible functions is impossible. The question and the possible answer imply a subjective component. The point of view of the person asking the question cannot be ruled out, as it can for the traditional question "What is this?"

Furthermore, the meaning of the question "What do I need?" – because it is tied to a subjective opinion and not a fixed object – may also shift. Those with whom I am speaking may introduce with their replies elements that may lead me to modify my objectives (and with them, I would change "what I need"). In the process of formation of awareness, an element of retroactivity is thus introduced. And the creation of these retroactions makes it impossible to represent design and cognitive strategies with simple models: the field of possibilities in which the designer now moves is a complex system, not only because it is extensive and changeable, but also because the individual exploring it is himself part of the system.

An essential point of contemporary science is to assume that the observer is an integral part of the observed system, while developing some reflections complexity, later extended to various areas of knowledge, ranging from biological to social systems. Questions previously interpreted through the filters of simple or simplifying solutions can now be considered from another standpoint. In this new atmosphere the act of design can be reconsidered on the basis of its characteristic rationality which stems from a process that is neither completely haphazard nor entirely systematic, but which gradually leads research to take form through a series of contacts and communicative exchanges.

In order for this to take place effectively, however, it is necessary for the designer to know or intuit how and with whom he must communicate. This is the specific foundation of transverse technical knowledge, determining the right people to communicate with. Succeeding in communicating with them requires a special form of organization of knowledge and awareness which, to paraphrase Edgard Morin, could be defined as a "knowledge of knowledge" or "awareness of awareness." Which means knowing who knows what, knowing what part of that knowledge may be of interest, and succeeding in communicating with that person about it.

Simple and complex

For Michelangelo, sculpting consisted in extracting the form that the artist's intuition told him was trapped in the block of marble, liberating it from all its excess parts. Designing, too, means giving form to matter, but today this act is far less straightforward. Greater emphasis is given to the knowledge that the designer conditions the process, but is also conditioned by the system in which he operates. Furthermore, it becomes clear that the form of the finished product is always in some fashion influenced by the cognitive process of the designer, prior to or during his design activity.

Just as in the past, there is a flow of information at the basis of all design activity. Designers work upon that flow by introducing their capacity to foreshadow and invent, by managing both the information that others supply and the information that they find "frozen" in the materials and components that they employ. Between the original block of marble and the statue by Michelangelo there exists an intermediate set of information that the artist has conferred to the matter by transforming a more probable form (the block) into a less probable one (the statue).

The new quality of matter, however, lies in the fact that the information to be managed is more complex and theoretical, and it is hence more difficult to interact with a range of options that appear as a growing number of signals emitted in a multitude of different codes. Given the lack of suitable interpretative instruments, there is a danger that the possible may remain merely potential, and fail to become thinkable for the designer, due to difficulties in communicating. Signals that are not decoded do not become information; they remain little more than noise.

On the other hand, it is impossible (in conceptual as well as in practical terms) to attain total understanding, that is, awareness of the sum of everything that is transmitted in the various codes. Anyone attempting to do so would find himself in the same position as the emperor's mapmakers described by Jorge Luis Borges. In order to represent the territories of their sovereign in the greatest possible detail, they produced a map as large as the empire itself.

Any approach to reality that intends to make it understandable must involve the use of a filter, a way of organizing raw information according to a model appropriate to the specific sort of information that one intends to extract. The quality of what is known depends on the quality (that is, appropriacy) of that model. Furthermore, different goals call for different models. To cross Europe, one needs a map of its system of highways (with a scale of 1:5,000,000); in order to find one's way through the heart of Venice, one needs a map of the *calli* and canals (1:5,000).

One of the obstacles to increasing and rendering more organic one's knowledge of all that technology makes possible is the lack of a "cartography" that offers maps in different scales, so that the designer/traveler can both survey the continents (that is, understand the general dynamics) and find his bearings in the alleys of more specific areas of activity. In short, almost the entire enormous task of organizing information – specifically oriented to the user's needs – remains to be done.

The reorganization of the various specialized areas around given functions, and the creation of data banks and expert systems capable of aiding the designer in decision making (*Computer Aided Material Design*, see 1.2.2) constitute an important and imposing task of reordering knowledge, and by no means are these the only problems facing a designer when working with "new matter." Even were we to suppose that the necessary tools were available (and they will not be for some time to come), not always does that which is known practically correspond to what is theoretically possible. A data bank is nevertheless a world to be explored, just as

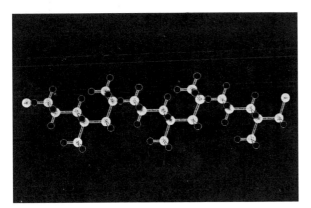

Fragment of a polypropylene chain.
Software for molecular graphics
permits one to simulate the spatial arrangement
of many atoms (shown in different colors)
within a macromolecule.
(Doct. Montedison-Istituto G. Donegani)

an expert system can answer certain questions – but those questions must first be asked. They can only be based upon an initial image of the problem, which the interested party must, in some fashion, formulate.

The designer's chief problem, then, remains that of asking the correct questions by forming mental images that are appropriate to the reality on the basis of which he will then organize his exploration. Whether this exploration consists in time spent visiting factories and laboratories, or reading through books and journals, or chatting with specialists, or dialoguing with a computer, the problem remains the same – how to make information emerge from the noise, how to develop filters and interpretational codes capable of extracting, from the mass of available data, the data endowed with meaning.

Since the term "design" refers to an extremely complex and variegated set of mental and practical activities, a designer is in need of an equally complex and variegated set of filters and reference models. Those that are outlined in the following paragraphs certainly do not constitute an exhaustive assembly, but they are sufficient to indicate the way in which the new qualities of matter test the traditional foundations of technical thought, tracing the features of a knowledge that is appropriate to the new technical and cultural atmosphere in which the designer now works – the "knowledge of knowledge" to which we previously referred to.

Models of thought

Problem setting and problem solving, that is, establishing the terms of a problems and organizing the means to solve it, are the two aspects of all design. They correspond to very different mental activities and practices, based on equally different styles of reasoning and forms of knowledge.

In the traditional layout of the design process (above all in areas that are chiefly oriented toward engineering and manufacturing) all the problem setting takes place in advance, or "upstream," and is often taken for granted, while the problem solving is "downstream" and is considered to be an activity that can be mastered with a functional, straightforward, and theoretical sort of reasoning. This is a simplified outline that is far from actual practice.

It is true that there always exists a point of departure in which the problem is set, but it is not true that problem setting is entirely confined to this initial phase – during the entire development of a design, the need arises repeatedly to define partial problems linked to various components and subcomponents, and out of these problems and their solutions, the need may arise to redefine the problem as a whole. This introduces into the design process new values based on chance and that cannot be codified. These values are typical of the problem setting phase, and they in turn make the problem solving phase far more complex to codify.

Indeed, problem setting always originates from a mental image, a metaphor capable of generating other images and, thereafter, actions, interactions among individuals, and action upon matter. It is this leap of imagination that provides the problem with its initial definition and that sets the stage for the solution. "Solving a problem," according to Her-

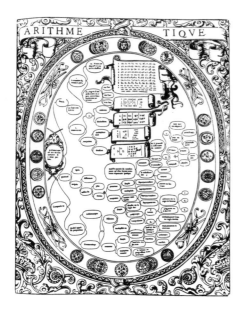

bert A. Simon, "means simply presenting that problem in such a way as to make its solution crystal clear." In other words, at the origin of each successive development (problem solving) there is always an event that cannot be formalized, the creation of a generative metaphor, the appearance of an idea that is simple but endowed with the ability to create a synthesis of many complex elements.

The quality of this idea, the generative capacity of the metaphor, should by no means be taken for granted. This is an element of chance whose probability of proving effective depends on many factors, but chiefly on the cultural background of whoever formulates the idea. That background is a complex set of specific technical knowledge and reference models, two components that are mixed differently and in varying proportions, but that are always present simultaneously.

A designer therefore needs two instruments with opposite qualities – a "microscope" and a "macroscope."

The "macroscope" is used to examine techno-science as a whole, to observe its movements, its relationships with society and culture, the transformations that it induces in the quality of objects and in the relationships between objects and individuals. The "macroscope" is a technological culture that emerges from the use of appropriate models of thought. The quality of the mental image, which is the point of departure for the problem setting, and the overall map of the possible, whence one can progressively derive other more detailed maps upon which to trace the path of the problem solving, originate with the macroscope.

They originate there, but they do not end there. It is typical of the design process that

an inspiration, the intuition of a solution may also move along the opposite path, rising from the observation of a detail, of a unique case, to an image that has a more general value to a designer. Therefore, alongside the "macroscope" a designer also needs a "microscope"; if the former serves to satisfy his curiosity about what is happening (a curiosity common to the designer and other decision-makers working in areas such as economic planning and regional planning), the latter satisfies a type of curiosity that is more specific to a designer – how things work, down to the smallest details.

While curiosity is a fundamental quality for a designer, it must be accompanied by the acrobatic skill necessary to be interested simultaneously in the social and cultural transformations that will be induced by the spread of artificial intelligence, in how brilliantly the leg of a table has been joined to the table surface, or in the solution employed for the

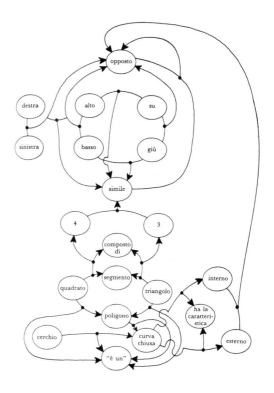

opening mechanism of the folding solar collector for the space shuttle. From these minute local observations, in fact, the designer can gather ideas and inspirations to be deployed in another context.

The process of transverse penetration of new technologies is based on the capacity of designers to use what has already been accomplished as a basin of ideas from which to nourish their own creativity. This capacity to observe details, in turn, requires an analytic ability based on a system of references appropriate to the qualities that "new matter" presents. In other words, the "macro-scope" and the "microscope" must have both overcome certain models of thought that are central to recent technical tradition. It is in this very area that adaptation to the new is most difficult. Traditional technical thought is largely based on implicit models that were formed in a cultural setting that is now quite distant. The beginnings of modern science and the successive beginnings of industry were based upon a mechanical and reductionist vision of reality, as well as upon a form of reasoning that always seemed crystal clear and unique. The astounding success of science and industry confirmed the correctness of this approach, rendered it absolute (by making it seem to be the only possible approach), internalized as something certain that did not have to be called into question each time it was used. Today the landscape of cultural references offers a less certain picture (see 1.3.1), and relationships with technology also tend to modify. The need that emerges to revise existing models of thought is therefore not only a basic cultural need, but also a need to produce more adequate working tools in a narrower sense. Four aspects of this situation are especially important: the crisis in the knowability of materials as a classification of elements, the need to overcome simplistic thought in the conception of highly integrated objects, the non-linearity of the design process, the non-singularity of the forms of reasoning.

The unclassifiable

Any organic taxonomy is formed on the basis of a limited set of objects that differ one from another and that are stable over time. This is a form of knowledge that has been of great importance in the history of culture — the great classifications of the mineral, vegetable, and animal kingdoms were fundamental in the construction of modern knowledge. Though they are useful under certain conditions, that does not, however, mean that their principle can be extended to just any area of study. They were useful, for instance, because according to the time scale on which we operate, the elements to be arranged in a system could be considered to differ one from another and to be stable. If we imagine, however, a great acceleration of biological and geological history, we can see that the task of the classifier would become impossible — each category would change constantly.
That situation would not necessarily bring

about a crisis of what is knowable, but it could create a crisis in a given model of knowledge. It would still be possible to develop knowledge about the "fast reality" that we have imagined, but by other means — by singling out flows, trends, and interpretative models of the factors that imply stability and of the environmental conditions that induce transformation and rupture, much like what current theories of evolution attempt to do.

Contemporary science proposes numerous cognitive models of this sort. Technical knowledge as well, if it intends to face up the new reality of matter, must develop appropriate models to capture qualities in a system

where identities overlap, and change prevails over stability.

If we consider the world of plastics, for instance, we note (see 2.1.) the difficulties involved in classifying them by properties. The designers and technicians who work closely with these materials have long since (and with considerable difficulties) adopted cognitive strategies that have little to do with rigid classification in families and sub-families. The new strategies are based on singling out dominant characteristics and their fields of variability, limits and intervals between limits, intuitive as well as anti-intuitive interactions. On the other hand, this form of knowledge — which accommodates the complexity and variability of the object of study — is becoming less and less a prerogative of plastics and increasingly a form of knowledge appropriate to the entire field of materials. The simple index file of (cultural and physical) objects upon which modern engineering thought has constructed its knowledge and practice must now be replaced by more mobile references, by "objects" that vary in smaller or greater intervals. To paraphrase Michel Serres, technical thought must be capable, when necessary, of abandoning the strict world of Mars for the fluid world of Venus.

Synergies

An advanced composite is a material in whose design one plus one does not equal two. Its qualities are not given by adding up the properties of its components. They are the product of a far more complex interaction, which takes place on the surfaces in contact. Designing a composite, therefore, means working with a system of relations and possible synergies.

The central role attributed to synergy is a new mental attitude with respect to traditional engineering thought, which for two centuries was built and consolidated upon a diametrically opposed foundation: for traditional thought design hinged upon the breakdown of the problem into simple elements, and their successive mechanical recomposition.

Nevertheless, the need to move beyond traditional engineering thought is not limited to the field of advanced composites. This need involves the entire system of objects, thrust along by the tendency to integrate functions, one of the most important trends in contemporary engineering. The entity of the cultural leap required can be seen indirectly by comparing the image of an object typical of the mechanical phase, with the image – which we defined above as quasi-organic – of an object in which there is a more extreme integration between materials and functions. The latter object seems dense, difficult to break down into component parts, ruled by phenomena that are not easily understood by an outside observer. The earlier object instead seems "crystal clear"; even with complicated objects from the earlier age, such as a watch or a steam locomotive, the complication is at least legible to anyone who is familiar with the elementary grammar and syntax of mechanics. Components and functions can be clearly linked, the parts are macroscopic, the connections are evident, the relationships of cause and effect are straightforward.

Beneath this leap in the image, lies an equally considerable cultural leap that has to do with the formulation of the initial idea underlying the design and the ways in which that design is developed. The object born under the sign of the mechanical is the product of design processes based on functional strategies, which in theoretical terms means breaking the problem down into elementary parts, establishing a function for each along with a component that can perform that function. This process can be represented by a tree-shaped graph. There is a single trunk upon which numerous branches converge. Atop each branch stands a function with its corresponding elementary component. With these elementary ties, an object can be constructed. The quality of the design is based on the qualities of the elementary components. Their successive assembly will certainly require adjustments and a certain amount of effort in order to make them consistent, but the point of departure remains the single qualities. Following this functional strategy means moving up and down from the branches of the "tree of functions," which implies that those branches may be considered to be independent one from another.

When the result being sought is a highly integrated object, this is no longer possible. The graph representing the links between functions and parts contains more intricate connections, which must be kept in mind from the outset – the tree of functions becomes a network of relations. The fundamental elements are no longer the single elementary components in their specific physicality, but the relationships between the parts, the system of which they form part and the "interfaces" they encounter.

The crisis of the mechanical-reductive model, which has general consequences, emerges in the area of technology and manufacturing, driven by the thrust of the possibilities offered by new materials. Technology calls into question the cultural cradle from which it sprang and was nourished.

Retroactions

We have already indicated that the introduction of a new material into a field of applications usually involves two phases. The first is a phase of substitution and imitation, while the following phase leads to a reexamination of the object as a whole (see 1.3.1). The potential for new developments on the part of the generation of materials and processes currently available exerts a certain pressure on the consolidated cultural and manufacturing structures, pushing to redefine drastically the approach with which objects are resolved technically.

A designer, therefore, in the course of whatever exploration he is carrying out on the basis of a given approach to a problem, may find himself faced with an engineering possibility that, in order to be used in full, requires questioning the original image, the approach with which he began work. The presence of materials with high potential for innovation is capable of making the design process non-linear. The underlying model, therefore, must be capable of capturing the complexity that derives from the frequency with which, at all levels, these rings of retroaction occur.

Of course, the possibility of reexamining the technical and formal structure of an object does not depend alone on the designer's ability to overcome mental inertia. Engineering and manufacturing inertia play an important role in the continuity of the formal sequences of objects (see 1.2.2). Nevertheless, the specific role of the designer is precisely that of picking up new possibilities.

The wave of potential innovations produced by the development of technology and science has prepared the terrain for a new era of inventions, capable of triggering a widespread and diffuse redesign of the system of objects and of the relationships between objects and men. The quality of the final results largely depends on the ability of designers to overcome the cultural inertia that can prevent them from "seeing" the new, and on their ability to direct design processes that can accommodate the new. All of this, however, depends in turn on the preparation of an underlying connective tissue made up of an awareness of the non-linear nature of the design process, as well as on the mental and organizational elasticity created by that awareness.

The panorama that we have sketched tends to emphasize the aspects that can be considered to be breaks with the recent past: physical elements are replaced by relationships, simple and static models are substituted by complex and dynamic ones. However, in order to face the complexity of these problems, as Edgar Morin puts it, it is not sufficient to move from reductionism, which emphasizes the parts, to holism, which emphasizes the whole. It is also necessary to keep in mind the relationship between the parts and the whole. On the other hand, the capacity to perceive the "circuit of relations" that links the two levels of the problem not only corresponds to a theoretical need, bound to the correct comprehension of the subject being studied, but is also a concrete practical need of the designer. Designing, in fact, means being able to move from the constituent elements to the whole and back again without losing sight of the wealth of relations, the potential of synergy that links the two levels.

The discovery of complexity that new matter generates, need not lead to a surrender before the unmanageable welter of relationships that is typical of the system. It means

rather moving within that complexity with the awareness that the models that one constructs are valid as long as they "function" with respect to a certain program.

In other words, complexity is not a datum of the problem per se, not something that the designer must master before beginning work, spending enormous amounts of energy in creating models for an infinite number of "objective" relationships in the system. Complexity is an open representation of the problem, constructed in a process that can be continually readjusted.

The quality of the designer lies in the quality of these representations, of the way in which they succeed in making the problem comprehensible in local terms, without however eliminating the possiblity of interacting with other representations and models.

Demonstrative reason and astute reason

Modern engineering developed in a world where reason was considered unique, the information available was considered complete, and the absolute optimum to be a result that could be virtually attained. Design practice, given those premises, corresponds to the journey of a traveler who was afforded the opportunity of seeing the land he was to cross from an airplane before setting out. At the start of his trip, the traveler/designer knows exactly where he intends to go and has had the possibility of evaluating various alternate routes in order to choose the best one. This approach, which corresponds to the functional strategy mentioned above, calls for the designer (or the design group) to be omniscient, endowed – when work starts – with all the information potentially available.

In practice, however, things never quite work out that way. At the outset, the designer possesses partial information, which is drawn from his cultural foundation and from the accumulation of his previous experiences. Upon this information he forms an idea, he sketches an initial conceptual structure of the topic, he performs reconnaissance that will allow him progressively to gather new information. The final design is not a product of the search for the optimum based on all available information. It is rather a product of a search for the satisfactory, which will be attained once the designer has accumulated a quantity of information that can be considered sufficient according to his cost/benefit balance sheet.

Furthermore, this solution will depend upon factors that are quite difficult to formalize and foresee, such as the quality of the initial idea on the cognitive process employed, which in turn depend on the initial approach, on intuition, and also on happenstance, which determines the designer's encounters as he searches for information.

This entire process, which is defined as a heuristic strategy or the strategy of learning, represents a description of the design process. The design iter always involves chance, subjective intuition, and the variability of the system of relationships. Rarely does the stategy that allows one to pick up the stimuli for creativity, or to gather and organize information for the development of a design, correspond to a clearly planned program, in which each phase can be clearly laid to entirely explicit reasoning which we shall refer to henceforth as demonstrative reasoning. The chief guide along this path is an interweaving of intuition, good sense, and happenstance which we shall now dub astute reasoning – the *metis* of the ancient Greeks.

Metis, in Hesiod's *Theogony* was the name of the goddess who was mother to Athena. Zeus devoured Metis in order to appropriate her qualities. As a common noun it implied series of mental aptitudes such as instinct, wisdom, multiple or polymorph talent, and was applied to mobile or slippery concepts devoid of exact measurements or strict reasoning (see Detienne Vernant). Metis has always been the basis of all practical knowledge. Both former and latter, as more lucid reasoning has prevailed, have been progressively shunted aside. Their outsider status with repect to dominant models of thought does not, however, mean that they have been entirely eliminated. Practical knowl-

ledge, in the shade of more formal and theoretical knowledge, has nevertheless remained the connective tissue in many operations: it is certainly metis that guides the hand in the complex physical and chemical process involved in making mayonnaise (to feel total conviction about this, it is quite sufficient to attempt to explain the engineering that goes into the process), and there is certainly a great deal of metis in the practice of designing and in the formation of the designer's technical knowledge.

The multiplication of materials and processes does not modify the structure of this process as much as the knowledge that we can have of it. The evident and growing gap between what is potentially possible and what is subjectively knowable underlines the fact that design, even when it involves the solution of technical problems, follows a path the various steps of which may not be determined *a priori*. One has only an idea of the direction in which one should proceed and a few landmarks. What the route is likely to be, who and what will be encountered – these questions can only be answered during the trip.

Of course, any smart traveler will climb a hill whenever possible to see farther ahead and to study the best route. In the same way the designer moves forward determining aspects and conditions of certain sub-systems, and from them deduces, rationally and directly, certain other consequences. These components of demonstrative reason are integrated and completed by a tissue of astute reason that serves as a guide whenever the lack of information or the need to find a shortcut make it the only practical path.

That more than one rationality exists, that design is a game played with less than complete information, and that the outcome is one among many possible outcomes – these facts may be looked upon as a loss. A loss of certainty, of clarity, of the force of reason. Based on the same awareness, it is possible to construct a more open approach to one's own relationship with technology and with the other actors in the design process. Working from the same premises, the component of astute reason in the practice of the designer is no longer necessarily rejected and hidden behind a flawless façade of demonstrative reason, but can be made use of and defended explicitly as a useful (if not the only) criterion with which to face the complexity of the systems with which one is working.

With one difference – in the past, metis could be employed, in the practical knowledge of the craftsman as well as in the practical component of the engineer's knowledge, upon the direct experience of a limited set of knowledge, present in all its physicality; today, faced with a material that tends to dematerialize, appearing along with a set of codes, languages, and specific techniques, metis is forced to find new paths and new forms.

The new terrain upon which astute reason must succeed in operating, integrating fragments of demonstrative reason, is that of language.

We have already seen how the growing distance between a thinking individual and the physicality of materials is being filled in by forms of abstract knowledge, that is, by languages. The same story could be narrated by placing at the center of the stage the figure of the designer seen as an actor that speaks, and by studying the development of his language.

In this story, the turning point that leads the designer to speak in a modern language, coincides with the effort of the eighteenth-century compilers of encyclopaedias to transform the technical knowledge of craftsmen, dominated as that knowledge was by symbolic and analogue communications, reproduced by imitation and initiatory education, into a knowledge that could be communicated in referential and prescriptive languages.

Ever since design entered the sphere of prescriptive knowledge, where it is necessary to say how things should be done and check how things have been done, the designer has become "an actor that speaks," in the narrow sense of the term. The designer speaks in order to acquire stimuli and information, in order to endow his work with meaning, in order to prescribe what should be done and reconcile his idea and the ideas of others... The final quality of the design is based on the properties of language — there are problems that cannot even be set because the language being used is inadequate to express their nature.

Faced with new matter, which takes the form of a set of encoded information, the designer's capacity to communicate increasingly becomes the central feature of design practice. The simplest solution would be to form an ideal new language spoken by all the actors involved in the design process; this hypothesis, however, which is entirely coherent with and complementary to the functional strategies mentioned above, not only runs into insurmountable obstacles, but even were

it practicable, would lead to an impoverishment of design. As far as the practicability of a new language is concerned, suffice it to point out that the most complete technical dictionary contains approximately four and a half million entries, compared with just over one hundred thousand words in a good general dictionary and the five thousand words in use in the spoken language. Aside from quantitative considerations, any attempt to unify the language spoken by all actors involved in the design process would create an elevated level of formalization. This would ease and simplify interactions between actors, and hence would also reduce the probability of the unforeseen emerging, and thus eliminate invention. In this atmosphere, in fact, invention is the result of an unprecedented linguistic game, created by the new contact of different languages.

The complexity of the designer's task, therefore, lies in the fact that he cannot speak all languages (or in the fact that he cannot hope that all will speak the same language). He must nevertheless, in theory at least, communicate with all, or at least promote general communication, lest another "Tower of Babel" be created. This impasse cannot be overcome by simplifying the problem with the introduction of a technical super-language, valid for all. Instead, paradoxically, the solution is to complicate the problem further by introducing a new language based on the questions "What is it used for?" and "How does it work?" – making it possible to translate mental images and formal intuitions into performances and parameters, which enable the designer to define practicable interfaces with a great number of languages.

PORTRAITS OF FAMILIES IN MOTION

Materials in transformation

To take a group photograph, one must have a camera and the subject must be willing to stand still long enough for the photographer to focus, set up the shot, and expose the film. These two conditions are fairly difficult to obtain if one is interested in photographing the current landscape of available materials.

First of all, it is far from simple to find the right camera – that is, an adequate system of classification to describe this panorama. The other problem is that the whole family refuses to stay put – a material is here one minute and somewhere else the next.

We can attempt to sketch a rough map – or overhead view – that will allow us to observe the shifting boundaries between areas traditionally occupied by various families of materials, the emergence of composite materials, the broad outlines of developing innovation, and technological transference among various sectors.

The decision to begin with a subdivision into families may seem to contradict the approach discussed up till now, which views materials as a continuum of options. The fact is, however, that we are living in a period of transition. Even though users experience growing difficulty in telling them one from another, families of materials still exist. A group photograph, in other words, can still be taken, although it will certainly come out blurred. The blurring should not be considered proof of poor photography, but rather an indication of the degree of transformation underway.

Let us begin drawing our map with plastics, a superfamily whose expansionistic drive has been one of the motive forces behind the revolution in materials that we have witnessed over the past few decades.

The word "plastic" is something of a catch-all, and the boundaries are far from clear. It is not idle curiosity to ask oneself just what plastics are today. The question is inevitable. An initial – and not entirely facetious – response might be that that plastics are like Zelig, Woody Allen's chameleon-like character who transforms himself according to his surroundings and the circumstances, donning a vast range of features.

The transformations of a Plastics fluid-solid

The lightweight cup in which coffee is served aboard an airplane is made of plastic. Part of the wing surface on the same airplane is made of plastic. The packing of a new computer is made of plastic, as is the medium upon which the circuits of that computer are printed. Certain medical prosthetic devices, meant to last for years, are made of plastic. Surgical thread for internal sutures, which must be absorbed rapidly by the organism, is made of plastic, as is the armored plating of a vehicle. The word "plastic" covers such a vast range of options that it tends to lose its meaning.

Nonetheless, the term possesses yet another meaning. Firstly, amiddst all its applications, the common feature is not what plastics are, but who works with them. The world of plastics developed outside of the crafts tradition of wood and the industrial tradition of metal, and has maintained its autonomy. The result of this heritage is that, against all theoretical

good sense, a manufacturer of plastic supermarket bags often has more in common with a manufacturer of sophisticated mechanical components in engineering plastics, than the latter has in common with fellow-technicians specialized in metals.

Historical roots aside, all plastics share certain features that distinguish them from other industrial materials. To work with plastics, one must employ a special relationship between the theoretical and the empirical. No other material, of common usage, is so reliant on scientific research, but no material is so tied to practical testing of the results. Furthermore, no other material is sensitive to so many factors that, for now at least, cannot be checked theoretically.

And that is not all – no other widely used material is called upon so frequently to operate under close-to-borderline conditions, where

plastics are sensitive to variations in parameter that would be considered unimportant if applied to other materials.

The qualities of any plastic object, furthermore, are determined – more than any other material – by time-related parameters: the thermal cycle of the process, the curve according to which loads are applied, strain duration... The relationship between plastics and time also forces one to take into consideration this fourth dimension of design, which the traditional knowledge of engineers – founded as it was on structural analysis and material science – basically ignored.

Plastics, in short, share the exhibiting of their special status as fluid-solids (glass too is a fluid-solid, but shows it to a far lesser degree). Hence, they call for a different technical culture. The clash between the world of metals and the world of plastics is also a sign of the difference between the technical culture of a solid and the technical culture of a fluid-solid. Certainly, as time passes, boundaries will blur between the two opposed camps. The spread of composites, which merge different materials and cultures, will serve as a bridge between two different cultural traditions. For now, however, the transition is still under way.

The brief but intense life of plastics began in an area of the "space of properties" characterized by modest mechanical and thermal performance but by excellent, cheap workability, good resistance to many chemical and physical agents but poor resistance to stress, excellent electrical resistance and good properties of thermal insulation, and hence very low thermal and electrical conductivity.

This point of departure ensured that plastics would have – from their initial appearance right up to the Seventies – ample possibilities of penetration in two fields. The first field involved volumetric and decorative uses, which require fairly modest mechanical and thermal properties, while the formability, low cost, and excellent mimicry of plastics made them a perfect material for substitution and imitation. The second was a technical field – use in electrical equip-

ment, where the qualities of plastics immediately made of them an insulating material *par excellence*. At the same time, other uses began to appear, linked to new forms of consumption – the packaging of mass-produced items, early experimentation in the fields of furniture and construction.

From these strongholds plastics began to deploy their attacks on new territories – first of all by consolidating and expanding their applications into fields neighboring the fields of traditional use. This invasion, as it were, took place through new processing methods, new surface finishes, new formulations (newly developed polymers, for example; but, above all, new alloys, i.e. new combinations of polymers and new additives). This led to an explosion in the number of ways in which plastics found a new equilibrium between different – and at times apparently antithetical – performances and properties. These areas of innovation were far from spectacular, but it was here that plastics made their silent and fine-toothed penetration into the world of objects. The bodies of appliances, the soles of running shoes, or packaging for food – these are hardly the sort of applications to astonish the public, but underlying each of these applications was a remarkable level of technical complexity. The world of plastic responded to this complexity with sophisticated options, that are all too easily overlooked.

During the Seventies, more technical uses began to appear – plastics began to invade the areas of performances and properties traditionally occupied by

Plastics in search of an identity.
Top: A television with a phenolic resin body (mfg. Bush, 1949).
Above: Table 4010, designed by Anna Castelli Ferrieri, 1983 (mfg. Kartell).
It is made by fitting together five components, all injection-molded.

structural materials (metals and wood). The first mechanical components appear; though in this initial phase, the structural qualities of plastics were chiefly static — they were used for furniture, building components, tanks, pipes and tubing, appliance bodies, rigid containers. Specific qualities were also exploited, for instance, in manufacturing foamed insulation or creating a barrier effect to gases in certain packaging.

From this broad and fine-toothed expansion into the system of objects, a few remarkable episodes began to emerge in which plastics abandoned their traditional territory entirely and moved toward areas ever further from their original properties. The principal goal of this offensive was to penetrate into fields of application that, because of the mechanical or thermal performances required, had heretofore been the uncontested domain of metals and alloys. It was a complex offensive, that tended to squeeze the adversary in a pincer movement — with on one side improved performances and on the other a descent toward more common uses.

The chief actors in the first jaw of the pincer were engineering plastics, whose strong point over metals was the combination of good mechanical properties with qualities typical of plastics — the capacity to create complex forms, weight reduction, resistance to chemical and physical agents, reduction of friction.

During the Eighties, plastics not only reinforced the positions they had occupied in the preceding phase, but also began to establish themselves in the sector of transport and especially structural components subject to dynamic stress. This happened in various fields, ranging from electrical appliances to sports equipment, but the chief field of conquest was that of the automobile. Nowadays, after having taken over the interiors and consolidated their role in bumpers, plastics are — so to speak — eyeing the body and the engine. This area has an importance that goes far beyond the automobile per se. The automobile sector is the traditional stronghold of metals, a stern test bench for the technical and economic qualities of options. For plastics, victory in the manufacture of automobiles means complete recognition of their qualities as technical materials, a recognition that will certainly have repercussions in other areas of manufacturing.

The second front in the battle with metals is being fought at the highest levels of technology, in the fields of applications where performances (in terms of performance-to-weight ratios) must be exceptional, while acceptable cost thresholds can be equally elevated. Here the enemies to be defeated are aluminum and light alloys, and the fields of battle are the aerospace industry — which includes numerous military applications — some sports equipment, and racing vehicles of various types. In the ranks of the challengers, we find advanced composites and, coming up fast, several superpolymers.

The expression "advanced composites" indicates a vast series of combinations of matrices and fibers of different materials, which may even be extraneous to the superfamily of plastics (carbons, ceramics, metals). Polymer matrices, however, are by far the most common.
Superpolymers, on the other hand, are a small group of materials, still partially in a phase of development. This is such a special field of applications that it is at times difficult to draw the line between experimental applications and commercial applications. Certainly, however, many applications have crossed the threshold during the Eighties (especially in the field of aeronautics) and processes have been developed and perfected that allow fairly simple manufacture of oriented fibers, thus broadening the future for economically plausible applications.
The increase in process productivity and the drop in costs bring the battle with metals onto the territory of automobile manufacturing and, in general, means of transport. Suspensions made of advanced composites are already being manufactured, and experimentation is being conducted on their use for parts of the chassis and for intermediate drive shafts. Also in the field of automobiles — and especially in the area of the engine — experimentation is being done on composites and superpolymers that are resistant to

Left: Engineering-plastic gears.(Doct. Bayer)
Top: Cross-section of the Lancia Prisma bumper, made of modified polybutylene terephthalate (PBT), with a strip of ethylene-propylene rubber (mfg. Comind-Stars). (Doct. Montedison-Dutral)
Above: Running shoe containing several materials with different performances (mfg. Adidas).

68

A POSSIBLE CLASSIFICATION

Consumption (%)	Price level (1 = 1.000 Lire/Kg)	Performances	Families
Mass Polymers (Commodities) (M)			
80	1-2	Acceptable performances over a wide range of applications; costs not too heavy; usually easy to work.	Polyvinyl chloride (PVC) Low-density Polyethylene (PELD) High-density Polyethylene (PEHD) Polypropylene (PP) Polystyrene (PS)
Intermediate level (FI)			
15	2-5	Slightly greater performances than mass polymers; particularly interesting in those applications where one particular quality is needed	Special formulations of the previous families (ex.: glass reinforced) Cellulose Fibers Methacrylates (PMMA) Acrylnitrelebutadenestyrene (ABS) Styrene acrylnitrele (SAN)
Engineering plastics (T)			
< 5	3,5-20	Satisfactory mechanical qualities even at high temperature	Polyamides (PA) (of greater usage) Saturated Polyesthers; Polyethileneterephtalate (PET) Polybuteleneterephtalate (PBT) Polycarbonates (PC) Polytetrafluoroethylene (PTFE) Polyoxymethylene (POM) Poly (phenylene oxide) (PPO) Polysulphones (PPSU) Polyacrilates
Super-polymers (S)			
Negligible (estimate 0,15% in 1990)	50-500	High mechanical and thermic qualities, difficult workability. Their field of application is similar to that of advanced composites, of whom they sometimes make up the matrix.	Polyimides (PI) Polyetherketone (PEEK) Liquid crystals polymers

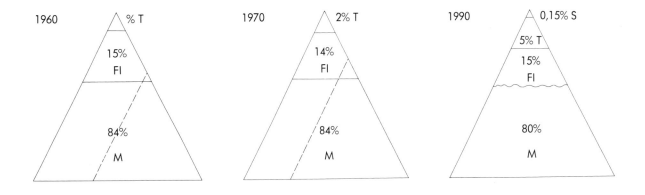

The three triangles represent the share in total consumption of the different groups of plastics - mass polymers (M), intermediate level (FI), engineering plastics (T), super-polymers (S). The data concern the Sixties, the Seventies, and forecast for the Nineties. The slanting dotted line separates "consolidated" products (at right) from products that can be considered innovative (at left). One should note that innovation concerned both the peak (high-performance polymers) and the base (mass polymers) of the triangle.

high temperatures. The most spectacular example is an engine in which almost all the parts are made of epoxy-matrix composites and polyimides reinforced with carbon and fiberglass (see 3.2.2).

A possible classification

The variety of the plastics superfamily can be viewed in other terms than the difference in the performances offered by each of its member materials. Another set of indicators is provided by the incidence of plastics on total consumption and by their prices. In Italy consumption ranges from well over 500,000 tons yearly at a price of about 1,000 lire per kilo (low-density polyethylene) all the way to national consumption measurable in kilograms, with prices on the order of half a million lire per kilogram. It is therefore necessary to subdivide the field in some fashion.

The operation is not simple, because performance, price, and consumption do not increase proportionately for the various plastics. For thermoplastic materials, which are also the most common, there does exist a widely accepted classification which takes into account, with a certain approximation, these three parameters. The subdivision indicates four groups: mass polymers (Commodities); an intermediate level between them and the following group; engineering plastics; and superpolymers. The table on the previous page refers to the situation in Italy, which is fairly representative of industrialized nations.

As for thermoset materials, it is not possible to perform an analogous division into groups. Since they are always either heavily loaded or reinforced, they present a continuous range of options from the bottom to the top of the scale, both in terms of performance and price. On the whole, they enjoy a tenth of the consumption of thermoplastics.

In the Nordica NS 850 ski boot each individual part, according to the specific performance required, is made of a different material: the shell is polyurethane (PU), the front flap is polyamide (PA), and the rear flap is high-density polypropylene (PP). Yet other polymer materials are used for various moving parts and for the soft inner slipper. (Doct. Nordica)

Among thermoset materials, the most significant category is that of polyurethanes, which alone constitute half of the consumption of thermosets, followed by unsaturated polyester, generally reinforced with fiberglass, and by phenolic, ureic, and melamine "molding masses." Lastly, with low consumption but great engineering importance, come the resins which are mostly used as matrices in advanced (epoxy) composites.

There remains a category – that of elastomers – which forms a group on its own, alongside the plastics and, in a few applications, in competition with plastics. This group contains at least fifteen different types of polymers (among which natural rubber) that offer an almost continuous range of variations in the relationship between elasticity and other properties.

Materials and processes

The dynamic world of plastics provides a good terrain on which to observe the complex relations between invention and innovation, and the paths along which the latter imposes itself. In this context, a characteristic of invention and innovation is the profound integration between materials and processes. Thus, the new does not emerge from above, from the laboratories of molecular chemistry, to descend to applicative fields. Rather, it appears at all intermediate levels. Innovation may consist in a new polymer or a new formulation of polymers and well-known additives, or a new process, or even a new

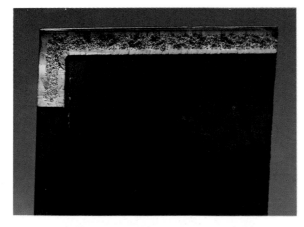

Material with sandwich structure (compact outer layer, foamed inner layer) made of polypropylene (PP). (Doct. Montedison-Himont)

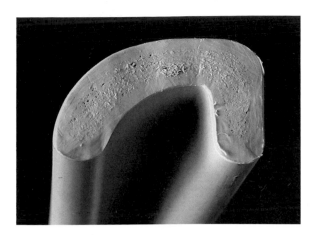

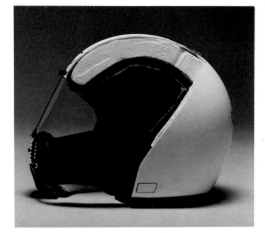

way of applying a well-known process in a hitherto unexplored field of use. The phenomenon is that much more evident if one moves from cutting-edge applications to mass-market applications.

In the area of new polymers, it is first of all necessary to distinguish between the moment of invention and that of the first application; between the first application and application on a mass scale. Among the polymers that have become mass-market products in the last twenty years, several already had a long history behind them (PVC, low-density polyethylene, and polystyrene were all formulated and introduced before World War Two). Others have more recent origins (polypropylene dates back to 1958; high-density polyethylene dates back to 1953). All of

these materials, however, entered production directly with mass-market applications.

For a polymer, the possibility of becoming a mass-market product depends on many factors. Some of these factors are intrinsic to their chemical nature, such as the ease with which certain qualities can be modified. PVC in this area is a champion transformer, since it can take on all degrees of rigidity, from maximum to minimum flexibility. Other factors might be the ease and cost of the transformation processes, and in this area the champion is probably low-density polyethylene. Lastly, a crucial consideration is the cost of raw materials, that is, the cost of producing the initial monomers.

In the field of mass-market applications, the prospects for future innovation do not in-

The helmet's outer shell is made of polycarbonate (PC), while the interior is made of foamed polystyrene (mfg. Nava). (Doct. Montedison)

71

clude the introduction of new polymers, while it is possible to foresee the passage of relatively uncommon polymers into the area of mass-market polymers. This is now happening, for instance, to polyethyleneterephthalate (PET), which has entered an expanding market (especially for bottles for carbonated beverages) and is made with monomers that can be produced cheaply.

Behind these fairly evident movements, however, there is a more diffuse activity of innovation, which really constitutes the most significant aspect of the matter. Even the most substantial part, in quantitative terms, of the trend toward made-to-order materials shows up in this framework. The reorientation of the chemical industry toward service activity that is responsive to the specific needs of users is based on the introduction of new polymer alloys , new combinations, new primers, new fillers, and new reinforcements, variously combined one with another. No less important is the innovation in transformation processes. From the introduction of information processing (to improve molds through the simulation of lines of flow) to robotics (to accelerate and automate molding

**A polypropylene chair and, above, a cross-section of a part of the chair.
Co-injection molding of a foamed interior with a compact outer layer ensures improved resistance, weight reduction, and good surface quality (mfg. Ravergarden). (Doct. Montedison-Himont)**

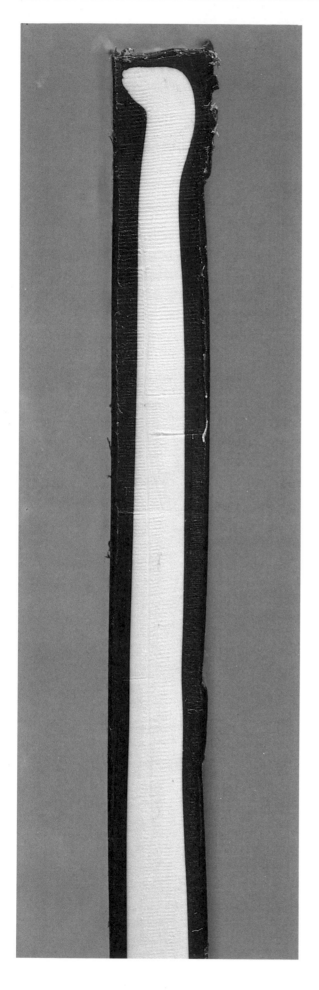

A sandwich-structure component manufactured through co-injection of polystyrene (interior) and acrylonitrile (exterior). (Doct. Montedison-Montedipe)

operations), to the promotion of new processes that have hitherto been little used, the competition among processes is no less lively than that among materials, and it too contributes to innovation. The technique of blowing, for instance, developed for the production of containers, can be used as a substitute for injection molding in the production of complex objects (such as automobile bumpers), while injection can be a substitute for traditional extrusion in the manufacture of pipes and tubing. Technologies developed for other materials, such as sintering, from the field of ceramics, are integrated into the world of plastics. Another example is the use of presses similar to those used for sheet metal in the forming of reinforced thermoplastic

Running shoe (mfg. Superga).

resins (Glass Mat Thermoplastics, GMT). Lastly, we should mention all the processes, new, or old but re-evaluated, that emerge from the need – imperative in all manufacturing sectors – to make production more flexible. These range from diverisfying surface treatments (painting, coating) to the improvement of inexpensive processes for limited production (rotary pressing, automated production of composites, etc.)

We should also mention, in relation to innovation in the field of mass applications, the research being done on degradable polymers. The results are of great interest, especially in the area of several mass-market products. The problem of degradability has been pursued for some time now, and results are still quite uncertain. The attempt is to mix existing polymers and additives so as to make them resolve under the action of solar rays. The shorter molecular chains that are produced are then subject to attack by common bacteria. Today development is proceeding on new polymers produced biologically (by means of selection of special microorganisms), which are in turn biodegradable. It is still too soon to predict their future or to say how wide an application they may enjoy as biodegradable prducts. We can be sure that one of their most intriguing qualities is biocompatibility, which may open the path to use in biomedics (in constructing prosthetic devices, for instance).

Limits to innovation

The fields in which special qualities of mechanical and thermal resistance are required, where the conflict between plastics and metals is most evident, constitute the area for the testing of superpolymers and advanced composites.

For superpolymers, the strategy followed in order to obtain the performances required is the creation of macromolecules in which, alongside the great thermal stability of the various chemical bonds, there coexists an intrinsic structural rigidity of the molecular chain. In certain cases a well-defined arrangement of the macromolecule to obtain polymers with liquid-crystal structures is looked for.

The last-named (in general, polyesters or aromatic polyamides) are also defined as self-reinforcing since their liquid-crystal conformation presupposes a privileged orientation of the macromolecules in one direction: the result is an anisotropic material that possesses great mechanical resistance in the direction of orientation.

There are two types of liquid-crystal polymers: the *lyotropic* and the *thermotropic*. The former cannot be thermally treated and their transformation process permits the production of only fibers and films. Des-

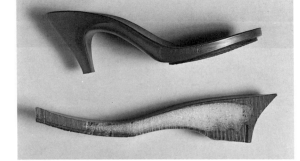

Shoe soles made of semi-foamed polystyrene with differentiated density.
(Doct. Montedison-Montedipe)

pite this limitation, one of these superpolymers has already enjoyed considerable commercial success. The superpolymer in question is an aramid fiber (known as kevlar), the market for which, both as simple fibers or as fabrics, finds outlets in numerous applications that exploit Kevlar's exceptional thermal and mechanical resistance. Thermotropic liquid-crystal polymers, on the other hand, can be thermally treated with certain processes typical of plastics, although there are considerable technical complications.

Compared with the more common polymers, all of the superpolymers tend to be more difficult to transform, and require appropriate modifications of equipment and operating conditions. This means, aside from a limitation of the forms that can be produced, that there is a higher processing cost. This is the price that plastics pay in their pursuit of metals on the terrain of high temperatures and high mechanical performance.

Nevertheless they will very likely find applications in various fields where good thermal resistance is required. They should replace, in particular the epoxy thermosetting resins in the matrices of the advanced composites. Their principal limit now is their high cost, which depends on the cost of the initial monomers.

A refrigerator wall is a composite made up of a sheet-metal outer layer and a vacuum-stamped polystyrene inner layer, while the space between the two walls is filled with foamed polyurethane (PU) (mfg. Candy). (Doct. Montedison-Montedipe)

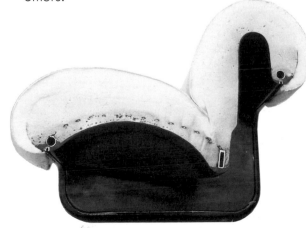

"Bonanza" easy chair, designed by Afra and Tobia Scarpa, 1970 (mfg. D & B). The metal framework is integrated into the cold-foamed polyurethane; the covering is Dacron.

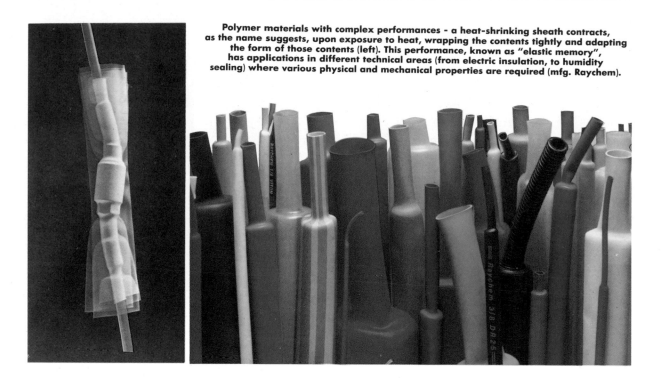

Polymer materials with complex performances - a heat-shrinking sheath contracts, as the name suggests, upon exposure to heat, wrapping the contents tightly and adapting the form of those contents (left). This performance, known as "elastic memory", has applications in different technical areas (from electric insulation, to humidity sealing) where various physical and mechanical properties are required (mfg. Raychem).

Playing with electrons

Mechanical and thermal properties are not the only field where plastics are competing with metals. Plastics are also expanding into the field of electrical properties. Alongside their traditional and consolidated position as excellent insulating materials, plastics are today attempting to move into the area of conductivity. The problem is now being resolved by adding in their mass appropriate conductive materials, such as carbon fibers and fillers or metallized aggregates. This technique is at any rate an intermediate step. The material treated with these additives is sufficiently conductive to meet the needs of several applications (such as the elimination of electrostatic charges or the shielding of electronic equipment) though it still cannot compete with metals.

That is a result that should soon be attained by research into the formulation of intrinsically conductive polymers that, once they have been produced and are on the market, may lead to remarkable uses.

An emblematic example – the possibility of producing light accumulators could set the whole matter of electric cars on a new basis. The formability of the material would make it possible – among other things – to give the accumulator any shape desired, and integrate it directly into the body of the vehicle.

Furthermore, since it is no more difficult to produce a conductive polymer than to produce a semiconductor polymer, once this research meets with concrete and reliable results, plastics would have new and interesting possibilities in the field of electronics.

A plastic semiconductor is still a long way off as a commercial product; but on other terrains, that are already practical, the encounter of polymer materials and electricity produces surprising results. One of these applications is represented by electroluminescent systems.

These are made up of a thin film of polymer material in which particles of doped zinc sulphide have been dissolved. This film is inserted into a sandwich of other protective plastic materials and subjected to alternating current. It then emits a uniform luminosity across its entire surface. The system has existed for several decades, but only recently has a process been perfected that allows easy and inexpensive production.

Another possibility has to do with the production of piezoelectric films.

The piezoelectric effect is the property of certain materials to transform mechanical impulses into electric impulses or vice versa. On this basis, it is possible to produce sensors or actuators, microphones or loudspeakers. Piezoelectric (in general ceramic) materials have existed for quite some time. The new development is the possibility of obtaining thin, light plastic films with broad surfaces, which greatly broaden the fields of application of this principle.

In these exemplary cases, plastics have moved away from their traditional image of a volumetric and structural material, taking on the image of complex components that provide special sophisticated performances due to the very properties of the material.

The second childhood of traditional materials

An enormous steel locomotive charges forward in a cloud of smoke across a steel bridge. This is the historic image of technology that dominated our recent past. Materials were measured by the ton. In this image, the predominant aspects were size and quantity. New technology, instead, speaks to performance and quality. The crisis in the use of metals, and of steel in particular, is a cultural crisis. It is essentially an inability to make the leap from quantity to quality.

This passage, amidst great difficulties and travail, is nevertheless being made. The response of metal to the shrinking market and the simultaneous attack of plastics consists in a tendency to put more information and less matter in their products as well. The forces directing this change are numerous. Several strong points are consolidated, other weak points are abandoned.

The strong points consist largely in the multiplication of special materials designed for specific applications: superalloys that resist high temperatures (for the turbines of airplane engines); high resistance steels (which have won a place for themselves in the sector of the automobile); an entire range of light titanium alloys with the prospect of lithium alloys (several experts feel that lithium alloys will be strong runners in the field of aeronautics); aluminum used in precision foundry work which, since it produces a very tough product, opens the way to the automobile engine for this metal, as a replacement for cast iron.

Again in the area of lightness combined with resistance (although in terms of lower levels of performance) there is a tendency toward the formation of metal-plastic-metal sandwiches, in an attempt to unify the advantages of both materials.

A proposal for a composite of this type for automobile bodies could be the response from the world of metals to the aggressivity of plastics in this specific field. Apart from this possible application, the sandwich approach is already widely used in building with sandwich panels, generally made of prepainted fretted sheet metal and with an interior of foamed plastic material.

Metal precision components
made by sinterizing (mfg. Samo).

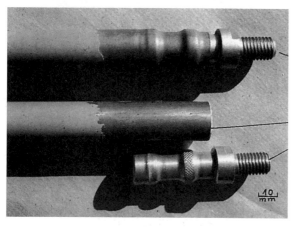

**Magnet forming makes it possible
to perform, simply and cheaply,
a wide range of operations
such as decorative etching (top)
or joining metal components (above).
(Doct. ICP-Ensam and Techmachine)**

**Superplasticity makes it possible to
manufacture metal components with
complex forms through procedures similar
to those used with plastics. (Doct. MBC)**

The new metallurgy

The world of metals is proving to be remarkably dynamic in the area of processes as well. There is a strategy of innovation that is attempting to halt the advance of plastics right on their strongest area – cheapness of transformation and easy formability combined with lightness. Even cast iron, the oldest of industrial materials, is acquiring new vitality through processes that make it possible to form cast iron in complex geometries with much thinner walls than previously, resulting in lighter products than traditional methods were capable of creating.

The possibility of manufacturing components that can integrate several functions and therefore reduce the number of assemblies necessary is generally tied to precision foundry work. The same can be said of the entire field of powder metallurgy, or sintering.

Sintering is a procedure by which it is possible to obtain metal products with complex forms. The engineering involved derives from ceramics processing. The first step involves a mix of metal powder that is sufficiently ductile to take on the form of a mold. When put under pressure at a high temperature, this material "sinters": that is, a diffusion of the atoms takes place which leads to the formation of a compact product with charateristics analogous to those of metals treated with traditional methods.

Other new techniques also tend to allow the molding of metal components into complex geometries, with lower costs and less use of energy. These techniques exploit the superplasticity of certain alloys at very specific temperatures, and what is known as magnet forming.

Superplasticity is the state of extreme ductility of certain alloys at a temperature that corresponds to approximately half that of melting point. Under these conditions their properties are remarkable: the metal can be hot pressed or blown like any other thermoplastic material. A zinc alloy, for instance, can be pressed with procedures similar to those used for plastics (hence, at lower costs than normal metal pressing at a temperature of just 26 °C). This solution allows the alloy in question to compete with ABS whenever its greater properties of rigidity and impact-resistance justify the slightly higher price.

Magnet forming consists in using a powerful magnetic field to accelerate violently the piece of metal to be molded, forcing it to strike a matrix mold. The metal becomes viscous on impact and assumes the form of the mold right down to the smallest details. This technique makes it possible to replace huge and bulky presses with light, fast (an item every three seconds) equipment that uses less energy. Not only does this make it possible to draw components with greater freedom of form than traditional systems, but it can be used as a way of welding metal pieces or of ceramic-coating metal.

Apart from these special processes that still correspond to relatively rare applications, the world of metals is witnessing widespread innovation at all levels, ranging from the development of the new alloys mentioned previously to the automation of shop labor and assembly processes.

Though robotized welding lines are today the most common image of that process, the prospect of an automatic and flexible machine shop is an objective of those working with numerical control machine tools. No effort is being spared in the research and experimentation toward this goal, and the chances of success seem quite good.

Furthermore, the spread of structural adhesives as replacements for other more costly assembly systems, or the introduction of the laser in place of traditional machine tools, constitute other important areas where innovation is radically transforming the traditional image of machine shops. Lastly, in the field of metals as well, some new products are appearing whose surprising performance is far from the properties one normally associates with them. This is happening in two specific cases: alloys with "memory of form," which have already found commercial applications; and amorphous metals, still in the stage of development.

Alloys with memory of form possess the property of taking on notably different configurations (with far greater variations, for instance, than in elastic deformations) when they pass in either direction a given temperature threshold. These alloys, which may be a binary or ternary combination of various metals (depending on the characteristics required), have the property of storing in their crystal lattice information about their original form, so that they keep that form even though deformed at an appropriate temperature. Current commercial uses lie in the field of thermal actuators (switches, relays) and heat-shrinking sheaths (which make it possible, for instance, to join pipes efficiently without welding). Other applications have been proposed in the biomedical area (for traction or compression in orthopedics or traumatology).

Amorphous metals acquire their unusual characteristic (metals are by definition considered to be crystalline materials) through an extremely rapid cooling process of the molten mass which, by preventing the formation of crystals, gives the material's structure a vitreous quality. The properties attained are interesting in mechanical terms (they are ductile and remarkably tough), in electrical terms (their resistivity, unlike crystalline metals, does not vary with temperature), in magnetic terms (less energy is required to magnetize and demagnetize). The most promising applications would seem to involve the latter property.

Facing page, bottom: microcasting by means of the "lost-wax" process. Through this process, it is possible to cast with precision components that integrate several functions. (Doct. MFI)

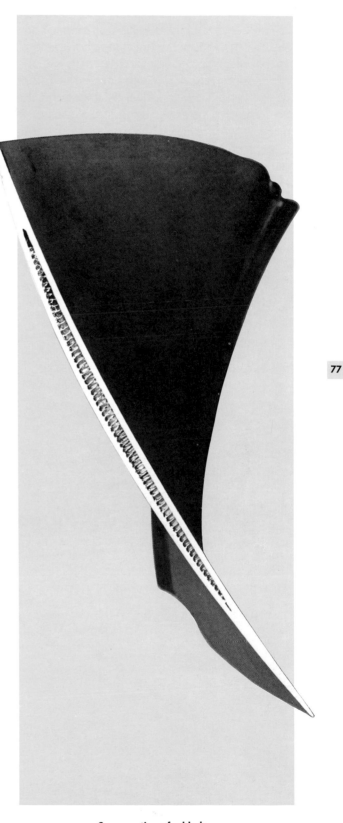

Cross-section of a blade from the Rolls Royce RB 211 turbine. This blade was made with a honeycomb core and two outer titanium shells joined by diffusion bonding.

High-performance ceramics

The second childhood of ceramics is taking place in the area of high performance. Their principal quality is resistance to high temperatures, at levels which not even the most sophisticated metal alloys could survive. They combine with this quality lightness, surface hardness, resistance to wear and corrosion, as well as excellent qualities of thermal and electric insulation. Attempts are being made to counter their weak points (fragility and processing difficulties) with new formulations of the initial powders and by improving the pressing processes by sintering. Research is now concentrating on powders and sintering, which is the only path open to ceramics, although fraught with difficulties. These powders have a very slight propensity to sinter, and tend to leave spaces between particles which lower the performance of the final product. If this problem is solved, it will be possible to widen the field of applications from the current electronics uses and other spot uses towards fields that call for greater mechanical reliability.

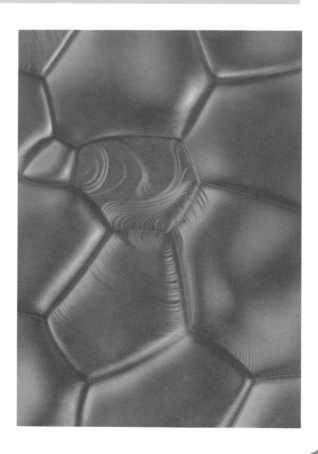

In this page: high-performance ceramics range from technical applications to everyday use. Left: Several technical components (mfg. Kyocera). Above: A pair of scissors (mfg. Kyocera). Top: Enlargement of the material's microstructure.

Facing page: Specially treated wood can provide remarkable performance. Top left: Mechanical components made of pressed wood laminate (mfg. Rochling).

The most ambitious goal is the automobile engine, where the replacement of the metal alloys used currently with ceramic materials would make it possible to attain higher temperatures, thus increasing yield and reducing bulk (the elimination of the cooling system that would ensue could cut an engine's size in half). This is still a distant goal, though engines do exist with ceramic parts. The most extensive application so far was on a Japanese sports car.
Aside from these uses, which chiefly emphasize the thermal resistance of ceramics, there is the prospect of applications that emphasize the surface hardness, resistance to wear, biocompatibility, and the capacity to dissipate impact energy. Possible products include ball bearings, mechanical joints, parts of bulletproof clothing or of armored vehicles.

Wood as an advanced material

Plywood and chipboard (which can by now be considered historic materials) are the solutions that technology developed long ago to obviate the problems of non-homogeneity and anisotropy common to wood. Wood is also the subject of new and advanced ideas. There is first of all a tendency to enrich the possibilities of "ennobling" chipboard panels (laminated plastics and paper treated with increasingly varied decoration and textures). What is more (and this is the most significant element) wood, with respect to problems of manufacturing flexibility, appears to be an excellent material for manufacturing limited numbers of objects with flexible automated machinery.

The use of panels thus acquires new relevance, but there are a number of other quite interesting technical advances. There are slabs of sawdust impregnated with polypropylene that can be hot pressed. There is the production of woods with special esthetic qualities (obtained by assembling laths or sheets of less prized woods). There is the technology of bonded laminated wood strips, which take on many of the qualities of a sophisticated composite material, with oriented fibers if needed.

79

Left and bottom: Structural components made of lamellated wood, designed by Renzo Piano, for the Exhibit (1982).

Managing complexity: Composites

In the landscape of materials many of the paths of innovation lead to composites. The development of plastics and the new developments of traditional materials both lead to composites. In order to grasp the importance of composites, however, it is necessary to forget about their origins in plastics, metals, or other substances and consider them as a whole.

The term composite has various definitions. The most common definition among specialists is also the narrowest: it implies the adjective advanced and indicates those techiques that, by composing through extremely sophisticated procedures matrices and fibers of assorted kinds, attain exceptional results in the performance-to-weight ratio.

Another definition indicates composites as any material whose macrostructure displays non-homogeneity and anisotropy. This is a wider but less precise definition. According to it, to be quite strict, any object that is not made of just one material is made of a composite material. In effect, when faced with the specialization of materials and the resulting increase in their numbers, the concept of composite helps to highlight the growing multi-material aspect of objects, the increase in the number of materials that are present in each new object. This is a definition that proves useful to indicate a new quality of materials, a new cultural and manufacturing atmosphere, but it is too loose for operational use.

In this volume, the term composite is used to indicate a material created in one or more phases of the manufacturing process, during which different elementary components (that is, components made up of materials with different properties) are profoundly integrated, so as to constitute a new element whose performance exceeds those of the single materials employed in its production.

This is certainly a definition that puts emphasis on the manufacturing process. It sets the composite in an intermediate area between traditional production of materials and the phase of design, molding, and assembly of parts. Designing and manufacturing a composite implies two levels of problems. The compatibility of materials and the possibility that, by integrating them, a result will emerge that heightens their qualities (that is, that a form of synergy will ensue) pose problems of microstructure, while the design and manufacture of the macrostructure pose problems of a macroscopic nature. The latter problems must be resolved with a single process, possessing characteristics that are more reminiscent of the production and transformation of materials than of the traditional assembly operations with which components are made into a final product.

In manufacturing advanced composites, careful production is as important as the quality of the materials. Here, a helicopter rotor made of an oriented-filament composite. (Doct. BASF)

Composites and form

Creating a composite means putting the right quantity of the right material in the right place. It means, that is, choosing the materials with the most appropriate characteristics and arranging them according to an adequate geometry in the resulting macrostructure. In practice, of course, this means coming to the best compromise between a theoretical optimum arrangement and what can be produced.

In current use, certain configurations are typical and occur frequently.

In the first of these, the material is made up of a matrix and a fibrous reinforcement.

The quality depends in this case on three factors – the sort of matrix employed (usually thermosetting resins – polyester and epoxy resins — or thermoplastics, engineering plastics, and superpolymers; in unusual cases inorganic ceramic or carbon matrices); the type of fiber (fiberglass, aramid fibers, boron or carbon fibers); the geometric characteristics and the spatial arrangement of the fiber (fragmented, spun, woven, arranged at random in order to create an isotropic material, or else oriented and arranged according to the directions of the stresses).

In the second configuration, thin resistant sheets are separated by a light material that serves as a spacer. This makes it possible to obtain considerably light and resistant two-dimensional components.

There are many different possible combinations of materials that form the skin and materials that form the core. The fields of application range from the most sophisticated aerospace technology to construction, depending on the materials used. The skins can be made of fabrics of fiberglass, aramid fibers, carbon fibers, aluminum sheets, and prepainted fretted sheet metal. The cores can be made of polymer or aluminum honeycomb material, foamed plastic material.

The third configuration gives rise to quasi-organic aspects, in which it is possible to identify the bone, the flesh, and the skin.

Here too it is possible to have a great variety of combinations of different components, reinforced with inner or outer metal or structural plastic; the skin is made of plastic material or fabric, which may or may not be preformed; filler of foamed material of a density that varies according to the function that it is intended to fulfill.

There is a fourth configuration in which the composite takes the form of film, plates, or structural shapes made by layering different materials through co-extrusion.

We might recall, lastly, the configuration produced by overmolding, in which two or more materials are intimately welded by being formed in the same mold.

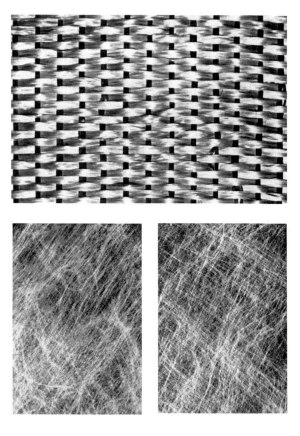

Semi-finished materials for the manufacture of advanced composites.
Top: Fiberglass fabric (mfg. Vetrotex).
Above: Two types of non-woven fiberglass fabric (mfg. Vetrotex).
Below: Mixed-fiber fabrics (left, carbon fiber and fiberglass; right, carbon and aramid fibers). (Doct. Hoechst)
Bottom: Enomex aluminum honeycomb.

Composites and the manufacturing process

The characteristics of the manufacturing process provide us with another possible classification of composites. This classification distinguishes between continuous and discontinuous processes, and within the context of the latter, those with high, medium, and low productive rates.

It is fundamental to determine the quality of the manufacturing process. The unit cost of the final product largely depends on this, as does the range of possible fields of application. For instance, extrusion is a process with such a high productive rate that a four-layer extruded material (each layer confers, respectively, effects of a barrier against gases, mechanical resistance, moldability, hot weldability), even though it is functionally sophisticated and boasts a high concentration of properties, is economically so banal that it is used in extremely common food packaging.

At the extreme opposite end of the scale, the high cost of composites with made-to-order geometries depends, more than on the price of the raw materials, on the intrinsic degree of work involved in the lamination processes or the orderly laying out of fibers. Not even the most advanced automation can work fast enough to allow mid-to-large scale consumption.

It is possible, nevertheless, that some of these technologies will find wider fields of application through the development of cheaper machinery or through the adoption of processes that will lead to greater productive continuity.

Let us consider, for instance, the technology of filament winding. It consists of winding a filament reimpregnated with resin around a form that, when the resin has hardened, is removed. The operation can be performed by a mechanical arm whose movements must be programmed with great precision. The drop in cost of this machine, linked to the general development of robotics, will make it possible to manufacture greater quantities of objects made of oriented-fiber composites.

Another example, which is perhaps more significant in terms of opening new possibilities, is that of the technology known as "pultrusion" and "pulforming." Pultrusion makes it possible to obtain oriented-filament composites with a process analogous to extrusion. Thus, elements with varied cross-sections and long forms can be manufactured (pipes, structural elements, bars, etc.).

If these semi-finished rectilinears are then shaped in curved geometries, the process takes the name of pulforming. Since the most commonly used matrix is a thermoset material, this forming can only be done immediately after the extrusion, before the material itself has completely hardened.

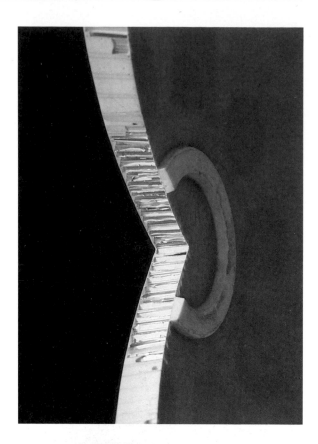

Advanced composites offer the highest performance-to-weight ratio.
Above: section of a honeycomb structured component.
Below: Radar dish antenna (mfg. Monfrini). (Doct. Montedison-Monfrini).

Contrariwise, the adoption of thermoplastic matrices, which is an option now being developed, will make it possible to form the semi-finished materials any length of time after extrusion, greatly broadening the range of possible uses.

Between the mass-market nature of co-extrusion the elite nature of advanced composites, there is an entire range of options mentioned earlier when discussing the development of materials — including the almost continuous manufacture of sandwich panels of all sorts, all the products of current molding technology, thermoformed coatings, foams, and overmolding of various materials, metal inserts, and the integration of external metal parts (outserts).

The idea of a composite
material spreads:
a growing number of objects
are conceived in terms
of synergistic integration
of different materials.
Above: Gasket, made through
coextrusion of metal,
compact rubber,
and foam rubber
(mfg. Continental).
Below: Cross-section
of a steering wheel
and overall view.
The metal core is integrated
into a polyurethane body
with a foamed interior
and compact surface
(mfg. Comind-Stars).
(Doct. Montedison-Montedipe)

Composites and manufacturing sectors

The glass and plastic sandwich used to make the windshields of automobiles is usually referred to as "glass." On the other hand, the blanket of fiberglass impregnated with polyester resin used to make the hulls of boats is usually called "plastic." Similarly, the layering of two sheets of metal separated by a plastic core, used in making auto body components, among other things, is referred to as "metal," while the arm of a chair, made of foamed polyurethane with a steel insert, is called "plastic."

The tendency to give simple and familiar names to a reality that is objectively more complex is a mere case of linguistic inertia, a refusal to abandon well-known classificatory models. The matter also presents a more practical aspect – every composite is created in a technical and cultural area that revolves around a specific material. That is why whatever emerges from the world of metals is called a metal, while whatever emerges from the world of glass is called glass, and so on for plastic, wood, etc.

This is an important phenomenon because when a culture prevails over a composite it tends to impose the processes and design methods that are closest to its tradition.

For instance, the layered metal and plastic composite mentioned above is processed as sheet metal would be (pressed and welded), while the composite made of foamed polyurethane and steel reinforcement is produced with molds typical of plastics. Chipboard (which is a composite of wood and resin), "ennobled" with laminated plastics, emerges from the world of wood and is processed like wood; the composite of wood and polypropylene comes from the world of plastics and is processed according to the tradition of plastics.

At this point, one might theorize a classification of composites based not on the question "What is it?" but on the question "To the technical and cultural tradition of what material does the manufacturer belong?" This classification works within certain limits, but it

The idea of composites expands to applications in which they can provide complex "solid-state" performance, that is, according to the specific properties of their constituent materials.
Top: An electroluminescent system. A layered assembly of several films of different materials, stimulated by a variable electric field, produces a uniformly luminous surface (mfg. Sinel).
Center and bottom: A self-regulating heating cable. When current passes through the cable, it maintains a constant temperature, despite variations in ambient conditions. The cable integrates metal parts with several polymer parts, including a conductive polymer that provides the performance required (mfg. Raychem).

does not cover the entire manufacturing area. Advanced composites, for instance, are not born of one of the "worlds" of materials. Ever since their origin, they have been a direct emanation of the aerospace sector. The companies that are specialized in these materials have cultural (and often financial and organizational) ties with the fields of the end-users rather than with the traditional materials manufacturers.

The native territory of a composite, the initial technical and cultural tradition, can in short be found among materials manufacturers as well as among materials users. Both the former (determined to earn money and defend market shares) and the latter (intent on finding options as close as possible to their needs) are potential forces for innovation. On the other hand, by the very nature of composite materials, no one possesses *a priori* all the necessary know how for their design and manufacture. A landscape derives whose complexity is not only a result of the multiplicity of the materials, shapes, and processes employed, but is also – and chiefly – a result of the multiple and variegated set of engineering and manufacturing cultures that interweave on the terrain of composites.

Composites and complexity

The central place acquired by the idea of composites in the manufacturing landscape seems to conduct the path of materials back to a position that is not far from its point of departure. Non-homogeneity and anisotropy are indeed characteristic of such natural organic materials as wood, bone, skin, from which technics set out. In fact, one of the most ancient building materials, a mix of clay and straw, is a composite whose underlying idea is precisely the same as that underlying advanced composites. The mix exploits the tensile strength of the fibers, leaving a matrix with inferior mechanical qualities to maintain the desired shape.

Men have worked with composite materials during the entire history of technology. For centuries craftsmen have measured their skill in working with pieces of material whose structure they had to discover anew, in order to then work with that structure and exploit it. When compared with the long history of this type of relationship between engineering and materials, the period in which a different, non-experience-based knowledge, and a different way of treating materials, not based on manual ability, set homogeneous and isotropic materials at the center of the

stage, appears as but a fleeting instant. The development of machinery and computing methods today does little more than to continue the most ancient tradition of human technical skills.

Furthermore, even in the interval dominated by homogeneity and isotropy, materials continued to exist with different properties, either because the original pre-industrial materials never disappeared or because materials such as reinforced concrete, reinforced fiberglass resins, or multi-ply boards were introduced, all of which were extremely non-homogeneous and anisotropic. These materials, however, during the period in question, did little to hamper the culture of homogeneity and isotropy. Reinforced concrete had a history of its own, with its own specialists and computing instruments confined to their own specific field of application. The first composites came in on tiptoe, as it were, long thrust to the outskirts of technical development and, above all, of the thought and debate on that development.

If the situation has changed today, that is the result of a set of factors in which technical and cultural aspects are closely linked. The development of composites and the management of the complexity of the materials required are possible because of the current availability of theories on matter and its operation, of experience accumulated and tested over time, of machinery capable of dealing with this complexity cheaply – a body of techniques that can be summed up in the term neo-technics. The management of complex materials means complex thought, it means abandoning the simple and mechanical reference models upon which modern technical thought is essentially based. The development of materials toward composites is bringing about a new form of technical knowledge and is taking shape as a component of a wider knowledge and is taking shape as a component of a wider cultural evolution, which has led Western thought to discover, in a vast range of fields, the theme of complexity.

PLAYING WITH THE POSSIBLE

"Masai Warriors", Angela Fisher, 1984.

Creating the light and resistant

Matter and the loss of weight

The bones of birds are made of a light compact exterior, given stiffness by an interior cellular section; wood is a combination of resistant cellulose fibers and a plastic matrix, called lignin. Every time that natural selection has exerted genetic pressure for a combination of lightness and mechanical resistance, nature has responded with "technical solutions" typified for the most part by complex and composite materials.

When compared with natural structures, (highly anisotropic and non-homogeneous but highly integrated into multifunctional elements), technology appears as a set of quite rudimentary solutions. Nonetheless, the solutions discovered by culture are coming closer and closer to those found in nature. This convergence is especially evident in the field of "creating the light and resistant," for the precise reason that this field has been present throughout the history of technology.

From the trilith to filament composite structures, one can clearly discern a dual process. The materials employed are increasingly unlike those provided by nature, while the engineering strategy increasingly resembles the approaches used by nature.

The efficacy of a rock smashing across the skull of one's prey or one's enemy was certainly proportional to that rock's weight. The weight also determined the stability of a trilith or a stone arch. The oldest technical solutions, for the most part, have hinged on strategies (at times rudimentary, at others remarkably clever) for the utilization of weight, that is, of the most immediately detected property of the materials employed.

By refining the materials themselves as well as the instruments for computation, today man has succeeded – following the example set by nature – in creating light and resistant structures, the materials of which are distributed in the most appropriate fashion, so as to produce controlled anisotropies and to specialize each point of the structure.

Creating the light and resistant should be viewed as an area that does away with the traditional divisions of expertise between the chemist (who works with the properties of materials) and the designer (who works with the form of the finished product). The problem instead must be taken as a whole, and must be expressed in terms of form: the form of the object, the form of the macrostructure of the material (that is, the arrangement of its internal anisotropies and non-homogeneities), and the form of the microstructure of the individual component material (the spatial arrangement and quality of the atomic and molecular bonds).

The form of light objects

A crease made lengthwise in a sheet of paper transforms a flexible object into a structure endowed with a certain stiffness. The material undergoes neither a qualitative nor a quantitative change. The new stiffness is a product of a change in the form.

If we shift the mass of an object away from the flexural axis (or, to be more precise, if we increase the moment of inertia of the object's cross-section) there is a consequential, and greater than proportional, increase in that object's stiffness. In a section that is exposed to a flexion load, the maximum stresses (both tensile and compressive) take place in the areas furthest from the inner axis, and lessen progressively as one approaches that axis, approaching zero at the axis itself.

Selection among different forms, that is, selection among various strategies for creating the light and resistant, today involves diverse options. Certain technical and cultural phases, however, have made certain forms more common and emblematic.

Therefore, it is safe to say that latticed structures (in which stresses are concentrated on linear ribbing) formed the image of lightness when construction science was at its beginnings and the materials for creating the light were wood and metal tie rods, struts, and rafters – in bridges, in large roofs, in automobile chassis, in the structures of the earliest airplanes.

Continuous, box-type, or membrane structures (in which stresses are spread over components with a continuous surface) provide the image of the light in a phase in which technology offers resistant two-dimensional materials (ranging from bonded plate sheet metal to plastics and composite materials), and structural analysis has developed systems of computing capable of modelling extremely complex forms and of evaluating their behavior under stress.

The range of forms, of course, is not limited to the two extreme poles made up of latticed structures, on the one hand, and continous surfaces, on the other. It is equally possible to imagine various hybrid forms, ranging from membranes created with fine lattices (geodesic domes, for instance), and lattices made up of box-type structures (such as in frames made up of large tubes), all the way to integrated multifunctional components. Housings, pins, reinforcements, and outer surfaces are assuming complex – and therefore stiff – forms (this is the special field of application of plastics and of die-cast and sintered metals).

In the face of this variety of possibilities, the selection of forms follows no exact rules – even when the technical aspects are prevalent. It is nevertheless obvious that, given the same conditions, a continuous structure will be more effective if the conditions of use are such that the surface that is automatically created by that structure can be used: for instance, in containers, structural frameworks, roofings. For the frame of a touring bicycle, instead, a traditional light tubular structure is probably the best solution. That could change for a speed trial bicycle with its special aerodynamic requirements; in this case a shell frame may be the best solution.

As for the relationship between the selection of the form and the selection of the materials

employed, tradition indicates that metals are best adapted to lattice structures while plastics (and in this case reinforced concrete becomes part of the group) are best for continuous structures. Here too, however, the situation is far from iron-bound. Airplanes have long employed metal structural shells, just as the bearing body of an automobile is made of metal. By the same token, composite materials have been used to construct lattice structures and frames.

The form of a light and resistant object possesses a constant characteristic: that of increasing rigidity, by spreading the mass as far as possible from the flexural axes. The materials available, the types of processing, and the new computing methods all contribute to breaking new ground for all sorts of forms – the image of the light object can be as airy and transparent as a spiderweb, as smooth and curved as an eggshell, or as dense and compact as a beetle.

The form of the macrostructure

Each of the materials that make up the form of an object may be homogeneous or else it may possess non-homogeneities and anisotropies. In the latter case, it is necessary to consider their form. One examines a cross-section to see how the anisotropies are arranged, one analyzes the quality and arrangement within the object of various identifiable materials (the presence of fillers and additives, or the fact that the material is an alloy made up of different materials are not pertinent to this level of analysis, and are instead taken into consideration in an analysis of microstructure, that we shall examine further along).

It is possible to attain rigidity by arranging materials in the most appropriate points in terms of their mechanical properties. For instance, if we take a cross section of a reinforced concrete pylon, we find a matrix of concrete along with reinforcing rods whose quantity and arrangement are determined by calculations involving the structure as a whole. The same is true of an advanced composite in which filaments or fabrics are arranged so as to follow the stresses. These are materials whose macrostructure is calculated and created *ad hoc*, point by point, according to a given system of stresses.

If on the other hand we consider a building panel made up of a foam core and two sheet metal skins, we are faced with a semifinished product endowed with a macrostructure whose non-homogenity and aniso-

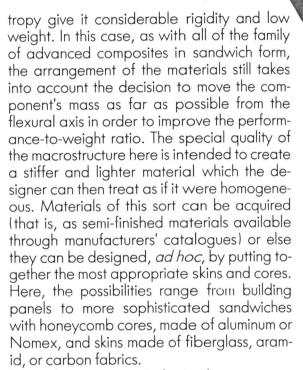

tropy give it considerable rigidity and low weight. In this case, as with all of the family of advanced composites in sandwich form, the arrangement of the materials still takes into account the decision to move the component's mass as far as possible from the flexural axis in order to improve the performance-to-weight ratio. The special quality of the macrostructure here is intended to create a stiffer and lighter material which the designer can then treat as if it were homogeneous. Materials of this sort can be acquired (that is, as semi-finished materials available through manufacturers' catalogues) or else they can be designed, *ad hoc*, by putting together the most appropriate skins and cores. Here, the possibilities range from building panels to more sophisticated sandwiches with honeycomb cores, made of aluminum or Nomex, and skins made of fiberglass, aramid, or carbon fabrics.

In another instance, similar to the cases considered above but different in terms of manufacturing and application, a single material is employed (with a homogeneous macrostructure, therefore), but when viewed in cross section, that material is made up of compact skins and foamed interiors. This solution, referred to as structural foam, may be employed with various polymers (especially polyurethane, PU, polystyrene, PS, and polyphenyloxide, PPO), and makes it possible to manufacture components with considerable thickness and mechanical resistance along with relatively low weight.

A last case is that of the ancient building technique of mixing clay and straw – the clay is the matrix and maintains the form of the straw fibers, which provide mechanical resistance. This model governs all polymer-matrix composites with fiber or non-oriented filament reinforcement (which appear in the form of non-woven fabrics). The macrostructure is non-homogeneous (because it is made up of different materials) but not anisotropic, because the fibers have no special orientation. These composites, in macrostructural terms, do not depend on the form factor. They create a material that can be treated like normal polymer materials, while possessing better mechanical properties (depending on the type and amount of reinforcing fiber employed).

Managing anisotropy

Placing the right material in the right place (that is, producing controlled anisotropies in a material) implies the management of a huge amount of information. There is a certain economic cost involved which in the end is decisive in determining the feasability of the proposed option.

The high-intensity information required may, for example, be put in the material through manual processes, that is, by calling into play the attention and practical ability of a technician. That, however, means high costs and a slow manufacturing rate. Nonetheless, many of the advanced composites for the aerospace industry or for the manufacture of structural components for racing vehicles are produced – for lack of an alternative – in this fashion.

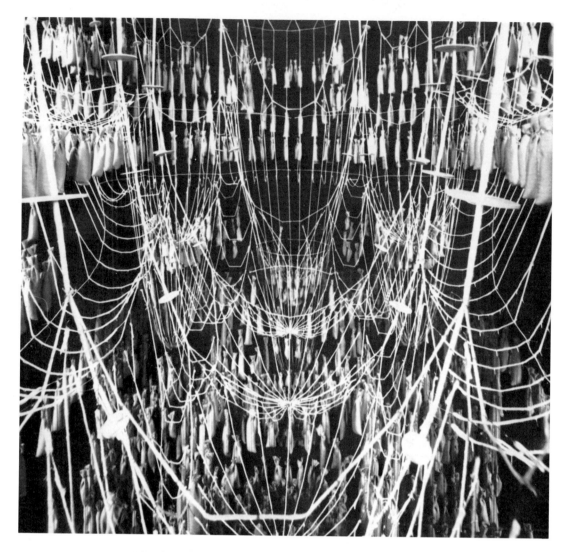

"Gaudì" structural model. Reconstruction directed by Otto Frei.

On the other hand, cutting costs or increasing productivity both involve extremely complex automated machinery, or else a willingness to accept a loss of accuracy in managing the anisotropy.

For instance, robots that "spin" with micrometric accuracy the filament involved in the process of filament winding (see 1.2.5) are available for the production of holding tanks and cylindrical components — but also for more complex components (on an experimental basis, even parts of an automobile chassis). There are tailor robots that cut and arrange fiberglass carbon and aramid fiber fabrics (this operation is known as lamination). These processes, however, require large investments and result in fairly low levels of productivity.

Other systems tend toward a compromise between positive anisotropic qualities and economic necessity. Among them, the most widespread is pultrusion (see 1.2.5); the outlook is promising for hybrid systems that link aspects of the manufacture of advanced composites with other aspects of more common forms of manufacturing. For instance, or-derly arrangement of fibers by means of a robotized filament winding system for the manufacture of slabs that can then be thermoformed.

Alongside this area of relatively glamorous activity — though limited in terms of applications — there are other areas where the technical ability to manage anisotropy has developed more quietly, although the commercial phase has long since been reached. This is true, for example, of reinforcements obtained by extruding a short-fiber filled polymer material, or by creating appropriate flows inside the mold in injection processes. The formation of the latter type of anisotropy, when not intentional, is considered a design defect. When it is controlled, instead, in certain cases this process can be useful in improving a component's mechanical qualities. In the injection molding of a motorcycle wheel, by putting the injection nozzles in the hub, the flow of material enters the spokes with an orientation of the fillers. In this way, the fillers are largely oriented in an optimal direction — parallel to the spokes themselves. Just as it is possible to orient short fibers, it is

possible to orient the yet shorter fibers that are the very macromolecules of a material, thus creating preferential orientations during the process itself. For certain polymer materials, especially semicrystalline ones, it may be possible to create preferential orientations along the lines of flow.

Another form of molecular orientation is often produced with a mechanical action, i.e., stretching and deforming a material as it comes out of the extruder. This stretching technique (which can be applied in one or more directions) makes it possible to obtain films – of polypropylene or other materials – with much greater mechanical resistance than films that have not been stretched.

The form of the microstructure

In a complex building, the quality of the bricks is important, but what is most important to the overall quality of the structure is the binder that holds together the various parts, and – above all – the structure according to which these parts are arranged in space. Likewise, the intrinsic qualities of a material depend on the capacity of its atoms to form structures with certain spatial configurations.

Materials that are traditionally called natural bear the same relationship to artificial materials as does a furnished cave to a structure designed by an architect. The development of science and technology has led to increasingly sophisticated adaptation of what exists, and in the end has produced the construction *ex novo* of the entire edifice of materials (see 1.2.1). In the latter case, the design of mechanical properties of materials truly begins with the bricks and mortar – by examining the quality and arrangement of atomic and molecular bonds.

It is therefore necessary to imagine, first of all, the spatial arrangement of the bonds,

keeping in mind that nature is fond of economy and therefore tends to prefer compact (and, where possible, orderly) forms, which correspond to the lowest energy levels. This tendency toward compactness with the greatest possible level of order is hindered by the fact that nothing stands still (unless the temperature is absolute zero), and that the resulting state of continuous movement, linked to the temperature, generates energy that tends to move atoms and molecules away from each other. Above a certain level, any increase in temperature generates movements that destroy any existing structural order.

The form that matter assumes at a given temperature is the product of these two opposite tendencies. Experience has shown us materials with a range of structures, from the maximum order (spatial repetition of identical geometric units, such as with crystals) to extremely haphazard configurations (such as in amorphous materials and fluids).

Different materials at different temperatures can move from one to another of the possible structural configurations while maintaining their chemical properties, but radically altering their physical properties.

It should be noted, nonetheless, that if all materials can easily acquire disorderly structures, not all materials attain order, and certainly not all attain the same levels of order. By increasing the temperature atoms vibrate and eventually molecular bonds break, thus weakening crystal lattices. By lowering the temperature, certain materials can be made

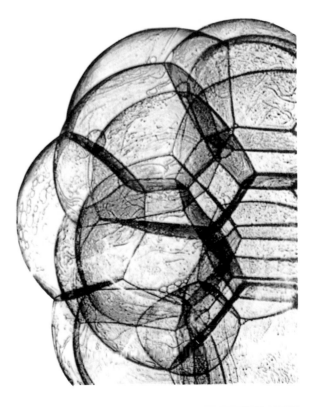

to take on an orderly structure; others cannot. The molecules that make up these materials are geometrically so irregular that they absolutely cannot be made to take on a repetitive configuration.

The system of loads that the material is called to support is then applied upon this dynamic and more or less orderly edifice. The more the thermal vibration separates atoms and molecules, the weaker the bonds become, while the possibility that external loads will succeed in breaking them increases, thus provoking a modification of reciprocal positions and, as a result, permanent deformation of the material.

In this general context, we see today various materials as chief actors in the creation of the light and resistant. These materials have emerged from the development of traditional materials and from research into new materials.

The quality of metals

At the beginning of this century the maximum acceptable tension for a good type of steel was less than 9 kg/mm^2; in 1960 that level reached 16-18 kg/mm^2; today we have reached a level of 27 kg/mm^2. These figures are a demonstration of the development undergone by the most ancient materials used in creating the light and resistant.

Another evident indicator is the simultaneous lightening of two products of industry that constitute typical applications of steel: reinforced concrete structures and locomotives. From the beginning of the century until today, the quantity of steel needed in a reinforced concrete structure has diminished five-fold, while the weight-to-power ratio of a locomotive has gone from over 1,000 kilograms per horsepower delivered to less than 20. Obviously, in both cases (especially the latter, in which the steam engine has been replaced by an electric engine) there is a convergence of factors. Nevertheless, the availability of higher-performance steel has certainly been a determining factor.

At the basis of this development has been the steel industry's ability to obtain an increa

singly closely controlled material in terms of homogeneity and regularity, with a corresponding reduction of alien elements.

High-resistance steels are today replacing traditional steels in many applications that call for a reduction in weight. Other metals and alloys have taken the same avenue and are enjoying considerable success (such as aluminum) or moderate success (such as magnesium, which is not used widely even though it has been available for many years now). More recently, alongside these young but already historic materials, a new generation of metals and alloys has appeared that is the product of great improvements in metallurgy. These new materials possess exceptional weight-to-performance ratios (see 2.2). Some examples can be seen with titanium, which is beginning its industrial phase (and can be processed efficiently with the technology of superplasticity), and a few special aluminum alloys, such as the aluminum-lithium alloy (still undergoing development), one of metallurgy's great hopes in its competition with composite materials.

The quality of composites

The search for lightness, in the sector of composites, centers around fibers. Whether they are short or long, oriented or not, in bundles or fabrics, and made of a wide variety of ma-

terials, fibers are the drive shaft (and not merely in a metaphorical sense) of almost everything that is manufactured in this field.

Any material that can be manufactured as a fiber presents in the fibrous state far greater mechanical resistance than in a simple mass state. All fibers have a configuration of their inner bonds that allows them to resist a strain exerted in the direction of those bonds. There develops a sort of economy of bonds, by virtue of which a relatively limited mass may withstand great stress, provided that stress is exerted parallel to the fibers. Polypropylene (PP), for instance, when it is pressed in fibrous form, multiplies its resistance by ten. This is true of many different fibers, ranging from common textile fibers all the way to the most sophisticated single crystal fibers.

In advanced composites the most commonly used fibers are those of fiberglass, aramid fibers, and carbon fibers. Each type of fibers is characterized by different properties of tensile strength and flexural rigidity (carbon fibers are the stiffest, while fiberglass is the most flexible) and even greater variations in terms of cost (carbon fibers can cost as much as a hundred times more than fiberglass, that is, several thousand dollars a kilogram). Often, in order to obtain the most appropriate cost–to–performance ratio, hybrid options are adopted, using various percentages of different fibers.

Aramid fibers (see 2.1) rapidly found a wide range of uses, in the area of light advanced composites, as well as in such other fields as replacing asbestos in brakes and in heat barriers and in the production of bullet-proof armoring.

Alongside this group of fibers, there are others with more specific uses that are nonetheless quite interesting. At one end of the scale there are ceramic fibers, which are especially used at high temperatures; at the opposite end of the scale are whiskers.

This term is used to indicate a certain configuration that can be taken on by various materials. Microcrystals form filaments with diameters on the order of a micron or a fraction of a micron, free from the imperfections that can normally be found in ordinary crystal structures. They are therefore endowed with tensile strength that comes close to the theoretical levels of crystals. Whiskers are not new (they even occur in nature) but only recently have their mechanical properties been fully noted, and only in the past few years have they been proposed as a reinforcing material in advanced composites. Research activity ensued, producing whiskers of various materials, both metal and ceramic. Silicon carbide whiskers, for instance, used as a 30 percent reinforcement in an aluminum matrix treble its toughness and considerably increase its strength.

The quality of a composite, however, depends on the characteristics of the matrix and – this is a crucial point – on the quality of the interfaces between its components. The transmission of stresses takes place in these interfaces. The matrix, which possesses a certain degree of plasticity, undergoes deformation and thus transmits the stress to the fiber. The fiber consititutes the resistent component of the composite. In order for this to happen, there must be no detachment phenomena. In other words, the interfaces must ensure adhesion between the two components. This is a delicate phenomenon, and must always be taken into consideration. This problem involves the wettability of the

surfaces, the quality of bonds, and mechanical and chemical stability.

As for the matrices, depending on the specific applicative field, a great variety of materials have been used, ranging from metals and carbon to ceramics. When the chief consideration is creating the light and strong, polymers are the most common.

Thermosetting resins (epoxy resins, when high performance is required; polyester resins in everyday applications) are the most commonly used today. Other thermoplastic matrices with high thermal and mechanical performance (superpolymers, see 2.1) are being developed, both for mass-market composites (for instance, in the automobile industry) and for advanced composites.

The quality of polymers

In manufacturing light objects, polymers play a broad role. The loss of weight, especially in the last century, has been a widespread phenomenon that has changed the entire system of objects. In the last few decades in particular, plastics have penetrated the system greatly and transformed areas ranging from packaging and containers all the way to the automobile. Plastics, even those with

relatively modest mechanical properties, make it possible to manufacture lighter and more compact obejcts, due to their low density and high formability. Even ordinary polyethylene, used in manufacturing plastic supermarket bags, can be considered matter for creating the light and resistant.

Let us see how the form of the microstructure of polymers has been modified in order to obtain materials with superior mechanical qualities.

It was necessary to create conditions that would prevent – under the effects of a system of loads and a given operating temperature – the slipping of molecules (breakage of macromolecules is a highly unlikely eventuality with the materials in question).

In order to prevent this slippage, it was necessary to promote the closeness and the bonds (chemical or physical) between the

molecules, while blocking the thermal agitation that weakens those bonds. Three chief approaches were taken toward this goal.

1. Creating transverse chemical bonds between the macromolecules, which come to form a stable three-dimensional lattice.

The lattice remains largely stable until heat is sufficient to break the bonds, resulting in a depolymerizing of the material. Materials that are organized in this fashion are known as "thermosets," and are traditionally the most widely used materials for technical applications that require a certain level of mechanical and thermal resistance. In particular, epoxy resins are the commonest matrices in the most advanced composites used in the aerospace and electronics industries.
The main limitations are the long processing times, the fact that wastes and scraps cannot be recycled, and that the material is somewhat fragile (this fragility however can be reduced by using certain fillers).

2. Producing crystalline zones, in which the shape of the molecules leads to a dense and orderly packet, thus restricting the degree of movement.

The thermoplastics known as semicrystalline polymers fit into this group, and certain of them have considerable thermal and mechanical resistance. An extreme case of the formation of orderly zones is that of liquid crystals. Here, large zones are created in which the molecules are closely packed and orderly, and the result is a material with excellent thermal and mechanical properties.

3. Creating macromolecules whose shape makes them intrinsically rigid, hence unlikely to move when exposed to thermal agitation.

This group includes the thermoplastic polymers referred to as amorphous, and in this direction, other materials have been developed that are endowed with great heat resistance and excellent mechanical properties.

Each of these three typologies reacts differently to variations in load and temperature (we shall return to this topic further along, see 3.2.1). Here we shall limit ourselves to proposing a model that is valid only for the two thermoplastic typologies, making use of

a prosaic but quite pertinent image.
These materials are like a plate of spaghetti covered with meat sauce. The welter of macromolecules, linked internally by solid chemical bonds, are held together by weaker forces (the meat sauce) that vary according to temperature. If the food is hot the sauce is fluid and the spaghetti slip over each other. When the food cools off the sauce becomes denser and the contents of the dish take on a certain solidity. If we put the plate of food into the freezer the whole becomes quite rigid. We could expand on this example by comparing a semicrystalline thermoplastic to a *pastasciutta* cooked badly, with too little water. Some of the pieces of spaghetti are glued together at places and continue to adhere one to another even when the sauce is quite fluid. Lastly, one might say that liquid crystal polymers, with their rigid molecules in parallel order, are like a package of spaghetti before cooking, if we are willing to stretch a comparison.
The problem of research in the field of plastic materials therefore involved making "a plate of spaghetti and meat sauce" into a reliable technical material (that is, endowed with appropriate mechanical properties) even at temperatures much higher than room temperature.
From the first plastics — rigid but fragile, like the first generation of thermosets, or tough but easily deformed and temperature sensitive, like the first thermoplastics — we have progressed to materials that, in a simple state or appropriately reinforced, can not only compete with metals in common uses, but as matrices of advanced composites, can even yield performances that are beyond the reach of metals.

Light objects

A thousand dollars a kilogram of reduced weight – that is the price that, according to a French study performed in 1985 (Euroconsult, *Etude sur l'allègement des produits industriels*), the aerospace industry is willing to pay to lighten a satellite.

This strange reverse bargaining, in which one pays to have less, takes place in other markets at other prices as well: 215 dollars for a kilogram less of helicopter, 140 for commercial airliners, from 7 to 70 dollars for sports equipment, and from 2 dollars to 3.50 for trucks...

The value of lightness – this matter with a negative sign – is determined by demand at least in commercial uses. Since launching satellites became big business, an aerospace sector has existed that operates by and large like any shipping company, computing its prices according to how much it costs to move a kilogram of merchandise from one place (the earth's surface) to another (the desired orbit). This value serves as a basis upon which to evaluate the highest price that the "shipper" can spend to reduce the price of the launch vehicle (the tare, in shipping terminology), and hence increase the payload; or else the most that a shipper can spend to lower shipping costs. The same logic applies to all other sectors, with lower prices as shipping costs drop.

In certain markets there is a sort of genetic pressure, if you will, toward weight loss. The thing that is new about the current state of affairs lies in the precision of the economic quantification, rather than in the pressure in and of itself. The push to uncover ways of making objects lighter is as old as technology itself. The reduction of weight in prehistoric flint tools can be taken, according to André Leroi-Gourhan, as an indicator of the level of technology. The progress from the bulky amygdaloids of the Mousterian Age to the microliths of the Mesolithic involves the manufacture of longer, less massive blades (i.e., finer points or tools), which in turn demands an increasingly complex series of technical operations and knowledge.

In general, any increase in the number of performances obtained from a given amount of material (or any reduction in the quantity of material needed to obtain a given performance) can be seen as a response to an elementary economic tendency that – though on rather different terms in the past – has always been part of technical activity.

The Voyager is such a light aircraft that it can carry enough fuel to go around the world non-stop.

In relation to the long wave of weight loss, which involves the entire system of objects, other trends develop that involves specific sectors, creating numerous openings for interaction.

There are, first of all, objects for which the reduction of mass is first and foremost an operational imperative – bows, vehicles of all sorts, automobiles, satellites, to name a few; or, in a neighboring field, triliths, geodesic domes, and tension fabric structures. Objects in motion (that is, objects subjected regularly to alternate phases of acceleration and deceleration) and objects that must support their own weight (roofing and airplanes, for instance) have been the privileged subjects of untiring technical experimentation in search of ways to make increasingly light objects.

From these areas, where strength and lightness are at a premium and command even extreme prices, new techniques spread rapidly into other applications, until they run into countertrends.

There are objects whose chief reference is a linguistic system. A king's throne, for example, is not the result of functional needs. Rather it is the product of a need to communicate – it must be imposing and so it must be (or at least seem) heavy. Likewise for other common and useful objects, each in varying degrees, but each laden with symbolic significance.

The equation weight = importance is of course not applicable to all cultures. A nomad culture, for instance necessarily develops a system of light portable objects, and builds its meanings upon that system. Japanese history reveals, for that matter, a refined culture of lightness. In European culture, on the other hand, the value of weight (and the equations that derive from it, such as weight = quality, longevity, solidity, safety) is rarely rejected, and has certainly left its mark on the quality of our physical surroundings.

As we speak of the light object, we must necessarily keep track of which of the three areas it falls into – objects that offer lightness as a primary performance, toward which goes much of the work in engineering them; objects that become lighter as a secondary effect of economic advantages provided by improving technology; or yet again objects that become lighter in reality without showing it, because a deeply rooted linguistic code requires that they possess an image of weight.

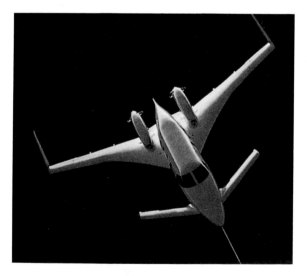

Top: The Gossamer Condor, a muscle-powered airplane, has a wingspread of almost 30 meters and weights only 34 kilograms, by virtue of a carbon- and aramid-fiber structure covered with a thin but strong film of thermoplastic polyester. Above: The Starship, manufactured by the Beech Aircraft Corporation, is a "canard" shaped airplance, largely made of a carbon-fiber composite.

Flying with composites

The Gossamer Condor, which was feted in 1977 as the first human-powered airplane, and which, after some improvements, was the first human-powered airplane to cross the English Channel, is an object with one of the highest performance-to-weight ratios ever achieved. This is a machine that provides all of the primary performances of an airplane and that – with a wingspan of close to 30 meters – weighs only 34 kilograms, due to the use of an extremely light carbon and aramid fiber structure covered with a thin but tough film of thermoplastic polyester.

"The only way we had of knowing when it was not strong enough was when we saw that it broke," admits with candor the plane's designer, Paul B. MacCready, in explaining the great number of accidents that marked the phases of engineering and development. This statement should interest everyone. The introduction of radically new materials, and the full exploitation of the properties that one can infer in them, opens a vast territory of non-knowledge. One realizes that everything one has learned to do and compute was based on a model that had been used previously and had proved to work. If the materials and technical strategy are completely altered, however, (beginning a new sequence of steps) it means that one no longer has a point – or form – of departure. And so design, at first, becomes a strange hybrid process that wanders from technical refinement to total hit-and-miss.

Obviously, one cannot always adopt the MacCready's design approach. The Gossamer Condor flies slowly, just a few meters off the ground (at least in the tests) and is so light that, when it falls, it falls rather gently. When one is asked to design an aerospace component or part of a real airplane, one must be certain of being able to depend on it right from the first test.

The entire crash and repair sequence that leads to the definition of a truly operational solution must therefore be rendered abstract, performed in advance, calculated. A mathematical model will survive any crash it encounters. But first you need the model, and it must efficaciously simulate future operating conditions.

An example of the new concept linked to the introduction of new materials is offered by the following circumstance — with traditional, homogeneous, and isotropic materials, once one has established the shape of a component, one has also automatically determined the ratio between flexural strength and torsional strength. This creates problems because the very frequencies at which the component vibrates may differ among themselves. With composite materials, in contrast, by appropriately distributing and orienting the fibers, one can engineer torsional and flexural strength as one likes or needs, obtaining non-coupled (torsional and flexural) frequencies. The advantages of the final product are evident, but they require far greater sophistication in creating models and in computing.

Furthermore, when one is faced with materials that have no history of their own, the problem of long-term reliability and behavior under fatigue becomes the central question, and the answer is not easy to find. In extreme operating conditions such as aerospace industry, even for materials with a relatively long history, the knowledge about their resistance to fatigue is fairly scanty.

From the testing heretofore carried out, it would seem that composites perform well in this area as well. If there are no sudden shear loads, they behave even better than metals because the cracks, or microfissures always present in materials, are prevented from propagating. More widespread testing is necessary however, and given the lack of solid practical experience, the only path to follow is that of creating models and laboratory testing.

Amidst technical and computing difficulties, composites are penetrating slowly into the field of airplanes.

In an imaginary map of the zones that are vi-

tal to the proper operation of an aircraft, composites began a long march in the Fifties from the outskirts to the center (at ever increasing speed). From pieces of interior furnishing, to secondary structures, aiming all the while at the more important ones. And these essential components are now the battleground in the competition with traditional materials.

The traditional materials in the aviation Industry, as far as structural components are concerned, as high-performance steel, light aluminum alloys, and titanium. For the same applicative areas, the composites that are now competing with those materials are organic-matrix carbon, fiberglass, or aramid material long-fiber composites (other carbon-, ceramic-, or metal-matrix composites are more specifically appropriate to engine components, see 3.2.2).

A tougher battle is taking place between aluminum and aluminum-alloy composites. Steel, after all, especially after reaching its high performance levels, is no longer questioned, while titanium is too expensive a material and excessively difficult to use; hence it is seldom used.

In replacing metal materials with composite materials, the savings in weight is generally estimated on the order of 20-30 percent. Under the pressure for this potential lightening (for an Airbus, a 320 passenger plane, for example, a kilogram reduction of weight is worth a 35-dollar savings in operating costs each year), it is estimated that in the aviation industry the presence of composites, which today hovers around 6 percent, at the turn of the century should reach 20 percent.

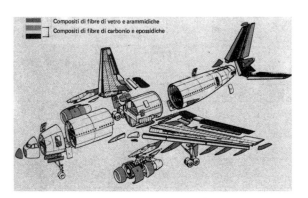

Composites make up 20 percent of the total weight of the Airbus 320. The use of composite materials in commercial airplanes makes it possible to reduce operating costs sharply.

Light mechanics

Kronotech, a speed trial bicycle, has a continuous-structure frame (a light honeycomb core that separates and stiffens the two carbon fiber fabric skins reinforced with other uniaxial fibers, oriented in the direction of maximum stress); the lenticular wheels and the wing-shaped load-bearing handlebars are made of carbon; crank, gearshift, and brakes are integrated into the structure. Even the bicycle seat is structurally integrated and streamlined.

This is certainly a special bicycle. It was created not only to set speed records, but also – and explicitly – as a testing ground for innovative technical results. The fact that it is unusual, however, does not make it less intriguing. Its shape – so radically distant from the bicycle with which we are familiar – reflects the general transformation of the system of objects.

A bicycle is an object that is emblematic not only of a technical system, but also of a conceptual system that we are now abandoning – the phase that we earlier dubbed the mechanical phase. A bicycle is, indeed, a metal object, in which the objective of simultaneously obtaining lightness and strength is reached through a frame made of linear elements (a lattice girder, such as in iron bridges and the Eiffel Tower). The various subsystems

(brakes, transmission, gearshift) are conceived as separate units, visibly connected to the frame. The system can easily be broken down to its component parts, in accordance with the model of mechanical thought (see 1.3.3).

This structure certainly constitutes one of the most successful objects of the mechanical phase, one of the products that has varied least over time. After a few initial oscillations, a shape prevailed – a few details changing as new materials and processing techniques were introduced – that has never been seriously called into question since. Now the pressure of new materials on the traditional problem-solving strategies has become powerful, and Kronotech provides an exemplary image of the shape that springs from the new possibilities. Without the new material, it would be impossible to make the structure so streamlined, with the integration of other mechanical components.

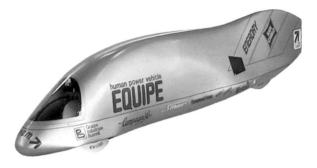

Top: Equipe Enervit is a muscle-powered speed-trial vehicle designed to go faster than 100 km/h. Made of carbon- and aramid-fiber composites, it weights 28 kilograms. The maximum height of 76 centimeters forces the athlete to lie on his stomach. Visibility is provided by a monitor and a video camera (prototype developed by Logos Compositi). Left: the introduction of innovative materials can transform even the best established formal and technical archetypes. In the Kronotech speed-trial bicycle, the traditional lattice structure is replaced by a load-bearing shell that combines good mechanical performance with excellent aerodynamic qualities. The structural elements (shown above) are made of a honeycomb core and two thin shells of a reinforced composite material with uniaxial carbon fibers, arranged to correspond to stress. (Doct. Montedison-Monfrini)

Similar thoughts are prompted by UFO II, an engine-driven vehicle developed by Ford to break the world fuel economy record. Weighing a total of 22 kilograms and with an aerodynamic coefficient of 0.113, the UFO II traveled at a speed ranging from 20 to 30 kilometers per hour with an average fuel consumption of 0.074 liter per 100 kilometers, equivalent to 1,351 kilometers with a liter of fuel. In order to achieve those results (35 watts is enough to push the vehicle at 24 kilometers per hour), the body was engineered in terms of materials (carbon and aramid resin composites) and shape right down to the smallest details; even the tires were specially engineered, and with special Kevlar reinforcement, have reached very low weight (81 grams each) and low rolling resistance.

Aside from the curiosity value, this object is interesting because of the way in which the mechanism has been minimized in favor of a shell the chief of whose qualities is performance – it contains a pilot and transports him on wheels with the least possible friction. This is a trend that can be seen in the development of all means of transport.

The relationship between vehicles such as the UFO II and mass-produced automobiles is at best tenuous. And yet, while in the past they both could have been described as engines equipped with wheels and room for passengers, today – in both cases – the engine is almost invisible. The engine no longer exerts influence on the overall structure. The predominant aspect is the interface with the ambient and the user. UFO II looks like a streamlined space suit built to fit the pilot; a mid-sized automobile looks like a small stream lined drawing room built to suit the needs (both in terms of function and image) of an average family.

Testing the possibility of introducing new materials in the automobile industry can reach the level of extremely advanced experimentation. With an image reminiscent of speed-trial vehicles developed in the Sixties to attain high speeds on two wheels, the Ford UFO II (above, without body) takes a concrete approach to a very realistic objective, lowering consumption in order to break the world's record for fuel economy.

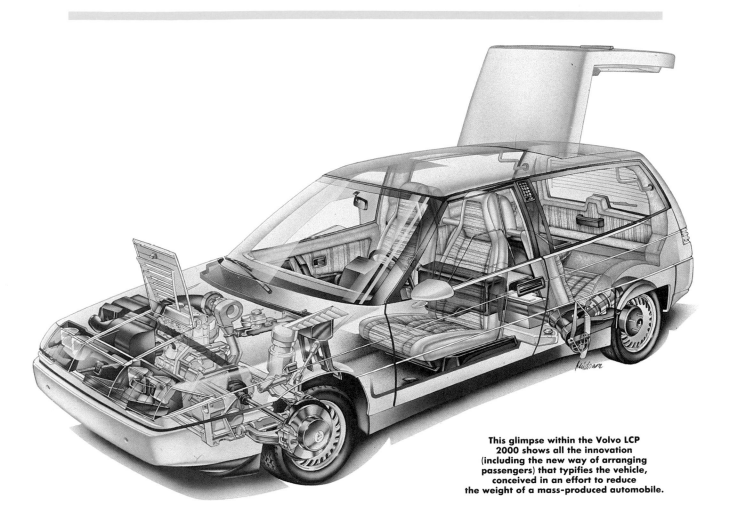

This glimpse within the Volvo LCP 2000 shows all the innovation (including the new way of arranging passengers) that typifies the vehicle, conceived in an effort to reduce the weight of a mass-produced automobile.

Automobiles: lightness, and other performances

An automobile can weigh as much as 1,000 kilograms and transport no more than a few hundred kilograms. The weight ratio between transporter and transportee is not among the most efficient. Lightness, however, in the automobile industry, is a goal that must be achieved within a complex system where it conflicts with other performances and other bonds. Lightness, except for a few experimental cases, is not the constituent organizing factor in the engineering. The appearance on the market of a light approach to automobile manufacturing is just that much more significant, inasmuch as it indicates that the technical solution was filtered through the very fine screen of mass-market manufacturing.

In this context, the role of experimental automobiles may be important but rarely is it decisive. The automobile system (due to these economic bonds) is too stable to accept a new idea wholesale, no matter how brilliant it may be. Experimental automobiles remain, nevertheless, a stimulus and testing ground for options that, in the long run, may enter in mass production.

The goal of weight reduction, together with the overall objective of reducing the total e-

nergy cost (both in terms of energy consumption in manufacturing and operating the automobile), finds very interesting expression in the case of the Volvo LCP 2000.

This automobile was conceived realistically in manufacturing terms, but differs with currently produced models, in that reduction of weight and consumption is approached by radically rethinking the entire vehicle typology, instead of simply adapting the existing.

The most innovative step was that of changing the seating arrangement so that the rear passengers are facing backward. This modification, although it makes the interior of the vehicle less comfortable, creates the space for a large structural beam in the triangle that is opened between the backrests, within which the fuel tank is housed. The structure, due to its shape, possesses great strength and makes it possible to save on material while keeping the same stiffness, thus reducing the weight.

The body itself, as is common practice with experimental automobiles, has undergone a change from the traditional load-bearing body that is prompted by the introduction of plastics. The traditional structure of stamped welded plate, in which the outer skin contributes to the structure's strength, is abandoned in favor of a return to the load-bearing chassis and a non-structural body. In this model of Volvo, the panels of the body were made of injection-molded thermoplastics, much like many bumper shields in mass-produced automobiles now on the market. The chassis is made of stamped and welded aluminum plate, a concept that has already been tested in racing cars. It was only through vast improvements in computing and materials that it became possible to apply this solution to an automobile that could be mass produced and that could stand up to the strict impact testing required in the United States.

The use of structural adhesives makes aluminum plate better adapted to industrial manufacturing, resolving the problems with welding that have always hindered the capacity of this material to compete successfully with steel. Stronger but more expensive materials (such as carbon fiber) are used only in such critical areas as the door frames, where the reduction of cross-section while maintaining the same strength yields such functional advantages as reductions in bulk.

Furthermore, the development of innovative treatments makes it possible to exploit the lightness of several well-known materials by eliminating some of the shortcomings that had previously prevented their widespread use in manufacturing. One surface treatment process (*plasma-spraying*) has made it possible to use aluminum for disk brakes instead of the tradition steel and cast-iron disks, which are heavier and less adapted to dispersing heat. Similarly, the development of anti-corrosion treatments has opened the way to intensive use of light magnesium-based alloys used in casting wheels, engine support frames, engine blocks, and suspension arms.

All of the glass, except for the windshield, is replaced with slabs of polycarbonate, the surface of which is protected by an abrasion-proof sheath. The pedal group, made of plastic reinforced with fiberglass, lends itself to pre-assembly off the assembly line, and can easily be adjusted by the end user.

Even improvements in minor details contributes indirectly to lightening. The development of safety tires, capable of moving at reduced speed even after a blowout, has made it possible to eliminate the spare tire.

A few years after this model was manufactured, we can see that (aside from the aluminum chassis with the large transverse stiffening beam) many of the innovations applied in this prototype have entered the realm of economic manufacturability, and some are already in production.

If we give special consideration to structural aspects – i.e., to the most decisive aspects in determining weight – the fundamental steps in the evolution of the automobile go from the primitive configuration inherited from the horse-drawn carriage (wooden ribs, and a skin of canvas or sheet metal on a load-bearing chassis), to the great development of the load-bearing body, introduced in Lancia automobiles in the Twenties and adopted in mass production in the Fifties and Sixties.

In this last phase, plastics began to win ground on the interiors of automobiles, and the first experimental plastic bodies were produced (generally in polyester reinforced with fiberglass and made entirely or partially by hand). It was chiefly in the Seventies, however, that, thanks to the development of polymers and special formulations, plastics began to move into more significant parts of the automobile.

The first area where they gained a foothold was in the bumper, which was completely redesigned (with an effect that has altered

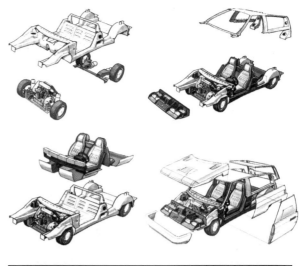

The use of sophisticated materials
may lead to a total rethinking
of the techniques used in making
automobiles.
Top: The four successive stages
of assembly planned for the Volvo LCP 2000.
Subassemblies made out of "specialized"
materials constitute separate large-scale
components with complex functions,
which are introduced, pre-assembled,
in the final stages of assembly.
Above and below: Prototype of the platform,
the finished body,
and the vehicle being tested.

104

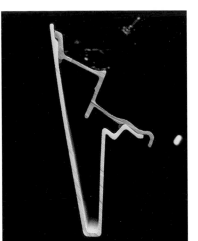

In mass production plastic materials have taken over many components, providing reductions in weight and other improvements in performance. Top: Lamp for automobile headlights made with a sandwich of coinjected normal and modified polybuteleneterephthalate (PBT). The lamp incorporates all sockets and adjustment mechanisms. (Doct. Montedison-Dutral)

Right: High-molecular-weight polyethylene fuel tank. Blowing makes it possible to generate complex forms, and to adapt the tank to the available space in the automobile (mfg. Safiplast). (Doct. Montedison)

Above and below: Hatch of the Fiat Uno Turbo, made of BMC (molded unsaturated polyester and fiberglass). The two shells, molded by an injection/pressure process, are assembled by using hot epoxy adhesive (top center, cross-section). The assembly, stiffened with glued crystal, weighs less than 8 kg and its appearance fits in well with the rest of the metal body (mfg. Comind-Stars). (Doct. Montedison)

the entire image of automobiles), becoming a subsystem of the automobile that is formally but also functionally different from the initial component (see 3.3.2).

In the production of the new bumper, different materials and transformation processes come into contact: injection molded thermoplastic polymers, thermoset composites reinforced with fiberglass (SMC), reinforced and non-reinforced reaction injection-molded polyurethanes (RIM, RRIM).

A second and unquestioned conquest of plastics is in the area of fuel tanks. With blow-forming processes, it is possible to obtain extremely complex shapes, to make the best use of the spaces available within the vehicle.

As for the car body, when working with plastics it is important to keep in mind the different levels of strain to which the horizontal elements (roof, hood, trunk hatch) are subjected when compared with the vertical elements (fenders, grill and nose). For each category, materials are required that are adequate to the performance needed.

For instance, nowadays, fiberglass-reinforced, injection molded (BMC) is used for horizontal parts, while polyurethanes or injection-molded thermoplastic reinforced engineering plastics are used for the verticals.
One of the features that blocks the success of plastics in this field is the quality of the surface that can be obtained. A "class A" surface, easily obtained by correctly painting sheet metal, is difficult to obtain with plastics, especially if they are reinforced.
Furthermore, during the present phase, with its auto bodies partly made of metal and partly of plastic, one of the chief problems is that the painting of the metal calls for a treatment in a phosphating oven (150-170 °C) and a treatment in the paint oven (130-150 °C). In order to install plastic parts "on line" as well (with considerable manufacturing advantages and greater certainty of uniform painting) one must either use plastics capable of withstanding those temperatures without undergoing deformation (at least in the paint ovens); and not all materials can meet this standard. The problem is quite important, and can be solved only by a simple and drastic change in the method of painting cars, shifting to paints that need lower temperatures (such as polyurethane dual-component paints).
Another problem grows out of the presence in the same product of materials with different heat expansion, which require appropriate engineering and manufacturing measures.

Where resistant structures are concerned, the use of high performance composites – the only materials capable of successfully replacing steel – is not currently feasible for economical mid- to mass-market industrial manufacturing. Nevertheless, both race cars and small-market sports cars are now being made in this way, and studies have been done on the manufacturing of auto bodies through filament winding or by using components made by pultrusion or other hybrid processes that merge advanced composite technology with other characteristics more in line with mass production.

When these processes become economically and technically feasible, we can really sit down and start thinking about an all-plastic automobile. Saying all-plastic does not mean that the whole car would be made of the same material. In fact, the most typical feature of a plastic automobile could be no other than the multiplicity of materials employed. It is not hard to imagine an automobile with a structural cage surrounding the passenger compartment made of high-resistance composites, zones of honeycomb structure for the absorption of impact energy, an outer skin made of large plastic panels (more rigid for doors, hood, and trunk, more flexible for bumpers and protective strips), transparent surfaces made of polycarbonate (PC) or polymethylmetha acrylat.

For that matter, it is not necessary to wait for the metamorphosis to be complete to be able to see the level of the multiplication of specialty polymers in automobile manufacture. Even in the present hybrid phase when a traditional material is replaced with a new material, the latter is always a special formulation of some sort, a material (or process) developed for that specific use. Automobiles provide the most important test of hyper-selection, engineering, and multiplication of materials (see 1.2.1).

Load-bearing body (top) and spoiler of the Alfa Romeo Formula One vehicle, made of carbon-fiber and fiberglass composite fabric and honeycomb composite. (Doct. Montedison-Monfrini)

106

Massive constructions

"In the Mediterranean tradition, whence most Western architecture descends," wrote Reyner Banham, "the need to make a shelter permanent or at least durable was usually met by making the construction massive (...) This type of construction brought about habitat advantages that have become so customary over three millennia of European civilization as to be usually considered as inherent in any structural solution" (*Environment and Engineering in Modern Architecture*). No consideration of "creating the light" in architecture would be complete without some reference to the three thousand years of history and roots that underlie the "culture of the heavy" in a context where symbolic components tend to prevail.

In this setting, which has been long rendered stable by the continuity in materials used, there are also a few conflicting elements.

First of all, the massive edifice to which Banham makes general reference, was in standard architecture of the western tradition really a hybrid of heavy vertical structures and mostly lighter horizontal structures, and therefore involved a vast range of static problems. The vertical structures chiefly function by compression, in a system of strain that is quite well adapted to the properties of traditional materials (stone and brick), while roofing is above all subject to bending stress which stone and brick are less readily able to withstand (both because of their own lesser resistance to tension stress and because of the difficulties with using them to construct joints capable of withstanding this sort of stress).

Certainly, the distinction is not always sharp. An arch (horizontal) discharges its load onto walls and buttresses (vertical), thus creating new problems and images. In architectural language, this takes on significance only when there are special functional or symbolic needs to be met by increasing the number of arched covered spaces (ranging from Roman aqueducts to baroque cupolas). In these cases, a horizontal structure performs more than just a technical function and becomes more than just a service structure, and goes on to become a true primary architectural element. Indeed, the roof becomes the very symbol of the art of building, the terrain upon which those who challenge matter and its weight offer the greatest possible expression of engineering.

When, however, there are no exceptional building requirements, the norm is to con-

The image of weight. Foundations of the mausoleum of Hadrian, Rome, by Giovanni Battista Piranesi.

107

struct boxes of which an observer/resident sees primarily the sides and the bottom. It is no accident that customary architectural drafting shows a building in two ways: elevation (i.e., the vertical outer portion) and plan (i.e., the interior seen without the roof, as it were).

In creating these forms, the separation between the architectural languages of the facades and the roof corresponds to a separation between two histories of construction, interwoven but quite distinct: that of the horizontal architecture of roofing and that of the vertical architecture of facades.

The latter, the chief field of architectural endeavor, has continued to offer an image typified by weight, while horizontal roofing, a far more functional and technical problem, has undergone a continual push toward lightness.

From trilith to tensile structure

A tensile structure is a roof so light that its problems tend more toward the area of fluid dynamics than to statics. It is as important, if not more, to keep track of depressions caused by wind and the tendency to lift like a wing as it is to work with the overall weight and load.

Its functional layout (based on pylons under compression, cables under tensile stress, and light covering surfaces) does have historical precedents – in terms of image and technical strategy – in tents, suspension bridges, the superstructure of sailing ships. It is nevertheless quite distant from all roofing offered by the history of Western architecture.

Tensile structures offer a construction image whose solidity derives from the effect of form and tensions that act on a membrane or a mesh of cables, strong but flexible by definition. They mark the conclusion of a long history of roofing, beginning with technical strategies based on rigid heavy materials subjected to pressure by their own weight, and concluding with know-how based on the use of light materials that work by tensile strength.

The weight per square meter of roofing, that different civilizations have used to provide horizontal cover to the shell of the edifice, progressively drops over time: from the 4 tons of Assyrian building to the 1.5 tons of Roman construction, down to the half ton of the Gothic period.

It should be emphasized that over this time span the ten-fold lightening that takes place is achieved more through the careful placement and use of materials than through actual changes in the materials. From trilith to arch and then to increasingly complex vaults, the chief structural problem is always how to arrange material so as to transform bending stress into compressive stress while maintaining tensile stress within the very modest limits allowed by the materials.

With the Industrial Revolution and its new materials, radically new solutions appear. Steel enters construction systems following the persistent tradition of wood trusses but extending the frontiers of this pre-existing building strategy.

Thus begins the era of light roofing, where the ratio between weight supported and the weight of the roof itself is less than one. Since, under average engineering conditions, the weight supported is approximately 100 kilograms per square meter, the weight of the structure itself is less than that value. With steel, used with the best possible weight-to-strength ratio, roofing can be lightened considerably. A metal truss can weigh as little as a tenth of

rials did not exist – from steel cables to light sheet metal or polymer covering panels and even coated fabrics. The last-named may involve various materials, depending on the loads and the durability required. The most widely used are PVC-coated polyesters, while the most sophisticated and long-lasting is fiberglass coated with polytetrafluoroethylene (PTFE).

Tensile structures, in various forms, have today come onto the landscape of construction, with their high performance and particular image. The special forms they create, however, are also a hindrance to their spread. That is why they are confined to special uses, where their very exceptionality and lack of a building tradition make it easier to accept their technical and formal novelty.

reinforced concrete beam over the same opening. With this structural framework, the problem of eliminating tensile loads is reversed. In steel lattice structures, the problem becomes that of limiting the compressive stresses that, in light frameworks, cause instability. The problem is usually solved by oversizing the compressed parts, which generates an increase in weight due not to a search for strength, but a search for stability.

The next step along the road to lightness could only be that of choosing methods that concentrate compression in the most appropriate points and keep the rest of the structure under tensile stress. This avenue may be taken with ease, due to the existence of steel cables and high-resistance fabrics and membranes. The resulting tension fabric structures are solutions in which material is so arranged as to work only – and at its best – under tensile stress.

By means of tension fabric structures, it is possible to construct roofing that, over the some space, weights less than a hundredth of a reinforced concrete beam and a tenth of a steel beam.

In the development of the lightest tension fabric structures, the principal matter employed is certainly the capacity to calculate and model their shape. The practical results would not have been able to go much past the level of a circus tent if the right mate-

Facing page and top: The roof of Jeddah Airport, designed by Studio SOM, is tied to the Arabic architectural tradition. Made of polytetrafluoroethilene-coated fiberglass fabric (mfg. Owens-Corning), it ensures natural ventilation and protection from sunlight.
Above and center: Computer simulation of a tension fabric structure of the Schlumberger research center, at Cambridge, England (Michael Hopkins Architects), made it possible to evaluate with precision such complex parameters as fabric elongation (3.2 percent along the weft and 0.6 percent along the warp), and surface geometry. Models derived from behavior of soap bubbles were employed.

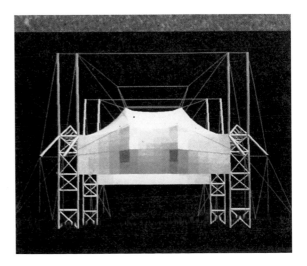

From pillar to pillar

"Far above the visitors' heads there is a luminous arch higher and more spacious than our most noble cathedrals. On every side, the view seems limitless." With these words a reporter for the London *Times* (2 May 1851) described his — and the other visitors — impressions of the Crystal Palace, the great construction designed by G. J. Paxton for the Universal Exposition of London.

Paxton's great glass edifice, as much as the latticework bridges and industrial sheds created by engineers of the period, gave a profound visual shock to contemporary Europeans. Constructions had always been thought of as massive objects anchored to the ground with solid walls. Suddenly they were taking on a transparent appearance. Indeed, the new constructions were becoming the very image of lightness.

This field, where ground was chiefly broken by engineers, was revisited by the architects of Modern Movement. Lightness borrowed its image from the world of engineering and machines, and was then proposed as a value to be introduced into architecture and the system of objects. Between the monumental eclecticism of the late nineteenth century and the constructions of masters of Modernism there is, even more than a technical difference, a difference in the image of weight. The esthetics of lightness thus took on in modern architecture an ideological significance that was diametrically opposed to what had long been the basis of the esthetics of weight — it was now a break with the past, an open assurance that the world of forms was taking the path of "Progress" toward which technology pointed the way. Today, nevertheless, the crisis of the Modern Movement reveals a thread of continuity that we thought was broken but that was merely hidden. In the name of a language that revives memory, the image of weight has reappeared on the design landscape. Technology's development toward the immaterial and the instantaneous has generated a countertrend toward emphasis on weight and "history." This "nostalgia for the heavy," however, plays more on appearance than on the effective physical nature of constructions. The columns and capitals of contemporary architecture are in reality merely thin strips of cement. The idea of a wall's solidity is given by the form of its covering more than by its actual construction.

Above, and top on facing page: Ricardo Bofill, El palacio de Abraxas at Marne-La-Vallee (1978-1983). Bottom left: Manolo Nunez and Henri Guchez, Psychopedagogic Institute of Wasmes. Facing page, bottom right: Site Group, Best Stores, Towson, Maryland (1978).

Innovation has penetrated the building sector almost unnoticed, transforming the materiality it encounters without effecting any deep changes in the organization of manufacturing processes or image.

Today, little remains of all those ideas of radical change in construction methods that were bandied about in discussions of industrialized building over decades gone by. Nevertheless, an accumulation of many minor transformations has generated a new context typified by materials that can be erected more rapidly and that are generally lighter. That lightness was not specifically sought and is indeed in certain cases antifunctional. It is often merely the result of an advantageous manufacturing situation: an outside brick wall is replaced by a sandwich panel; an inside partition wall, likewise made of brick, is replaced by a plasterboard partition, a marble floor is replaced by wall-to-wall carpeting, a metal plumbing network is replaced by plastic pipes... By a thousand different minor paths, new materials are filtering onto the construction site, bringing with them reductions in mass and thickness. And so a gap is created between the actual material nature of constructions — affected by economic considerations that call for

weight reduction – and their image, which often proffers the idea of solidity in terms of weight and quantity.

On the other hand, of course, this separation between a light signifier and a meaning that hints at weight, this "rêve d'épaisseur," or dream of thickness, in the words of Bernard Hamburger and Alain Thiebaut, has more to do with European buildings than with construction in other cultural areas less rooted to the idea of massiveness – both in terms of learned architecture and everyday architecture.

And so it happens that architecture offers a growing range of images, and that the wide selection of technical alternatives and available materials, along with their adaptability to different performances, serve as a medium for a variety of languages, which flourish during the crisis of the Modern Movement. Therefore, "creating the heavy" – or perhaps more correctly "simulating the heavy" – is joined by a second parallel tendency that is ironic and provocative, where counterfeiting weight becomes an evident design element. Here the weight is destabilized or suggested in images that are devoid of materiality. On the other hand there is the use of an image of lightness that breaks with building tradi-

tion and embraces the mechanical tradition. Here the column's role in nostalgia for the heavy is taken over by the lattice girder, which becomes a symbolic, rather than a functional, element. The lattice girder is a reference to a consolidated image of a technological avant-garde that is already an image of memory, a monument to a hypothetical future mechanical world that has already become history without ever creating a full-fledged present.

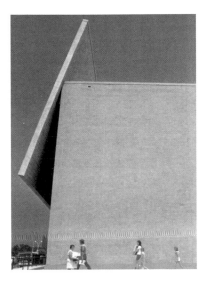

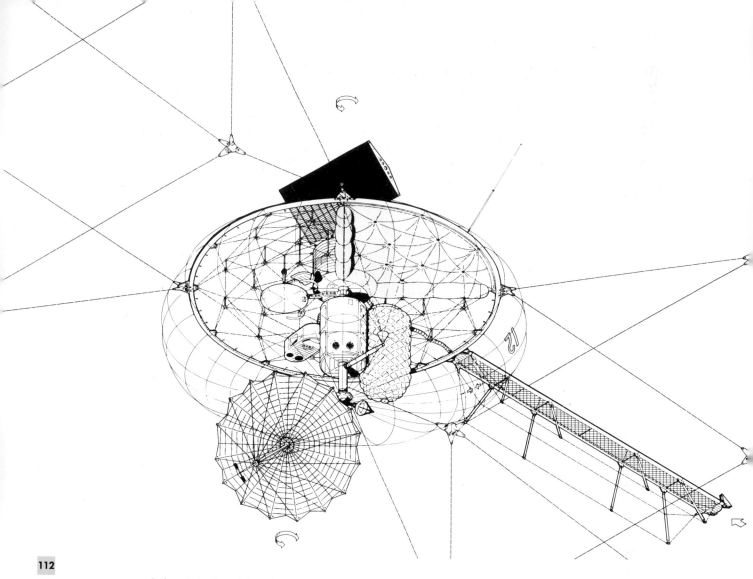

Other inhabitable objects

In the projects of Jan Kaplicky the houses — or perhaps we should say, the living cells — are always depicted amidst a savage wilderness, set in the most improbable positions, with the relaxed and delicate poise of an insect sitting on a blade of grass. Indeed, *Project 019*, referred to as a "45° house for a family of four," has the air of a caterpillar on the shore of the sea, while *Project 117*, a living cell suspended from a system of cables, cannot help but make one think of a spider. Both of these projects, and everything designed by Kaplicky, are technically feasible. The materials and technology involved are derived from the automobile industry, if these dwellings were produced in sufficient quantities, the same economic considerations used in the automobile industry could be applied to them.

Houses, however, are not automobiles. The history of constructions is as long as the history of technology or culture, and any consideration of how buildings could change should take into account the complex system of values and interests that has consolidated around the idea of the house. This system may provide an explanation of why the se-

The dream of a technological house/machine. Designs by Jan Kaplicky for his *Future Systems*: inhabitable objects made with aircraft technology. Top: Project 117, (1983), aluminium structure, inflatable cupola made of transparent PVC. Facing page: (top) Project 019, house for sloping land. Below, bed/capsule by Kisho Kurokawa in a hotel in Osaka: made of phenolic resin, it takes up only about 3.3 sq.m. instead of the 15 sq.m. of a traditional hotel room.

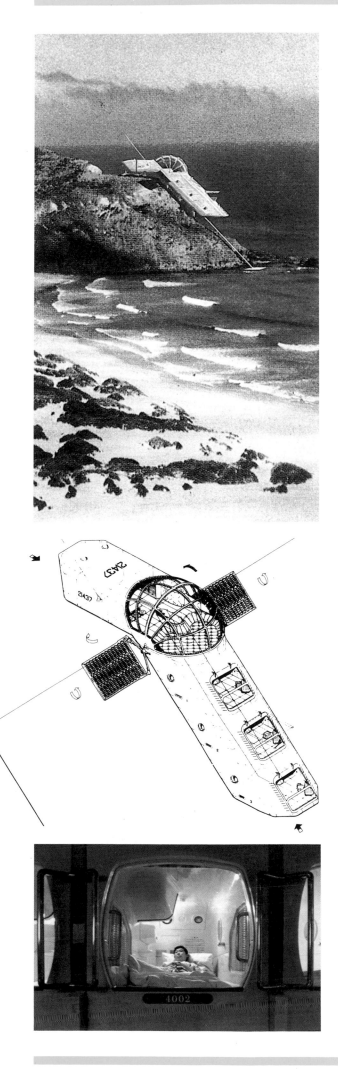

ries of proposals of designers like Kaplicky and many others (beginning with Buckminster Fuller with his *Dymaxion House* in 1927) have been quite important in the cultural debate over living spaces but have been virtually ignored in building.

This observation, which is widely accepted, is certainly accurate if we consider these new ideas as proposals for the future overall state of living spaces. In reality it is difficult to imagine a city constructed with the living cells described above. In the past few years, however, we have become familiar with the principle of coexistence of different cultural choices and attitudes. Models of living space and architecture differ and often conflict, but they all describe in some way possible alternatives. So that if in some geographic and cultural areas nostalgia for weight will continue to exert its influence for some time, that does not mean that in the same areas (and to a greater degree elsewhere, where the tradition of weight is less powerful) other paths can be followed at the same time, and that other "inhabitable objects" may be proposed, outside of the boundaries of the European tradition of massive constructions.

In the past, the homogeneity and limitations of available materials and techniques in a given area and time led to a certain uniformity in the material substance of everything that was built. Today the multiplication of materials and techniques, on the one hand, and the multiplication of behavior, on the other hand, make it possible to break down the habitat into different shapes, that fit different cultural and functional needs. City homes and vacation houses, permanent homes and temporary residences are the most obvious extremes, but we could mention commune/homes for the young, hotel homes for singles, houses with a rapid turnover of tenants, all the way to the "home" of a few hours, long a familiar fixture in certain Japanese hotels with capsule-style room/beds.

Different inhabitable objects that are not necessarily the wave of the future, but that are available within an increasingly articulated and differentiated environment: perhaps this is the terrain upon which innovation will emerge from the narrow context of process innovation – currently the overriding form in the building trades – to become true product innovation. New materials for new inhabitable objects that succeed in establishing a link with tradition (and so coexist with the older inhabitable objects) while proposing new functions and new relationships.

Frontiers of lightness

Astronauts tell us that it is not all that difficult to become accustomed to objects without weight. That may well be, but the fact remains that our movements are controlled by a nervous system that is calibrated (i.e., genetically evolved) to perform those movements in an ambient where mass is subject to the force of gravity, so that objects possess weight. A world of feather-weight objects, of objects so light that they would practically hover in the air, would not only be light-years away from our cultural framework (and this framework could always change), but very difficult to live in. Already there are objects (in the area of home appliances and equipment, for instance) that, due to considerations of manufacturing economics, are made of a light material, and have to be ballasted in order to remain functional. In other words, the basic trend of "creating the light" may pass a boundary beyond which any increase in the performance-to-weight ratio proves non-functional.

Not all families of products however lie at the same distance from this physical limit. Vehicles, large-scale roofing, packaging are all areas where lightening has been going on for some time. There is still considerable room for development, which should move in directions that can be pretty clearly seen even now. For many other industrial products, on the other hand, lightness as a consequence of a reduction in the material used already seems to have reached the limits of functional acceptability, and now varies only according to differing engineering and market trends (for instance, according to preferences for esthetic lightness or nostalgia for the heavy).

This is true only if we are considering the families of traditional objects, that is, if, in the performance-to-weight ratio, the performance is a given. Actually, this is not true, and it is here that there emerge some of the most interesting aspects of the new meaning of lightness.

From a situation in which the performance index rose, with a loss of weight for the same

level of performance, today we are moving toward a condition in which the weight is a given (because it can drop no further) while the performance level rises. Thus a pattern of "relative lightening" commences, born not of function or economical drives, but which nevertheless leads in the same direction — the integration of functions made possible by the miniaturization of electronic components tends to condense in the same object functions that would otherwise involve separate objects. The lightening of a computer, a typewriter, or a watch can be measured up to a certain point by the decrease in the object's weight. From a certain point on, lightness is chiefly expressed in terms of the increase in functions incorporated. An intelligent object is not light only in terms of its weight in absolute terms, but also — and chiefly — in terms of the range of functions performed.

Hence there arises an image of "creating the light" that is more mental than physical — a lightness in terms of the quantity and degree of the performance (see 1.1.1). The physical form of a light object is neutral (keyboards, displays, "black boxes" without any formal hint at their functions) or parasitic (in the sense that their calculating and memory capacity is often integrated in the shape of a watch or credit card, but can even take the

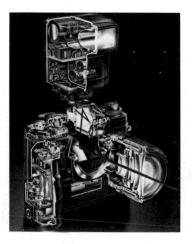

form of pens, shoes, and so on). In reality, the true form is that of the set of relations that the high density of performances establishes with the user and the ambient.

Stability, nomadism, sensitivity

Tents and mobile homes, with all the accompanying system of transportable objects, have roots as ancient as nomadism and a lesser modern history that runs parallel to the history of objects of more stable cultures. These historical objects of nomadism are joined by others, to whom portability is a novelty, the product of a marketing leap made possible by the reduction of weight.

Integration and miniaturization of functions lead to the relative lightness mentioned previously. A Walkman is a prime example – it is a hi-fi system whose reduction of weight and bulk creates an entirely new use. This changes the market quality of the product, but it also changes the way in which we relate to music. The sound space created by a Walkman is unprecedented, and creates a new dimension of experience.

The same is true of everything that electronics and materials progress make light and portable or superportable. Today is it possible to carry (on one's wrist in the form of a watch, or in one's wallet in the form of a credit card, or else just in one's pocket) objects whose range of performance is limited only by lack of imagination or by caution.

The new availability of these high perform-

ance-density extensions of our body, joined to an equally high variety in means of transport, creates an important overall result – a high-tech nomadism that, moving with equal ease by airplane, car, bicycle, or on foot, creates a new idea of space and a new relationship between space and time (see 1.1.1). The two traditional systems of objects created in the past by nomadism and stability – over which the two values of lightness and weight prevailed – now tend to merge.

On the other hand, the growing artificialization of the ambient we experience, leads to a quest for greater immediacy in the relationship between our physical bodies and nature – this is the reason for the success of objects such as windsurfs and hang gliders (both creations of advanced technology) which are products of the development of sporting equipment that have little to do either with sports or with their direct forebears. Certainly, windsurfs descend from sailing ships, while hang gliders descend from airplanes. They are both, however, totally new

objects – in terms of the way in which they are used (they are not means of transport, they are extensions of the body), because they are used for gratuitous reasons (neither is used to go somewhere, they are used solely for the pleasure of riding wind or waves), and lastly because of their remarkable spread (made possible by the joint factors of moderate cost and high sensitivity, the cultural development defined by John Naisbitt, in *Megatrends*).

"Creating the light" thus fits in different ways into the meeting/clash between high technology and high sensitivity – on the one hand, by causing objects to lose materiality, it creates a yearning for physicality, for direct contact with the environment, for the "real weight" of things; on the other hand, by virtue of the lightness produced by the loss of materiality, there are now lightweight extensions of the body, with which to plunge into nature.

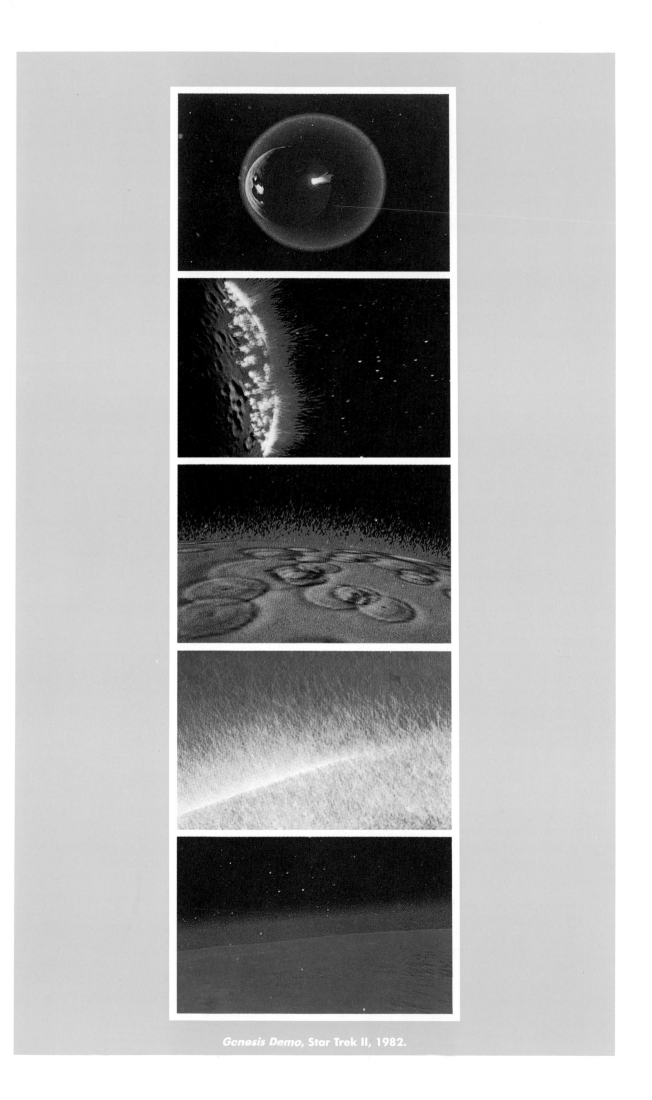

Genesis Demo, Star Trek II, 1982.

Creating the heat resistant

Matter and temperature

From the first use of fire to cook food, the earliest metallurgy, all the way up to space travel and nuclear fusion, the history of technology has always been linked to the mastery of high temperatures.

Of course, the exact meaning of the adjective high varies according to the period in question. Leroi-Gourhan describes as a "Promethean ascent" the succession of techniques used in working at temperatures ranging from the few hundred degrees required to fire terracotta up to the thousands of degrees used today in processing certain advanced materials.

On the other hand, Leroi-Gourhan points out, the history of fire generally has at its origins myths that would seem to hint at a sort of curse. In his words, "The myth of Prometheus at once reflects a victory over the gods and a fettered captivity," (Le geste et la parole. Technique et language); Vulcan forges the arms of heroes, but he is a ridiculous, lame god. The mastery of fire, and of high temperatures in general, is shrouded in a mysterious aura that passes from mythology to alchemy. Not even modern thought, which always tends to depict observed reality in terms of perfect clarity, has entirely eliminated that aura.

The thread of continuity lies in the property of fire, and of high temperatures, to modify the substance of things. Ignis mutat res was the motto of alchemists and ancient chemists. The changes that fire produced, however, by refuting the stability of things, conflicted with the belief that everything is at all times what it is: a belief, upon which not only common sense but the dominant philosophical thought of the Western world was based — as was science itself at its outset.

"The science of fire," observe Prigogine and Stengers, "became part of experimental science during the eighteenth century. This was the result of a conceptual transforma-tion that forced science to reconsider what it had at first rejected in the name of the mechanistic view of the world, and especially irreversibility and complexity" (La Nouvelle Alliance. Métamorphose de la Science). Since then scientific attention has been riveted on fire's ability to transform matter, make it react chemically, spread it, melt it, make it evaporate, and in the end create another matter, or produce mechanical effects capable of generating motion. The achievement of these results, however, implies a substantial problem — it is equally necessary to develop materials that can contain the phenomenon. Heat-resistant materials have always been the hidden face of fire technology. In order to have fire alter things without triggering a catastrophe, one must have something that fire cannot change.

117

Today we know that temperature merely indicates a state of agitation in matter. An increase in temperature corresponds to a tendency toward destabilization of matter's structures, and to a potential loss of the orderly forms that those structures possessed. Temperature is therefore a decisive feature of the structural configuration of a material. Whether the material appears in a solid crystalline state, a solid amorphous state (which is merely a liquid state with extremely high viscosity), or a gummy, viscous, liquid, or gaseous state — all this depends on a great number of factors, but it is always tied to temperature. What is more: temperature is a decisive factor in promoting or inhibiting chemical reactions between a material's components, or between those components and the ambient, thus prompting transformations that alter not only the physical structure of the material in question, but even its chemical properties — in short, turning it into something else.

To sum up, let us say that if increases in temperature correspond to increases in motion, then what we refer to as heat resistance is the capacity of atomic, molecular, and inter-molecular bonds to resist, without breaking, the increase in agitation in the particles that they hold together.

Hence, a material is thermally resistant within a given range of temperatures if no unacceptable variations in the macroscopic qualities that typify that material occur within that range. If the chemical and physical composition of the material prevents the microscopic motion from altering the respective positions of atoms and molecules, then that material displays sufficient macroscopic stability even under stress.

A material's resistance to various temperatures is therefore a value that has to do with the very structure of that material, the temperature interval in question, and the system of loads to which the material is subjected. For materials science, developing something that is more heat resistant means producing (by modifying something that already exists or by engineering it anew) a structure whose parts – atoms and molecules – are as closely bonded as possible, and possess a form and bonds that are capable of restricting motion even at high temperatures.

On the other hand, the most heat-resistant material is also, in general, the most troublesome and tricky to work with; the task that awaits engineers is therefore to find a balance, a compromise between thermal resistance and workability.

High-temperature materials

For a very long time, fire-resistant materials were not required to possess other properties. A furnace, a crucible, a pot, or a pan were not often subjected to mechanical actions. When they were, the quantity or mass of material used in their construction could usually take care of any problems with thermal or mechanical quality.

The situation changed with the arrival of engines. These are objects with moving parts and that, often, are themselves in motion, with interior sections at high temperature. New heat-resistant materials must now ensure greater mechanical performance along with the least possible use of mass (mass, with its inertia, is an enemy to be shunned whenever acceleration occurs). Furthermore, a heat-operated engine is more efficient at higher operating temperatures.

This set of requirements provides a push for research into and the adoption of new materials. If heat resistant was once practically synonymous with refractory material of argillaceous origin, in this new field of fire technology the expression heat resistant has practically become synonymous with metal, with steels and alloys that can resist temperatures of hundreds of degrees (up to a thousand degrees in the combustion chambers of turbojets) while conserving an acceptable percentage of their mechanical qualities. The steel in a steam engine is not only a symbol of power and speed, but also a symbol of a management of fire that has nothing to do with the static and clayey cavern of Vulcan.

Steel is a product of fire (the blast furnace, after all, is an old-fashioned image) but provides us with a new mastery of fire. Now fire does not modify just things – it produces acceleration, it changes the kinetics of phenomena, it provides new performance.

In this new context, metals too have developed, acquiring properties of thermal and mechanical resistance that have made possible the manufacture of reliable and ever lighter components. The superalloys are at the peak of this family of materials that fire is so hard put to transform.

The dominant role of metals in the management of high temperatures in moving parts, however, is now being impinged upon by other materials that were traditionally excluded from this field of application, but that now, thanks to new materials science, have become plausible and advantageous.

By different paths and for different reasons, ceramics on the one hand and plastics and composites on the other are able to move closer to the searing core of machines. New technical ceramics are maintaining and increasing their heat resistance while shedding the fragility that once typified them, thus becoming materials that can be used in manufacturing mechanical components. Likewise, plastics are maintaining their workability while offering superpolymers that can go right up the temperature scale and still provide satisfactory performance.

Ceramics have a long history as refractory materials, that is, as materials that can resist high temperatures. It is a history of furnaces and blast furnaces, where temperatures reached 2,000 °C, where quantities were measured in hundreds of kilograms, and where the levels of stress were fairly modest. The powerful metal/non-metal bond that characterizes their structure gives ceramics extraordinary technical resistance, but also makes them fragile and difficult to process.

Their image is based on this set of qualities: if we think of refractories or the more commonly used ceramics, it requires a genuine leap of faith to believe that a slim white ceramic turbine, whose blades and axle are integrated in a single unit, can stand up to the regimen of dynamic loads to which it is subjected in operation. In other words, while the ability to stand up to great heat is a quality that is in line with the genealogy of new ceramics, their current ability to function as components in mechanical systems is absolutely unthinkable if one is to rely on tradition.

Naturally, fragility is still the Achille's heel of these materials. It requires extreme technological sophistication in the manufacturing process to reduce that fragility (peak tenacity is obtained with ceramic-fiber composites, which are complex and costly to manufacture), but the results are worth the effort. It is possible to obtain components that can operate at far higher temperatures than the best metal alloys, and that are endowed with such additional properties as high surface hardness (there are ceramics that in this area are second only to diamonds), a low friction coefficient, electric resistivity and thermal conductivity

that can be varied according to need by simply using different type of ceramics. All this comes at a density (hence, a mass) that may be as low as half that of a metal alloy with comparable heat performance.

Research, lured on by this remarkable potential, has rapidly developed a whole new family of products specifically formulated for special applicative fields. And so we have ceramics that are engineered to achieve the maximum heat resistance, other ceramics in which a compromise is struck between heat resistance and a low friction coefficient, good resistance to thermal shock and mechanical strain, heat conductivity, resistance to abrasion and chemical agents, manufacturability in complex shapes and with great dimensional precision...

Carbon-based materials, unlike ceramic-based materials, have a very brief history, exclusively in the area of exceptional lightness, mechanical resistance, and heat resistance. All carbon-fiber composites possess these characteristics (see 3.1.1), but the highest level is attained with composites whose fibers are integrated in a matrix that is also carbon-based. A carbon-carbon composite is thus an extremely light and stiff material, that can withstand temperatures ranging from 2,000° to 3,000 °C. On the other hand, however, both the raw materials used and the working processes employed are quite costly, which makes these materials plausible only where satisfactory alternatives are lacking (engines, brakes, structural components in certain very large vehicles, etc.).

Ceramic materials and advanced composites provide the most spectacular features of research into high temperatures. Nevertheless most of what is now manufactured still involves metal. Indeed, metallurgy has made much progress in this area, and has developed new alloys that combine remarkable properties of lightness with heat resistance.

The descent of new ceramic materials and of composites toward more widespread applications thus runs up against metallurgy that not only boasts a long tradition, but has also succeeded in developing new, high-performance products.

Moving down from the area of high and extremely high temperatures to more modest temperatures (on the order of a few hundred degrees), the metal kingdom extends all the way to the far border with the land of low and medium temperatures. This is another lively field of competition. Here plastics have launched an attack on metals, beginning at room temperature and rapidly reaching higher thermal levels.

Solid meets fluid: plastics

For the more common plastics, 100 °C is already a critical temperature; but so is 0 °C, for different reasons.

That is not all. A plastic component can successfully stand up to a load for a brief period of time, but may flex and deform irreversibly if the load is applied for a longer period. The degree of this deformation from continuous loading (known as *creep*) is in turn largely dependent on the temperature at which the phenomenon occurs. For the most part, as the temperature increases, the component may deform in an unexpected fashion, because internal tensions are freed that had been "frozen" at the time of manufacture. In brief, there is a complex relationship between plastics and temperature.

It is for this very reason that, if we are interested in innovation that leads to a superpolymer capable of operating at temperatures of over 300 °C, we are equally interested in

an innovation that allows a mass polymer to operate at over 100 °C, or an engineering plastic to attain a temperature of 200 °C, or in an innovation that permits an increase in their dimensional stability or a decrease in the deformations that take place under a continuous load.

The problems involved here are similar to those involved in creating the light and resistant (see 3.1.1): considering the heat resistance or mechanical resistance of a polymer material in the final analysis means observing from two different points of view the same phenomenon. In both cases, increasing performance means preventing heat agitation from compromising the stability of a component subjected to a system of loads.

Classifications of polymers according to heat performance, by and large, mirror classifications by mechanical performance. Even at the top of the pyramid (for temperatures above 200 °C) there are a few thermoplastic superpolymers: polyimides (PI), polyetherketone (PEEK), liquid-crystal polymers. They still enjoy only limited use, but they can open the way to a wider use of plastic materials in mid-to-high temperature ranges (used alone or, more often, as matrices in advanced composites), where what is required — aside from mechanical resistance — is con-

siderable dimensional stability (such as for engine parts, electronic components, etc.). Apart from these thermoplastic polymers there are many engineering plastics which can attain 200 °C in special formulations; here again the final goal is the automobile engine, but the problem has some pertinence as well to designing automobile body components that can be put together on an assembly line and painted in the standard drying ovens, which reach temperatures of 140-160 °C.

Lastly, although heat resistance is essentially linked to the intrinsic properties of materials, the final outcome in this field may also depend on certain aspects of product design. They may allow the use of a material at temperatures that at first might seem too high for it to withstand.

If, in fact, the high temperature occurs in brief cycles, one may take advantage of the low heat conductivity of plastics and, by increasing thickness, be certain that only the hottest layer of material, the closest to the heat source, will lose its mechanical properties, while the underlying layers, further from the heat source and hence cooler, will maintain those properties, ensuring the product's stability.

Hot objects

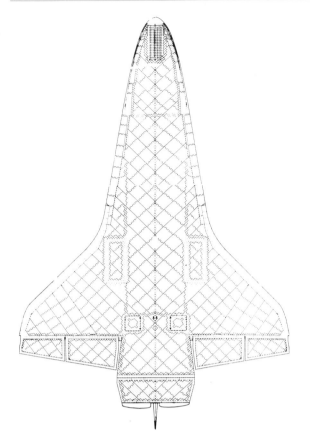

The use of new materials has
changed the image of "hot objects."
Above: The heat shield made of
ceramic tiles gives the Space Shuttle
an unusual appearance for an aircraft.
Below: In steam irons,
heat-reistant thermoplastic materials
have replaced thermosets
and have covered the metal parts.
The "iron" is now just a thin, almost
entirely covered piece of metal.
Top: A 1956 Rowenta iron. The handle
is made of bakelite. **Bottom:** A 1984
model made by the same company.
The grip is made of ABS,
the water tank is injection-molded
— in polycarbonate (PC) — or blown —
in polypropylene (PP).

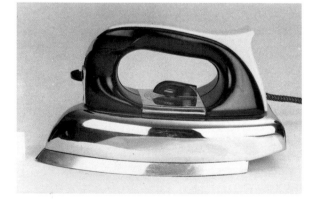

In the landscape of the home, the steam iron is an emblematic hot object in everyday use. At the beginning of its history it was a metal product with a handle upon which, set well away from the heat source itself, was a grip – at first made of wood, later made of thermosetting resin. Over time the resin grip spread and was transformed into an entire handle, absorbing other functions (thermostat, on-off switch, socket for the electric wire). Later still, the plastic segment spread down the sides of the metal body to the plate and thermosetting resins began to give way to thermoplastic resins.

Today we are faced with an object of a vaguely sculptural shape, in which only a thin plate of metal is visible (which, to cap it off, is often covered with a plastic material that lessens sliding friction). This heat plate is entirely encapsulated in bodywork that integrates various functions and clearly reveals the thermoplastic nature of its constituent material through shape, color, and surface quality.

The replacement of metal with plastics (first thermosets, later thermoplastics), the increasing proximity of the plastics to the heat source, and all the set of technical possibilities and shapes that results, is a trend in an ongoing transformation that touches much of the terrain of engineering and heat in the everyday environment.

Let us move on to another, less banal situation, where much higher temperatures are involved. Here too, at times, the transformation brought by new materials is quite evident. The thing that struck us about the first photographs of the space shuttle – rather than its technical features – was the non-metallic image of its heat shield – strange white ceramic scales that seemed so improbable on the surface of a machine.

Heat innovation is not always so clearly legible in terms of image. Indeed, here more than elsewhere, it can be hidden, just as heat sources can be hidden. Close observation however allows one to identify an important pattern to the transformations that are profoundly altering the features of new hot objects.

Engines (from those of missiles to mass-production automobiles) certainly provide the most significant example. If one traces the penetration of innovative materials, it is tantamount to drawing a map of new potential in creating the heat resistant.

121

Missiles and carbon

The nozzle of a missile is where exhaust gases are accelerated to generate thrust. Temperatures reach 2,000-3,000 °C, and are too high to be withstood by metals.

The method employed in the past (for instance, in 1970 for the French delivery system "Diamant") was to use composites made of fibers of refractory materials stiffened with resin. During ignition the resin was consumed by heat (through a pyrolitic effect) and it was necessary to apply a layer several centimeters thick so that it would not be entirely consumed before the launch was complete. Today, the solution employed for the engine of the "Ariane" delivery system involves use of a carbon-carbon composite (carbon fibers in a carbon matrix). This is a light material that is neither consumed nor degrades during operation of the engine. It therefore becomes possible to reduce the cone's thickness to a few millimeters, reducing its mass to a tenth of the initial value.

This example lends itself to a few more general considerations. Use of this material, in fact, made it possible to lengthen the nozzle, since the ensuing increase in thrust now more than offset the increase in weight. It then proved appropriate to reshape the engine itself in order to make the best use of the new configuration. The entire layout of the booster was thus modified, beginning with a minor but decisive change.

In the case in question, the initial innovation was based on a carbon composite, but other sophisticated materials endowed with similar qualities of heat resistance are under study or in the early stages of industrial development.

Cerasep turbine wheel. Cerasep is a silicon carbide composite reinforced with fibers of the same material. (Doct. SEP)

Worth pointing out among these materials is the family of ceramic composites (ceramic fibers of various types in matrices that may also be ceramic). These materials may play an important role in the manufacture of components for the turbines of jet engines, which are subjected to great mechanical stress and temperatures on the order of 1,500 °C.

Working with these materials and under these engineering conditions is like putting together a puzzle in which each piece corresponds to an area of research that is being pioneered. This applies to ceramic fibers themselves (still extremely complex to manu-

The use of carbon composite reinforced with carbon fibers in the nozzle of the engine of Ariane, the European Space Agency rocket, led to improvements that increased overall efficiency by 10 percent.

facture); it applies to the computing methods; it applies to product testing.

It is, in short, necessary to found a technical culture of high-temperature non-metallic mechanical components. From this culture, there might emerge a transformation of hot objects far more radical and widespread than anything we have yet seen.

Engines will once again provide a privileged arena for this transformation, but this time they will descend from the sky to the ground and from high-powered vehicles to the lower levels of power used in earthbound transportation. This descent is already starting to take place, because earthboud motion presents fewer technical problems and fewer safety requirements. To counterbalance those advantages, while earthbound experimentation and proptotypes are still important, in order to obtain an effective result, it is necessary to pass through the narrow doorway of mass production and, hence, to become economically feasible for applicative fields with very narrow margins.

Ceramic engines

The internal combustion engine is a machine that long ago entered a phase of maturity, when innovation is normally limited to refinement of well-established techniques. The challenge of ceramics is to shatter this state of things. This could be accomplished by following one of two avenues. The first would mean developing engines with radically different operating temperatures that would allow considerable increments in efficiency. The second avenue offers an alternative — high-temperature gas turbine engines, competing with today's internal combustion engines.
The former hypothesis stems from the observation that in diesel engines only 30 percent

A piston with an extremely heat-resistant ceramic insert. This allows higher operating temperatures and prolong the components lifespan. (Doct. Volkswagen)

The use of ceramics in the rotor of a turbo supercharger reduces the mass and therefore inertia, thus increasing the engine's speed of response. (Doct. NGK)

of the energy introduced in the form of fuel is transformed into mechanical energy; a part (40 percent) is lost in the hot exhaust gases and another part is absorbed by the cooling system. If one wishes to reduce the latter category and increase efficiency proportionately, one must utilize materials that resist much higher temperatures and that reduce heat transmission. It is along these lines that research on the adiabatic engine is proceeding, in an effort to limit energy loss through the engine walls. This is done by

coating the areas where heat is produced, with an appropriate material (and only ceramics are appropriate), so as to contain the heat.

It should be noted that recently some doubts have been advanced on the likelihood of obtaining the expected results by this method. Ceramizing all surfaces, and creating a heat barrier, would profoundly modify the engine's internal metabolism and create a whole new set of problems that would in the end prevent the increase in efficiency. Research is therefore currently devoted to determining whether or not to continue along this path.

The latter hypothesis is more radical and involves long-term planning. Gas turbine engines are today only plausible for very high-powered engines, because they require costly and complex cooling systems. The temperature of the gases can reach 1,400 °C, while the metal alloys used can tolerate little over 1,000 °C, and therefore must be cooled continually. The introduction of ceramics, only a tenth as costly and with no need for complex cooling systems, could make it quite profitable to manufacture small turbine engines that would be far more efficient than internal combustion engines.

Road testing performed in a Ford/General Motors research project showed that an increase of 350 °C in the operating temperature of an engine of this sort leads to about a 30 percent improvement in efficiency.

As we wait for the most advanced results, the penetration of ceramic materials in the engine is for now limited to experimentation (and in a few cases to commercial applica-

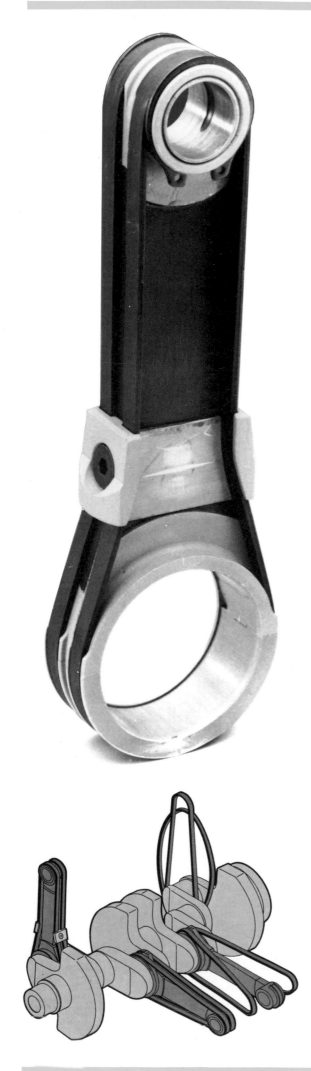

tions) with ceramic parts placed in ideal locations, such as the production of a heat-insulating barrier on the head of a piston (prolonging its life) or in the turbine of a turbocharger (by lightening it, one reduces its inertia, improves its responsiveness, and improves overall efficiency).

Though these components are small, they represent a weakening of the dominion of metals over heat-operated machinery. They are the spearhead of new materials, new interests, and new cultures.

Plastic connecting rods

Plastics march ever closer to the engine, attacking the opposite flank from ceramics. On a hypothetical map of temperatures, ceramics first appear in points where the heat level is at a peak, and then spread toward areas where temperature is less of a consideration. Plastics instead made their appearance at the coolest points and move toward areas where the temperature is higher.

The drive to do research is guided by two criteria – first of all, reduction in weight, and second, the prospect of developing new techniques that, when taken out of the experimental phase and applied to mass production, would considerably lower manufacturing costs.

A reduction in the weight of a mechanical part can vary in significance, depending on whether it is a stationary or moving part. For stationary parts, there is only a direct advantage. Any reduction in the weight of a component helps to reduce the overall weight of the product. For moving parts, the advantages are many. They include reduction in inertia and, consequently, an increased speed of response of the engine, the possibility of lightening the entire system, thus limiting stresses caused by masses in motion. Furthermore, by employing plastic mechanical moving parts, it is possible to reduce engine vibrations and noise, creating greater comfort. That is why the first parts being developed are the connecting rod and the piston, the parts that – more than all others – are subjected to alternating motion.

This terrain has been surveyed for some time by different research programs, based on different possible forms and combinations of materials. One research program, conducted in Germany by the Volkswagen company, for instance, has shown the feasability of a version in which both connecting rod and piston are mostly made of a carbon-fiber polymer-matrix composite that would be resistant to high temperatures (tests have been done on polyester, polyimide, and epoxy resins). The initial objective was to succeed in obtaining a 50 percent reduction in weight. After a preliminary phase, it was decided to maintain a metal (aluminum) piston and completely re-engineer the connecting rod. In the new connecting rod, the core is a bar made of seventy layers of pre-impregnated carbon fabric, pressed together by a bundle of carbon fibers under tensile stress. The weight reduction thus obtained was on the order of

60 percent. The results, in terms of mechanical performance and resistance to fatigue, were judged more than satisfactory. Study is underway on the economic feasibility of mass production.

Another, more spectacular example is an experimental engine for race cars, produced in the United States by the Polymotor Research Corporation, with sponsorship from the Amoco Chemicals Corporation. Most of the components of this engine are made of plastic materials. The result is an engine that can develop 320 HP, weighs 76 kilograms (as against the 143 kilograms of a corresponding engine made of traditional materials) and has yielded satisfactory performances even under racing conditions. The only metal parts remaining are the cylinders, the piston heads, the crankshaft, the camshaft, the springs and heads of the intake and exhaust valves, and the exhaust manifold. The oil sump and the carburator cap are made of epoxy resin reinforced with carbon filaments, while all the other parts are made of a thermoplastic polymer — a polyamide imide called Torlon, manufactured by Amoco. The piston head is made of metal and the piston skirt is made of resin. The greatest obstacle to overcome was how to bond the two materials. In the end the bonding was achieved both with an adhesive and by mechanical means. Still, someday we may be able to mold the polymer directly onto the metal piston head. It is safe to say that since all the other parts (piston rings, distributor and alternator gears, rocker arms, intake valve stems, etc.) now weigh less, they all have less rotational inertia as well as excellent resistance to wear and corrosion.

In this application, the most interesting and innovative feature is the use of a polyamide imide, as this demonstrates the possibility of using a thermoplastic material in components that are exposed to conside-rable prolonged mechanical stresses at temperatures that can reach 260 °C. Indeed, while a composite part, such as the connecting rod, requires extremely refined processing which cannot easily be applied to mass production, polyamide imide parts can quite easily be treated, with a few small adjustments, just like normal thermoplastic polymers. Therefore, though the material itself is more expensive, the ease in processing could in the future make it cost-effective in many applications. It is already being used in the gears of new diesel engines in the United States, in virtue of its qualities of resistance to fatigue and thermal shock, along with reductions in noise and vibrations.

125

Reduction in weight of moving parts in an engine makes it possible to reduce inertia, and thus lighten the system (less exposed to stress caused by moving parts), and reduce vibrations and noise. Facing page: A connecting rod made of a composite material (polymer matrix and carbon fibers) alone and (bottom) with its assembly. (Doct. Volkswagen). Below right: Cutaway view of the engine developed by the Polymotor Research Corporation, indicating the parts made of thermoplastic materials (Torlon polyamide imide made by the Amoco Chemicals Corporation) and a reinforced carbon-fiber composite. The engine was tested on racing cars. (Doct. Amoco) Top: Torlon polyamide imide gears made for diesel truck engines. They withstand fatigue and heat shock particularly well, and reduce noise and vibration. (Doct. Amoco)

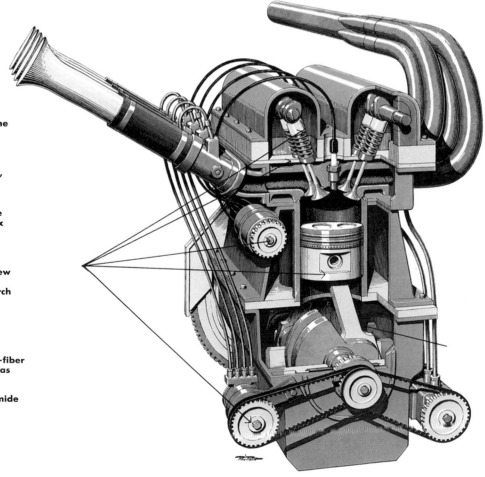

The transformation of mechanisms

Engines, electrical resistance, moving mechanical parts that generate friction are all sources of heat within a machine. This technical ambient, traditionally the realm of metals, is being progressively overrun by plastics. the new materials enter by various paths, each time offering a formulation that solves the problem at hand by reconciling different – and at times conflicting – requirements.

Brakes are an extreme case because of the level of mechanical and thermal performance required, and engineers designing brakes tend to call on the most sophisticated materials, such as carbon-based and aramid fiber composites. Ball bearings or bronze bushings, however, may also be made of plastics, with considerable advantages (weight and friction reduction), as long as the material is capable of withstanding the high temperatures that may be encountered. Furthermore, in the field of electronics, miniaturization is generating an increase in the density of concentrated power, and therefore an increase of the temperature that the materials must withstand. In this field, the board of a printed circuit has to pass through a bath of melted tin at 220 °C, during manufacturing, and during use must provide maximum dimensional stability even at the very high temperatures that can be attained.

In all these cases, a range of temperatures of up to 150-200 °C is involved. Only a few special polymers and special formulations of engineering plastics can withstand those temperatures without loss of mechanical properties and dimensional stability.

In a few special cases, other performances may be required, generating problems that are in turn exacerbated by high temperatures. Thermal and mechanical resistance may have to coexist with resistance to hostile chemical environments (for instance, all the under-the-hood components of an automobile must be able to withstand gasoline fumes) or resistance to wear (such as parts exposed to friction) and fatigue (all the parts exposed to continuous cycles of dynamic stress).

In this complex area of applications, aside from the liquid-crystal polymers mentioned above, liquid crystals, and polyimides (PI), materials with various qualities compete. To list a few: polyetherketone (PEEK), polyphenylsulphone (PPSU), polyethersulphone (PES), polyphenylsulphate (PPS), acetyl resins (POM), and special formulations of polyester or polyamide (PA) resins filled with fiberglass, carbon fibers, or aramid fibers.

Without fanfare, as if someone were tunneling in, the world of machines is pervaded by a transformation that affects the most delicate points, the components most exposed to stress. Shiny steel gears, the noise and vibrations of rotating parts, greasy lubricants all were typical of a stereotypical image of mechanisms that is rapidly being rendered obsolete. New mechanisms are opaque, compact, dry, silent, and vibration-free.

Polymer materials are exposed to operating conditions in which mechanical resistance, heat resistance, and resistance to hostile agents pose increasingly complex requirements of performance. Top: Friction-proof gaskets for aramid-fiber brakes. The new material replaces asbestos quite well, and poses fewer problems. (Doct. Dupont) Above: Gears made of engineering plastics: they reduce friction and vibrations (mfg. Rowenta). (Doct. Bayer) Facing page, top: Ball bearing with a polysulfone retainer, which provides excellent long-term resistance even at operating temperatures of 200 °C. (Doct. BASF) Facing page, bottom: The tank of a Candy washing machine, made of polypropylene (PP), with a fiberglass-reinforced rear shell (mfg. Faini). (Doct. Montedison-Dutral-Himont)

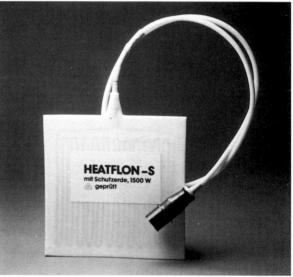

HEATFLON-S
mit Schutzerde, 1500 W
geprüft

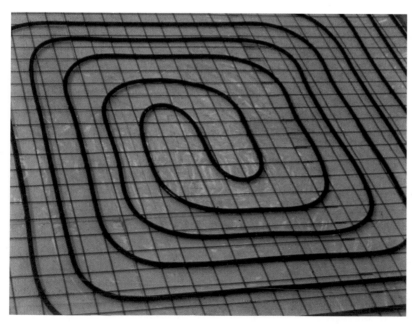

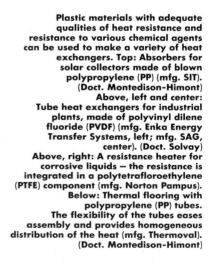

Plastic materials with adequate qualities of heat resistance and resistance to various chemical agents can be used to make a variety of heat exchangers. Top: Absorbers for solar collectors made of blown polypropylene (PP) (mfg. SIT). (Doct. Montedison-Himont)
Above, left and center: Tube heat exchangers for industrial plants, made of polyvinyl dilene fluoride (PVDF) (mfg. Enka Energy Transfer Systems, left; mfg. SAG, center). (Doct. Solvay)
Above, right: A resistance heater for corrosive liquids — the resistance is integrated in a polytetrafloroethylene (PTFE) component (mfg. Norton Pampus).
Below: Thermal flooring with polypropylene (PP) tubes. The flexibility of the tubes eases assembly and provides homogeneous distribution of the heat (mfg. Thermoval). (Doct. Montedison-Himont)

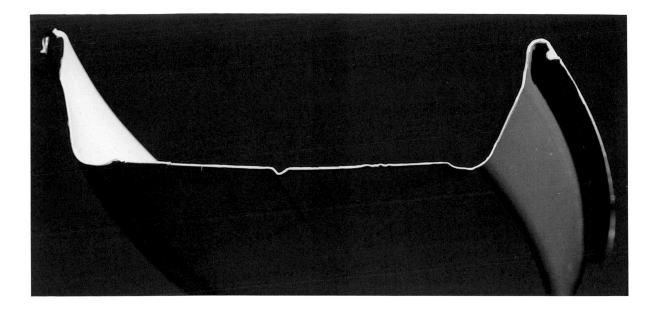

Everyday objects

Oven-ready food container manufactured by vacuum-molding with an extruded sheet of polyethyleneterephthalate (PET). (Doct. Montedison-Montefibre)

Today it is possible, though certainly not common, to cook in an all-plastic pot. It is difficult to say whether and to what degree this application will become commonplace, but the fact remains that one of the first commercial applications of liquid-crystal polymers was in maufacturing a line of oven containers.

The idea, entirely aside from its marketing success, is striking for various reasons. First off, we see in a very common object the point reached by polymers in their "Promethean ascent" toward high temperatures. Second, it modifies one of the most stable images of our everyday environment.

The pot is an elementary object, whose operating principle has basically not changed from the Neolithic right up to the present. This functional stability over time has been expressed in various materials in different technical phases (from terra cotta to copper, aluminum, enameled iron, stainless steel, ceramics, heat-resistant glass). These materials have introduced – alongside the prime objective of cooking – secondary performance increments that are nevertheless quite significant: lightness, ease in handling, uniform heat distribution, easy cleaning. Plastics had heretofore approached the area of pots and cooking rather circumspectly. Thermosetting-resin handles had long been an outpost for polymers moving toward the home fires. In this context, the manufacturing of non-stick pots (with an inner surface to which food did not stick) introduced a performance that was as hard to see as it was significant in functional terms. They were manufactured through various systems, the most common of which is the formation of a polytetrafluoroethylene (PTFE) skin that has good thermal qualities and creates non-stick surfaces. This is an object that has not made headlines as an advanced technology, but it is nevertheless an example of an intelligent use of materials. Each material used performs its function well – the metal withstands and spreads heat, the surface prevents adhesion between container and contents.

Perhaps there will never be an all-plastic pot, the traditional tool of cooking. Today other cooking methods are available, and that changes matters a great deal. For instance, the food processing sector that ranges from the industrial preparation of frozen food all the way to home or institutional kitchen microwave ovens is a field that poses a whole new series of containing and heating problems. The cooking or heating of foods by microwaves profoundly alters the thermal dynamics of food preparation, and hence the task performed by the pot/container. Heat is no longer conducted from the surface to the interior. It is generated directly within the mass of the product being heated. The task of the pot is to contain the food and allow the flow of microwaves to pass undisturbed. If these are the terms of the performance required, they can be met by the very packaging of the food. The qualities needed are no longer the ability to withstand high temperatures, be washable, and be solid. What is needed is now cheapness, hygiene, and the ability to pass from the low temperatures of the freezer to the 200 °C of the microwave oven, and to be as transparent as possible to the passage of the radiation.

In this field, plastic oven containers are certain to be mass produced. The most common materials are polypropylene (PP) and more recently poly crystals (PET) which are already used in the thermoformed trays employed in microwave ovens.

Aside from pots and oven-ready packaging, the problem of containers capable of withstanding relatively high temperatures arises for all applications that call for sterilization (requiring temperatures on the order of 110-120 °C). These applications range from the packing industry (where the heat cycle takes place once only) to laboratory and medical equipment, where the performance required is greater and where it must be possible to repeat the sterilization cycle many times without product deterioration. In this case, the material selected must be a high-performance material. In the medical field, for instance, polysulfones (PPSU) are an appropriate material because of their biocompatibility and their ability to withstand as many as ten thousand sterilization cycles.

The hearth, for a long time and with few exceptions, was the only hot point in the house. Only recently have we seen the progressive spread of hot and warm objects, that translate into practical terms the ideas of comfort and practicality suggested by new technical and energy options. Today houses are filled with objects of this sort, which attain modest levels of heat. Here problems can arise with such heat sensitive materials as plastics.

There exist, as we have mentioned, heat-resistant polymers that go well above the limits involved here, but these are special materials that are relatively costly and therefore for limited uses. In the production of more common objects, one tends to work with cheaper polymers which have a more delicate relationship with heat.

It is therefore important to keep in mind a very exact map of heat levels so as to know in advance the operating conditions that each product must face. A few dozen degrees of difference could endanger the product's solidity and dimensional stability (if there has been an underestimation of the heat levels involved) or else cause one to use higher-performance material than required (in case of overestimation).

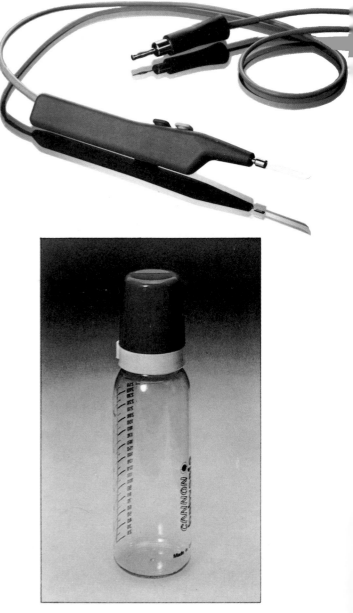

It is important to know, for example, that an incandescent light bulb generates temperatures of up to 100 °C, while the parabola of a halogen lamp reaches temperatures of 200 °C. Or it is necessary to pay close attention to the different heat levels to which various parts of a hair-dryer, an electric kettle, a steam cooker, or an oven are exposed. Then there are such special effects as the greenhouse effect that windows exposed to sunlight can generate on nearby surfaces. This is especially important in automobiles. Between the windshield — increasingly angled for streamlining and visibility — and the top of the dashboard, temperatures of up to 100 °C can be generated during the summer. If the engineering does not take this into account, there is some danger of heat deformation resulting.

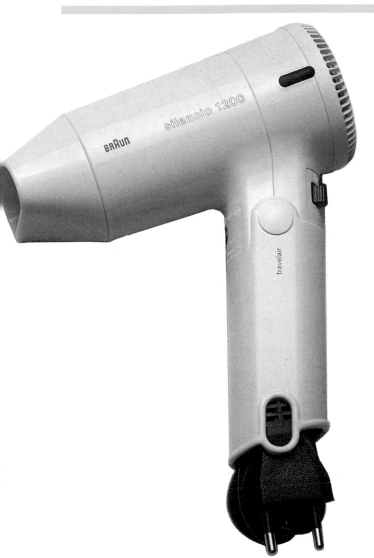

It is diffuse heat of this sort that plastics most often encounter; this is where hidden innovation, together with refinements in technical engineering, is slowly modifying the substance and the image of the hot domestic object.

Domesticating fire

The development of the clothes iron, described at the beginning of this chapter, is emblematic of a whole family of objects – metal, metal and thermosetting resins, metal and thermoplastic resins, thermoplastic resins alone (in exposed parts, but often on the interior as well). The steps in the transition from a metal/mechanical to a plastic/integrated substance and image can be easily traced. The hot domestic object has lost its traditional image (and also its identity) and has been integrated into the formal world and language of "good plastics design" of household objects.

In effect, the conquest of hot objects by thermoplastics has acquired a sort of uniformity of image; a departure from the references provided by traditional materials and no longer afforded by new materials. If we think of the difference that existed thirty years ago between an electric kettle and a blender, and compare that with the substantial identity of the two appliances now, we can register the degree of the transformation that has taken place in household fire engineering.

The kitchen had long maintained a link with the smithy of Vulcan – both material and tools were specific and recognizable by their function. There was an old and well-established relationship between fire and the materials that could contain it. That link has been broken. New engineering approaches and new materials bring about a proliferation of hot points in a house, until they are taken for granted. Heat can be produced and modulated as needed, the image can be normalized. The domestication of fire that started so many thousands of years ago is now complete. The new hot domestic object no longer burns the finger.

From this point onward, the indication of the heat quality of a warm object, if there is an indication, is no longer a necessary consideration but a free linguistic choice.

Sterilization requires temperatures of 110-120 °C, to which many plastic materials can be exposed without problems. Facing page, from top: polypropylene (PP) containers for the food industry (Doct. Montedison-Himont); a surgical instrument with grip made of polyestersulphone (Doct. Basf); baby bottle made of polycarbonate (PC). (Doct. Bayer)
Hot objects in the everyday environment, no longer tied to metals and thermosetting resins as in the past, can assume a vast rage of forms made possible by thermoplastics. Above: A Braun hairdryer. Below: Hairdryer designed by Denis Santachiara (1979). The stream of air can be directed by squeezing and bending the flexible tip, and the air can be scented as desired by inserting filter-bags in the appropriate slot.

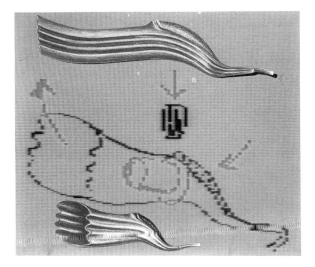

Danzatore, Rebecca Allen for "The Catherine Wheel", 1981.

Creating the elastic and pliable

Deformable matter

As in a series of mirrors, man projects human qualities upon objects, while taking those same objects as metaphors for his own behavior. The way in which materials and structures react to mechanical stress is a feature of their identity that, more than any other, lends itself to this anthropomorphic game: the character of bamboo and that of stubble are clearly different from that of an oak tree. While an oak is the very image of positive values (consistency, solidity, clarity of intention), materials that are either flexible and elastic like bamboo, or flexible and pliable like stubble evoke images to which our culture attributes ambiguous, or even negative values (opportunism, duplicity, weakness). A snake is flexible. It would seem that the world has always been dominated by the values and esthetics of the rigid.

And yet the rigid, the nondeformable, does not exist. The performance to which we attribute this quality is, in common parlance, pure approximation and, in technical language, a conventional term. Something is rigid if we do not notice its deformations or, to be more precise, if, given a system of loads, it deforms in a way that is acceptable to, or expected by, the designer.

Strictly speaking, then, we cannot speak of flexibility without speaking of rigidity. Nevertheless, from the viewpoint of end use, the options in terms of form and materials can be grouped according to different objectives. In order for the chassis of an automobile to be light and resistant, it must also be elastic and tough, but other aspects of that chassis revolve around the first set of qualities. Suspension and seats, on the other hand, must undergo an appropriate level of deformation, and all other aspects of these parts must be considered as a function of that objective.

Of course, just as poplar and acacia wood lie between the extremes of oak and reed, it is possible to find intermediate engineering requirements among objects. A helicopter blade and a ski both require a carefully balanced combination of rigidity and extensive flexibility. In the following pages we shall examine cases where elasticity or pliability take on a clear value, and become dominant aspects of the engineering.

This area opens up numerous possibilities that involve a wide range of engineering problems and applications areas. An archer's bow, an easy chair, an inner tube, or the boot of a cable all require a deformable material. What varies is the performance required, that is, the way in which that deformation should take place, and the final result to be attained — whether the deformation should involve an accumulation of energy that is then yielded with the least possible loss at the appropriate moment, or else by opposing the least possible stress and maintaining the deformation. In any case, the deforming action calls energy into play, and the various natures of materials correspond to the different ways in which they store or dissipate that energy.

In other words, a material (in practice, one always refers to a component, that is a structure made of a certain material and endowed with a certain form) can behave as an accumulator of energy, as a dissipator of energy, or as a cross between the two. In reality, one always encounters some hybrid between accumulation and dissipation, but the specific case may be so close to one of the two extremes as to be considered an accumulator or a dissipator, that is, a material with elastic or else plastic behavior.

In this context, the new possible brought about by the latest generations of materials does not consist of an increase in the elasticity or plasticity of traditional materials. It lies in the greater ease with which one can manufacture and distribute elasticity, plasticity, and pliability within the system of objects. Elasticity, softness, and pliability have long existed, but they have been confined to very special applications, scattered throughout a

133

system of prevalently rigid objects, with hard surfaces and forms that cannot be modified. New materials and new manufacturing processes have instead opened huge new fields of application to elasticity, they have spread softness over surfaces much vaster than would previously have been thought possible. They have generated pliable objects that do not require complex assemblies, but only a certain care in design and manufacturing.

The historic development of this quality in materials offers no threads of continuity; but this area has been the theater of an endless series of astute design approaches, of small and large inventions to bend the "spirit of reed" or the "spirit of stubble" to a certain goal.

Matter according to Hooke

"Ut tensio, sic vis," a spring stretched resists with a force proportionate to its extension. With those words Robert Hooke enunciated in 1674 the law of behavior of materials under stress that bears his name. As the force increases, the material is deformed proportionately, accumulating within it elastic energy. When the force is removed, the material releases the accumulated energy and returns to its original form.

This law, which is the basis of all computation of structures, is at once general and partial: it can be applied to all solids, but — for all solids — it applies only as long as the deformations and tensions remain within a given interval, which differs for each material.

A material's aptitude for elastic behavior is determined, aside from the range of the interval mentioned above, by its resistance to the deforming force (the amount of force required to reach a certain variation in its form): a measure of this resistance is given by the modulus of elasticity. This is defined as the ratio of stress and strain. Stress as a function of deformation is graphed as a section of straight line the gradient of which is given by the *modulus of elasticity.*

If one wishes to use a material as a spring one must therefore accentuate two factors — the modulus of elasticity and the range of acceptable deformations (for instance, one may opt for a high modulus of elasticity with slight deformations, or else great deformations with a low modulus of elasticity). In practice, however, a third factor becomes essential in the selection of the appropriate material — tenacity. The conditions of use of any spring implies variable conditions of loading with great and rapid transfers of energy. The material used therefore cannot be fragile (it is possible to make a glass spring, but it would have no practical use).

As in the fields of resistance and lightness, it is necessary to employ atomic and molecular edifices that can withstand certain stresses without breaking. It is

A spiral spring made of a fiberglass-reinforced composite. (Doct. Vetrotex)

necessary to search for a compromise between rigidity and tenacity, and the modulus of elasticity is vital to this search. The difference is that here it may be appropriate or necessary to use a material with a low modulus of elasticity — especially if it is necessary to accumulate energy with great deformations, or if one wishes to deform the component without subjecting it to great stresses.

The form of elasticity

A piece of bamboo cane ten centimeters long is generally considered rigid. If the piece of bamboo is two meters long it will certainly be called elastic. Elasticity (like rigidity) is less a property of materials *per se* than a property of their structure, of their form, and of how they are located with respect to a system of loads. Creating the elastic generally means giving the correct form to a component.

This form can be obtained by reversing the considerations we made about creating the light and resistant: if, in order to create rigidity, the problem was to create cross-sections in which the mass was as far as possible from the flexural axis, now the problem is to put the mass as close as possible to that axis; if previously the three dimensions were to be more or less equivalent, now it is necessary to manufacture elongated components, with one dimension far greater than the other two.

Setting out from these considerations, tested daily, technicians have developed a vast range of forms that fit various applications. Indeed, the expansion of the field of application of "creating the elastic" is a direct result of the capacity to play with forms (and manufacture them on an industrial basis). Whatever the form may be (sheet, spiral, or other less common and more elaborate shapes), the overall elasticity of the component always depends on how the deforming action is translated into stresses over each section. The form determines the distribution of stress; the material determines, section by section, the infinitesimal deformations that, integrating one with another, lead to the overall deformation.

The ideal form of an elastic component is one that, at the maximum level of deformation expected by the engineer, creates uniform distribution of stresses within the component itself, that is, a uniform distribution of the elastic energy accumulated in the material. The typical form of an archer's bow (with the grip far thicker than the extremities) is an ancient, intuitive expression of this fundamental rule. In order for

Rubber conveyor belt (mfg. Cigo).

everything to operate correctly, however, it is necessary that the peak stress on each section not exceed the acceptable level for the material employed.

The "elastic-plastics"

For plastics (unless special reinforcements are employed) Hooke's Law has limited and approximate validity. The law is valid for stresses that fall within a very narrow interval, and even within that interval, events do not follow the theoretical predictions exactly. The behavior of plastics under stress is called "elastoplastic": a combination of accumulation and dissipation of energy where the equilibrium of the two aspects is greatly affected by ambient temperature, by the way in which the deforming force is applied, and by its duration.

There would certainly be a number of problems with using plastics to create elastic components. The freedom of shape offered by plastics has led to their use in a wide field of elastic applications, especially those where the structural qualities of steel or of the best woods are not necessary, while low costs and ease in manufacturing are essential.

Plastics have brought about unheard-of elastic applications: every container that has an integrated click-shut seal, every assembly system that works on the elasticity of a joint are made possible by the special qualities of plastics. That is not all — at times the low rigidity of plastics has been used profitably to confer, with their elasticity, an added performance to certain components. The back

of a chair and non-structural parts of an automobile work much better if they are endowed with a certain elasticity.

The selection of the most appropriate polymer material for the creation of the elastic is a search for a compromise between the required qualities of rigidity and those of flexibility.

It is therefore important to be familiar with the conditions of use, operating temperatures, and type of load. The load may be static, such as with a spring that must provide continuous pressure, or it may be dynamic-impulsive such as in the case of a spring that must trigger a click-shut fastener. Each type of load creates certain risks — in the first case mentioned, relaxation and creep may ensue, in the second case it is necessary to keep in mind the fatigue created by a great number of loading-unloading operations.

The selection of materials must also take into account the appropriate modulus of elasticity (a high modulus for small deformations, and vice versa); and among the various moduli, favoring those that yield the greatest elongations at break, so as to design components that can withstand the greatest possible deformation without breaking.

It is essential that the form of the component prevent the tensions at peak deformation from exceeding the field of elasticity of the material used.

Polymer materials are appearing — apart from areas where limited structural qualities are required — in high-performance elastic components, as the matrix of composite materials. These materials comply closely — and over a wide range of stresses — with Hooke's Law, and are capable of accumulating great quantities of elastic energy and deformation. Research into advanced composites (see 3.1.1) is thus laying new groundwork for creating the elastic.

The elasticity of rubber

If one subjects a small bar of a material that complies with Hooke's Law to tensile stress, the maximum dimensional variations that can be attained before exceeding the boundaries of elasticity are on the order of 1 percent of the original length. In this case the chief factor determining elasticity may be the form (such as in a steel spring). There are other materials, called elastomers, with intrinsic elasticity that permits deformations that can double or even increase ten-fold the dimensions at rest (as in the ordinary rubber band). Their use is limited, since their very low elastic modulus renders them unusable in those components in which elasticity must be combined with structural stability.

Elastomer technology is relatively new. Although the elastic capacity of the latex of certain plants found in the Amazon basin was observed by the earliest European explorers, only in 1823 was natural rubber finally used commercially (by MacIntosh to waterproof fabrics), and it was not until 1839 that Charles Goodyear perfected his vulcanization process, and elastomers began their career as materials that resolved many technical problems of energy accumulation, and shock and vibration absorption.

Elastomers are made of very long flexible polymeric macromolecules, which create a typically amorphous structure. The temperatures at which they must operate are well above the temperature of glass transition. Under these conditions, the material is a viscous fluid that cannot be used in the production of elastic components.

What Goodyear discovered in 1839 was that natural rubber, acquires a certain degree of stability when a small quantity of sulphur is added by a special heat process (called vulcanization). Vulcanization indeed creates a series of bridges between the different molecules — vulcanized rubber (as indeed all successive synthetic elastomers) can be compared to a net with a wide mesh, each section of which, when the material is in a state of rest, is tangled and in continuous motion due to thermal agitation. Stretching of the material forces the free sections of the macromolecules to distend, while the fixed bridges between them prevent reciprocal slipping.

The elasticity of elastomers has nothing to do with the elasticity of solids. While the latter is a product of the deformation of atomic and molecular bonds, the elasticity of vulcanized elastomers is of kinetic origin, and follows the law of thermodynamics according to which, in a complex system where haphazard motion is prompted by thermal agitation, the most probable configuration prevails. In this case, the tangled configurations are more probable than the stretched configurations (the greatest distance between the ends of the polymer chain corresponds only to one shape — a straight line).

That is why elastomers lose their elasticity as the temperature drops (i.e., as the freedom of motion of the macromolecules decreases) or when the process of vulcanization is carried even further (there is an increase in the number of bridges and a corresponding decrease in the possiblity of movement in the chains).

The development of elastomers has followed various paths. The point of departure was the replacement of natural materials (subject to supply limitations) with synthetics. Re-

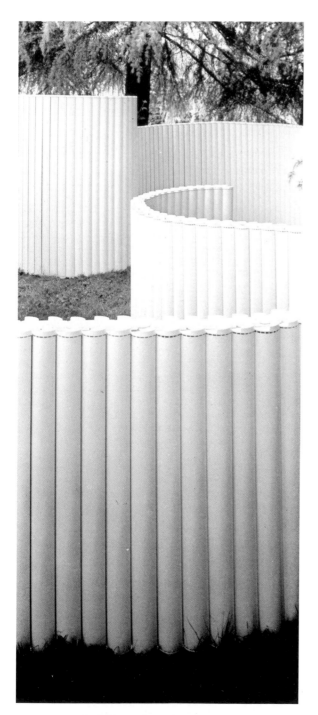

Variable-configuration partition wall for offices. Designed by Isao Hosoe, 1984 (mfg. Snake).

search then aimed at specific performances. The family of elastomers has acquired members capable of withstanding high or low temperatures, tolerating various chemical agents, and ensuring great durability.

Another direction in which research is moving is toward the creation of materials with good elastomeric qualities, but with the processing characteristics of thermoplastics.

The chemical bonds produced by vulcanization do not break down with increases in temperature, unless they reach depolymerization. Normal elastomers, therefore, behave in this case like thermoset plastics. That means that the manufacturing process is fairly complex, and that scraps cannot be recycled.

A thermoplastic elastomer, instead, obviates both these problems. It has a structure just like that of normal elastomers, but with the following difference: the bridge that links the free molecular chains is a physical and not a chemical bond. Vulcanization is unnecessary, and with an increase in temperature the bond breaks so that the material becomes fluid and can be recycled. On the whole, this material can be processed with the same equipment used for thermoplastic materials, with an end product that can compete with vulcanized elastomers in numerous applications.

Soft matter

The idea of softness implies complex physical performances that have to do with the way a material deforms and its reaction to deformation, the distribution of pressure, the texture of the surfaces. The history of softness is one of refinement and diversification of technical options, as well as of a gradual spread from limited uses — in areas such as comfort and rest — to other fields of application, that range from the protection of fragile objects to the manufacture of gaskets for technical uses.

The production of softness may involve the assembly of systems of springs, wire nets, elastic fabrics or ribbons, but the chief role has always been played by materials that provide these performances by their intrinsic properties and by their macrostructural form. From vegetable or animal fibers haphazardly woven together, there is a gradual descent to cots, mattresses, quilting. These ap-

plications have been refined over time and until the recent appearance of flexible foamed materials, have had no alternative. Through those materials, softness has achieved wider distribution (due to greater manufacturability) and improvement in quality (due to greater calibration of performance according to specific demands).

The characteristics of a flexible foam derive from the combination of a number of different factors: the properties of the material itself, its density (which indicates the relationship between the material and bubbles), the size of the cells, whether or not they communicate (whether, that is, they are open, closed, or somewhere in between), and the strain strength (which indicates how the material reacts to deformation).

The curves that describe strain strength in terms of deformations occuring during phases of loading and unloading, known as hysteretic curves, supply much significant information on the behavior of material. From the loading curve, for instance, one can see how a foamed material behaves when it is subjected to a certain amount of weight (it is important to keep it from deforming either too much or too little), while from the unloading curve one can see how the material returns to a state of rest when the load is removed. The configuration describes the combination of elastic and plastic properties of the material, that is, the part of energy accumulated and the part of energy dissipated. The closer the two curves come to each other (hence, the less area contained between them), the more elastic the material becomes. If the curves are spread, the energy-absorbing function prevails.

In many applications it is important to consider how long the material takes to regain its original shape, and the fact that prolonged compression brings about plastic deformation sufficient to prevent the material from returning to its original form, thus causing the loss of elasticity and softness.

In other cases, whether the cells are intercommunicating or not is significant. If they are, ventilation is good and there is poor thermal insulation. If not, the reverse is true.

By choosing an appropriate formulation, foamed materials can be produced that are well adapted for various specific applications — from upholstered furniture to mattresses, the packing of fragile objects, quilting, inner linings of ski boots, applications in vehicles, and window sealing.

The first foamed material in chronological order is *natural latex foam rubber.* The cellular structure of this material was at first produced mechanically, by mixing latex and air until foam was created. Later, better control of the cellular structure was achieved as foaming was done with a gas-developing agent. When the process is complete, the material appears spongy, and this is still the preferred treatment when an especially well-ventilated material is required (such as in mattresses that must permit the greatest level of transpiration), or for a material that is particularly soft to the touch. Another of its qualities is the practically straight hysteretic curve. Deformations grow in direct proportion to the increase in loads. Latex foam rubber is manufactured in different densities, in slabs of varying thickness, to be cut and shaped when needed.

Later, various plastic and elastomer materials were produced as flexible foams. The most widely used is *polyurethane* The great spread of softness over the past thirty years is to a large degree the result of this material's popularity. With it, one can produce foams of any density (from the lightest — 12 kg/cm — to an almost compact material), of various degrees of flexibility (from rigid to elastomeric), with open or closed cells, with or without a compact outer skin. The manufacturing process may employ the production of blocks from which to cut slabs and parts needed for use, or it may involve the direct molding, hot or cold, of a component with a complex form.

The versatility of polyurethanes spring from a series of research projects that have improved both their manufacturing and performance. In the first area, ways were found of speeding production cycles, to produce finished products with a single molding process (with the manufacture of parts with integral skin or by foaming the material directly within preformed plastic films or fabrics which become the outer skin). One of the newest and most interesting innovations is the manufacture, in a single molding operation, of a material with differentiated density (important for automobile seats, in order to give different degrees of strain strength to different parts, depending on whether or not they need to sustain human weight).

In the area of performance, materials have been developed that have special hysteretic curves, for different fields of applications. Particularly significant cases are encountered when a soft component is employed in a dynamic situation (for instance, car seats). When this is the case, it becomes important that the material dampen oscillations. It therefore becomes necessary to control the shock absorption factor by altering the form, the specific quality of the material, and by keeping in mind that the problem may be approached differently from case to case (in the example of automobiles, according to the type of suspension, wheels, and distribution of mass).

Flexibility provided by the form: blown polypropylene (PP) "accordion" component for a motorcycle engine (mfg. SIT). (Doct. Montedison-Himont)

Pliable matter

Manufacturing a pliable component means creating an anisotropy of behavior: achieving high resistance in certain directions and low resistance (that is, a capacity to deform without accumulating energy) in others. The "spirit of stubble" (and, in general, the qualities of vegetable and animal fibers) consists in resisting tensile stress while opposing minimal resistance to all other types of stress. The observation and utilization of this property are ancient, and have given rise to a history of mats, fabrics, and non-woven fabrics which include paper (also a two-dimensional pliable fibrous product).

Alongside this evolutionary line of low-structural pliable materials, from a certain point onward, another technical strategy arose, capable of making pliable objects that required greater structural qualities – for instance, hinges, which are pliable elements connecting rigid parts (one of the oldest areas of engineering, which has generated a succession of applications based on the use of leather and metal).

The introduction of plastics has uncovered new potential for pliability. Some plastics can indeed operate blithely outside of the area governed by Hooke's Law. They deform plastically without reaching breaking point. On the other hand, since the field of creating the pliable has to incorporate considerations that have as much to do with the intrinsic properties of materials as with the form of the component, here too, the good workability of plastics can determine their success.

Flexibility as an intrinsic property of the material: Pratt-Chair by Gaetano Pesce (1984) is an enquiry into the relationship between form, material, and qualities. Using the same mold and the same ureic resin, and by varying the additives, nine different chairs are obtained. They range from an ultra-rigid chair to a chair so flexible that it collapses when used.

The same considerations apply to form as to elastic components: the form of the component must reduce to a minimum the moment of inertia of the section with respect to the flexural axes that one desires to reinforce. The most appropriate forms are therefore films and flexible membranes, but also corrugated three-dimensional elements that are accordion-shaped or with other forms that improve deformability.

The materials in turn must be characterized by a certain degree of intrinsic flexibility and reciprocal mobility of molecules. We can therefore apply, in the opposite sense, the observations made previously about the rigidity of polymeric materials (see 3.1.1).

Here materials with a polymeric chain that is in itself not terribly rigid and in which the molecular bonds are rather weak will prove most appropriate. The latter aspect can also be produced by using the appropriate plastifiers, i.e., substances that introduce themselves between molecules and act as spacers, reducing the force of attraction between them (forces that depend on proximity), and thus increasing the possibility of reciprocal molecular slippage.

Another special but extremely widespread application permits the manufacture of *integral hinges*. With a single molding operation, it is possible to produce two or more movable parts united by a thin flexible element that operates as a hinge. Here too, the pliability is attained by exploiting the intrinsic flexibility of the polymeric chains, while the structural quality is provided by their orientation in a perpendicular direction to the axis along which the bending takes place. This orderly arrangement is created both by correct orientation of the flow of the material in the mold and — above all — by the stretching that takes place when the component is bent for the first time. Not all materials are equally adapted to the production of integral hinges. If it is not necessary to ensure a long and active product life, many adequately flexible polymers can be used (such as PVC); otherwise the most appropriate materials are the polyolefins: polyethylene (PE) and polypropylene (PP).

Flexible object

At its origin, the bow was just a curved strip of especially elastic wood. The ancient peoples of the Mediterranean basin, however, developed an extremely refined and efficient object. This bow consisted of a wood core whose convex face (the side being stretched) was covered with a layer of dried tendon, while the concave face was covered by a layer of horn. Tendon is a material with great tensile strength, while horn has equal compressive strength.

Technical skill and a gift for observation, confronted with the task of improving the performance of a vitally important object, hit upon a composite with properties specifically created for a precise use — the assembly of tendon/wood/horn is something quite similar to a material made to order — specially manufactured to provide extremely high performance (see 1.2.1).

The bow is certainly not the only historical example of skill in using materials to create the elastic. James E. Gordon, in his book *Structures*, described the qualities of a composite bow, but he also mentions the carts used by archaic Greeks. These vehicles were equipped with light wheels made of curved willow, elm, or cypress wood. The hubs and four spokes of these wheels were so elastic that they gave the cart a certain degree of suspension, making it possible to travel at a gallop along the very rough roads of the time. Similar considerations apply to the catapults that the Romans copied from the Greeks, and to their energy-efficient operation (based on elastic torsional energy accumulated in two springs made of tendon, attached to the arms of the machine). In short, very early did man grasp the possibilities offered to him by the "spirit of reed."

The same can be said of the "spirit of stubble," that is, the use to which one can put certain fibrous animal and plant products that are easily bent and braided. Weaving, which dates back to the Neolithic, is such an efficient technique that, on the whole, it remains unchanged to the present day. Furthermore, nomadic cultures very early perfected a set of very refined objects that were not only light, but pliable.

This technical development came about early, due to the availability of appropriate natural materials. The organic world, indeed, offers excellent materials in this field. Therefore, while technology required many long centuries to attain today's levels of perform-

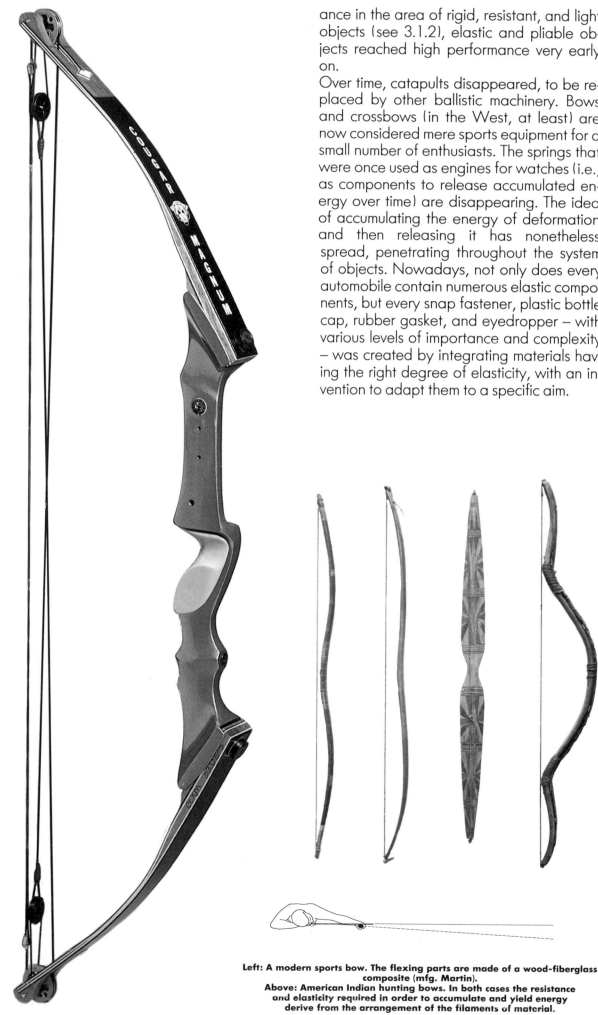

ance in the area of rigid, resistant, and light objects (see 3.1.2), elastic and pliable objects reached high performance very early on.

Over time, catapults disappeared, to be replaced by other ballistic machinery. Bows and crossbows (in the West, at least) are now considered mere sports equipment for a small number of enthusiasts. The springs that were once used as engines for watches (i.e., as components to release accumulated energy over time) are disappearing. The idea of accumulating the energy of deformation and then releasing it has nonetheless spread, penetrating throughout the system of objects. Nowadays, not only does every automobile contain numerous elastic components, but every snap fastener, plastic bottle cap, rubber gasket, and eyedropper – with various levels of importance and complexity – was created by integrating materials having the right degree of elasticity, with an invention to adapt them to a specific aim.

Left: A modern sports bow. The flexing parts are made of a wood-fiberglass composite (mfg. Martin).
Above: American Indian hunting bows. In both cases the resistance and elasticity required in order to accumulate and yield energy derive from the arrangement of the filaments of material.

The leaf springs of trucks

The leaf spring of a heavy truck may be the point in which creating the elastic is required to provide the highest performance. A leaf spring must support considerable weight, deform to accomodate uneven roads by accumulating energy, withstand shear stress whenever the vehicle brakes, accelerates, or turns, withstand the temperatures that develop in the engine and exhaust pipes. Lastly, the leaf spring must provide this performance for some time, with great dependability, even in the presence of chemical agents (such as salt on winter roads).

Ever since the leather suspension of carriages was discontinued, steel (or, more accurately, certain types of steel, specifically designed for these applications) has been the only material endowed with sufficient mechanical resistance, elasticity, and tenacity for this use. The composites, however, have recently made their debut in this area.
In order to understand the terms of the comparison more clearly, let us consider the task performed by the suspension of a transport vehicle.
The variations in the road surface tend to impress vertical accelerations on the wheels, and thence on the chassis — the suspension system must reduce the quantity of force transmitted while, within that system, the springs or leaf springs operate as elements that accumulate energy. The chief engineering objective is to accumulate this energy in the most efficient way possible.
The idea of leaf springs made of composite material (fiberglass filaments in an epoxy matrix) is powerful chiefly because of this material's capacity to store elastic energy. Testing shows that, with parity of weight, its efficiency in this area is 13 times greater than that of steel. Therefore, the same performance can be achieved with a component that is far lighter. A composite leaf spring tested by General Motors, for instance, weighs only 3.8 kilograms, versus the 18.6 kilograms of its steel counterpart. They are smaller, which means less bulk, and therefore more compact motor vehicles. They last longer, because they withstand fatigue better, and are not subject to corrosion. Furthermore, they provide a greater degree of comfort for passengers, because they operate silently, and thus reduce the noise level within the vehicle.
Most of the stresses are flexural, which the composite withstands quite successfully. Nevertheless, as mentioned above, there are also shear stresses. This is

Leaf springs for heavy vehicles and automobiles made of a fiberglass-reinforced composite (mfg. Isocar).

141

the Achille's heel of composites in this application. Shear stress tends to separate the longitudinal fibers from the matrix. Very careful engineering is required to prevent this from happening; indeed, this area is receiving close attention from manufacturers. Among the various possible approaches, there are hybrid composite/metal springs, where the former material chiefly provides the flexural resistance while the latter material provides shear resistance.

Perhaps truck suspensions will be one of the first mass-market applications of high-performance advanced composites – the reduction in weight that they allow can be translated into more payload transported. Penetration into the broader field of passenger automobiles implies considerable problems, both because it calls for a revision of the vehicle itself (as most automobilies have adopted helicoidal springs), and because manufacturing processes must be developed that are consonant with the manufacturing standards of the automobile industry.

Currently, the "leaves" are manufactured both by filament winding and by pultrusion and pulforming technologies. The latter process can be used to form curved or variable shapes at a rate of one or two minutes per item.

Opening and closing

At the far end of the field of elastic performance, we find the family of elastic fasteners, and in general, of snap fasteners. Here elasticity is required of a component in order to join two parts in the simplest and most immediate way possible. More than ever, we can see a wealth of small and ingenious innovations suggested by the workability of plastics, with the aim of solving the same problems as screws, bolts, and other systems of joining or fastening, but with a simple and faster motion.

The result has been the growth of a large and prosperous family of systems that can be adapted to a wide range of operating conditions. They can be used in a reversible form (open-shut), irreversible (in order to release the joint, one must break the assembly), or semi-reversible (in order to release the joint, a special tool is needed).

A snap fastener may be found as part of a small component specially designed to join things, or it may be an integral part of a component with other functions (such as a system for closing a box). Of course, not all plastic materials are equally well adapted for these elastic joints. A fragile, stiff material such as polystyrene (PS), for instance, encounters problems that polypropylene (PP) or polyamide (PA) do not. Contrariwise, in the production of a fastener, the selection of the best material depends on the mechanical performance one wishes to obtain. The fundamental parameters are the modulus of elasticity, acceptable elongation, tenacity, coefficient of friction, and – especially if the fastener is subjected to tensile stress – creep.

The shape of plastic snap joint springs varies from a lamel to a ring joint (which operates more or less like a bottle cap), and to springs in which an element operates by torsion, or various clever combinations of all three types.

The elasticity of the material makes it possible to integrate different functions and performances in the same item. Above: A polyamide (PA) cable support. Below: Detail of an ABS that incorporates the hinge guides and the elastic closure snap. (Doct. Bayer)

An automobile hubcap made of polyamide (PA), easily removed without tools and corrosion resistant. Below: An irreversible snap-shut fastener clip. (Doct. Bayer)

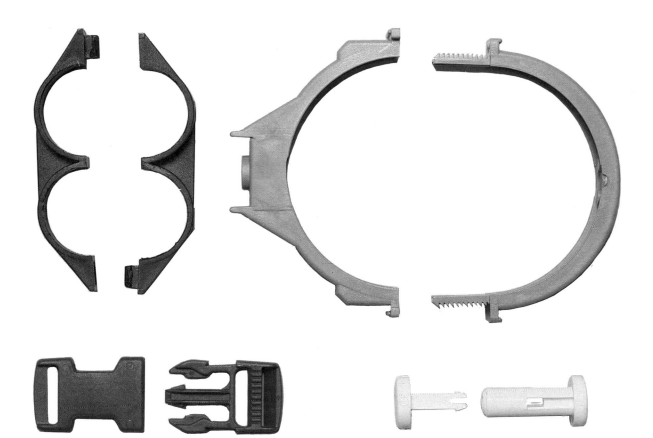

Above: Different types of elastic snap closures used in pipe clamps, buckles, and fastening nails (Doct. Montedison) Integral hinges and snap fasteners, when correctly designed, can withstand a great number of open-shut cycles, and will last as long as the product itself.
Below: Snap fastener for a polypropylene (PP) valise. (Doct. Montedison-Himont)

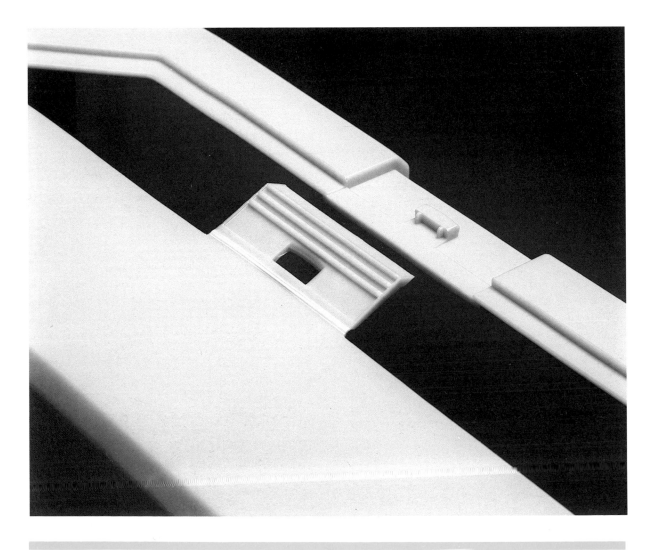

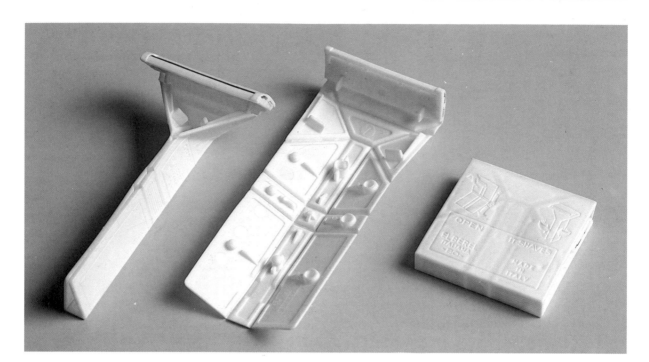

Among the many solutions adopted by nature to promote the dispersion of the seeds of plants, there is one that endows the seeds with small elastic hooks that can easily snag the fur of a passing animal. This method of achieving a fastening has been copied almost exactly in the creation of one of the most inventive and efficacious new fastening systems – Velcro. This technique is the fruit of a gift for observation and the possibility of mass producing, at a reasonable cost, broad surfaces covered with small elastic hooks (generally made of polyamide, PA) and other surfaces covered with tiny rings made of fibrous material, onto which the hooks attach.

Once the fundamental feasability was determined, the system developed to take into account various factors such as rip-resistance and long operating life. Therefore, differently shaped hooks were developed (ranging from the simple flexible type to the complex rigid type) that can withstand various levels of tensile strength before losing adhesion, and different numbers of open-shut cycles. Other shapes have been developed to hook onto other materials (foamed cellular materials, fabrics, non-woven fabrics).

This invention has a fairly unassuming appearance, but it has penetrated rapidly and deeply into the system of objects – from spacesuits to diapers. Through an infinite range of hidden technical uses, this application has created a new gesture – simple and immediate – involved in opening and closing. Velcro is a significant – but not unique – example of a diffuse and fine-toothed transformation of the way things are done, based on the flexibility and formability of plastics.

Above: The tradition of origami when combined with the possibility of creating integral hinges may lead to the creation of new pliable objects, such as this razor (mfg. Elberel).

The elastic hooks produced by nature (above) are artificially reproduced in manufacturing Velcro, one of the most efficient and common fastening systems (below).

Tightening and loosening bolt and screws, tying and untying knots, buttoning and un-buttoning – these ancient motions, often charged with symbolic meanings (for a child, tying a shoe is an important step on the path to personal autonomy), are now joined, and at times replaced, by other simpler and faster motions – pressing shut, tearing open. Development began with metal clips and zip fasteners (another remarkable and largely unrecognized invention), but it exploded with the advent of plastics. The world around us, from assembly lines to supermarket counters, is now populated with objects that close, hook, open or shut with a simple motion – all through the elasticity of the material.

In parallel (though to a more limited extent) the flexibility of certain plastics has increased the number of pliable objects. The integral hinge (see 3.3.1) cannot be used when great stress is likely to be encountered, but for all other applications (and there are plenty), it is a cheap way of giving an object the quality of changing shape, of opening and closing as needed, of flexing without resistance an infinite number of times.

The integral hinge was first used to reduce costs and increase production (e.g., in containers for many mass-consumption products). It soon spread to numerous other applications, that include clothes pins, travel bags, and a vast range of products sharing only the use of plastic, and the presence of moving parts – integral hinges – manufactured with a single molding operation.

In this landscape, a few products stand out for transforming pliability into a new market quality, for having given new quality to a

product through pliablity. To mention only a couple of cases, there is a pocket slide viewer that can be carried flat and then popped into shape for use; then there is a razor that is packaged like a box of matches but that folds into shape, ready for use.

The razor is particularly interesting in terms of image – the passage from flat to three-dimensional, in fact, takes place through folds that follow a logic similar to that used in origami. The ancient art of folding paper joins the integral hinge so as to develop a new line of objects, and thus "create the pliable."

145

Some innovative solutions deriving from the use of integral hinges. From top: A one-piece electric plug with an openable shell (mfg. B Ticino); a portable stereo headphone - the pliable part is made of polyamide (PA) (mfg. Yamaha).

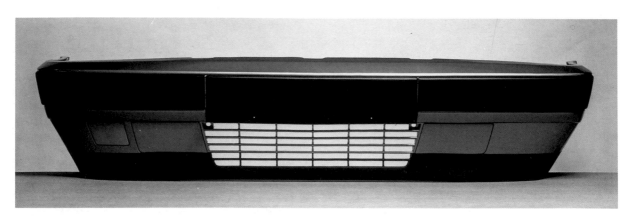

Bumpers must meet complex technical requirements - they must absorb energy without permanent deformation. Top (this and following page): Lancia Prisma bumper, made of modified polybutyleneterephthalate (PBT), with a protective strip of ethylene-propylene rubber (mfg. Comind-Stars) (Doct. Montedison-Dutral). Below: Diagrams of cross-sections of a high-impact bumper that does not deform permanently.

Bottom: The almost organic structure of the dashboard of the Lancia Prisma. The skin is made of vacuum-molded PVC/ABS, the ribbing is made of filled polypropylene (PP). Between the two materials, a mass of polyurethane foam absorbs impact energy (mfg. Comind-Stars). (Doct. Montedison-Montedipe)

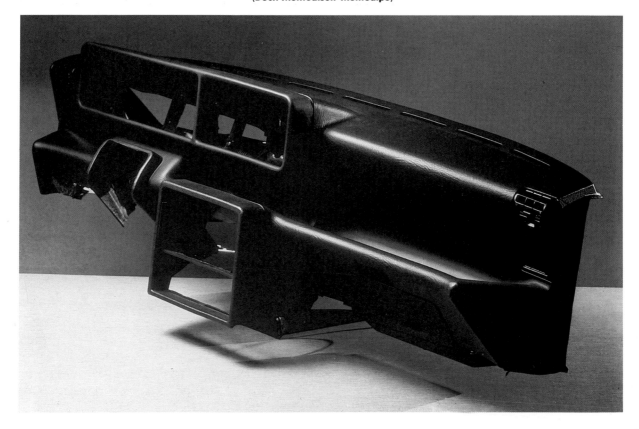

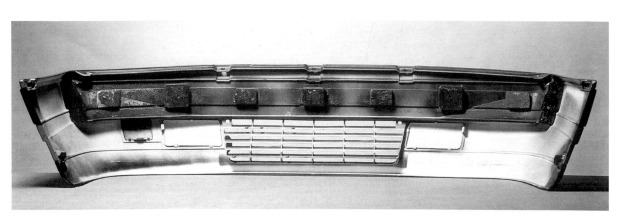

Beyond the bumper

The bumper was once made of metal plate solidly attached to the automobile's chassis. Its task was merely to prevent small impacts from ruining the car body, by absorbing elastically or plastically (depending on the force of impact) a certain amount of energy.

Since then, the bumper has undergone a profound modification both formally (perhaps more than any other automobile component) and functionally. Today, bumpers are conceived as refined systems capable of dissipating, without excessive damages, growing quantities of energy.

The approaches used are many. In some cases full-fledged mechanical components are set between the bumper and the chassis, to function as shock absorbers. Otherwise, a simpler (and hence more reliable, since there is no chance of mechanical failure) approach is that of dissipating energy with some particular deformable materials: semi-rigid foams (polyurethane) or semi-rigid structural girders of deformable plastic materials (often polyethylene or polypropylene), set between a resistant material nearer the car and a flexible material in view.

A problem is created by the fact that the performances required of the component are contradictory. On the one hand it must absorb energy and hence deform; yet, it should be able to withstand numerous impacts without losing its functional and esthetic features (i.e., not deform). A compromise has been attempted with the adoption of an energy-dissipating element whose behavior can be defined as temporarily irreversible — it deforms upon impact, dissipating energy without elastic spring-back. Then it slowly returns to its original shape.

This sort of system was adopted, for instance, in the bumpers of the Lancia *Thema*: a core of a special polyurethane with temporarily irreversible deformation is inserted into a polypropylene box element, the rear section of which has been greatly reinforced (and is therefore extremely rigid) while the other three sections are very flexible.

Another approach involves replacing the elements made of plastic foam, with air bags connected by special valves (that are calibrated to open at certain pressures). When a deforming pressure acts on any point of the bumper, it compresses the air in the bag directly behind that point. If the pressure exceeds a certain level, then air passes into adjacent bags, dissipating the energy. When impact is over, the air filters in the reverse direction, bringing about an equilibrium of pressure and restoring the original shape of the bumper.

Bumpers aside, an entire automobile – if it is engineered according to criteria of peak safety – can be viewed as a complex dissipator of energy. The entire body, in this spirit, should be considered as a system with differentiated deformability, made of a rigid cell around the cockpit and of components that can deform and absorb great amounts of energy, in front and back.

One crucial feature of a hypothetical all-plastic automobile is the ability to absorb a sufficient quantity of energy upon impact, rather than to achieve resistance or rigidity. With aluminum bodies, which can absorb great quantities of deforming energy, this result could almost be considered as a by-product of normal engineering. With automobiles made of plastic and composite materials, this area must be treated specifically, and may lead to specially conceived deformable systems.

Moving from the automobile's exterior to its interior, we find another terrain where the need for greater safety has led to profound changes. From the dashboard to the steering wheel, arm rests, roof lining, and door panels, the interior of an automobile has changed from a prevalently metallic environment to a place made of plastic – more or less foamed and yielding as needed. Nowadays what we see is a cushioned space where almost every surface, aside from glass, is covered with a layer of impact-resistant deformable material. The result is a *soft* micro-environment with rounded edges, yielding and warm to the touch; a setting that has been entirely designed on the parameters of safety and the image of "softness" that is to be transmitted.

Tires and other wheels

Tires, by virtue of their spread and history, their symbolic value (humanity moves on rubber tires), and their sophisticated engineering, have acquired for us the same emblematic role that the composite bow had in ancient Mediterranean cultures.

From Dunlop's first experiment in 1888 on, an uninterrupted series of tests, empirical improvements, and theoretical studies have flowed into the production of an object made of a highly complex composite material, in which each component plays a specific role — fabric and metal reinforcements oriented according to the lines of stress, in order to provide the whole with structural resistance while maintaining a high level of flexibility; an elastomeric matrix made by mixing different rubbers, in order to give different zones the necessary qualities — high wear and skid resistance to the treads, flexibility to the foot of the tread and the sides of the tire.

148

Today a tire is a mature product. Research continues, resulting on the one hand in improvements in the standard typologies (that is, for the average passenger car), and, on the other, in a proliferation of special product types.

A significant innovation in this landscape is a tire designed so that, even when it is flat, the car can move (though slowly). This innovation, based on a difference in the relationship and attachment of the tire to the rim, could, among other things, abolish the historic requirement of the spare tire.

Then there are special ideas — from the tire of elastomeric polyurethane for the driving wheels of tractors to the tires without air pressure for bycicles, whose elasticity is based on the interior configuration of septa made of elastomeric materials (polyester based).

The above example, apart from its eventual spread, indicates an interesting expansion of technically viable solutions. If in the past, the elasticity of a tire could only be produced by a complex system (the set of inner tube and tire) and the only alternative was a rigid iron or wooden wheel (at the most, softened with a layer of solid rubber), today, in-

termediate options, based on the intrinsic elasticity of a material and on the factor of form, have become practical.

The properties of these alternatives cannot, of course, hope to compete with the sophisticated performance of an automobile tire, but since performance at that level is not always necessary, the alternatives could become feasible due to their cheapness and safety (obviously, a tire without air is not subject to blowouts!).

**Top, left: Pirelli racing tires (mfg. Pirelli).
Above: Safety tire that allows a car to move
even when the tire is flat; the bead is
anchored to the rim (mfg. Continental).
Below: An equally innovative system applied
to a bicycle tire. An elastomer spiral
replaces air as the elastic element.
(Doct. Dupont)**

From the inflatable muscle to the bionic muscle

The arm of a robot designed in Japan moves by means of rubber actuators that expand and contract according to the air pressure within them. These actuators are cylinders of reinforced rubber, whose shape is modified by fluid pressure – they grow and shrink, exerting force on the "tendons" that then act on movable mechanical parts.

The arm equipped with these "inflatable muscles" (designed by the Bridgestone Corporation and Hitachi) has seven degrees of liberty, is light (68 kilograms total), and can operate accurately and delicately. The last aspect, in the opinion of the manufacturers, might be the most intriguing.

The inflatable muscle is extremely intriguing, perhaps even more than its real technical advantages would indicate, as an actuator for a mechanical arm. In reality this solution is in competition with others that would seem easier to apply at present. The same principle, however, has long been applied successfully in other fields – variable-pressure pneumatic springs and pneumatic jacks are, after all, nothing but large muscles, a bit simplified and requiring far less precision in their operation. For instance, an inflatable cushion made of aramid fiber spread with an elastomeric material operates as a pneumatic jack capable of lifting up to fifty tons of weight.

Robot "muscle." The pneumatic approach makes it possible to perform delicate motions (mfg. Continental).

149

On the other hand, the intrigue exerted by an artificial muscle can be sensed in research into other applications that, when they emerge from their current preliminary stage, will make it possible to manufacture sophisticated actuators made of organic material. There are laboratories that are now studying the mechanical and chemical properties of polyelectrolyte gels. These materials, when they interact with an electric field, undergo microscopic modifications in their structure that, taken overall, create a macroscopic size variation in the system.

This research, still short of possible engineering applications, hints at the possibility of producing mechanical actuators that would bear a considerable functional similarity to living systems (a similarity limited to the macroscopic level, since the basic chemical and physical mechanisms involved are quite different).

What has been proven for the moment is the existence of the physical properties needed for the phenomenon to take place. The system must be made up of a polymer matrix containing the appropriate combinations of substances characterized by a change in phase, and hence by a variation in size, if subjected to the appropriate stimuli (such as the ionization due to chemical, electrochemical reactions or photoionization).

The final aim of this research is the development of *soft* actuators controlled by electrical stimuli. This would open new horizons, heretofore impracticable – mechanics similar to what science fiction has sketched out for bionic robots.

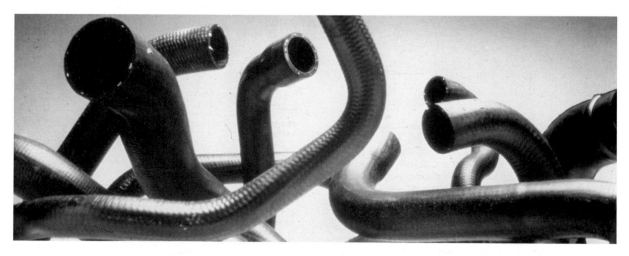

Transmission of mechanical energy by means of the resistance and flexibility of elastomer materials.
From top left: An engine belt that ensures long product life and can withstand chemical agents (Doct. Dupont);
an elastomer polyurethane belt reinforced with aramid and polyamide fibers, to replace
the traditional bicycle chain (Doct. Bridgestone); two industrial conveyor belts (mfg. Cigo).
Flexibility and elasticity as solutions to various technical problems: tubes and gaskets (mfg. Continental)
and (bottom) flexible tubes of ethylene-propylene elastomer. (Doct. Montedison-Dutral)

Seats for spaceships and seats for cars

The seat that an astronaut occupies is an object that must provide acceptable levels of comfort under very special conditions of use: the apparent weight of its occupant may vary, for instance – depending on acceleration of the spacecraft and the intensity of the gravitational field – from zero to many times its normal earth value (in this specific instance, the engineering involved calls for the possibility of an impact of 20 Gs, that is, with accelerations twenty times the value experienced on the earth's surface).

In order to meet these unusual conditions, a modified foamed polyurethane padding has been developed that has some very unusual behavior.

When subjected to impact, it behaves like a semi-rigid foam with great strain strength, and withstands the load without much deformation. As a result, during phases of powerful acceleration, the occupant is not "jammed" down into his seat. Furthermore, 85 percent of the energy of deformation is dissipated, and so does not produce a ricochet effect (the "return" is slow, and transmits relatively little energy to the body it is supporting). On the other hand, while a traditional foamed material (like any elastic material) reacts to a deforming force with a pressure proportional to the deformation itself (and hence, is stronger on the projecting parts of the body than elsewhere) in this material the heat of the seated body produces a softening of the constituent cells, thus permitting a more uniform distribution of pressure in all apparent weight conditions.

This seat is certainly an extreme case, but it has affinities with many other applications in which the aim is the comfort of a seated person. Normal chairs, seats for long periods of use, seats for use in any situation involving special acceleration or energy changes (from spacecraft to ordinary passenger cars).

Strain strength, mentioned above, elasticity (i.e., the way in which a deformed object tends to regain its original form), shock absorption (i.e., the capacity to extinguish oscillations) combined with air permeability (i.e., the ability of the body to transpire), insulation (resistance to the passage of heat) – all become parameters that are increasingly closely controlled to meet the physiological needs of a seated person: blood must circulate, bundles of nerves and muscles must not be compressed, skin must breathe, the position of the body must be correct but also relatively free to change.

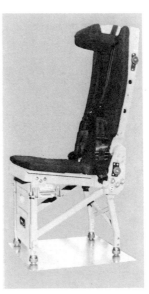

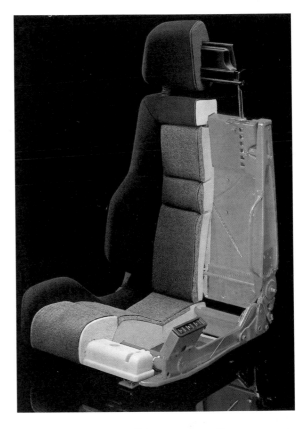

The special operating conditions encountered by a seat in a space vehicle (top) have led to the development of special padding. This is a modified polyurethane capable of providing acceptable levels of comfort even when it is subjected to great acceleration (seat: mfg. AMI; foamed material mfg. Specialty Composites Co.). Above: The structure of a sophisticated automobile seat, with differentiated padding, climatizing cloth, impact-absorbing structures, and electric regulation (mfg. Recaro). Below: simplified alternative for the seat. Spring are replaced by a fabric with elastomer monofilaments. Weight, cost, and bulk are all reduced. (Doct. Dupont)

This refined system of ergonomics often must be incorporated in low-cost mass-produced objects. Seats for passenger cars, which must meet these conditions more than other products, have become extremely complex objects.

The car seat is in fact an easy chair that must furnish a high level of ergonomic performance (comfort here translates into highway and road safety), but it must also be adjustable (there are car seats with three degrees of liberty, plus another provided by adjusting the headrest); it must be easy to adjust the seat (at times, with just one hand). The system must be light (it must be contained in a vehicle) and resistant in a crash. And the whole must be planned so as to integrate the system of suspension/body/seat, with no unexpected resonance effects.

The wide range of performances required has been met by auto manufacturers with various applications, in which the tasks are divided between a rigid structural component, parts that provide elastic support (made with strips of elastic fabric or with elastic components made of plastic) and cushions of foamed material. In order to improve the ergonomics of these cushions, wrap-around differentiated-density shapes are generally used, so as to attain the greatest possible strain strength where they touch or restrain the body. In particular, in the lumbar-supporting area, where the ergonomics of a seat is critical, the correct relationship between comfort and support is achieved through plastic inserts, small yielding "baskets" made of polyamide or even little inflatable cushions made of rubber-coated fabric, the rigidity of which can be adjusted by increasing or reducing the air pressure.

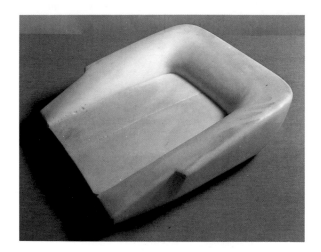

Above: a car cushion made of a differential density expanse polyethylene (PU) (mfg. Comind-Stars). (Doct. Montedison-Montedipe) Below: Automobile bench seat in its metal structure configuration. Bottom: The same component, made of polypropylene (PP) and produced in a single molding operation, integrates various functions (mfg. Zanussi Componenti Plastica). (Doct. Montedison-Himont)

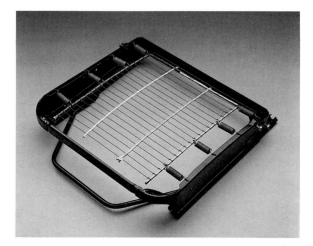

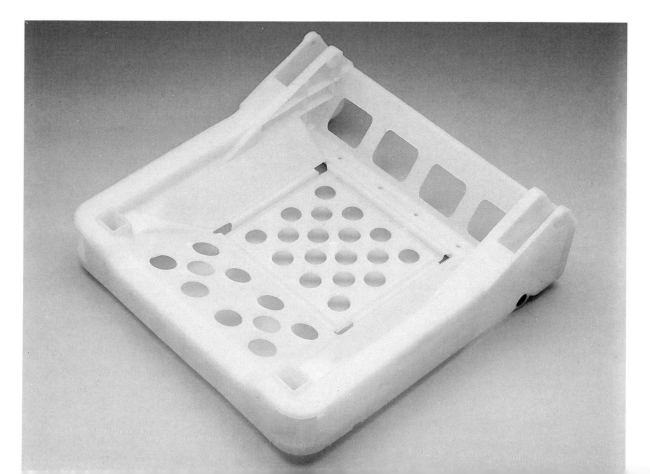

Domestic comforts

During the Sixties and Seventies, we witnessed a wave of radical innovations in the field of "soft" household objects. A long tradition of upholstery, padded materials, springs, and their support structures was swept away by the appearance of a material that alone could perform all of their functions. Flexible cellular foams, and above all polyurethane, were the chief players in this tranformation.

Materials that are highly formable and adjustable in terms of performance can become at once the flexible element and its support structure, freeing the production of comfort from many of the formal and technical limitations that had hindered it.

The first attempt to manufacture easy chairs and sofas, during the early decades of this century, chose the path of simplifying the structure while attempting to recuperate the performance lost as a result, through the properties of the new materials employed. For example, in the first small metal armchairs designed in the Bauhaus period, the yielding qualities of the natural materials assembled by craftsmen was substituted by the elasticity of an industrial product like steel tubing. The quality of industrially manufactured comfort, nevertheless, was still fairly low; the padding was still largely done by hand.

In the Fifties, the development of materials that could be transformed industrially broadened the field of experimentation. The structure remained similar to the traditional structure, with a separation between the load-bearing framework, the yielding structure, and the soft padding and covering, but materials that were new to the sector began to spread — curved welded metal tubing, cloth-covered elastic strips, foam rubber padding, and padding made of cut slabs of polyurethane.

In the Sixties, the development of synthetic foamed materials opened the door to the economic and industrial manufacture of seating comfort. Natural foam latex rubber (better known as foam rubber), which was, as the name suggests, still a product of natural origin as well as being relatively costly, was joined by foamed polyurethanes that rapidly spread because they were cheap, easy to transform, and provided structural performance as well.

The design of those years enjoyed a period of great openness to technological innovation, and rapidly made the most of the expressive and technical potential of the new material. The first easy chairs whose

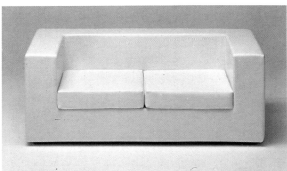

From a complicated mechanical construction to the simplicity of foamed padding - the mixed metal-frame/elastic-strap structure of the *Martingala* easy chair by Marco Zanuso (mfg. Artflex, 1954), top; *P 40* by Osvaldo Borsani (mfg. Tecno, 1957), bottom; center, the *Throw-away* sofa by Willie Landels (mfg. Zanotta, 1965), made entirely of foamed polyurethane, without a load-bearing structure.

153

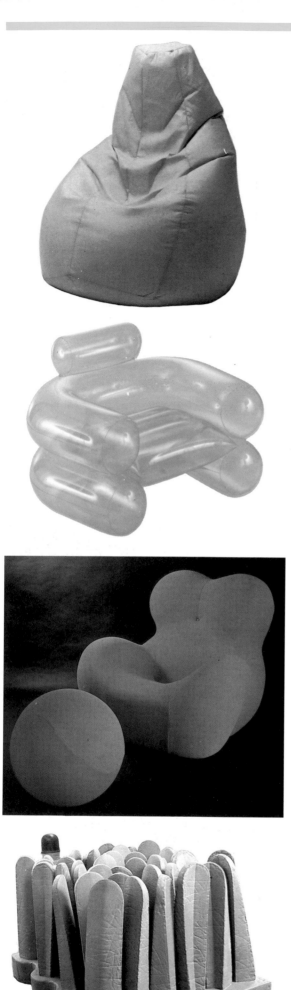

structure was entirely supplied by the foamed material were created, and the concept of cheap total softness gave rise to the prospect of mass-market comfort.

The idea of comfort, aside from the natural impulse to have something soft to sit on, is profoundly marked by its historic origin. It is a specific system of images and meanings that consolidated in the Victorian era, produced by a wealthy middle class that developed a system of objects, and formal and functional solutions, as a tool and representation of its own well-being.

This model, at first limited to an elite, later spread and as Andrea Branzi observed, "the conquest of comfort in both private and public spaces can be measured in centimeters of thickness" (*Confort e democrazia*). Furthermore: this soft thickness has the form of the middle class parlor with all its attendant values of home, family, and the social relations that it embodied.

In this context, the Sixties and Seventies constituted an attempt to break with the past. The enthusiasm over the new possibilities offered by plastics was linked to the cultural atmosphere of that period – experimentation went beyond a new system of forms in an attempt to create a new system of life. In all their variety, the images generated during that period share a common feature – they are impossible to reconcile with a middle class drawing room. Not only did the new "padded furniture" have a different form, but it called for a new concept of sitting down, of communicating with others, and, in the final analysis, a new concept of the home.

Within this shared framework, ideas varied wildly: from the geometric and rigid softness of *Throw away,* to the organic and anthropomorphic softness of *Up,* and the ironic pop playfulness of *Pratone* and the *Sassi.*
Solutions were also tested in which the potential of the materials permitted unusual interactions between the object and the user: *Sacco* is an object practically without form, which can take on a wide variety of shapes; *Blow* is an imposing easy chair, but is inflatable and deflatable; *Up* was purchased flat, compressed in a sort of vacuum container – it then grew and softened (one might even say "was born") before the eyes of the purchaser who opened the box...

Later, as we know, many aspects of this landscape changed, and in the world of sofas and easy chairs this radically experimental phase was followed by a return to objects with more traditional structures. Interest shifted to the possible linguistic variations on the theme of sofas and easy chairs, without rejecting the historic identity of these items of furniture. The new developments – when there are any – are subtler, and the technical aspect is used with greater discretion.

As a formal result, easy chairs grew legs again. After total softness, a more restrained and composed idea of comfort developed. From the informal evocation of a big pillow on the floor, padded furniture returned to the family of true furniture, which it had momentarily abandoned.

Once again, in technical terms, there is a subdivision between the load-bearing elements and the soft and elastic elements, but the bygone experimental fervor has left its mark. Technical reality, all questions of image aside, is radically different from that of the Fifties. For instance, in the field of differentiated strain stength, what earlier required different materials can now be made with a sole material (polyurethane) and by acting on a sole parameter (density), cutting the parts from foam blocks with different densities, overmolding in later phases the foams of different density, or even creating in a single molding operation a double-density foam, determining its shape through a precise control of the flow of material in the mold.

The innovation, in this context, has more to do with the process than the product, but thanks to linguistic tolerance there is also room for research in which the performance potential of a technical solution is used in a clear fashion, as a quality that typifies the product's image. *Transformer* is a paradigmatic example of this line, which certainly has roots in the previous experimental phase, but which is also conditioned by the current cultural atmosphere, where the relationship between willingness to accept the new and preservation of memory has become more complex.

If *Sacco* accepted all forms, and if *Up* was a mother's womb that received birth before our eyes, *Transformer* performs the opposite voyage: from a plastic container of small free elements, the air is emptied, forming a stable vacuum that preserves the shape that has been given it. A frozen imprint of someone's passage, an interweaving between the possibility of change (which is always possible) and a track, the memory of a presence that can be preserved.

Facing page: the Seventies and the destructure of the drawing room. From top: Sacco, by Gatti, Paolini, and Teodoro (mfg. Zanotta, 1968) - the interior is made of high-resistance foamed polystyrene balls; Blow, by De Pas, D'Urbino, Lomazzi, Scolari (mfg. Zanotta, 1967), an inflatable transparent polyvinyl chloride (PVC) structure; Up by Gaetano Pesce (mfg. B B, 1969), made of polyurethane foam; Pratone, by Guardi, Ceretti, Derossi, Rosso (mfg. Gufram, 1969 and again in 1986), made of integral foamed polyurethane.

In this page: sofas of the Eighties. Above, Transformer, by Ron Arad (mfg. One Off, 1983), a polyvinyl chloride (PVC) shell, sealed, containing granules of a foamed material. A valve makes it possible to suck the air out of the container, which stiffens the chair around the body that is pressing on it. Bottom: Torso, by Paolo Deganello (mfg. Cassina, 1982) - the overall image emerges from the juxtaposition of different languages and materials.

Intelligent flexibility

The flexible object may be the forerunner of the intelligent object. If, by this term, we mean something that has been manufactured and programmed so as to interact with the user and the ambient, flexible objects in many ways meet this description.

In them, unlike in information-rich objects, the operating program is not contained in a digital memory, but is inscribed in their shape and in the very structure of the material of which they are made. They contain, as it were, an analogue program which permits them to modify themselves simply and directly and to alter their form (and therefore their performance) in relation to the needs of the ambient. The program of a bow or a spring permits it to interact with the surrounding ambient by following a cycle of energy accumulation and discharge which the programmer/manufacturer has impressed in their structure with a set of design choices. Or, from another point of view, a pliable object (a tent or a chair) carries, inscribed in its components, the capacity to interact with the ambient in a more complex fashion than a shed or a rigid chair.

As we have seen, in this field the recent wave of innovation has led to no spectacular new developments, no miracle materials with unheard-of properties. It has led, however, to the spread of "elastic strategies" or "flexible strategies" in developing a theme. Thus, the ground has been prepared for a new type of micro-design capable of inventing new solutions. At times these solutions are contained within the confines of a technical and manufacturing area, and only a trained eye can detect them; at other times they emerge with an improvement in performance conferred to the product and offered to the user.

Thus, though the history of this type of interactive objects, rich in analogue information content, is as ancient as the first hunter with a bow or the first nomad people that folded their home microcosm and carried it with them, it is also true that the current availability of materials opens new vistas for inventivity, in directions that have yet to be explored.

This and facing page: the possibility of bending or flexing elastically a material, may provide objects made of that material with new performances. This happens in a wide variety of applicative fields - from simple kitchen objects to aerospace components.

Stars lamp by Remo Buti. The flexible transparent tubular parts are made of polycarbonate (PC) (mfg. Targetti Sankey).

Sikuro hang-everything made of polypropylene (PP). The yielding quality of the slots make it possible to hang up objects of different weights and shapes (mfg. A.C.E.A). (Doct. Montedison)

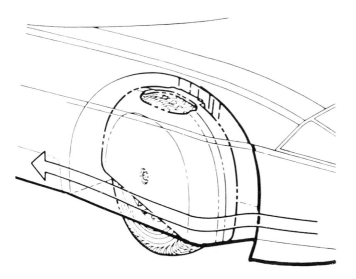

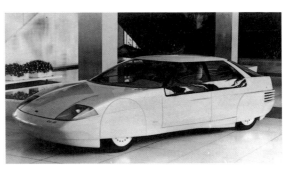

The experimental vehicle Ford Probe IV, an innovative approach to the covering of the front wheels made it possible to improve the car's aerodynamics. An elastic membrane, perfectly integrated with the rest of the body, deforms (diagram at left) as it is pushed by the mobile mudguard as the wheel turns.

The *Dilungo* table by Giancarlo Piretti (1985) upsets traditional typologies of extendable tables, by using a flexible material (polyurethane - PVC) for the table surface (mfg. Castilia).

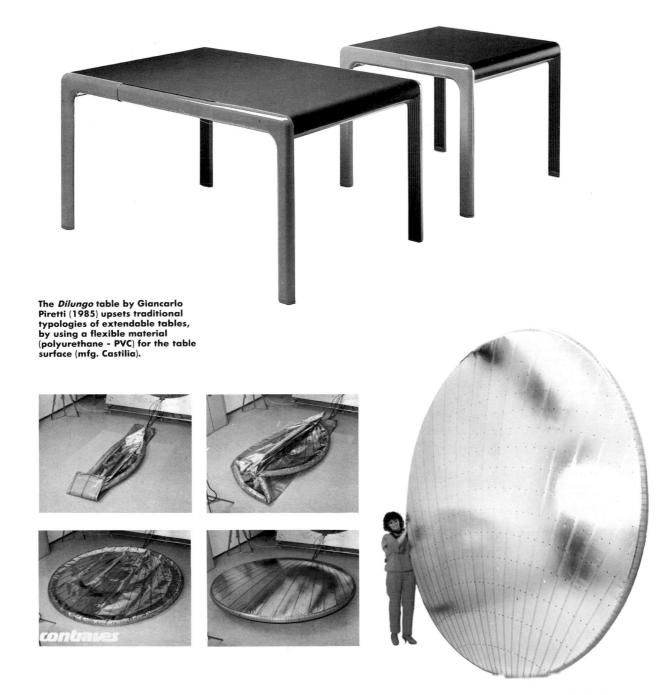

The dish antenna Load 3, developed by the Contraves company for the European Space Agency (ESA), travels folded within the satellite, and is inflated once the appropriate orbit is reached. The composite material, developed by Ciba-Geigy, is then hardened chemically or by the sun's rays, in order to give it the required dimensional stability.

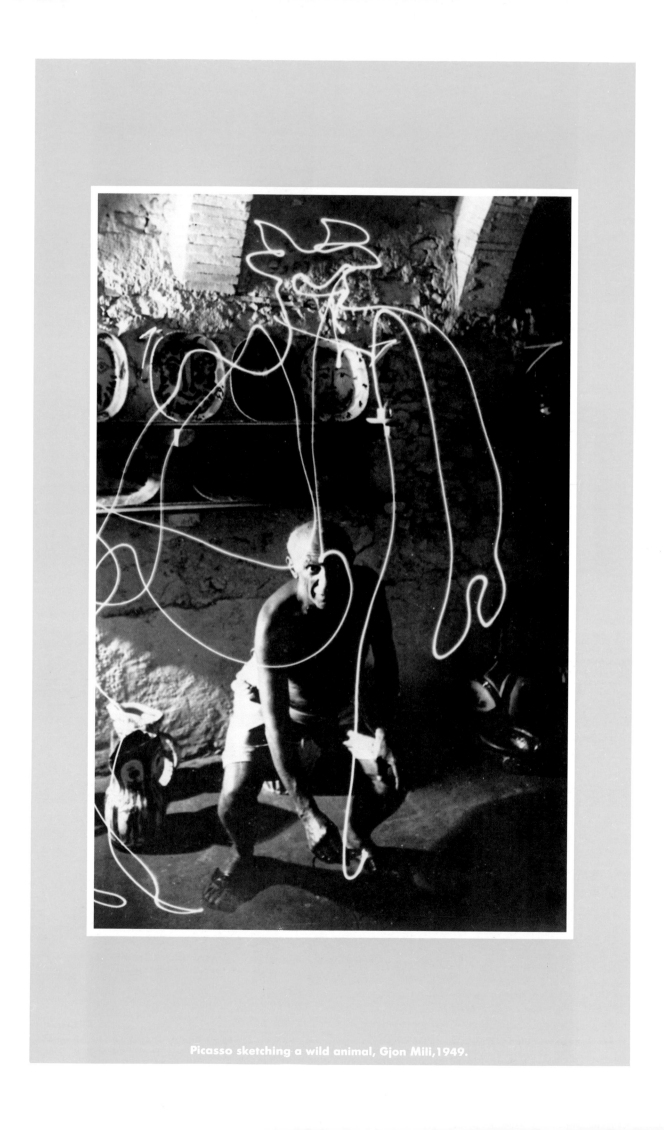

Picasso sketching a wild animal, Gjon Mili,1949.

Creating the transparent

Transparent matter

A transparent object exists, but not as far as light is concerned. It must contain, separate, protect, insulate, and support without imposing in visual terms its materiality. Or else a transparent object may proffer its materiality with delicacy – in the form of opalescence, reflections, luminous colors.

Traditionally, "creating the transparent" chiefly meant bringing daylight indoors (as is, or with a modification of color), producing containers that allow one to see the contents (bottles, laboratory equipment), and creating esthetic effects around this special invisible and glowing materiality (let us think of crystal chandeliers or Cinderella's glass slippers).

Until recently all this was linked to the use of glass: the long dominion of this material has created a cultural image in which transparency is one with other specific properties of glass. In particular, a bond has been created between the almost magic quality of the performance, and the delicacy of the material that provided that performance. It seemed right that glass, a noble material, should also be sensitive – hard and fragile. "Fragile as glass," sounds even today like an expression of respect more than the description of a flaw.

Then plastics, many of which are transparent, arrived on the scene, and not only did they enter into competition with glass in traditional sectors, but they also spread transparency to new marketing areas: packaging, furniture, clothing... The traditional image of a transparent object has changed profoundly – transparency can proliferate. Moreover, it has shed its historic fragility. Transparency's connotation of nobility disappears – because the performance is no longer exceptional, but also because the use of transparent objects no longer requires the care and reverence demanded by glass. Glass, we might say, paraphrasing Walter Benjamin, loses its aura in the era of its technical reproducibility.

Of course, glass has tried to emphasize its history, and is offered as a noble and delicate material. Transparency, however, has long since lost this connotation, and glass itself keeps its market chiefly due to its functional qualities (unalterable surfaces, high-quality transparency) and to a reduction of its historic limitations (fragility, weight, difficulty in processing).

The relationship between matter and light has become more complex and articulated. Transparent material takes on new performances – it has become possible to use it as a selective filter (of color and of energy); the prospect exists of changing it from a static filter (as it now is) to a dynamic filter, whose performances can vary according to the appropriate stimuli from the environment or user. More recently, the field of optical electronics opened up to creating the transparent, utilizing light as a means of transmitting information. Thus transparent materials should soon become strategic elements in one of the most advanced sectors of technology.

Thus, the creation of the transparent displays a dual tendency: on the one hand, the elementary performance has become commonplace (transparency no longer presents obstacles); on the other hand, there is a greater range of possibilities in new fields, where the relationships that reveal themselves make up for the loss of the traditional aura.

The path of light

Light is one of the most difficult physical entities to pin down – it can be thought of as a ray if we are speaking of lenses; as a train of electromagnetic waves of varying length if we speak of color; as a flow of energy particles (photons) if we are dealing with a photoelectric cell. Furthermore, the geometric aspects of light, aside from the direction and sense of its propagation, also concern the

plane of oscillation of the waves — haphazard oscillations on all planes (such as in normal light emission) or else on a sole plane (polarized light). The relationship between light flow and matter involves all these aspects — transparency is a product of these interactions.

If a material presents a homogeneous structure (we shall return to the practical meaning of this homogeneity further along) a light ray can travel through it without disturbance. The medium in this case is perfectly transparent. In general, however, no material exists in this condition; hence, light flow is split up. Radiations with a certain wavelength pass through, others are blocked, and the quality of flow transmitted is thus changed.

Transparency does not mean only the passage of that range of electromagnetic waves that our eyes are capable of perceiving, but also of waves that are outside the field of visible light: ultraviolet (low wavelengths) and infrared (high wavelengths). In the field of visible light as well, material may be transparent to the entire spectrum (that is, it may allow the passage of white light) or only to a few bands (transforming white light into colored light); or it may also present dispersion phenomena, that is, it may break down a flow of white light into the various chromatic components (splitting up a ray into monochromatic rays). Material may also create a polarization effect, allowing only electromagnetic waves on a specific plane to pass.

When a light ray passes from one transparent medium to another, at the moment in which it strikes the surface of the second material, part of it is reflected while part of it penetrates. The quantity and quality of the light reflected depend on the optical characteristics (expressed by the index of refraction) of the pair of materials, and on the angle of incidence.

The part that penetrates into the second medium may be totally absorbed and transformed into thermal energy — the material then proves opaque. Otherwise, the light may only be partially absorbed; the remaining part continues on, but in a different direction from that of the incident ray. The angle of this deviation is called the angle of diffraction; it may differ for different wavelengths, giving rise to the dispersion mentioned above.

The absorption may be identical along the entire spectrum of the incident flow (in which case there is a quantitative reduction of the light flow) or else it may be differentiated according to the various wavelengths (the material, for instance, may prove opaque to ultraviolet or infrared radiation or to part of the visible spectrum, and thus transmit colored light).

The parameter used most widely to evaluate the effects of absorption is transmittance, that is, the ratio between the intensity of light exiting from a sheet of material and the light incident upon that material.

Another relevant phenomenon is that of total reflection: when a ray of light encounters a surface separating two materials (where the index of refraction of the second is less than that of the first), it may happen that instead of being partially reflected and partially refracted, it is entirely reflected. This occurs when a ray reaches the surface at an angle to that surface's perpendicular that exceeds a given value (definable for each pair of materials) that is defined as the critical angle. If this occurs, even if the second material is transparent, the separating surface functions as a mirror.

Furthermore, a material's transparency depends not only on the quantity and quality of the energy that passes through it, but also on its ability to transmit images, that is, to maintain the order of a beam of rays. An opalescent material, for instance, transmits light with good energy efficiency, but causes the loss of the information carried in the images.

The transmission of an image is faithful if the material and its surface cause all the rays to travel in parallel paths, or (as in a lens) paths that preserve the initial order. This congruence may be lost either due to internal refraction and reflection in the material, caused by particles dispersed in its mass (some rays encounter these particles and are deviated, others do not), or else due to the shape of the surface (as different rays enter or exit from the material they encounter a surface aureole with varying inclinations, and thus undergo varying deviations). The tendency to lose the order of incident flow is measured by a parameter known as diffusion, or haze.

Materials and transparency

A material, in order to be transparent, need not be absolutely homogeneous — it must only be homogeneous with respect to the flow of light. Possible nonhomogeneities do not compromise the transparency if their size is less than the wavelength of the incident light radiations; or if the various components of the material, though greater than the wavelength, possess uniform indices of refraction (so that the ray of light undergoes no deviations when passing from one to another).

Therefore, single crystal and amorphous materials can be considered transparent. The path of single crystals, nevertheless, is not feasible. A perfect crystal is indeed transparent, but it constitutes a rarity, and a sheet obtained from an enormous quartz crystal would possess excellent transparency but would be extremely difficult to produce. Crystalline materials, instead, are generally found in a microcrystalline form, that is, as small orderly zones aggregated in a haphazard fashion, so that the interfaces constitute a nonhomogeneity that compromises their transparency. Therefore semicrystalline metals and plastic materials are not transparent.

A very thin metal film may nevertheless be transparent. Even semicrystalline plastic materials such as polyethylene (PE) or polyethylene terephthalate (PET) can become transparent if they are "stretched": with this operation, in fact, the crystalline areas are oriented in a more cohesive fashion and the material becomes homogeneous with respect to the light flow.

The effects of light polarization are evidence of the internal stresses of a plastic film.

The main highway of creating the transparent, therefore, passes through amorphous materials such as glass and many plastics (not filled or pigmented).

Surfaces, however, still play a crucial role: their qualities determine the share of energy reflected, and — above all — they can cause the loss of that special orderly light flow that is essential to transparency. This depends as much on the type of processing as on the intrinsic properties of the material. Among these properties, one of the most important (in terms of lasting optical performance) is surface hardness.

Then there are cases in which the performance required of the surface is exactly the opposite — to allow light to pass without permitting visibility. The problem here is far simpler — to diminish order and increase entropy, particularly refined solutions are not needed. Any surface texture is sufficient to this end, as is demonstrated by the widespread use in the home of frosted glass.

Polarization

The filtering action of material on a ray of light passing through it may often occur in other ways, some of which have a particular bearing on our topic.

A material may interact with a ray, causing it to polarize. A polarized ray of light, as we said above, is a special flow of electromagnetic waves that all oscillate on the same plane; this effect is the product of many causes, and may be turned to various purposes.

For instance, the light of the skimming rays reflected, by a surface, is polarized. Light produced in the presence of a strong electric and/or magnetic field is also polarized. The most widely used system for generating polarized light employs the polarizing effect of filters made of specially modified and oriented polymer materials (e.g., a film of polyvinyl alcohol with the addition of iodine microcrystals, which is then stretched).

If the polarized light then strikes a second polarizing filter, it can pass through only if the plane of the second filter is parallel to that of the first; otherwise the filter absorbs part or (if the planes are perpendicular) all of the incident light. Two polarizing filters, thus paired, can work as a modulator of luminous intensity.

Other modulating systems can be based on other principles. There are systems that use liquid-crystal materials and the different spatial orientations that they can take on if they are appropriately stimulated. These different orientations can determine the transparency of the system. A liquid-crystal component is a sheet that can be alternately transparent or opaque according to an electrical stimulus.

There are also electrochromatic and photochromatic materials that vary their own capacity to absorb light rays according to the oxidation of certain of their components (metal salts in glass or special organic pigments in plastic). The variation may be creat-

ed with electrical stimulations (electrochromatic effect) or as a function of the intensity of the incident radiations (photochromatic effect).

The second effect has already found wide commercial use in the manufacture of lenses for glasses. The material in this application is glass containng silver salts, such as silver halides: these produce a variation in the absorption of incident light ranging from 10-20 percent to 60-75 percent, accompanied by a change in color from neutral to grey and dark brown. Response time, that is, the time required for a variation of the optical properties as a result of the change in ambient lighting, is under a minute. The technology involved in producing photochromatic and electrochromatic effects upon a plastic medium is still being developed.

The metamorphoses of glass

Ever since the Phoenecians discovered it accidentally (according to Pliny), glass has acquired ever greater mastery of the transparency, color, and shininess of its surfaces and optical qualities. Manufacturing processes have developed as well, and the line of products has swelled.

As early as 1300, the Murano glassmakers were capable of producing an extremely refined range of tones, and had perfected a method for manufacturing an especially clear glass with shiny surfaces that they dubbed "crystal." Only recently was this refined empirical knowledge translated into scientific terms — improvements in our knowledge of light phenomena and in our technical and manufacturing ability have opened new vistas in the area of controlling the qualities of transparency. It has therefore become possible to acquire increasingly precise control over the intrinsic properties of material and surface qualities, leading to the development of glass engineered for specific performances (from the building trades to precision technical and scientific applications).

In the field of manufacturing processes, the history of glass ranges from the secrecy of craftsmen's workshops that produced precious and rare items to the current state of affairs, where, alongside a few specialized processes that are used in creating precious and rare types of glass (such as a few types used in electronics applications), there are the great types of continuous manufacturing that have turned glass into one of the most common and — in the final analysis — cheapest of materials.

Alongside this enormous broadening of production, another line of research has developed in an aim to limit, if not obviate, a few of the historical limitations of this material. Its fragility and hazardousness when broken have led to the development of tempered glass, safety glass, to stratified plastic and glass, bulletproof glass (see below, 3.4.2). Athermanous glass, capable of withstanding elevated temperatures, has been in production for some time (this is a borosilicate glass with low thermal expansion; important because in normal glass it is the difference in the degree of the expansion that causes breakage). Attempts to reduce the weight of glass objects have brought about, through a chemical tempering processes, stronger glass (hence thinner and lighter objects), or else integration with plastic in sandwiches that combine the two materials to their best advantage.

Then there is the entirely new field of fiber optics, laser materials, and all the equipment that goes under the heading of optoelectronics. Here glass takes on the status of a new, high-technology product, rediscovering a link with its past nobility, revived in the new communications age.

Plastics and the spread of transparency

Plastic competes with glass in all areas – from that of artistic craftsmanship to standardized mass production and high-tech electronics, but along an opposed line of development. While for glass it was necessary to make the high-quality performance cheaper and easier to produce, the problem faced by plastics is how to raise the quality of performance that can be easily manufactured.

Many plastics are transparent – amorphous thermoplastics are transparent, and while semicrystalline thermoplastics are opalescent when used in thin layers, they can also become practically transparent (and if subjected to stretching, they can also attain quite respectable level of performance); lastly, many thermoset plastics, if they are not filled, are also transparent.

Plastics, therefore, open to "creating the transparent" the entire range of possibilities

generated by their remarkable workability: thus a complex three-dimensional object, a film, or a flexible component can become transparent (but still be easy to manufacture). Nevertheless, the transparency of plastic is not always as good as that of glass, especially in terms of durability. Many plastics are not clear; many yellow when exposed to ultraviolet light; nearly all are subject to scratching and chipping.

This does not pose serious problems in many

applications that require short-term use and for which less than perfect transparency is acceptable: packaging, containers, disposable products. Certain polymer materials stand out distinctly from this landscape of cheap throw-away transparency, offering properties that allow them to compete with glass in areas where greater levels of performance are required – from the production of lenses to the automobile industry and fiber optics.

The most widely used plastic materials are:

Polymethylmethacrylate (PMMA) – the thermoplastic material that most closely resembles glass in terms of transparency, surface hardness, and resistance over time even when used outdoors (when exposed, that is, to ultraviolet rays). It also shares with glass a certain fragility (it is not as fragile as glass, but it is more fragile than other plastic materials). In order to improve its tenacity an impact-resistant formulation has been developed (HIPMMA) in which the base polymer is mixed with an acrylic rubber coupled with methacrylate. This second component, which possesses the same index of refraction, increases the capacity of absorbing mechanical energy without a loss of transparency, although there is a certain drop in surface hardness.
It is produced in extruded sheets of varying thicknesses (for standard uses in building and in greenhouses), which in certain cases can then be thermoformed. If the sheets must possess good optical qualities, then they are cast. Extrusion generates surfaces that can produce effects of optical distortion. Only recently has extrusion technology been perfected to resolve this problem (sheets of this sort can be used, for instance, in the windows of public transport vehicles). The sheets can be further enhanced with the addition of reflective films (for building) or reflection-proof films (for instruments). Cast sheets can then be stretched (bioriented) in order to improve their mechanical properties (especially for use in aeronautics as cupolas or portholes).
Like all thermoplastics, PMMA can be produced in granules and then transformed through molding; this technology is used in manufacturing transparent three-dimensional objects, from laboratory test

tubes to automobile parking lights. Special formulations can be used in optical applications, for scientific instrument lenses or contact lenses, "light guides," fiber optics, compact disks, and even in the optical elements of lasers.

Polycarbonate (PC) – possesses transparency that is slightly inferior to that of PMMA and, if it is not protected, tends to yellow when exposed to ultraviolet light. On the other hand, it is very tough. Like PMMA, it can be manufactured in extruded sheets of varying thickness or molded with traditional processes. It is the most widely used transparent material in technical applications that require mechanical resistance. PC is also used in manufacturing compact disks.

Polystyrene – (PS) has good properties of transparency, and has a moderate cost. In its standard form it is rather fragile, though some transparent and impact-resistant types are also available. It is used in glasses, disposable products, toys, as well as in manufacturing lenses if costs must be reduced.

Cellulose fibers (Cellulose acetate, CA; Cellulose acetate butyrate, CAB) – have good optical and mechanical properties. Their use is limited due to their relatively high price, and is concentrated in applications where the texture must be agreeable (for instance, glasses frames).

Polyvinyl chloride (PVC) – has lower mechanical quality and transparency than the above materials, but it also costs much less. It is therefore the most widely used polymer when especially high levels of performance are not required (for instance, in mass packaging).
Aside from the materials mentioned above, there are less widely used materials destined to specific fields of application — for instance, styrene-acrylonitrile (SAN), which is resistant to chemical agents and is used in appliances; poly-diallil-diglycol-carbonate (better known as CR 39), a thermoset which has as its sole but important application the manufacture of lenses for glasses, where use is made of its remarkable qualities of impact- and abrasion-resistance.

Transparency as immateriality - after shrinking to a minuscule size, the calculator becomes transparent. The Casio TH-10 uses an invisible conductive deposit for the contacts of the keyboard.

Transparent objects

Transparent objects have always possessed three different personalities, often integrated one with another – one is hygienic and functional, one is information-related, and the third is esthetic and emotional. Bringing sunlight into a dark space makes it more healthful and improves visibility; seeing through a wall or door means receiving information on what lies on the other side. Playing with light, creating sparkles, colored light, and bundles of rays that cut through the shadow has always meant designing a quality that we would today call (in Italian) *soft*, that has to do with an immaterial entity (light) but which is extremely evocative.

All this is still true, but attainment of the objectives in question is no longer blocked as it was in the past by difficulties in working glass and by its fragility. Transparency has therefore become a common quality – if there were a reason to do so, we could easily produce an artificial habitat that was completely transparent.

In this new context, therefore, transparency is no longer a performance to be conquered as much as a possibility to be managed, by calibrating its extension and by linking it as needed to a complex of other performances.

The crisis of the giant crystals

Building has historically implied a compromise between the need to close an environment (making it functionally and psychologically protective) and the need to open it to sight and sunlight – the interweaving of technical and cultural factors in the development of this equilibrium is nicely illustrated by the history of the window.

The possibility of industrially manufacturing sheets of glass, of making buildings with thin structures, and of developing air conditioning systems, has eliminated the principal technical obstacles that governed the relationship between opaque and transparent – from Paxton's Crystal Palace on, transparent architecture became a practical solution.

This sudden freedom from opacity has given rise to new architectural languages, and especially the glass architecture of the International Style. In this context, the delight with building structures that resemble giant crystals has led architects to sacrifice an entire tradition of sensitivity and skill in managing light functionally and culturally. The window, a fundamental architectural element in

developing the rhythm of facades and in modulating the flow of heat and light, by extending itself to the entire skin of a building, in fact becomes a transparent continuum, and is lost in a flat curtain wall, in which the individual parts no longer stand out — the architecture of transparency has often turned into almost total uniformity with respect to light, a total rejection of any design approach to light.

If a crystal skyscraper constitutes one of the most emblematic representations of twentieth-century culture (rational, transparent, essential, unambiguous form, indeed, perfect as a crystal) it is also in a certain sense an emblem of the contradictions and the crisis in this culture — a glass prism that glitters in the sunlight is hot on one side and cold on the other, and even the most powerful and energy-hungry air conditioning system has a hard time creating acceptable living conditions within it.

Now that this approach to architecture has

Glass roof coverings create intermediate settings, neither indoors nor outdoors.
Above: The great central "court" of the Zublin building in Stuttgart, designed by Gottfried Bohm (1985).
Bottom: The use of polymethylmethacrylate (PMMA) sheets in restoring the Stazione Centrale in Milan. (Doct. Montedison-Vedril)
Facing page, top: A covered walkway in the Psychopedagogic Institute of Wasmes, design by Manolo Nunez and Henri Guchez. (Doct. ICI)

166

been roundly and widely criticized, the topic of creating the transparent in buildings can be approached in a more diffuse and articulated fashion. It is thus possible to rediscover a tradition of transparency that is not limited to the ancient and variegated culture of light (from Gothic cathedrals to a certain type of Arabic architecture). In this tradition, there is also a more recent architecture of glass, the delicate and careful expression of a thermal culture overshadowed by the International Style coupled with air conditioning. This tradition has nevertheless survived in the form of spontaneous and commonplace architecture – from the small scale of winter gardens and bow windows to the larger scale of urban arcades and covered passages. The articulation of all these possibilities enriches both the single architectural object and parts of entire cities with ambients that vary in terms of quality of image, microclimate, and lighting; architectural elements but also technical components of a more complex thermal system, capable of interacting with the changing climatic qualities of places.

This aspect, made more urgent by the economic and ecological problem of cutting energy consumption, in such that in the area of creating the transparent in buildings, the upper hand passes from an emphasis on quantity as in the recent past (creating more transparent) to an emphasis on quality (designing the quality of transparency). This transition can be observed as well in the development of materials, which progressively tend to emphasize the role as filter, and the capacity of interacting with light. Materials are no longer required to be merely transparent. They are now expected to filter in an intelligent and sensitive fashion the flow of incident radiation.

Sensitive windows and other filters

Let us imagine a transparent architectural component that in winter captures as much energy as possible and in the summer instead works as a heat shield. During the day it modulates its transparency to attain the light intensity desired. It can orient light so as to distribute it more efficiently throughout the ambient. Perhaps it can vary the color of this light. Lastly, it has the thermal resistance of an opaque object.

The traditional window with its outer shutters, inner hatches, light curtains and heavy drapes was not, after all, so distant from this "sensitive window." The possibility of acting separately and gradually upon the different elements in the system enabled one to obtain a varied combination of performances. What is emerging today from the development of materials is the possibility of concentrating many of the subsystems of the complex traditional window system in one or more sheets endowed with equivalent performances.

From the thermal standpoint, a window is always a "hole" in the skin of a building, that is, a surface capable of providing (in summer and winter) lower levels of performance than the opaque elements of that skin. Producing transparent components with better thermal characteristics has therefore long been an objective of primary importance.
A consolidated result are the windows with air chambers (simple or double) and sheets of honeycombed plastic material (polymethylmethacrylate, PMMA; polycarbonate, PC) which greatly reduce winter heat loss due to conduction or convection.
More recently, attempts have been made to resolve the problem of heat exchanges due to radiation. Here the filtering role played by transparent surfaces is more complex, and the solution must meet various

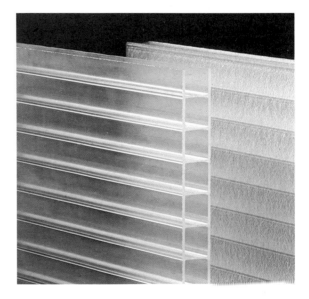

**Double-wall heat-insulating sheets
of polymethylmethacrylate (PMMA)
(mfg. Vedril). (Doct. Montedison-Vedril)**

needs. On one hand, for instance, there is the problem of the loss of heat energy which in winter is radiated from the inside out – in order to limit this phenomenon, windows with low emissivity have been produced in the following way. On the inner side of a sheet of air–chamber glass, a film of reflective material is deposited, which then returns most of the heat radiation to the room. On the other hand, there is the need to reduce incident radiation in the summer. With this goal in mind glass has been manufactured with a mirrored outer surface, capable of reflecting much of the incident energy. This result is attained by depositing a thin metal film – or, any way, a reflective film of some other type – on the outer surface (coating). This application, nevertheless has the disadvantage of lessening the energy contribution that the sun's rays can provide in the winter.

In effect, when faced with cyclical climatic and energy conditions, which require a transparent building component to provide

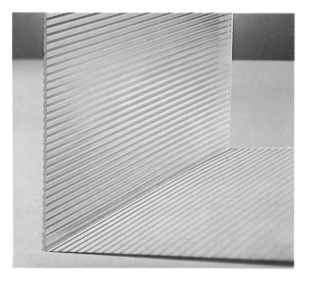

Halfway between an optical polarizing filter and old-fashioned shutters, the "sensitive window" makes it possible to improve energy economy in buildings by adapting the transparency to climatic conditions. A PMMA solar batcher under two different conditions of light incidence. Note the difference in light intensity on the sill. (Doct. Montedison-Vedril)

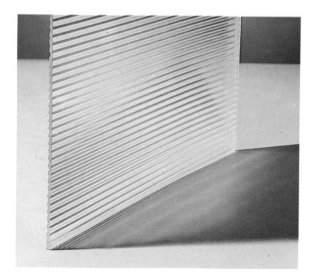

opposite performances in winter and summer and at night and during the day, any static filter must necessarily provide only a partial response. Interest has therefore concentrated on dynamic filters, that is, on components whose optical and energy qualities can vary in accordance with the cycles of radiation flow.

An example can be given: the "solar batcher." The principle consists in controlling the transmission of light through transparent sheets that have been faceted – it is the same basic idea as that underlying the Venetian blind or the *Brise-soleil*, which are solid however, and integrated in the transparent component, exploiting the phenomenon of total reflection (see 3.4.1). In the context of a research program on energy saving sponsored by the European Community (Solar Energy Applications in Dwellings), the Vedril company developed a sheet of PMMA, flat on one side and faceted on the other, which is transparent when the sun is low on the horizon (winter) and opaque when the sun is high (summer). In this case, the rays that penetrate the sheet strike the inner surface with an angle such that they are almost totally reflected. The attainment of this variation in behavior naturally requires a very precise definition of the shape of the cross-section, and an equally exact manufacture. These aspects are still being studied.

The transmission and reflection of light in a sheet with a faceted surface can be exploited as well in order to provide good natural lighting even well inside a building. One solution proposed by the Siemens company consists in a sheet of methacrylate composed of many prisms with a reflective metallized face, arranged so as to focus the light at zenith (that is, the radiation that is highest on the horizon) onto the ceiling of the interior space. The ceiling, which in turn is reflective, sends the light up to 6 or 7 meters' distance from the window.

Another system, proposed by the Corning company, calls for a sheet of transparent glass in which light-breaking laminae are integrated. These laminae are also made of glass, but have different optical qualities.

Transparent surfaces that function as dynamic filters – currently being developed – exploit an interaction between their shapes and the motion of the sun; but there is something to be said as well about filters that are dynamic due to variations in their very transparency. As we mentioned earlier, the principles of liquid crystals and electrochromatic and photochromatic phenomena could be exploited in the production of variably transparent building components. The challenge is to make technically and economically feasible on large surfaces what is feasible today only for small surfaces. That would open a vast range of possibilities to the creation of the transparent.

These technical difficulties (and their solutions) do not apply only to architecture. Even the transparent portion of a welder's mask is, after all, a small window that must act as a filter between an outer environment with unfavorable light conditions (the intense flame generated during welding) and an interior ambient that must be well protected (the eyes of the welder). On the other hand, when the flame is off, the operator must be able to see what he is working on. The need for a variably transparent component has been met with a liquid-crystal "window." An electric eye set on the mask transmits an electric impulse upon the lighting of the flame which modifies the position of the liquid crystals and, hence, the transparency of the system. All this occurs automatically and immediately, ensuring optimum conditions of visibility when the flame is on and when it is off, without any action from the operator, who can use both hands for his work.

A similar result can be obtained in other ways; for instance, by exploiting the electrochromatic and photochromatic effect mentioned earlier (see 3.4.1): photochromatic eyeglasses, which have been on the market for some time, are also small variably transparent "windows."

Another strategy for interacting with a light flow employs polarizing filters, currently in use in laboratories and in manufacturing sunglasses. The operating principle of the latter is based on the observation that much of the light that reaches the eyes is reflected from flat horizontal surfaces, and hence is powerfully polarized. If the lenses are polarized on a perpendicular surface, they operate as a filter that absorbs these radiations, though they remain transparent to all others.

The availability of polarizing films opens the way to other fields of use — by juxtaposing two of such films and rotating them with respect to each other, it is possible to move with a continual variation from a condition of transparency (when the planes of polarization are parallel) to a condition of opacity (when they are perpendicular).

Three cases of controlled transparency. From botton: A welding mask with liquid-crystal filter, capable of darkening in 80 milliseconds (mfg. Thommen); "one-way" transparency in a squash court enclosed by sheets of polymethylmethacrylate (PMMA) - two staggered grills of small dots, silk-screened on the sheets, along with special light conditions, make them opaque for the players and transparent for the spectators (Doct. ICI); sunglasses that are transparent to ultraviolet rays - neither the lenses nor the arms leave marks in a suntan (mfg. Fovs). (Doct. Montedison-Vedril)

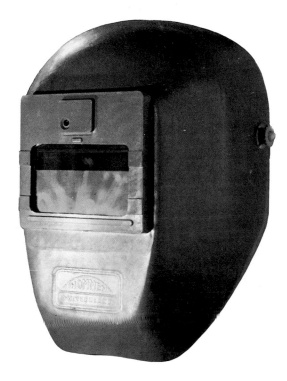

Special performances

A windshield that breaks without jagged edges; the rear window of an automobile that has an integrated heater against fogging; show windows that are smash-resistant and contain a sensor that triggers a burglar alarm; bulletproof glass which can absorb the energy of a high-caliber projectile... The proliferation of transparent materials makes it possible to create wiches sano in which transparency is combined with other performances.

Impact testing for a stratified windshield made up of a plastic-glass sandwich. It must give way, absorbing energy, without forming sharp fragments. (Doct. SIV)

The introduction of the idea of composites in the field of transparent materials developed out of the need to reduce hazards. The safety glass that has long been used in building, integrates fine wire nets. If the sheet of glass is broken, the nets hold the pieces of glass together and keep them from falling. This solution cannot be used when the problem is to provide good visibility under normal conditions, such as with an automobile windshield.

The windshield poses a very complex engineering problem. It is a large transparent surface that must be resistant, light, and scratch-proof; if there is an accident it must break in such a way as to limit the risk of cutting whatever hits it. The solutions adopted for the moment use differentially tempered glass (which breaks into small fragments with rounded edges in certain areas, while leaving other larger fragments that are still transparent, so as not to compromise vi-

sibility entirely) or plastic/glass sandwiches, made up of two sheets of glass joined by a sheet of plastic (polyvinyl butyral, PVB), designed to hold the shards of glass together in case of impact.

A recent application calls for the bonding of an outer sheet of glass with an inner sheet of polymer material. One advantage is the further reduction of hazards in an accident. The material employed is a film of highly transparent polyurethane which can be laminated directly onto the sheet of glass. The problem is to ensure long-term transparency, even under the effects of chemical and mechanical agents to which the surface might be exposed.

170

A heat-resistant micro-oven "window" that is opaque to microwaves - it is made up of two sheets of tempered glass containing a thin sheet of perforated anodyzed aluminum. A sheet of polymethylmethacrylate (PMMA) on the outer side completes the assembly (mfg. Philips).

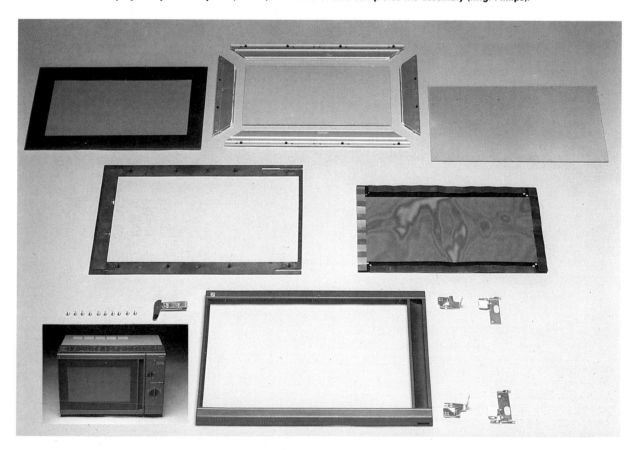

Another problem that has met with good solutions in the field of transparent sandwiches is that of loss of visibility due to condensation, most often encountered in automobiles and aircraft, but also in the windows of walk-in refrigerators (strictly speaking, this problem arises in building as well, but there the loss of transparency does not compromise essential performance).

The first solution, employed for the rear windows of automobiles, was to "print" on the glass an electric resistance that, by heating, increased the temperature, and thus prevented the formation of condensation. Then, on the windows of aircraft and walk-in refrigerators, and now in a few automobiles, a thin conductive film — which was also transparent — was applied. With respect to the earlier solution, the heating (hence, the defogging) was more uniform; furthermore, the elimination of the printed resistance improved visibility and made this system applicable also to the windshield.

A similar conductive film can be inserted between two sheets of safety glass as the sensor in an anti-burglary alarm system. If the glass is damaged, the interruption of continuity in the conductive film creates a variation in resistance, which in turn triggers the alarm.

In general, the field of security against theft and assault has provided an excellent arena for the development of increasingly refined sandwiches, capable of absorbing increasing quantities of energy. Bulletproof glass can be made by laminating layers of high-resistance glass to films of a plastic material (polyvinyl butyral, PVB), or by laminating glass and polycarbonate (PC) or polymethylmethacrylate, (PMMA), with a division of tasks in the absorption of mechanical and thermal energy required at the moment of impact.

Among the many possible additional performances that can be combined with transparency, let us cite just two others. One is the glare-proof quality of a surface, particularly important in the instrument systems for automobiles and airplanes, as well as in lenses for eyeglasses. The elimination of glare that could interfere with the reading of instruments and dials can be achieved either by covering them with a specially developed material (for instance, a glare-proof polymethylmethacrylate, PMMA, or a polycarbonate that has been appropriately filled with fiberglass) or else by applying a glare-proof film to another transparent material (in other words, by specially treating the surface of that material).

Another interesting case is provided by the window of a microwave oven — here visibility to the interior must be provided by a screen that serves as a barrier to the microwaves, as well as withstanding the heat generated in the oven. The solution is a sandwich in which two sheets of glass enclose a thin sheet of anodyzed aluminum that has been microscopically perforated (so as to provide a barrier to the microwaves); the system is completed by another transparent sheet of colored polymethylmethacrylate.

The liberation of the form

The introduction of plastics into the manufacture of transparent objects has provided a dimension that was almost unknown with glass — freedom of form. Even if the skill of a few master craftsmen succeeded in obtaining truly fantastic forms with glass, these were always exceptional cases — the glass that spread into everyday use over time, and that became a manufactured product, had simple forms, either flat or slightly curved.

Plastics, on the other hand, can be easily used to create complex forms, and, moreover, complex forms are often required in order to make up for the less-than-excellent mechanical qualities. For instance a flat sheet of plastic material can more successfully be manufactured with a complex honeycomb cross-section (which exploits the form in order to increase rigidity) than with a simple solid cross-section.

This aspect makes it possible, within the context of a general tenedency to integrate functions, to reorder radically the engineering criteria of transparent objects.

In the tradition of glass, an object that possessed transparent parts had to be conceived as an opaque load-bearing structure to which transparent zones could be added as needed, through complex assemblies. With plastics it is possible to conceive an entirely transparent object, and then decide whether it is wise to make certain parts of it opaque.

With plastic materials it is possible to manufacture transparent objects with complex shapes.
Top: The water tank of a steam iron (mfg. Rowenta).
Above: The framework of a polycarbonate (PC)
electric meter. (Doct. GEP)

Complex forms that integrate different functions are today common to products that derive from the ancient tradition of glass, as well as products that have never been thought of as transparent.

Among the former group, we find, for instance, three-dimensional enclosures (usually made of polymethylmethacrylate, PMMA, or polycarbonate, PC) which use a single transparent element to solve a problem that otherwise would have called for a masonry wall, a frame, and a flat sheet of glass. The same area includes the transparent elements in lamps that, if made with PMMA and PC, easily acquire complex shapes and integrate assembly functions. One of the most common cases is that of coverings for parking lights, turn indicators, and brake ligts on automobiles, made of polymethylmethacrylate, PMMA).

Greater difficulties are encountered in using plastic materials in manufacturing the lenses for headlights. The optical and mechanical performance required is quite elevated, because the material must at once provide certainty of dimensional integrity, must withstand the heat of the bulb, must possess surface hardness, and must withstand ultraviolet rays. This applicative field can be entered only by a few polymers; one of the solutions employed calls for lenses made of polymethylmethacrylate (PMMA) or polycarbonate (PC) protected with a special paint.

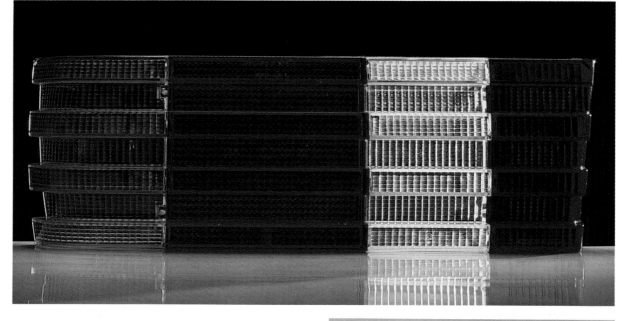

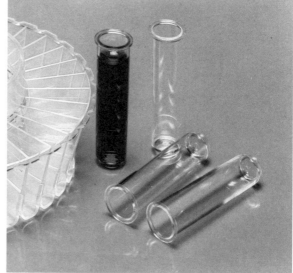

Transparency in objects with complex forms. Top: Two transparent roofs designed by Renzo Piano - modular skylights made of reinforced polyester resin and sheets of polymethylmethacrylate (PMMA) in the Olivetti factory in Scarmagno (1968). (Doct. Montedison-Vedril)
Below: Polycarbonate (PC) items in the shape of a pyramid give structural solidity to the roof designed for a travelling IBM exhibition Exihibit (1982). In both cases, the transparent components are manufactured by Caoduro.
Above: Rear lights of an automobile, made of polymethylmethacrylate (PMMA). The colors are produced in a single molding operation. (Doct. Montedison-Vedril)
Right: Test tube stand and test tubes made of polymethylmethacrylate (PMMA). (Doct. Montedison-Vedril)

Containers and visibility

Bottles, glasses, transparent vases, test tubes, and laboratory equipment are all objects in which traditionally glass has made it possible (at times due to a fuctional need, at times out of a cultural habit) to see the contents through the container.

Plastics have greatly enlarged the field of visible contents, and products (especially food products) have provided a privileged area of application. In this field, transparency has attained a high level of distribution, and has even become commonplace.

Paradoxically, the technical problems involved in transparent containers, and in particular in food containers, are far from simple. The performances required (compatibility with foods, impermeability, mechanical strength, moldability, and good surface quality) often call for sophisticated technology, and an ordinary packing film may be made up of many different layers, each serving a specialized purpose. An application that is of particular interest due to its complexity is that of bottles for carbonated beverages. While bottles for non-carbonated liquids rap-

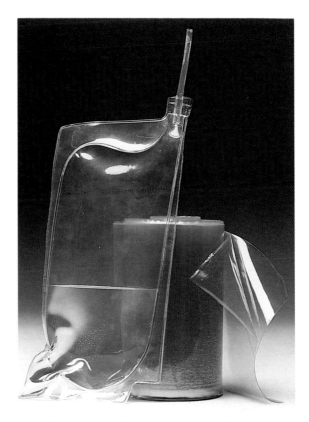

Single-use containers for medical applications. Top: Transfusion bag in a coextruded PVC-polypropylene film, with high-frequency sealing. (Doct. Montedison). Left: Transparent polystyrene basin for spectrophotmetry (mfg. Kartell). Bottom: Disposable containers and bottles made of cloruro di polyvinyl (PVC) and polyetylenephtalate (PET). (Doct. Montedison)

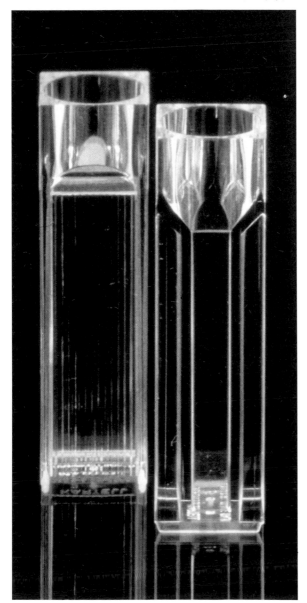

idly found an alternative to glass in PVC (which has the advantage of weighing less), for carbonated beverages the problem was complicated by the need to give the container greater structural strength in order to withstand pressure, to make a hermetic seal possible, and above all to ensure gas impermeability. The solution that is currently in use is "stretched" polyethylene terephthalate (PET) (the stretching renders it more resistant as well as more transparent).

The role played by plastics in the transformation of packaging, which in turn is linked to a transformation in the flow of merchandise, has been quite important. In a very brief period of time, the landscape of products on the market has gone from a situation typified by loose merchandise sorted into paper bags (or even wrapped in old newspaper) to the realm of products packaged in a great variety of containers. In this context, a growing number of products reach the consumer after a complex industrial and distributive circuit, placed anonymously on the shelves of a huge supermarket along with many other products of the same sort. Here, transparent packaging is probably the last trace of a direct contact with the product one is about to purchase.

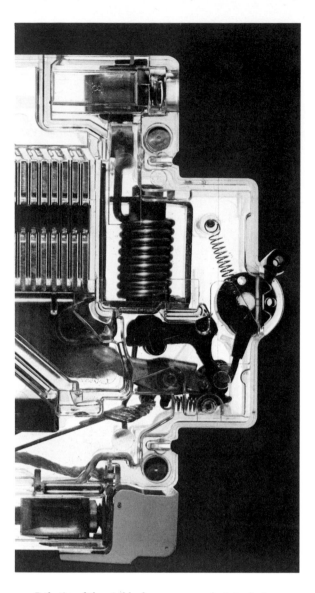

Esthetics of the visible, from supermarkets to design. Top left: A shell meat container in polyvinyl chloride (PVC). (Doct. ICI) Bottom left: A radio designed by Daniel Weil (1983) with a covering in the same material (PVC) (mfg. Parenthesis). Above: Electric switch (mfg. B Ticino). Below: A chest of drawers made of polymethylmethacrylate (PMMA), designed by Leonardo Fiori (1968) (mfg. Zanotta).

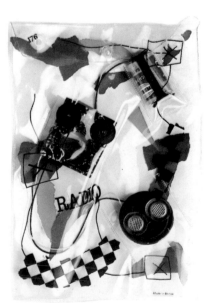

Contents as ornament

The plastic envelope in which ham is sold on the counters of a supermarket is a total negation of transparency as magic, as a way of playing with the senses and with light — the annulment of what remains in transparency of the ancient nobility of glass. Nonetheless, the pleasure of seeing inside, the esthetic value of the contents or internal mechanism has conserved a cultural space for itself. Many decades ago, the appearance of the first transparent plastics inaugurated a series of design experiments that had the glow of discovery. Albini's transparent radio truly meant to show the formal qualities of the inner components, just as the first transparent items of furniture of the Sixties and

Above: A glass radio designed by Franco Albini (1938). Left: A Swatch watch. Below: A television body made of polymethylmethacrylate (PMMA). (Doct. Altulor)

Seventies truly meant to dematerialize their presence into a play of reflections.

Today quite often the objects that play with the transparency of materials do so in a less whimsical fashion, and seem to desire, more than to reveal mysterious contents, to allude to their interior much in the same spirit as the plastic envelope in the supermarket — purses and transparent objects that include *Avant de Dormir*, for instance, are little more than transparent envelopes that contain various objects, no matter how surprising those objects may be. Even the radios and watches by Daniel Weil are little sacks in which electronic components are scattered as technology permits, but in the same way as they would be scattered in a shopping bag.

Alongside this area of creating the transparent, which finds more room for play on the

counters of retail stores than in references to the aura of ancient glass, there are certainly objects that display their operating mechanism in a "serious" fashion — a transparent Swatch watch is a good example. More than an amazement at the new, they seem to express nostalgia for the simplicity and visibility of machinery, for the ease with which one could see machines operate, now that everything has been compressed into surfaces and interfaces. With the Swatch, what we see is familiar. The watch is analogue, the gears are recognizable, everything is fairly sizable... If a digital watch were transparent, the effect would not be the same — inside there would be almost nothing to see, and certainly nothing that resembled a mechanism.

It is no accident that in Weil's watch the mechanism has become a set of small colored objects freely arranged. Displaying the components of the system in this case is less a way of understanding it than an ornamental choice.

175

Polymethylmethacrylate (PMMA) lenses. (Doct. Montedison-Vedril)

The objects of optics

The play of images created by the orderly diffraction of rays upon the surface separating two transparent objects was considered in the Middle Ages to be the work of the Devil. Magnifying glasses, which craftsmen had began to manufacture at the end of the thirteenth century, were symbols of deceit to the learned of the period, because they showed what did not exist. Nevertheless, the lenses spread, for the excellent reason that they were useful; indeed, the growth of knowledge and the spread of information which took place in the following centuries were at least in part a result of the lengthening "useful life" of a scholar or copyist, past the threshhold of farsightedness. The lens' first contribution to science was to allow farsighted scientists to read and write.

These first lenses were the product of empirical knowledge acquired in the craftsmen's workshops (in the fourteenth century, the driving force behind this area was Venice), but they were soon destined to merge with science as we now know it. Galileo's telescope is indeed the first modern optical instrument whose existence was based not only on practical experience, but came about through an integration with theoretical models and calculations. The lenses are located exactly where the calculations established in advance they should be. Since then, not only has optics remained instrument for scientific and technical advancement, but the "diabolic tool that shows what does not exist," has become, along with eyeglasses and contact lenses, one of the most common of man's prothesis.

Glass, refined and processed with micrometric precision, is still the chief actor on this stage, but here too plastics are competing, both in the manufacture of optical components with moderate performance but low prices and ease of production, and in designing materials and sophisticated methods capable of meeting the requirements of complex performance.

The strong point of glass lenses is their dimensional stability and surface hardness, which respectively ensure optical quality and long-term durability. Their weakness, on the other hand (aside from fragility and weight), lies in the complexity of processing, which requires long and costly mechanical grinding processes. Glass cannot be molded, because the resulting surface quality is poor, and internal tensions are created that produce optical distortions.

Plastics, instead (aside from their greater tenacity and lightness), boast the great advantage of being moldable. The processes (either casting or injection) needed to ensure high-quality products require precision molds and special thermal treatment, but they are nevertheless far cheaper and simpler than those required by glass. The disadvantages of plastic lenses are their lesser level of rigidity (they can be deformed by mechanical stress); their lower level of surface hardness (they scratch easily), and the variability of their optical and dimensional characteristics with variations in temperature.

These limits, for that matter, are not equal for all plastics. While the cheaper polystyrene (PS) is more sensitive, polymethylmethacrylate (PMMA) causes fewer problems, and CR 39 has almost the same qualities as glass while being tougher and lighter. Therefore, CR 39 is competing with glass in the manufacture of eyeglasses, and is unique when specially impact-resistant glasses are needed.

From this set of possibilities, the variety of optical objects that surround us emerged. Apart from the scientific uses, let us indicate just two emblematic cases: the lens of a camera (even the simplest pocket version), which is a precision instrument produced by the millions; and the contact lens, which has become so sophisticated an extension of the body that in some sense it can be compared to the bionic objects imagined in science fiction.

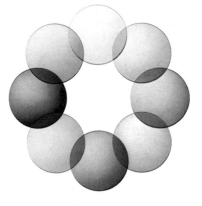

Above: maps for the definition of gradual bifocal lenses; the transition from the area for nearby objects to that for long-distance vision occurs in a continuous fashion, reducing distortions to a minimum (mfg. Solma). Below: Protective and colored sunproof lenses (mfg. Zeiss).

Fresnel lenses made of CR 39 - the enlargement is produced by a thin sheet of plastic material. (Doct. Ottica Matuella)

The first contact lenses were basically similar to the lenses of eyeglasses, but were smaller and shaped so as to adhere to the eye (they were generally manufactured with special formulations of PMMA). They were, however, oxygen impermeable, and so did not allow the eye to carry out its epithelial respiration. They further blocked the lubrication via lachrymal secretion. Both problems were solved by adopting gas-permeable materials that were extremely water-wettable (in conditions of use, they contain from 30 to 85 percent water). These lenses, which also have the property of softness, are manufactured with special formulations based on hydroxyethylmethacrylate (HEMA). Recently proposals have been ventured for contact lenses made of other gas-permeable materials, such as silicone-based materials.

Also in the field of lenses, we should note an application of great practical usefulness, rich in evocative qualities – lenses made of Fresnel. Their geometry makes it possible to manufacture flat lenses that traditionally would have required considerable thickness. Hence it is possible to produce large, light, thin lenses.

The basic idea is to segment the curved surface of a normal lens, and to transfer each segment onto the same plane. The result is a sawtooth surface, in which one side of each tooth exactly reproduces a section of the original curve. The greater the number of segments, the smaller each segment need be, and the thinner the lens.

The manufacturing obstacle is the precision required in producing this complex shape. If one uses glass, the problem arises separately for each lens; with plastic the problem arises only once – in the production of the mold from which all the lenses take their shape.

In their more technical uses, Fresnel lenses allow one to focus a beam of light produced by a lamp or the converging rays of sunlight onto the "boiler" of a solar energy plant. The number of non-technical uses is great: fish-eye lenses to put on windows, thus increasing the angle of visibility, pocket magnifying glasses, lenses to put on tv screens.

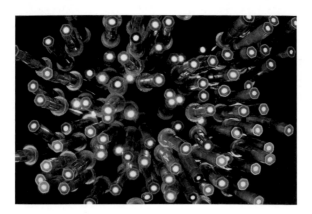

Fiber optics and light guides

A "monomode" fiber optic, with a core a few microns across and a laser beam as the source of the input signal, can transmit up to two thousand phone calls at once. A numerical laser disk (on which the information is stored in digital form) can contain 2,500 typewritten pages, or 500,000 if the text is specially treated. The transparency of glass, of polymethylmethacrylate (PMMA), and polycarbonate (PC) are the media for an information processing system that is so powerful – in terms of size and speed of access – that the very terms information storage and transmission are changing their meaning.

This field of creating the transparent, where light is the sole medium of signals and where the eye that looks through a transparent substance is the eye of a machine, exceeds the scope of this volume. Nevertheless, it is an important reference point just because the fallout of optical electronics research and manufacturing, above all in the area of communications fiber optics, will certainly increase the availability of these materials for other uses – first of all as light guides, i.e., as channels through which light can be transmitted for the traditional purpose of illumination, or else carrying an image which can be viewed directly.

The operating principle of fiber optics and light guides is that of total reflection (see 3.4.1): the rays that are projected into a fiber (or a transparent component, such as a bar or slab) can leave that fiber only when it encounters a surface that forms an angle with its perpendicular that falls below a certain value, which depends on the index of refraction of the optical medium in which the ray is travelling and on that of the external optical medium. If the ray encounters the surfaces of the fiber optic or light guide at angles such that it is always totally reflected, it moves forward in a zigzag from one surface to the other, and follows the path of the channel in which it is imprisoned, exiting only at the end of the channel (at the far extremity of the fiber, at the edges of the slab or bar, or at surface features such as scratches or cuts), that is, when it meets a portion of the surface arranged so that the critical angle is not exceeded.

In theory, if the material were absolutely transparent, there would be no limit to the possible length of the channel. In practice, each reflection causes a certain loss (depending on the surfaces) and every meter travelled in the material implies a certain absorption (depending on the material). The difference between a light guide produced by molding a transparent material into the right shape and a sophisticated fiber optic for long-distance communications lies in the absorption of material and in the loss of intensity of the light for every meter travelled.

Extremely low-absorption fiber optics are made of an especially transparent glass, with a sheath of plastic material (on the outside, there is a complex layering of other materials that ensure protection and mechanical strength). With fibers of this sort for communications, a relay is needed every 7-10 kilometers. Plastic fiber optics, instead, have greater absorption levels and are used for communications networks over short or medium distances (from several hundred meters to a kilometer) or for the production of light guides (over distances ranging from under a meter to a dozen meters or so). They are made of polymethylmethacrylate (PMMA), with an outer sheath that is also made of plastic (polyethylene, PE) with a lower index of refraction. As light guides they are available in multifiber cables (formed by several fibers with diameters of a fraction of a millimeter each), uniaxial cables (composed of a single fiber whose diameter can reach three millimeters), and tapes (in which many thin parallel fibers are held together).

On the other hand, a light guide can also take on the form of an appropriately shaped component, without a sheath (generally, in this case the material is also PMMA), capable of transferring the light from a lamp set at one edge, over brief distances (from a meter to several meters) to the other edges or else to cuts made on the surface. The cut deviates the light rays, causing them to exit from the material on the opposite side from the cut, which seems to light up. Thus, sign panels can be made with luminous writing or figures.

Light guides bring to the field of lighting a new possibility: the light source can be separated from the point of lighting. On this basis, it is possible to rethink both the problem of natural lighting in closed ambients and – above all – the lighting of areas where it is impossible or dangerous to bring a lightbulb.

The possibility of channeling sunlight have been tested successfully in technical terms, but there are still economic problems, tied to the cost of the fiber optics and that of the outdoor solar receptors. If greater production of these components for telecommunications should allow a reduction in cost, they could be very useful for lighting interiors with sunlight, superior to artificial light because of its chromatic yield and variability. This would also provide a sort of link with the outdoors.

The use of light guides is already common, however, where it is dictated by safety considerations (ambients where there is an elevated risk of explosions), or where the presence of light must not be accompanied by heat (lighting of preparations for viewing under a microscope). The widest use, however, occurs in the illumination of parts of objects where space is at a premium or maintenance must be kept as simple as possible. The spread of instruments (and the need to light them) on one hand, and the increase in the density of objects on the other, make it increasingly difficult to allocate a lightbulb for each signal or button that must be lit. It becomes convenient to

179

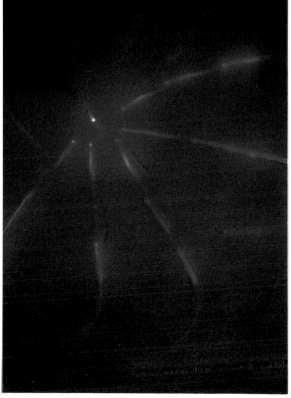

Luminous decoration = public uses of fiber optics.
Top: *Motel bed*, (1980). Left: Wallpaper with
luminous decorations (1980) designed by Denis Santachiara.
Above: raincoat with rainstorm effect obtained
through fiber optics, *Avant de dormir* project.

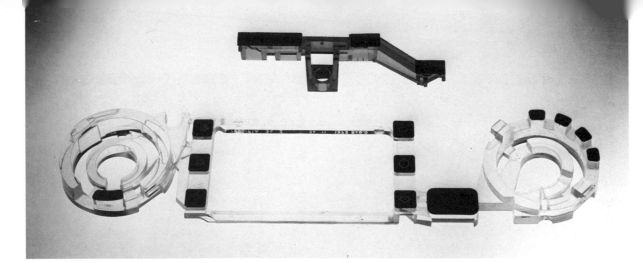

consolidate the light source and create a series of light guides that, following a more or less tortuous path, lead to the points that need light. Thus, bulk is reduced and maintenance is simplified to the replacement of a single lightbulb, set in an easily accessible location.

Another possible use of light guides is in creating panels with luminous points that can be used to form written words or images, which can vary as the light source varies.

Many designers have also begun to experiment with the expressive possibilities of this technology, creating a vast range of clothing, bedspread, upholstery, and similar products in which the fiber optics are used as decorative motifs. In this case, alongside a proper use of the fibers (that transport light to one point), another improper use has developed (a certain length of the fibers are freed from their sheath, and thus appear as luminous lines).

In a few cases, lastly, light guides become a medium for information, although in a simpler and more direct fashion than the digital signals carried by fiber optics for telecommunications.

For instance, a light guide can easily carry an on-off or open-shut type of signal, detected by a sensor or directly by the operator. It is therefore quite simple to use light guides as a speed gauge or item counter — every revolution or item that passes causes the interruption of a light beam, information which a fiber optic gathers and transmits to a sensor. Similarly, other systems have been developed that make it possible to detect flaws in a conveyor belt, or to monitor the level of liquid in a tank.

Fiber optics as bearers of information, lastly, are used in systems for direct transmission of images. It is sufficient to create a bundle of coherent fibers — that is, the position of the fibers at one end of the bundle must be the same as that at the other end. If this condition is met, the bundle works as a flexible optical instrument, which can be as long as several meters, making it possible to see the interior of inaccessible areas. This principle has been used to create endoscopes for industrial and medical use. These endoscopes are made up of a bundle of coherent fibers with a very small diameter (the number of fibers is quite high because the greater the number of fibers the better the definition of the image), completed with an eyepiece, a lens, and an auxiliary bundle of incoherent fibers to supply light to the ambient under examination.

Lighting with light guides is spreading to different fields of application. Top: Illumination of an automobile dashboard with light guides made of polymethylmethacrylate (PMMA). (Doct. Montedison-Vedril). Above: The controls of the television remote control box are illuminated by the channeling light from their sides (mfg. Telefunken). Facing page, top: Illumination on the edges as a decorative effect in *Fast Design* eyeglasses, made of modified polymethylmethacrylate (PMMA) with fluorescent fillers, designed by Alessandro Mendini and Jeremy King (1985) for Alchimia.

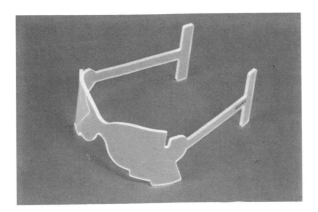

Light from the edges

Certain special substances absorb direct and diffuse light, and transform it into a light flow that is emitted in all directions, with an effect that is known as fluorescence. If this property is associated to that of light channeling, one can then develop components whose edges and cuts are far brighter than the surrounding environment.

Their surface, in fact, operates as a light receptor – the radiation incident upon it penetrates into the transparent material and part of that radiation encounters coloring molecules that perform a fluorescent action. While a normal coloring would absorb the light energy and turn it into heat, this one has the property of emitting the energy again after a very brief time (10^{-9} seconds) in the form of light at a shorter wavelength.

At this point the light guide effect comes into play – while part of the radiation that is re-emitted strikes the surface at angles such that it can exit, most of it remains trapped and channeled to the edges of the object or the cuts in its surface. There (given that their surface is smaller than the receptor surface) a concentrated light flow emerges that makes them seem powerfully lit.

A similar effect is obtained if other treatments are applied to the surface. Instead of cuts, printing in ink will modify the surface quality and interrupt the total reflection, causing the emission of the light at the non-printed parts. The greater the ratio between absorbing surfacing and emitting surface, the more evident the phenomenon.

This type of receptor has thus far found applications in the production of fixed displays with illuminated letters, numbers, and shapes, or variable information displays in which the receptor system is linked to a liquid-crystal display to increase its visibility. Alongside this technical use, a family of applications has developed in which these properties are used to create special lighting effects on the edges or other areas of objects.

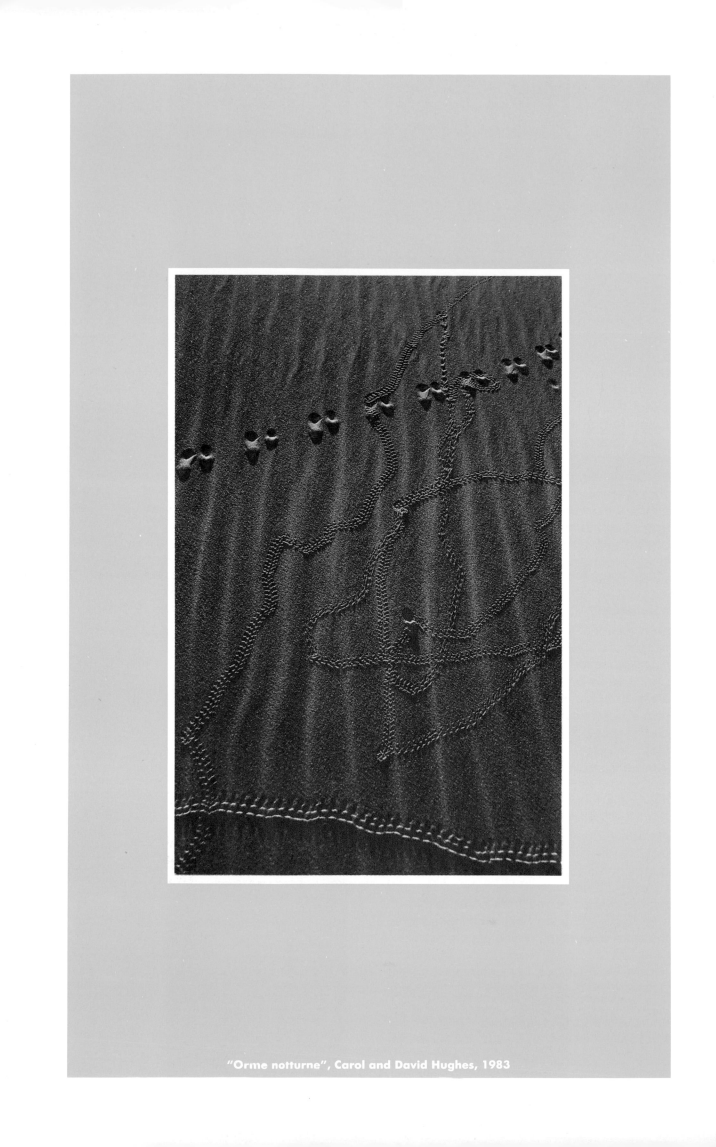

"Orme notturne", Carol and David Hughes, 1983

Providing surface qualities

Two-dimensional matter

There is a simple way of conceiving the surface of an object: it is the location of the points where an object's material ends and the surrounding ambient begins. This definition, however, is acceptable only in certain cases (for instance, a stone, or else a plastic object that emerges "finished" from a mold); furthermore, even in these cases the geometrical definition hides a more complex physical state. The "locale of points" is in reality a final layer of atoms and molecules called upon to encounter operating conditions that are quite different from the conditions of the inner layers. This front-line matter must withstand all sorts of stresses and mechanical, physical, chemical, and biological agents; what is more, upon this last layer is concentrated much of what is important in the object for an observer/user: sensory qualities (optical, thermal, tactile), symbolic and cultural values...

If we reverse our point of view, then we may say that, if the surface of an object is truly the last layer of a material that continues inward with the same properties, all in all we are witnessing a great waste. It is no accident that nature (which tends toward thrift) has equipped the more complex organisms wih a skin, that is to say, an organ specialized in the role of interface between the outside and the inside. In reality, most manufactured products also undergo a form of surface treatment that alters the last layer of material in order to help it withstand greater difficulties and provide superior performance.

It would therefore be well to develop another, more comprehensive definition, beginning with a rethinking of the role of a surface that emphasizes its character of autonomy from the rest of the object as well as the dynamic qualities that are concentrated in the surface. The idea of a mute and static border to matter is thus replaced by an idea of the surface as an interface between two ambients, with a role involving an exchange of energy and information between the substances put into contact. The surface as osmotic membrane capable of promoting or inhibiting such an exchange thus becomes itself a component of the object (a component that we may consider to be two-dimensional), capable of standing between the inside and outide of the object itself, or to provide a range of performances of its own.

In these terms, to consider the surface as a mere border of the object's material becomes only one of the many approaches possible. The range of performances which the surface system can provide is in fact quite broad and grows continuously. It extends from the most traditional and obvious performances (providing protection and esthetic or sensory qualities to the underlying materials) to performances that transform it into a medium for static communications (printed surface) or dynamic communications (surface made sensitive through the use of two-dimensional components for information input or output).

Depending on the performance required, the engineering and manufacturing strategy may shift. If it is necessary to maintain coherence between the underlying material and the surface quality, the material must be selected so as to allow the surface treatment desired or, contrariwise, the surface quality will be limited by the way the material is processed. This is the simplest path, and has found remarkable opportunities for development with plastic materials — with these materials the coherence between the material *qua* structure and the surface quality can be produced in a vast range of solutions.

The other line, diametrically opposed to the first, is that of a more or less accentuated incoherence between the underlying material and the surface quality. In this case, the surface becomes a full-fledged component, and the adjective "two-dimensional" applies only approximately. In truth, the surface *qua* component is truly endowed with a third, albeit limited dimension. Paints, enamels, lacquers all constitute the ancient tradition of this strategy, which makes it possible to protect perishable materials and endow poor materials with esthetic refinement.

This traditional strategy has once again become relevant the quest for an apparent variety in mass-produced products, the integration in the surface of growing range of sensory (high-touch, luminescence) and informative (from printed advertising and displays to sensitive films) performances. The role of the qualities and performances of the skin of objects is increasing.

The quality of the surface as a direct expression of the quality of the material - *Kartell chair 4875* by Carlo Bartoni, made of polypropylene (PP).

The border of material

Stone, glass, ceramics, stainless steel, and a few other metals and metal alloys can all face the ambient in which they are used without requiring any particular surface modifications, because of their intrinsic qualities. They are inert with respect to chemical, physical, and biological agents, they are hard enough to withstand the mechanical actions linked to use, they possess a surface workability that allows them to respond to culturally ingrained qualitative needs. These materials and their respective applications have long constituted a restricted group, flanked by other materials and situations whose surface required appropriate treatment, protection, improvement.

Then, with the arrival of plastics, the set of materials that emerge finished from processing has expanded, indeed, it has become the dominant tribe. Here, too, the winning cards of plastics were their workability and versatility, generally accompanied by the quality of being inert to aggressive agents. Furthermore, plastics in general can be colored in mass (the surface color, in other words, derives directly from the coloring applied to all the material); and can also "copy" the mold with great precision. Every surface quality that can be produced once and for all on the mold will be reproduced as often as there are numbers of items molded, with the greatest of ease.

This general sketch of the superfamily of plastics should, nevertheless, be examined specifically case by case. Each family may differ, at times radically; each polymer and each formulation has precise limitations of use (many plastics will not withstand ultraviolet rays; some are inert to one set of chemical agents, others to another set; all have continuous operating temperatures that cannot be exceeded); each possesses its own surface hardness, which is generally not very high (this sets operating limits that imply the possibility of scratching and abrasion).

The very esthetic quality of the surface is different for each, and depends both on the material and on the mold. As far as the material is concerned, here different aspects interact: the first is the propensity of the material itself to form free monomers (i.e., monomers that are not linked into long polymer chains). These free monomers flow to the surface and confer a waxy, or at any rate a non-shiny appearance to it (this occurs with the polyolefins, PE and PP). Another aspect is the capacity to "copy" the mold with great precision, a property that is largely linked to the plastic's fluidity during processing, but to other factors as well (for instance, polycarbonate, PC, is not very fluid but still replicates the mold quite well). A third aspect is the possibility that whatever reinforcements are in use (mica lamellas, glass fibers or spheres) may emerge on the surface. This is more likely to happen with greater size of the reinforcing substances and greater shrinkage of material at the end of the manufacturing process (as the material cools, it shrinks, pushing reinforcements toward the surface).

It is therefore possible to establish a hierarchy of plastic materials according to their capacity to provide esthetically pleasing surfaces, which we conventionally take to mean shiny surfaces. At the top of the ranking among the most widely used materials come polymethylmethacrylate (PMMA), polybutylene terephthalate (PBT), polycarbonate (PC), acrylonitrilebutadiene-styrene (ABS), polyamide (PA). Lower down come the polyolefins (PE, PP), plastified polyvinyl chloride (PVC), and polyurethanes (PU).

On the other hand, as we have mentioned, the final surface quality also depends on the mold. A shinier surface is obtained with chrome-plated molds that have been mirror-polished, used when shininess is considered a primary objective (furniture, appliances); the material most often used in these cases is ABS. A lower level of shininess, but acceptable in most applications, can be obtained with molds whose surface has been obtained through mechanical processes of smoothing and lapping.

Nevertheless, it should be pointed out that the esthetic criterion of surface shininess is open to question, and derives from a complex cultural heritage based on metals, enamels, and lacquers, that certainly predates the history of plastics. Over time, therefore, another surface image has developed which better fits with manufacturing necessities – that of the opaque or variously textured surface. In reality, this solution too derives from the imitative nature of plastics and from the tendency to propose surfaces that recall something familiar (the textures may recall leathers or textiles), but it also meets the practical requirement of developing a surface that is less sensitive to flaws and mechanical agents. The texture, in fact, which can be easily obtained with photoengraving treatments of the mold, makes less visible the minor imperfections that can be produced during molding, as well as the scratches that use inevitably produces.

Aside from the surface qualities that we have thus far considered, and which we could call geometric, there is also the question of color. Aside from the mass coloring of plastics, which we mentioned earlier, here too there are many possibilities.

Intrinsically transparent or milky polymers can obviously accept any coloring, and all that is necessary is to mix a pigment to the base material. It is however necessary to keep in mind that some polymers are sensitive to ultraviolet rays, and when exposed to them, tend to change color. This can be prevented by introducing, in the mass, an anti-UV agent along with the pigment, or else by applying a surface layer of protective material. Other polymers, instead, are intrinsically colored (polyurethane, for example, tends to be yellow) and therefore allow only colors that are compatible with the base color. Furthermore, quite often materials are modified or filled and therefore the coloring is limited by the color of the material itself. The range is from calcium carbonate (since it is white it sets no limitations on the range of colors that can be used) to talc (which is grey, and therefore sets no significant limits on the colors used but causes a loss in brightness) and carbon black (which obviously can be used only with a few dark tones).

Mass coloring may therefore be considered as a modification of the qualities of a material throughout its depth in order to bring a certain quality to its surface; a similar approach is traditionally employed in order to confer to the surface esthetic qualities that are more complex than mere coloring.

The tradition of plastics is rich in materials that are imitative (from alabaster to horn) and non-imitative (free or geometric patterns), the surface image of which is created by the haphazard or careful mixture of variously pigmented materials, so that it is possible to obtain "in-depth" designs in an infinite range of solutions. In particular, we can mention the case of block cellulose acetate (Rhodoid is its most common commercial name) and high-thickness layered laminates, whose edges show the colors of the various layers. Another case is that of the substitution of normal pigments with "special-effect" pigments — pearlescent, iridescent, fluorescent. In each of these cases, different surfaces can be obtained, endowed with special degrees of brilliance, luster, and depth.

Lastly, by a similar technological process, we should mention the possiblity of conferring special aromas to materials. In this case, granules of perfume concentrate are added to the mass of base polymer, and free their aroma over time. The concentrate migrates from the inside toward the surface, and thence toward the ambient, in the quantities and for the time period foreseen during the engineering phase. Often this solution is employed to neutralize unpleasant odors of the material itself, for uses where bad odors can be generated (garbage bags), or — in a positive sense — to give an olfactory quality to a product (from toys to watches).

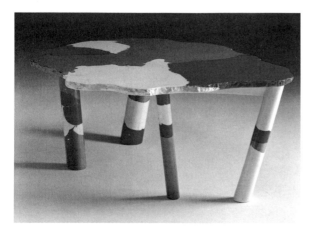

Sansone table by Gaetano Pesce (mfg. Cassina, 1980). The arrangement of surface colors is the fortuitous result of the flow of differently pigmented materials within the mold.

Kyoto table by Shiro Kuramata, made of a mix of cement and glass. The quality of the surface is provided by the combination of structural materials adopted (mfg. Memphis, 1983).

Modified borders

There are also intermediate approaches between, on the one hand, considering the surface as a simple border of the material and, on the other, applying a completely different material. The most evident case is that of integral foams. These are materials that, though they possess uniform chemical properties throughout the component, display radical physical differences between the surface and the interior. The surface is a compact skin, variously textured, flexible, or stiff; the interior is a foam that can also be rigid or flexible, varying in density as required.

This is certainly one of the best ways of exploiting the versatility of plastic materials. With a single molding operation, by acting on the thermal cycle, pressure, the formulation of the foaming agent, it is possible to obtain light components that are structural or flexible, and at the same time a finished surface.

This is a result that can be obtained with various materials: polypropylene (PP), polystyrene (PS), polyphenylene oxide (PPO). The first to be used, however, and still the most common is polyurethane (PU). When superior surface quality is needed, a similar product can be obtained with a process of double injection molding in the same mold: a compact material for the surface and a foam for the interior.

Other materials employ "intermediate" solutions of a similar nature. For instance, there is a process that uses an electrochemical action to oxidize the surface layer. This technique, which is used for protective and esthetic reasons, is especially applied to aluminum (anodyzed aluminum), but also to other metals (magnesium and zinc alloys, steel). It is performed by placing the item to be treated in a special electrolytic solution, which then acts as an anode.

Metals can also be treated by diffusion: in appropriate heat conditions, the surface layer of the metal is impregnated by another material (also metallic) set in contact with it. Thus a solid solution is created that greatly increases the mechanical qualities of the surface treated.

Added surfaces

The processes that we have mentioned up to now share the common feature of forming a surface layer with new chemical and physical characteristics, but created from the same material as the substrate. A surface may be made of another material, however – as it were, an added skin.

A two-dimensional component capable of covering an object may be produced by following different paths. The traditional approach is to create a film of organic or inorganic material, causing it to shape itself directly upon the material that is to be covered: varnishes, paints, enamels, and metallization were long ago developed along this path.

A second path (which we shall examine later) calls for both the interior structural part of the object and its future skin to reach a stage of partial completion and then to be assembled. This is true of traditional cloth coverings, of wood veneering, of plastic laminates, of thermoformed plastic films, or two-dimensional systems capable of endowing an object with complex performances.

Even if some of these technical strategies sink their roots in the distant past, all today form

part of the landscape of manufacturing composite materials. This still means combining different materials in order to attain synergy, an elevation of the respective performances.

Here too a central technical problem that is often underestimated is that of the interface between materials, a problem of reciprocal relations more than a question of the intrinsic properties of each material – matters such as coherence in elastic or thermal deformability, surface-tension ratio (wettability of the medium by a paint product), chemical compatibility (especially for solvents).

Paints, whether liquid or in powder, when applied to a surface in a thin layer, are capable of forming a solid, adhesive, continuous film. Varnishes form a transparent film, paints are pigmented and form a film with a color that is independent of the medium. If they form an especially hard and smooth surface, they are called enamel paints.

The intrinsic qualities of a paint product, and hence its applications, depend on its principal components. The film-generating resin, the pigments, and the fillers, solvents, and additives.

The film-generating resin determines the characteristics of the painting process and the final functional performances. In this field we have progressed from desiccatory oils and natural resins (now used only in very special cases) to synthetic resins, which have made it possible to generate a vast range of alternatives both in terms of processing cycles and in terms of performances obtained – alkyd resins, acrylic resins, epoxy resins, polyurethane resins, polyester resins, nitrocellulose resins, phenolic resins, and vinyl resins. Research in this field aims chiefly at increasing the productivity of painting cycles (reducing the number of phases necessary, the need for heat applica-

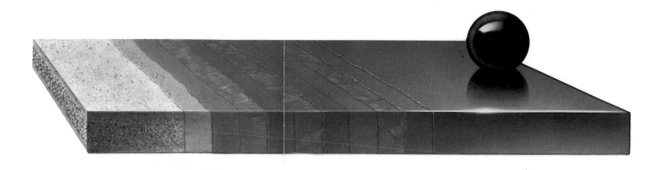

tions, etc.), at obtaining formulations appropriate to specific media and fields of application, and the production of new special effects.

In the field of pigments, as well, there has been a progression from a limited number of natural (organic and inorganic) pigments that produced a definite and restricted range of colors to a spread of synthetic pigments that, over the past century have not only widened but modified the chromatic landscape of the artificial ambient (see 3.5.2).

The fillers are instead white or light pigments that are used as bulk to reduce the cost of paint or to endow it with special qualities, such as making it opaque or more adherent.

Lastly, the additives are substances made necessary by technical aspects of the painting process (preparation, storage of the product) or to provide certain performances (anti-mold agents, water-repellent agents, agents that absorb ultraviolet rays). In certain cases, the additives can endow the product (and thus the surface treated) with qualities that are more immediately perceptible. The grains of sand included in slip-proof paints are additives, as are the microscopic glass spheres that make a surface retroreflective.

Operating on this set of factors, many possibilities are posed — the optical quality of a surface that runs the gamut from opaque to shiny, the various chromatic tones and saturations, the special effects.

The metallized effect is obtained by including flakes of aluminum in the paint. Depending on the arrangement that they take on with respect to the surface, they give the impression of polished or hammered metal, or else create iridescence.

A 3-D effect is obtained with special binders and additives. The cracking that is created is used to produce textures and depressions.

Velvet finishes can be obtained both by working with the normal components of the paint product or else

The possibility of painting all sorts of materials makes the internal structure of the object less transparent. This cross-section shows a flexible foam for use in the automobile industry, protected with a velvety paint. (Doct. Tecnomax)

by a special process called "flocking," which consists in blowing short textile fibers against a surface of fresh paint. By appropriate use of an electric field, it is possible to produce an overall orientation of the fibers (perpendicular to the surface), thus obtaining the effect of true velvet.

Fluorescent and phosphorescent effects can be obtained by exploiting the properties of certain substances that absorb visible or invisible radiations. Instead of transforming them into heat energy, as normal pigments do, they re-emit them in the form of luminous radiation on special wavelength bands in the range of visible light. The phenomenon of fluorescence implies an almost instantaneous re-emission, while phosphorescence implies that the re-

emission continues for a certain time period (ranging from a few minutes to a few days) even after the incident radiation has stopped.

Chromatic variations based on temperature variations can be obtained, both reversibly and irreversibly. The former type is based on special pigments (such as cobalt salts) that change color once or more than once when the temperature rises. They are generally used in technical fields to visually indicate abnormally high temperatures in mechanical components or in heat plants. The latter type of change is based on the optical behavior of heat-sensitive liquid

In the field of protective treatments for technical uses, new processes make it possible to add more sophisticated new performances, such as in this detail protected by self-lubricating zinc-coating. (Doct. Dacral)

crystals. In a special form (cholesteric phase) the incident light radiation is reflected with different colors as the temperature changes. Considerable color changes can be obtained even over intervals of under 1 °C.

Another way of providing surface qualities is to deposit directly on the surface a layer of another material with protective or esthetic properties. This is the path of metallizing, which is the foundation of the culture of shininess and chrome-plating, of the ancient tradition of ceramic enamels, and the economical plasticizing of so many objects in everyday use.

The most widely used and most traditional system for obtaining a metal plating is electrodeposition — the material must be conductive (or, as with plastics, it must be made conductive with the application of a conductive varnish); the component acts as the cathode of an electrolytic cell in which the metal that is to serve as plating (chrome, but also nickel, copper, tin, and many other metals) constitutes the anode. Thus, a uniform and resistant metal layer is formed.

Another system is direct immersion of the piece into a bath of molten metal (zinc, lead, tin, aluminum), which obviously can be used only to plate the surfaces of metals with high melting points.

A third system consists of spraying molten metal against the surface to be treated. A particularly interesting variant is known as plasma spraying. A high-temperature, high-speed gas melts particles of metal, projecting them against the surface of the piece.

Lastly, there is a group of processes that are characterized by the production of extremely thin metallized films, that can be applied to any medium, through the deposition of metal ions or vapors in a vacuum chamber. Processes of this type are used to obtain, among other things, the metallization of reflective glass, the parabolic mirrors of headlights, magnetic tapes, and laser discs.

Ceramic, vitreous, or porcelain coatings are obtained by melting the constituent elements of the plating material directly on the surface to be covered. Thus, enameled surfaces of particular hardness and brightness can be created. More recently, a system for ceramic coating has been introduced, based on plasma spraying. It can be used with metals but also with glass and certain plastics. It allows the production of surfaces that can withstand a wide range of temperatures.

Plasticizing, too, can be done in various ways, ranging from direct immersion of the component in a bath of thermoplastic material maintain in its molten statement by means of on emulsion, to the "fluidized bed" processes, in which the component is heated and inserted in a chamber where powders of plastic material are in suspension. These powders enter into contact with the hot surface of the object and melt, creating a continuous film covering. The contact can be facilitated by creating an electrostatic charge of opposite poles for the powder and the surface.

188

The surface of a gear, hardened by vacuum depositing. (Doct. Leybold-Heraeus)

Printed surfaces

Demand for an imposing mass of containers, cans, bottles, and boxes of every shape and size, each of which must stand out in the circuit of merchandise with a name, a trademark, an image, has stimulated the technology of printing – traditionally applied to flat surfaces – to adapt itself to complex surfaces.

One approach is to print the surfaces while they are flat, and then create a three-dimensional container. With this method, however, only certain shapes can be obtained and only certain materials can be used. The next step therefore was to move on to printing (in general, silk screening) on the preformed object, but this application has fairly narrow limits – the surface being printed must be very regular.

The best technique, which combines ease of printing with greater formal freedom of the surface, consists in printing an image on a flat medium, and then transferring it onto the final, formed medium. The central operation is the transfer, which can be performed, for example, by using a flexible pad which gathers the ink from the flat surface on which it has been printed and then transfers it to the surface to be printed. Due to its flexibility, the pad can fit even relatively complex surfaces.

Another way of transferring the image, known as hot stamping, is based on the principle of the decal. A flexible film medium, upon which the image to be printed has been reproduced in ink, is passed before the surface which is to be decorated, and an appropriately shaped hot pad presses the image against the surface, transferring the image to it.

This system, used in many different variants depending on the type and shape of the medium, is extremely fast and "clean," and allows – thanks to recent developments – to produce not only legends and decorations on consumer goods, but even to provide more complex finishes that possess greater levels of performance. For instance, it is possible to mark letters and numerals on the keys of office machinery. It is even possible to mark an entire assembled keyboard, selecting the alphabet according to the country of destination. Furthermore, normal ink is replaced with a material that – due to pressure and heat – tends to sublimate (i.e., passes into the gaseous state) and spread into the interior of the polymer material, then solidify again. Thus the surface is marked in depth, and stands up to intense and prolonged use.

Another interesting development of hot stamping allows the use of conductive inks and magnetizable inks. With conductive inks, it is possible to create screening against electromagnetic interference for electronic equipment. Magnetizable inks can be used to create magnetic bands upon which codes and other information can be recorded (such as in credit cards with magnetic codes).

All of the methods mentioned have certain limits with respect to the shape of the objects to be printed – it is not possible to exceed certain curves, beyond which the film medium cannot cling. Nevertheless, there is a system (commercially known as Cubic Printing) which widens the field of application of transfer printing technology to entire surfaces with complex and even rough shapes. The pattern to be reproduced is printed by rotogravure on a water-soluble film which, after special treatments, is set in a tank of water. The film dissolves and the ink remains on the surface. At this point, the object to be decorated is dipped in the water, and the pattern adheres to its surface, following its shape with great precision. Each object, due to the nature of the system, bears a pattern that is slightly different from all the others in the series.

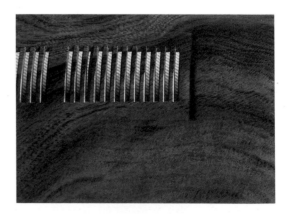

At the boundaries
of perfect simulation of natural
materials.
Above: The three-dimensional "fake-wood" decoration
of a dashboard, done through "cubic printing."

Printed circuits

In a certain sense, the manufacture of all electronic hardware can be seen as the conferment of certain qualities to surfaces. The spread of miniaturization leads one to construct any system with printed circuit boards, PCBs. Upon them, the circuit is created by printing and with the use of small components that, in the most advanced forms of manufacture, are first glued and then welded to the circuit itself surface mounting). The problems that one encounters are therefore those typical of surface treatments.

The printed circuit can be viewed as a special sort of surface treatment. This becomes even more evident, now that it is possible to print circuits on the surface of three-dimensional components, injection molded in thermoplastic materials.
Above: Supports with complex forms for integrated circuits.
Left: The body of a telephone receiver that integrates the routes of the electronic circuit.
(Doct. Seriglif-Union Carbide)

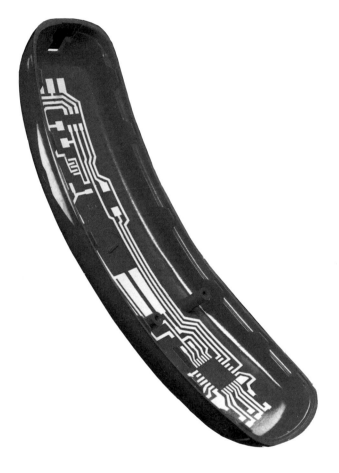

This innovation is a product of the meeting of advances in thermoplastic materials with advances in transfer printing technology. In the latter field, it has become possible to print circuits with a highly conductive ink on special paper, and then transfer it to the final medium simply by laminating. The final medium must, nevertheless, have exceptional qualities of heat and chemical resistance. Great success has been encountered with a polymer blend based on polyarylsulfone. It is easy to see that the advantages of these combined innovations will be considerable. Thermoplastic materials (unlike thermoseting resins, which are generally phenol and epoxy resins, used traditional in making the boards), thanks to their great formability, make it possible to imagine boards in which the connection functions are integrated with other elements of the system. Hence, one can create far more compact systems. One can even imagine going beyond the narrow field of electronic components to create structural elements or frames that specialize part of their surface so as to integrate a connection or distribution network for signals and power.
For that matter, we can point out that the technology of printed circuits began to filter outside of the field of electronics even before this innovation became available. To cite just one example, let us think of the printed resistance on defogging windows.

Applied coverings

Cloth for upholstery, wall paper, thin layers of wood for veneered furniture — these are the historical solutions of the strategy that begins with an existing material, and forms it so that it can become the skin of an object, supplying that object with its own qualities.
Here too, the possibilities have multiplied until great functional complexity can be obtained. In the field of ennobling wood, veneers have been joined by thin strips of processed wood, which not only reproduce every type of wood known, but can be used

This observation may seem exaggerated if we are speaking of normal flat PCBs (which are themselves full-fledged components), but not if we are speaking of some of the more recent proposals, which call for printing circuits even on curved and complex surfaces. Inside the receiver of a telephone or in the case of a watch, the component is no longer just the substrate of a circuit. It now integrates different functions that are inherent to the overall structure of the object in which the circuit has been inserted.

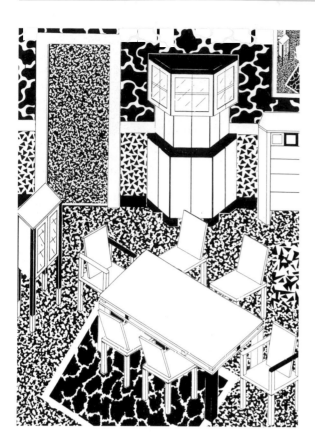

that of the interior coverings for automobiles. Here, beginning with a tradition of wood (for the dashboard), leather, and upholstery (for the interior coverings), it has been necessary to find cheaper and more easily produced solutions that would not differ too radically from what (rightly or wrongly) was considered to be a consolidated image that the public demanded.

For all of the components in question, the aim is to create something endowed with a certain structural strength, covered with a flexible layer (to absorb impact), covered in turn by a surface of textured plastic or cloth. In a few cases, the solution was provided by integral polyurethane foam, which we have already discussed. More often, however, manufacturers utilized the formation of a plastic film or cloth, made to adhere to the substrate by various systems.
This can be done in different ways. A sheet of thermoplastic material (for instance, polyvinyl chloride, PVC), that may be covered with cloth if so desired, is preformed and inserted into a mold into which is injected the material that will constitute the interior. Another approach, known as vacuum thermoforming, calls for an initial phase in which the inner structural part is molded, and then used as a mold

to create different and original ornamental patterns. The ennobling can also be done by means of paper impregnated with melamine, so as to create colored surfaces, smooth or textured with reliefs, or else by plastic laminates whose surfaces have great mechanical resistance, in any pattern and color.

Laminated plastic is manufactured by layering a certain number of sheets of kraft paper that have been impregnated with phenolic resin with a sheet of decorated paper (upon which the pattern desired is printed in color) spread with melaminic resin. High temperatures and pressure are applied to this laminate, causing the resins to cross link, and creating a sheet with great thermal and mechanical resistance, used to ennoble such modest materials as chipboard panels. Laminated plastic, which can take on any type of decoration at no additional cost, has been the privileged tool in linguistic design experiments since the mid-Sixties. Its versatility has made it the medium for experimentation that goes beyond graphics to obtain textured surfaces in relief and luminescent surfaces, which we shall discuss later.

Other coverings have developed parallel to laminated plastic. Rubber for flooring, moquettes, textiles for interior decoration, as well as the continuously growing range of adhesive films with a wide variety of properties – ranging from a simple protective esthetic covering, to filter functions, mirrored and retroreflective surfaces. The vastness of the landscape is in itself worthy of notice.
One area upon which technological research on surface quality is concentrating is

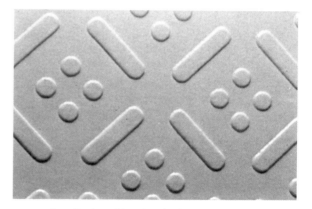

Top: Design of interiors by George Sowden (1983). Above: A Reli-tech laminate designed by Andrea Branzi (mfg. Abet Print, 1978).

upon which to form the finishing sheet (the formation takes place by means of air suction through the item itself, so that the sheet adheres perfectly to the substrate). A third approach calls for separate molding of the resistant part and the skin, so that when they are assembled, a space remains between them. Into this space, a flexible polyurethane (PU) is injected and foamed.

Beyond the covering

Membrane keyboards, touch sensors, electroluminescent systems, displays... a growing number of components with complex functions tends to take on the same form – a thin, often flexible membrane, made up of a layering of different materials. There is a thin layer of "active" material (which produces the desired effect when electrically stimulated) inserted between two conductive matrices printed on two sheets (or between two continuous conductive sheets); the latter, controlled by an electronic system, create the electrical conditions required. The whole is then sealed in a shell of protective films that make the product "monolithic." A printed circuit distributes power or signals, exiting from the system with a tape cable and a connector.

This scheme may undergo variations or additions, but in the final analysis the difference between one component and another lies in the chemical and physical qualities of the inner layer and in the electronic control system. This difference, though it may be considerable in terms of performance, is at any rate difficult to observe from the system's physical appearance. These membranes, which are physically so neutral and yet are so active in terms of relationships, are the new coverings of the emerging family of sensitive objects.

For instance, in a liquid-crystal display, the liquid crystals appear as a thin layer sandwiched between two surfaces upon which electrodes of a special shape are printed (and are controlled in turn by an electronic system) and two polarizing films. By selectively creating electric fields in different areas of the surface, one orients the liquid crystals, causing variations in their optical properties, so as to create legible figures through the contrast between transparent areas and opaque areas.

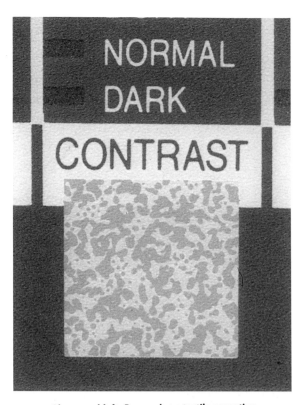

191

In a membrane touch system, between two electrode matrices, a piezoelectric film or a variable-resistance rubber sheet is arranged. In the first case, pressure is registered by an electric impulse created by a mechanical action upon the material, received by the underlying electrode. In the second case, the material contained between the conductive matrices is a rubber whose resistance with respect to the electric current changes with the deformations cause by a mechanical action. The system is therefore capable of locating and measuring the pressure according to the intensity of the electric current registered by each electrode.

In an electroluminescent system, instead, a sheet of special polymer material is placed between the two matrices. When a variable electrical field is created, this material is excited and emits luminous radiation. Thus, lit surfaces are obtained, either continuously or split up into parts that can be lit selectively, thus creating another form of display.

Lastly, let us make mention of the membrane keyboards that stand apart from earlier systems due to their great simplicity. Their conception is based on the elasticity of the materials: two films, on which appropriate circuits are printed, are separated by a third film that has apertures which correspond to the points where contact should occur. Pressure upon the "key," that is, upon an area indicated by a symbol, causes the upper film (and with it, the corresponding circuit) to touch the lower film, thus triggering an electric contact. Once the pressure is removed, the key elastically returns to its original position.

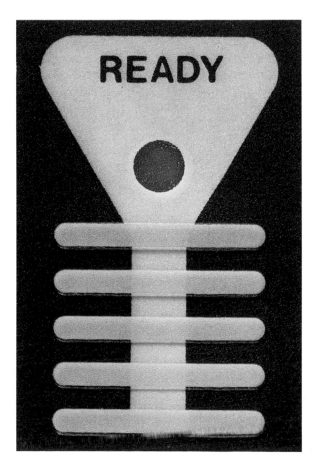

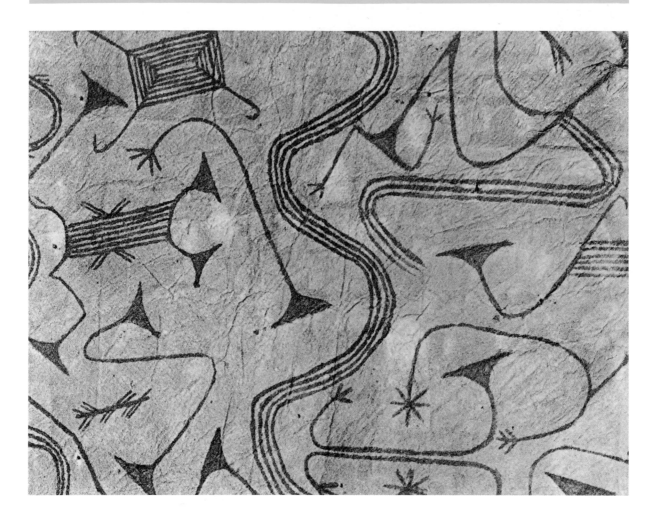

The skin of objects

The first objects manufactured by man were items made of a homogeneous material, extracted from nature and subjected to simple transformations in order to utilize intrinsic mechanical performances: rocks, bones, clubs... In this first technical phase, the surface, even though in functional terms it was no more than the border of the material, rapidly interested man because on it one could place the graphic signs of symbolic expression. The dawn of the image is represented by regular carvings on sticks and bone fragments. It is impossible for us to understand exactly the meaning of this proto-writing, thirty thousand years old. It is certain, however, that the writer intended to repeat the signs and link them one to another, that is, to create a rhythm. This rhythm was to remain one of the specific features of the representation which today we call decoration. Objects, as Leroi-Gourhan puts it, have "spoken" ever since the Paleolithic, expressing with their signs reality, characters, cultural references of a people in a specific phase of its history.

In that period typified by a scanty layer of artificiality (sec 1.1.1), when technology had a very limited control over matter and, consequentially, over the structure of objects, the surface constituted an area in which it was easy to express one's image and identity – from objects and walls to tattoos on one's own body.

Perhaps, if we observe recent history in this broader perspective, we could say that the Modern Movement, with its declared aversion for decoration and ornaments, intended to underline the newness generated by technology in the nineteenth century – an unprecedented ability to control the structure of objects. The downgrading of surfaces and of the messages that surfaces can bear was a result of the desire to eliminate anything that might disturb the geometric purity of shapes which could at last be produced and reproduced by machine. The skin of things, with its opacity, blocked the vision of their perfect geometric and functional essence.

Culture thereafter rediscovered the value of surfaces and of the sensory variables which surfaces can bear. By opposing the concrete and physical idea of sensory quality to the abstract idea of formal quality, culture rehabilitated decoration, which modernism had branded immoral, and is now emphasizing the designer's control over the *soft* qualities of objects – not only visual qualities but also qualities of touch, warmth, smell...

This many-faceted approach could not be understood overall if one were to ignore the simultaneous technical transformations that form its background, more or less unconsciously. The development of materials toward composites in which each layer has a specialized function sets the design and manufacturing problem of what qualities to give the outermost layer (the skin). The concept of a sincere image of materials thus becomes useless, in the way that the Modern Movement understood it. To the degree that materials have a skin their image is sincerely that of the skin, with the entire range of variations that the skin permits.

Surface and time

The lifespan of an object is linked to phenomena that affect all of its components. It is the surface, however, that displays the marks of transformation, and it is through the surface that most of the factors that lead to aging reach the interior.
Indeed, over time, due to the relationship between the ambient and the physical and chemical characteristics of the material, phenomena may emerge such as corrosion, oxidation, abrasion, cracking, biodegradation triggered by microorganisms, or damage from use. These possible sources of decay may lead to a loss of the initial qualities, which can be shown in a dropping performance curve, which we call degradation. The question "How long should an object last?" is a central concern in any design process. It immediately leads to a second question – "How much degradation is acceptable within a given period of time?" To find an answer, we may look at the strictly technical aspects or we can look at cultural aspects as well. In the first area, at least in principle, the answer is quite simple: the initial qualities of the object and the quality of

Loft verticale by Gaetano Pesce, a construction in ashlars made of rigid foamed polyurethane. The exposed sides have a variable form and create a bossed surface that should acquire quality as it ages.

the protections set on its surface should never fall below the performance level called for during the design phase.
In terms of cultural criteria, instead, the matter of the decay of a material's image, of the way in which an object moves away from the condition of brand new is far more complex. While the decay of some materials has been accultured (for instance, traditional building materials take on a special value as they age, the patina of time), for others (practically speaking, for all recently developed materials) there is a clear choice – either a plastic chair is brand new or it's ready to be thrown out. Surface quality in terms of protection therefore takes on a cultural dimension (which is largely unexplored) with respect to aging and the capacity to last over time, registering the marks of time without losing quality.
Certainly, most materials that have been introduced recently, show only a slight ability to do so, that is, to age in a dignified manner. Nonetheless, the equation "new material product that cannot age" need not al-

ways be true, and some designers have started working with the expressive possibilities of new materials over time. A great deal of work still needs to be done, however, and perhaps, more than work on materials what needs to be done is cultural work. What we need to do is overcome the recent design tradition that has mostly conceived objects as frozen in the image of their newness. One thus runs up against one of the most solid strongholds of the spirit of modernism, that which casts out the theme of decadence and death, replacing them with a dream of an eternal springtime of youth.

In the landscape of objects that travel at ever greater speed from the factory to the dustbin, proffering a non-lasting image, it is possible to think of inserting objects that last and "know how to age," acting as a medium for memory and functioning as slow analogue timepieces, that mark the passage of time by changing.

Surface and sensation

The quality of surfaces contains all that we can learn of an object, if we leave aside that particular mental activity that elaborates sensations in terms of shape. This operation (which leads us to say that a given object is "cubic"), although quite "noble," i.e., specifically human, is neither the sole nor the most exhaustive way that we have of gaining knowledge of objects. The wealth of space-time experience is far greater than that which would derive from a pure relationship with geometric or functional abstractions.

"We know of no organs of perception that man does not share with all other mammals," writes Leroi-Gourhan. "His sensory equipment — put to work for an apparatus that is well suited to transform sensations into symbols — functions like that of animals; and if animals lead a mental existence devoid of a symbol-creating apparatus, this does not exclude that man leads a life of the senses in all its density (...) and that, in short, the animal machine functions at a number of different levels, which, up to that of intellectual integration, are the same in other living beings" (*Le geste et la parole.*)

Recognition of a color, a texture, the quality of a smell or taste — these are all sensory activities at a different level from the recognition of a shape. They require less interpretation, they are linked to a relationship of direct proximity — color is the decoding of a wavelength, texture is the decoding of a precise mechanical action. The sensations that emerge are analytic, the synthesis of the image comes later, and sometimes never comes. Part of this sensory activity remains infra-symbolic, eludes language, sinks its roots deep into our zoological origins.

Emphasizing the importance of this in no way lessens our status as human beings. This is our foundation, the available information upon which the construction of symbolic thought rests. Surfaces are the site upon which this passage of information takes place.

Underestimating the importance of the surface in order to exalt the purity of forms can be a specific esthetic choice, but not a general law. A world of significant forms but of homogeneous and commonplace surfaces would completely lack a dimension of sensory relationships.

On the other hand, while in the past the predominance of the natural environment provided an inexhaustible wealth of diversified surfaces and the scanty artificiality of materials meant that choosing a material automatically determined most aspects of an object's surface quality, today the increasing spread of the artificial (see 1.1.2) implies that the variety of surfaces has become a design topic, and that surface quality is now determined for the most part independently of other formal and functional aspects.

We are encountering, in short, the design of the relationship of closeness with objects. Closeness here should be taken in its literal sense (with reference to touch, for instance) but also in its broader sense — as closeness in the process of elaborating sensory messages, in the way in which color is "closer" to an object than form, because perceiving color requires a lower level of mental elaboration.

Colored surfaces

The contemporary universe of color is potentially limitless. The design condition that we have called "hyperselection" (see 1.2.1), i.e., the loss of the technical and cultural limitations that in the past were confines within which possible design choices fell, has come about sooner and with greater relevance in the area of colors than elsewhere.

From the first red ochers found in human settlements dating back fifty thousand years, to the manufacture of synthetic colors in the nineteenth century, the choice of color was always limited by the availability of colored substances and natural film-generating resins. The number of these substances and resins had certainly grown with the passage of time, but so slowly as to allow the new arrivals to be absorbed culturally. Thus specific cultures of color formed for different ethnic groups and peoples, each with its own hierarchies, each attributing different symbolic values to each color.

The beginning of the manufacture of synthetic colors not only brought about an increase in the shades available, but also a rise in the level of color saturation that could be attained, with a rapid and overwhelming transformation of the chromatic system of reference. This system has also been enriched by the new colors of electronics, endowed with a special and hitherto unknown brilliance, which added a new dimension to the space of color variations.

What is more, this entire heritage now circulates through communications media, overlapping the local chromatic cultures with the new colors of international industry (the colors, that is, of industrial products) and the newer and more international colors of video.

The current chromatic culture, which is the fruit of this overlapping, presents shared features and aspects of local singularity, breaking down into different settings through which the chromatic experience of each of us passes. In that culture, elements of stability (colors that tend to last over time as a constant foundation) coexist with elements of change (new colors enter into the field of acceptability, others exit).

It is not easy for a designer to measure himself with this field — the relationship with color is, as we have said, largely infra-symbolic and is closer to our relationship with food than to our relationship with forms. Color allows no rational justifications or logical explanations (apart from the cases where there is a functional motivation). The only possibility lies in developing a strategy based on a phenomenological reading of reality (that is, of the trends of collective choices) and of its developing behavior.

Recognizing trends and interacting with them is the only attitude a designer can have with respect to the color variable that is not purely intuitive. "Trends," writes Clino Castelli, "indicate a tendency within a certain date, and apply to the time from now until that date. (...) It is a new form that embodies – in advance – the expectation of an object that is as much coordinated by subjective needs as by objective means." (*Il Lingotto primario*, p. 16).

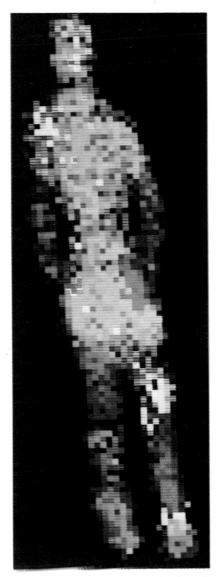

Above: Image of a jogger "seen" by the Ladar (Laser Radar) robot eye.
Left: Theoretical models of colorimetric solids.

Decorated surfaces

The oldest form of graphic human expression is the production of rhythms, or the regular repetition of signs. From notches cut onto clubs and bones, mentioned earlier, there emerged "closed" figures, that is, figures that are separate unto themselves, the expression of clearly delineated mental images. Rhythmic expression has not disappeared. It has been perpetuated to our time under the form of decoration which, based on the same sort of needs, finds its most characteristic feature in repetition.

"Unlike the surface of a painting," writes Andrea Branzi, "which always implies the existence of a border constituted by the very perimeter of the painting, within which the painted message is organized into units, a decorative surface implies infinite borders, and contains in each of its smallest parts the sum total of information in the entire system, since it contains the individual sign that is then repeated *ad infinitum*." (*La casa calda*, p. 117).

If decoration is linked to rhythm, and hence to an important moment in human behavior, the age-old discussion over the difference between painting and decoration could be resolved by observing the difference in the level at which the two forms relate with our

perceptive and representational system — that of the production of images and that of the production of rhythms.

This experience of visual rhythm is so deeply rooted that all of the stances assumed by the masters of the Modern Movement have not much limited the public's taste for decoration (nor their own, in the final analysis, given that the theories expressed have always been far more anti-decorative than the final products). On the other hand, the anti-decorative argument based on the idea that decoration was typical of manual craftsmanship, while a smooth surface was more appropriate to machinery, is no longer applicable (if ever it was): we have already noted (see 3.5.1) what current technology is capable of in the area of decoration.

Among the many possible examples, that of laminated plastics is exemplary for the role it has played in the cultural recovery of decoration. Created as cheap imitation products for other, more "noble" materials, used later for imitative decorations of the materials that they were to substitute, forced into silence by the neutral surfaces of the culture of modern design, laminated plastics exploded with their infinite range of graphic and chromatic possibilities on the crest of the wave of the cultural re-evaluation of the decorated surface.

If the broad lines of this process, however, form part of the development of the design culture with respect to decoration, underlying it all is another, far more common culture, which never really called decoration into question. Not only did most people continue to decorate their own home and purchase decorated objects, but (most important of all) industry always continued to manufacture decorated mass-market goods, inven-

ting new styles and languages that include those special informative decorations – labels, trademarks, advertising designs and legends on merchandise.

The field of decoration, rich as it is in possibilities, may lend itself to abuse. Rhythm as the basis of our existence extends over time and space – decorated objects must be replaced now and then with smooth objects; just as phases in which decoration is emphasized will be followed by other phases in which the decorative landscape empties out and takes, as it were, a rest.

The question of trends recurs. The masters of the Modern Movement who, after the decorative overload of the late nineteenth century, emphasized the geometry of shapes over the language of surfaces, expressed in terms of a moral imperative what, after all,

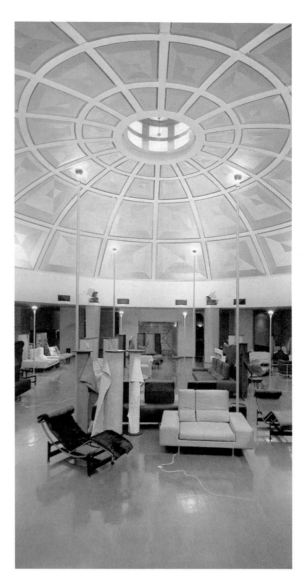

The image of decoration in the Eighties is made up of citations, imitations, and the discovery of new frontiers. Above and below: Cupola coated in retroreflective material, designed by Clino Castelli (Cassina Showroom, 1985), in which the shimmering pattern of the dome simulates three-dimensional depth. Left: A wall clock designed by Nathalie du Pasquier and George Sowden. The entire series consists of decorative variants on a few basic elements.

was just a correct intuition as to the prevailing trend of their period toward increasingly rarefied decoration.

Recently, the spread of decorated design has indicated another trend reversal. It is probable that an initial polemic and extremist phase, which has led design culture to proffer images with an extremely dense level of decoration, will be followed by another phase, in which decoration will become more restrained and well thought out – decoration will play more on subtle qualities and diffuse sensoriality.

Surface and touch

Touch is the most analytic of senses, the furthest from sight. The messages that it sends serve as a background to our system of representation – they do not become images. For this to happen, it is necessary first of all to eliminate the dominance of sight, go into a dark room or close one's eyes, and combine onès capacity for specific analysis with the mobility of the hand and explore in this way a surface or a shape. This operation is similar to the scanning that computers use to analyze images.

"Corporeal touch has to do with well-being and one's presence in space," writes Leroi-Gourhan, "and there is no purely tactile esthetics, except in the manual field. This esthetics remains quite close to the physiological level and revolves around the sensation of a caress; it has to do with polished materials, furs, pellets, ductile pastes, flexible and elastic materials." (*Le geste et la parole.*)

This brief sketch suggests two orders of considerations. What is the effect on one's well-being and presence in space of rapid modifications in the tactile landscape? How can we pose this problem in design terms, if its infrasymbolic nature is so strong as to deprive

The Braun Micron Plus razor, designed by Dieter Rams in 1980 (shown above in cross-section). The anti-slip decorative finish is produced by overmolding a soft elastomer thermoplastic polyurethane onto the polycarbonate (PC) body.

199

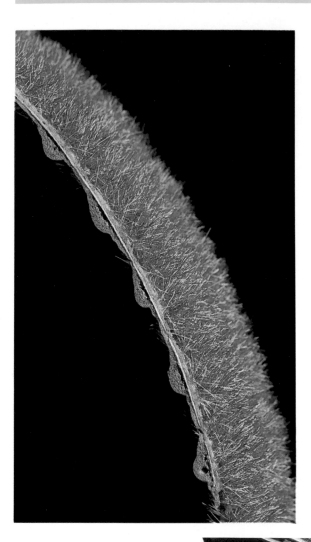

us of the words with which to speak of it? Of course, the second question has repercussions on the first. Intuitively, however, one would say that the basis of our behavior should be an attempt to ensure variety. If the spread of the artificial deprives us of opportunities to encounter the tactile variety that was always present in the consistency, texture, and thermal qualities of natural materials, then the new artificial must produce a comparable range and variety.

This principle has already been confirmed to a certain extent in reality: the predominance of the culture of the smooth/hard/cold industrial product — against which the culture of padded textured/warm/soft products are making headway — is beginning to show signs of decline. Intermediate solutions endowed with new qualities appear with growing frequency. As we have indicated (see 3.5.1), every system for providing surface quality winds up producing "high-touch" applications: the simplest texturizing of molded surfaces, the insertion of fabrics into molds, and all the ways of softening surfaces; "3-D" paints, velveted paints or (in the near future) paints that are soft to the touch; veneered woods, laminates with surfaces in relief, and the variety of surface shapes of rubber products; the vast area of "hairy" surfaces, from flocking to moquettes. These solutions are accompanied, in certain cases, by a reconsideration of properties that have always been thought of as flaws: the "waxy" quality of certain plastics (especially the polyolefins), the "sticky" quality of certain kinds of rubber...

Above: "Furry" surface obtained through flocking. (Doct. Maag Schenk)

The interior of an auto offers a huge variety of surfaces. A detail of the dashboard of the Autobianchi Y10: goffered polycarbonate/ABS blend structure, hatch created through injection overmolding of polypropylene (PP) on fabric (mfg. Comind-Stars). (Doct. Montedison-Montedipe-Himont)

The tactile landscape of the artificial environment technically possesses the ability to develop much the same way as the visual landscape has. It would suffice to imitate a well-known tactile quality, develop variations on it, and propose new qualities. In this case, however, new, semantic difficulties arise. "Velveted" paint, for instance, aside from a few similarities, has nothing to do with velvet; in the same sense the expression "laminate in relief" indicates the form of a surface, and we must try to imagine a tactile sensation to accompany the term. Again, the Braun Micron Plus razor designed by Dieter Rams, an excellent example of a tactile object, can only be described as a smooth surface that has projecting points that are relatively soft. This communications gap probably cannot be bridged, which puts the designer in a condition like that of the traditional artist – he or she creates something of which one can speak, but about the central aspect of which nothing can be said, at least until, with time, certain, more precise and communicable tactile typologies have been singled out so that, here too, trends can be examined.

High-touch furniture: A chair made of plastic material, the top half of which is covered with veleveted paint. (Doct. Tecnomax) Bottom: Textures on rubber (mfg. Cigo).

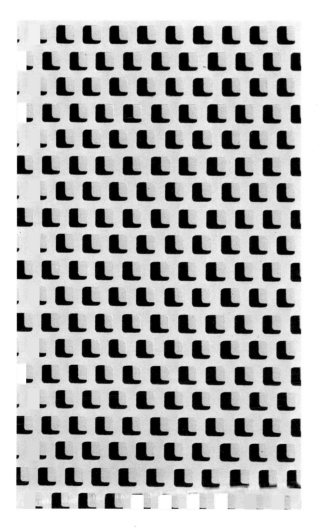

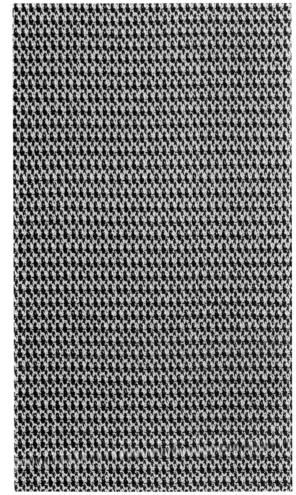

In the childhood memories of many of us, there is the intriguing image of a clock dial or a statuette that emanated a cold pale brilliance in the dark. The use of phosphorescent pigments is not new, but their communicative potential is far from used up. Their ability to mark the darkness with the memory of a light that is no longer present confers a special life to the surface of objects, linking that surface with the history of its surroundings.

A new sensibility has been generated with respect to these objects, which do not undergo events statically, but bear the mark of each event on their surface. Phosphorescent surfaces (which now use more efficient and more widely available paints and laminates) are the forerunners of the family of reactive surfaces (which relate with the ambient) and expressive surfaces (which communicate their state and the changes that have occured in it): another example is provided by surfaces coated with a liquid crystal-based material that is temperature sensitive, and expresses this sensitivity with a color change. Other reactive surfaces can be easily imagined, even using quite simple technology – soft surfaces that preserve for a certain time the shape of whoever touched or used them (one could use a flexible polyurethane foam with a delayed "return"); surfaces made to be used up, leaving a trace of the use that was made of them...

Put in these terms, these suggestions have a basically poetic nature; but there is a realm of functionality that merits exploration. There are (and indeed are in rapid expansion) fields of application in which function and esthetic and emotional qualities cannot be easily separated. A phosphorescent surface is also, and always has been, an element for signalling in the dark; a temperature-sensitive liquid-crystal surface can serve as an analogue indicator of an object's thermal state; a surface that is easily used up can be used to indicate routes.

The future of reactive and expressive sur-

The surface becomes keyboard - an exploded view of a membrane keyboard. From top: The outer silk-screened coating, the "snap-discs" to give a tactile sensation, and the two sheets of electric circuits, separated by an insulating layer. (Doct. Micro Switch)

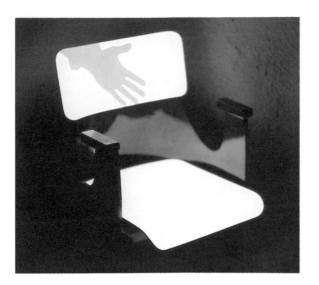

The surface becomes luminescent - *Glowing Chair*, by Clino Castelli (1972), made of photoluminescent laminated plastic.

The membrane keyboard, increasingly common in office machinery, toys, and appliances, today constitutes the most widespread case of a reactive surface that interacts in time with the actions of the user, sending signals to the interior components of the machine. The newness of this keyboard is not, of course, in the keyboard itself or in its role — as interface, but the different physiognomy that it gives any object in which it is integrated. A traditional keyboard is a "massive" physical component. A membrane keyboard is a portion of surface, the sensory instrument of a diffuse tactile quality of the machine, the first step toward a tactile sensitivity that is no longer only man-to-machine sensitivity, but also machine-to-man.

On the other hand, the field of artificial sensoriality involves far more complex solutions. Pressure sensors have existed for some time, but only recently have they evolved into membranes. The need to make the "hands" of robots more delicate, has led to increasingly subtle, light, and compact devices, capable of reproducing with greater accuracy the sensitivity of human touch. Piezoelectric films and conductive rubber (separately or used together) are leading to the production of artificial skins that can move on to other applications after their use for robot "hands": a tennis court that can feel and indicate whether the ball went out of bounds; a plate that can reconstruct the shape of an object that was set on it; the surface of an instrument for orthopedic exams that can produce a diagram of the pressure exerted by the patient's foot.

The time when we shall be able to write "sensitive skin" without quotation marks is not that far off. Indeed, models of artificial skin have been developed that can "feel" and locate pressure, "feel" and recognize surface textures, "feel" and evaluate the heat properties of the bodies with which they enter into contact (that is, recognize the specific heat through contact). With this end in view, a membrane has been produced which even resembles skin in its configuration, since it is made up of a dermis and an epidermis, each with specific properties and performances.

faces, however, goes well beyond all this. In the examples mentioned, simple coverings provide in an elementary fashion performances that are also quite elementary. The world of two-dimensional components that can become parts of other components may soon reach other levels of complexity, offering a great variety of combinations of functional logic and esthetic and emotional values.

Electroluminescent system, on and off (mfg. Sinel).

Here too the development of the expressive capacity of surfaces is following a similar route. Light bulbs, LEDs, displays, and cathode tubes have long been the chief forms of expression for machines, indicating visually, in a more or less profoundly encoded language, what is happening inside them. These components too tend toward two-dimensionality — a light bulb can become an electroluminescent system, that is, a flexible luminous film that is little more than a millimeter thick; displays tend to become thinner and flexible; cathode tubes are gradually being replaced by flat screens... And where can all this be heading but into the surface of other objects?

The surface generates electricity - solar energy (photovoltaic) cells integrated in the roof of the Saab 900 Turbo. (Doct. Saab)

Sensitive and communicative objects

In nature, there are living organisms without structure, but there are none without skins. On the first step of the biological ladder, there are microorganisms composed of only a membrane dividing the inside from the outside. Skin, with its specializations, is the privileged location of the exchanges of energy and information that characterize life.

It is no accident, therefore, that at a time when technical development creates artificial products that rival the organic world in complexity, the surface of objects should grow in importance, becoming itself an interface, filter, and privileged location of exchanges of energy and information.

Technology has reached this stage after recapitulating the avenue of biological development — beginning with membranes and reaching organisms with rigid structures (vertebrates); technology began with simple structures and in the end has developed dynamic surfaces.

When Reverend Edwin Abbot wrote *Flatland* in 1882, minutely describing the life and operation of a two-dimensional world, he certainly had no inkling that he might be describing what was to be one of the most important trends of technological evolution of the next century. Unlike Flatland, however, where the world was only two-dimensional, the new, real, two-dimensional world of today fits over the old three-dimensional world, becoming its skin.

With the design of these new objects endowed with interactive surfaces, we have come to the conclusion of our investigation. Their physical aspects are still within the world of materials, but their operation, their very state of being, is well beyond the manipulation of matter and has more to do with information exchange than with form.

In these pages, we have repeatedly approached this border; in many chapters we have noted that proper use of new materials could lead to objects providing performance that would define new types of relations — creating the light and a new idea of portability, creating the transparent and the availability of variable filters, creating the elastic and giving objects a sort of intelligence that would allow them to interact with their environment... In all these cases, however, the macroscopic organization of the matter in space is still the predominant aspect — it is here that the "genetic code," which allows the successive relation-oriented performance of objects, is visibly and concretely established. Instead, the future behavior of sensitive and communicative skin is entirely inscribed within miniaturized components, whose operation possesses physical aspects that escape our perception.

The design of this skin, and therefore of the objects that are made with it, is chiefly the design of interactivity with the environment — a scenario for which we must prepare the stage, the sets, and the actors. Imagining the nature of these "individual objects" is another, new chapter in the history of design.

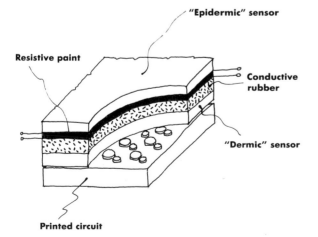

"Epidermic" sensor

Resistive paint

Conductive rubber

"Dermic" sensor

Printed circuit

"Artificial skin": various types of sensors reproduce tactile and thermal sensitivity of natural skin (research project performed at the Istituto "E. Piaggio" of the University of Pisa).

EXERCISES IN INVENTION

The following projects are the outcome of an experiment, or better, the outcome of a game. In line with the composite nature of this book, we asked several designers to comment, as it were, the topics discussed in the form that is most comfortable for them — that is, by proposing ideas that comply with the "rules of the game."

The rules, briefly, were the following: given the information on materials discussed in the book, and given the separation into five broad themes, corresponding to the five chapters of the third section (*Playing with the Possible*), the problem was to imagine ways in which a new material or a new technique could permit small or large extra performances, that is, small or large inventions.

We contacted designers with different cultural tendencies and professional experience. Many of them agreed. Each worked according to his own nature both in establishing the solution and in interpreting the spirit of the exercise.

The design ideas presented here obviously do not constitute a catalogue of the newly possible, nor do we necessarily endorse their worth or feasability by publishing them. Our editorial choice was to publish all the proposals that complied with the rules of the game, without questioning their worth. We believe that by so doing, we provide an authentic snapshot (ingenuous, perhaps, but realistic) of how creativity can interact with new materials today.

It seems to us that the set of projects offers a clearer idea than any long discussion could of a shared quality, which joins the esthetics and sensibilities of designers that are otherwise quite distant. This shared quality is the performance "extra" offered by new materials, a new character that tends to shift the way in which we judge an object from a simple formal evaluation of "what it is," to another evaluation of "what it does."

A generation of objects appears on the horizon. Here the new is chiefly sought by proposing innovative uses and new qualities of relation that broaden the functional, emotional, and sensory field of new possibilities.

**This is made of two light sheaths,
placed one inside the other.
The more rigid, internal, orange one
contains the hot water.
The more elastic, external, light blue
one is inflated with air.
In this way, the water is insulated and
emits the proper degree of heat without burning.
The two membranes are closed by a
simple knot.
Good night and sweet dreams!**

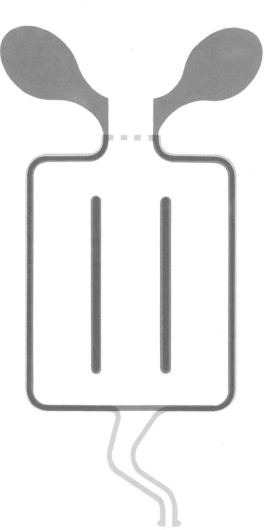

209

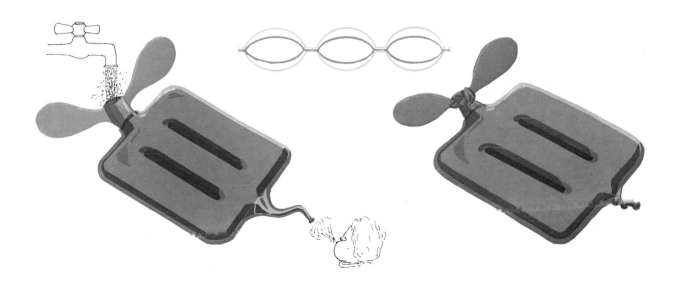

This design extends the "disposable" concept to a more complex object.

This is a cup that comes prepared with roasted, ground coffee and water (naturally chosen to guarantee a "good cup of coffee"). The user need only boil the water by electrical means.

The cup consists of four parts, i.e., a body with handle to hold the coffee once made, a container for water to be boiled, a cover for the latter, and a thin aluminum disk. The plastic parts are made of polypropylene and joined by ultrasound.

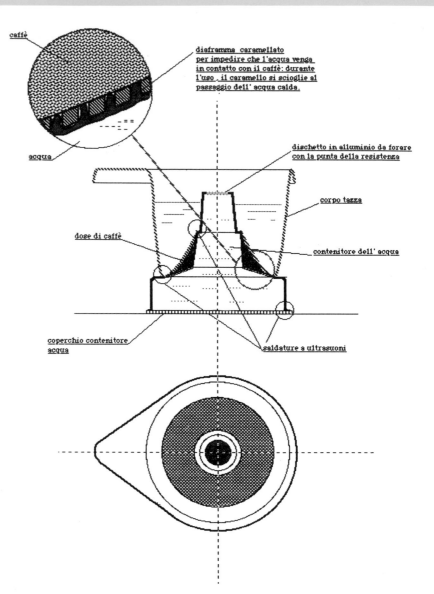

caffè

acqua

diaframma caramellato per impedire che l'acqua venga in contatto con il caffè: durante l'uso, il caramello si scioglie al passaggio dell'acqua calda.

dischetto in alluminio da forare con la punta della resistenza

corpo tazza

dose di caffè

contenitore dell'acqua

coperchio contenitore acqua

saldature a ultrasuoni

210

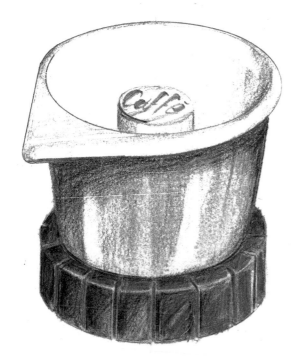

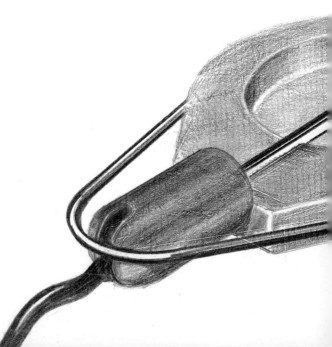

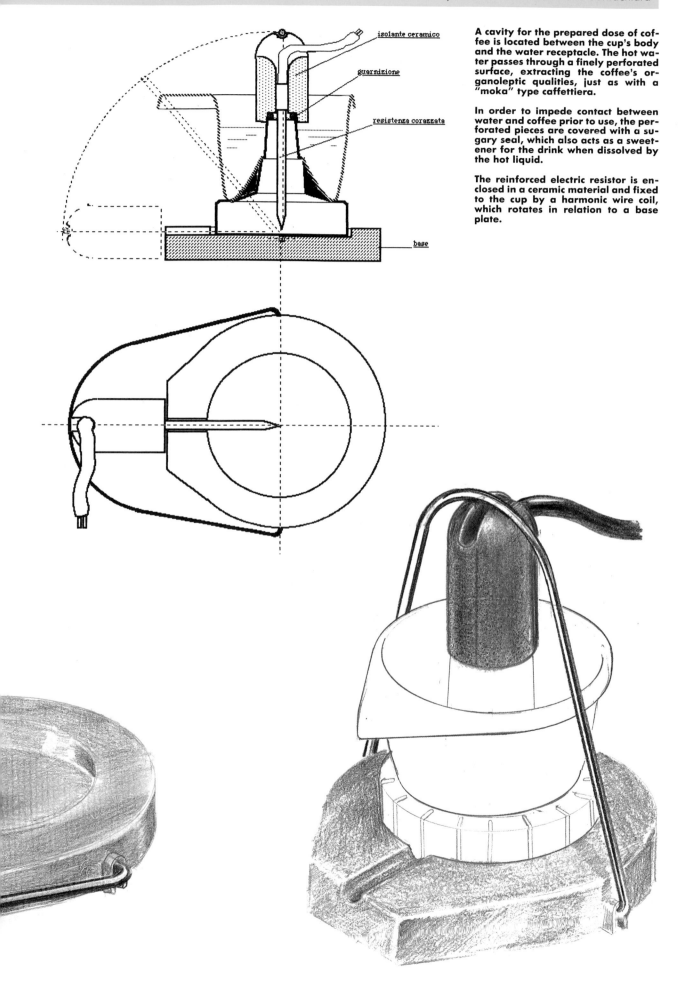

isolante ceramico

guarnizione

resistenza corazzata

base

A cavity for the prepared dose of coffee is located between the cup's body and the water receptacle. The hot water passes through a finely perforated surface, extracting the coffee's organoleptic qualities, just as with a "moka" type caffettiera.

In order to impede contact between water and coffee prior to use, the perforated pieces are covered with a sugary seal, which also acts as a sweetener for the drink when dissolved by the hot liquid.

The reinforced electric resistor is enclosed in a ceramic material and fixed to the cup by a harmonic wire coil, which rotates in relation to a base plate.

An object's surface is an interface rich in sensorial suggestions that are able to arouse direct and intense emotional involvement. In fact, color and surface behavior have always put us in imaginary contact with the profound substance of the material, and in empathy with the most intimate elements of the corporeal nature of things. Chromatic variation has therefore the effect of an alchemical metamorphosis, provoking us with the joyous enchantment of a magical act. Metamerism, as interpreted here, is a phenomenon expressed by superficial color changes in an object, caused by the spectral properties of incident light. Industry has, up until now, tried to avoid this, because of its duty to the laws of constancy and technical perfection. But where there is a "qualistic" product conception, this type of phenomenon gains much expressive and communicative value, and can therefore be used as a means

The color of an object depends on the interaction between incident light properties, and those of its own surface, which acts as a filter, absorbing some wavelengths and reflecting others. Materials which exhibit the same color under given light conditions can appear chromatically diverse with a change in illumination. We have called this phenomenon "metamerism".

of conferring new esthetic and perceptive quality.

The **METAMERIC CHAIR** is made of a material (for example, a plastic laminate) which is printed with colors and drawings, using highly "metameric" paints, that reveal themselves reciprocally as the light changes. This creates unexpected transformations in the chair's look.

As in other "primary" design projects, the formal choice is not the most important one. It is rather the possibility of exploiting some aspects of the color-light relationship, giving rise to rich and intense emotional communication with the product. The images shown here are, then, metaphoric; by playing with references and allegory, they emphasize the properties of this interactive skin, which changes the object's identity in rapport with the luminous characteristics of its surrounding environment.

Synthetic colors, obtained by mixing a number of pigments with diverse spectral absorbency qualities, are used for this chair. Therefore, altering light composition the percentages of each reflected wavelength vary, and this creates different chromatic sensations.

The spectra behind the chairs refer to two ideal lighting conditions. One is natural, the other, artificial.

Thomas Alva Edison did not invent the incandescent light bulb, as is often believed. He perfected it though, and made its industrial production possible. His studies and experiments with production systems and the transport of electrical energy to supply public and private illumination fixtures were really much more important.
Some decades passed, however, before electrical energy was used for motors, heating, telecommunications, and (even more recently) refrigeration, computer systems, et cetera.

Today only one tenth of the electricity produced in Italy is used for lighting. Standards have remained more or less the same for the last hundred years (tension from 100 to 380 volts, frequencies of 50-60 hertz). This is not only perhaps inappropriate for other devices (for example, compressed air is used in garages to operate tools more safely, quietly, and economically than would be possible with electricity), but has become obsolete for lighting fixtures as well. In fact, fluorescent tubes, sodium and

halogen lamps, as well as discharge-based lamps in general, all of which are not incandescent, are in use today. Frequencies between 50-60 hertz are too low for these, and cause stroboscopic flickering.
It is therefore necessary to consider new energy sources, new functional standards and, at the same time, reduce energy waste; some lamps dissipate heat which is not used, while certain heat generating equipment squanders precious luminous energy.

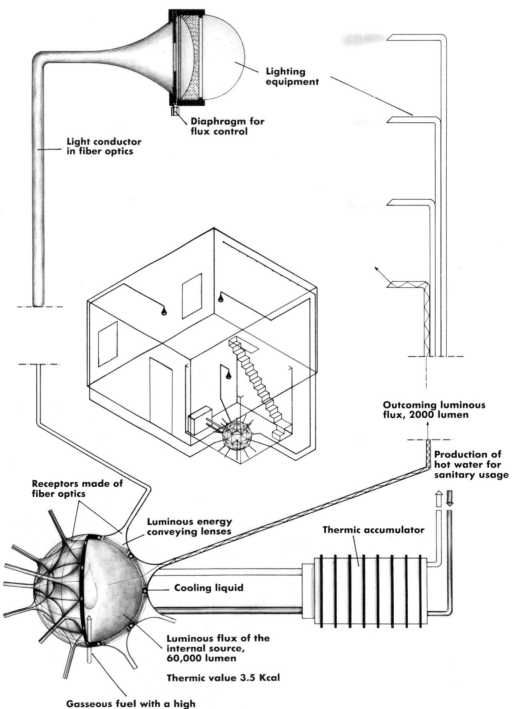

Lighting equipment

Diaphragm for flux control

Light conductor in fiber optics

Outcoming luminous flux, 2000 lumen

Production of hot water for sanitary usage

Receptors made of fiber optics

Luminous energy conveying lenses

Thermic accumulator

Cooling liquid

Luminous flux of the internal source, 60,000 lumen

Thermic value 3.5 Kcal

Gasseous fuel with a high pressure combustion substance

Materials
Alucobond is a composite panel material made of two 0.5 mm aluminum sheets and an extruded polyethylene core of variable thickness. It is a standard product which can be made available in tailored dimensions. It is easily cut, curved, sliced, bored, calendered, milled, and bent. It comes in thicknesses from 3-8 mm, weighing from 4.5 to 9.1 kg/m^2.
It is commonly employed for external finishes, and was used on Milan's Linate airport.

Design
The project exploits the panel's possibilities as an electrical conductor. Due to the relative rigidity of Alucobond, a self-supporting lighting system can be devised using low voltage halogen bulbs.
Wiring is almost unecessary; the current can be accessed by two metal plates held by a clamp, while the dichroic lamp is positioned right on the panel.
This project emphasizes the simplicity in working and applying this material, which can easily be used for do-it-yourself lighting systems.

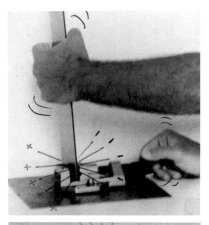

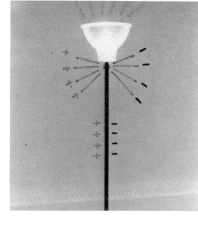

215

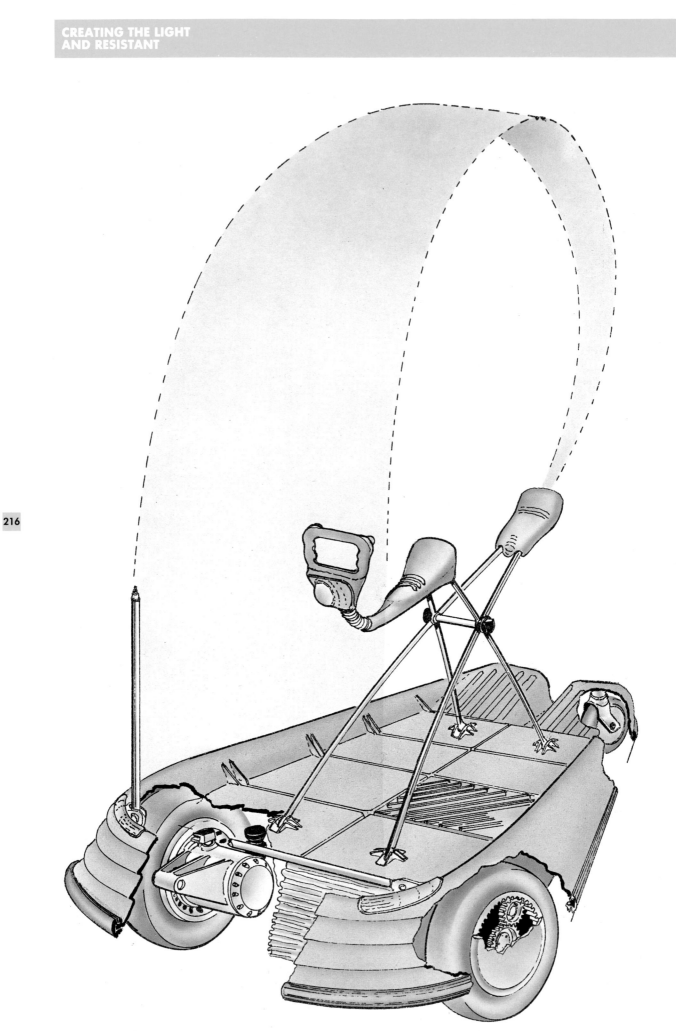

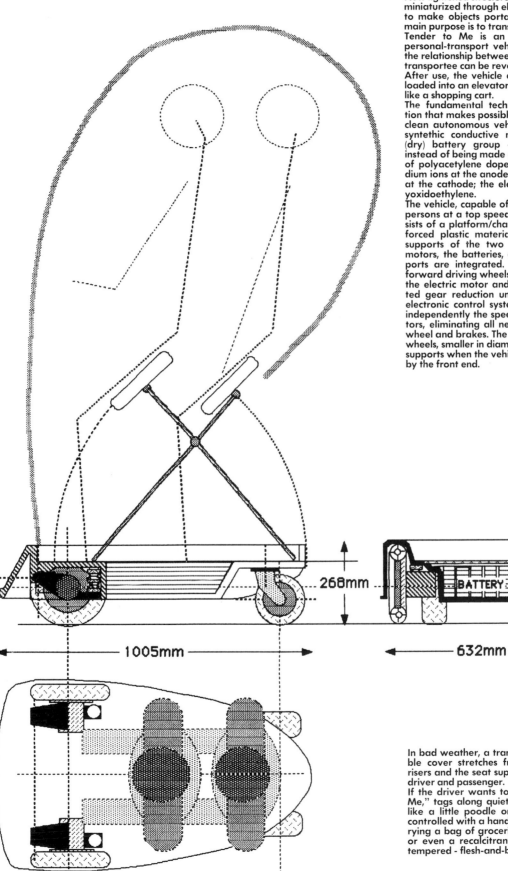

New lightened structures and mechanisms miniaturized through electronics allow us to make objects portable, even if their main purpose is to transport.

Tender to Me is an electric-powered personal-transport vehicle, so light that the relationship between transporter and transportee can be reversed if necessary. After use, the vehicle can be folded up, loaded into an elevator, and pulled home like a shopping cart.

The fundamental technological innovation that makes possible a very light and clean autonomous vehicle is the use of syntethic conductive materials for the (dry) battery group - the electrodes, instead of being made of lead, are made of polyacetylene doped with NA + sodium ions at the anode and I- iodine ions at the cathode; the electrolyte is a polyoxidoethylene.

The vehicle, capable of transporting two persons at a top speed of 30 km/h, consists of a platform/chassis made of reinforced plastic material into which the supports of the two wheels and two motors, the batteries, and the seat supports are integrated. Each of the two forward driving wheels forms a unit with the electric motor and with an integrated gear reduction unit in the hub; an electronic control system also regulates independently the speed of the two motors, eliminating all need for a steering wheel and brakes. The two pivoting rear wheels, smaller in diameter, also serve as supports when the vehicle is pulled along by the front end.

217

268mm

1005mm

BATTERY

632mm

In bad weather, a transparent and flexible cover stretches from two forward risers and the seat support to shelter the driver and passenger.

If the driver wants to stroll, "Tender to Me," tags along quietly after its master like a little poodle on a leash, remote controlled with a hand-held joystick, carrying a bag of groceries, a cranky child, or even a recalcitrant - and less even-tempered - flesh-and-blood poodle.

This is a redesigned "tajin", a primitive pressure cooker which I have had the occasion to use while travelling in North Africa. This object originates with the Berbers, nomads from the high Atlas region of southern Morocco. It is made of a refractory earthenware material which resists high temperatures, is well-insulated, and facilitates cooking by recycling vapor in its conical chamber. Its many advantages include the following:

1. It combines the benefits of cooking in an earthen material (which preserves flavor, and minimizes the amount of energy necessary for heating thanks to its thermic qualities) with those of steam cooking (which reduces the need for unhealthy amounts of animal fats and oils).

2. Its shape is simple and attractive. It consists of a cone set on a base whose walls are often decorated with plant motifs, or a bichromatic interplay of graphic patterns.

3. It is extremely easy to fill and clean, being made of two separate pieces, i.e., the pot and the lid.

4. It is a multi-use object; a pressure cooker when its conical cover and plate are used together, and a simple skillet without the cover. It can be brought directly to the table and used for serving and warming food.

The "tajin" cooks without destroying cellular structures, because, in contrast with steel pots, it has a "gentle" contact with the foods prepared within. The earthen material breathes, maintaining an equilibrium between internal and external, as if equipped with a myriad of tiny valves that regulate pressure and temperature, thus avoiding abrupt fluctuations.

SARHAOUI is a ceramic-fiber version of this object. Thermoplastic polyester and polytetrafluoroethylene are the other materials included in this technically integrated design.

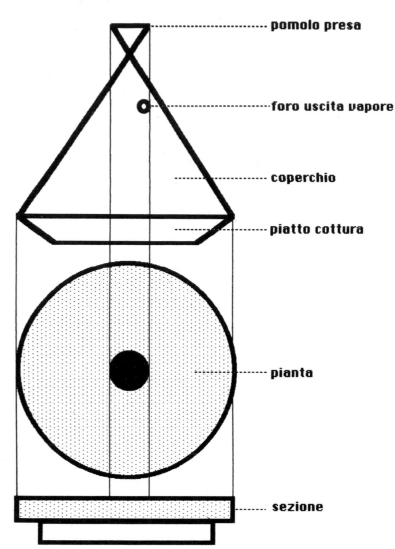

pomolo presa

foro uscita vapore

coperchio

piatto cottura

pianta

sezione

218

KAN was conceived as an instrument for domestic use. New approaches to food preparation, including macrobiotics and other special diets, have revolutionized our eating habits. The rediscovery of our organism has led us to consider the technical and esthetic value of foods, as well as the instruments they require.

A new "esthetic survival" nutrition philosophy is being developed; the symbolic and esthetic elements of food preparation are also important. Accessories have become decorative and symbolic, and the kitchen a domestic workshop. The computer has entered into the home environment. Materials are becoming more specific and "aware".

The knife KAN is an instrument made for the computerized environment. Its ceramic-fiber blade, precise and enduring, performs excellently. Thanks to the reduced friction of the blade, food cells and fibers remain intact. Nutritional value is therefore maintained at a high level.

This knife is equipped with reflectors so that it can be located in the dark; the handle, blade, and protective sheath are all differently colored. Its nylon grip makes it easy to manipulate. It is also very light, and much more durable than those made of traditional metal alloys.

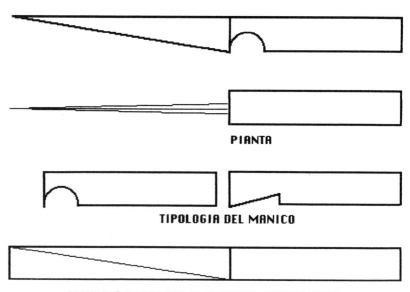

PIANTA

TIPOLOGIA DEL MANICO

ASTUCCIO IN GRAFITE O PLASTICA FLUORESCENTE

This is a personal, portable, "wireless" telephone.
CARD PHONE is part of a local, "cellular" system (in the office, at home, etc.) whose transmitting-receiving range is limited to twenty meters. The advantage of this is that little energy is required, and a "flat" battery can be used.
Thanks to the miniaturized and flat electronic audio components made available by today's technology, it is possible to make a flat, hand-sized unit that can be folded and placed in a pocket or wallet.

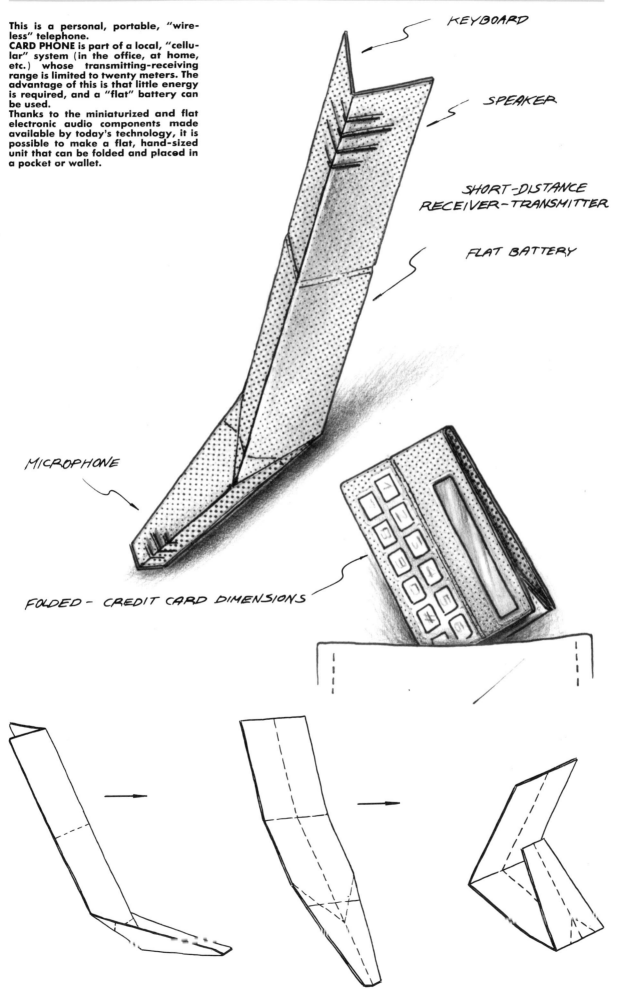

KEYBOARD

SPEAKER

SHORT-DISTANCE
RECEIVER-TRANSMITTER

FLAT BATTERY

MICROPHONE

FOLDED - CREDIT CARD DIMENSIONS

219

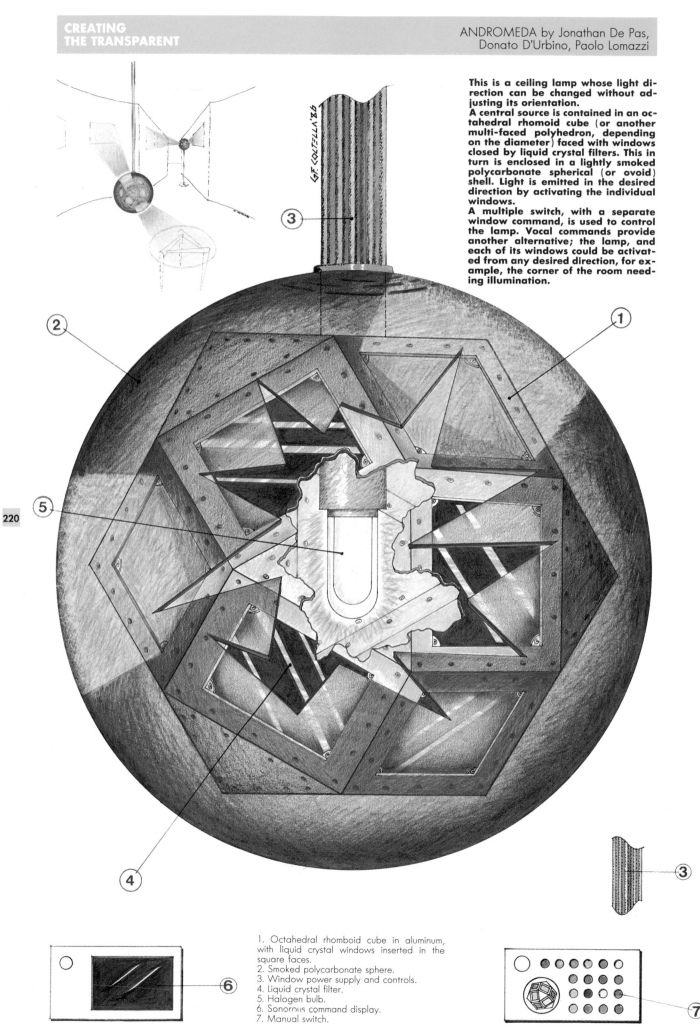

ANDROMEDA by Jonathan De Pas, Donato D'Urbino, Paolo Lomazzi

This is a ceiling lamp whose light direction can be changed without adjusting its orientation.

A central source is contained in an octahedral rhomoid cube (or another multi-faced polyhedron, depending on the diameter) faced with windows closed by liquid crystal filters. This in turn is enclosed in a lightly smoked polycarbonate spherical (or ovoid) shell. Light is emitted in the desired direction by activating the individual windows.

A multiple switch, with a separate window command, is used to control the lamp. Vocal commands provide another alternative; the lamp, and each of its windows could be activated from any desired direction, for example, the corner of the room needing illumination.

220

1. Octahedral rhomboid cube in aluminum, with liquid crystal windows inserted in the square faces.
2. Smoked polycarbonate sphere.
3. Window power supply and controls.
4. Liquid crystal filter.
5. Halogen bulb.
6. Sonorous command display.
7. Manual switch.

The holograms are reproduced on a plastic film, which is a few microns thick, applied to the piece of furniture's surface. The boundary between the decorated surface and the object's structure, though physically distinct, is figuratively subtle, unclear, and ambiguous; the decoration has its own three-dimensionality.

In the past, other means of simulating three dimensions, such as *tromp l'oeil*, have been used. But in this case, though simulated, the effect is "real", because it introduces the fourth dimension (time), through the movement of the observer.

The surface reproduces a virtual space superimposed on the actual depth of the piece; ample color variation is possible, depending on lighting conditions.

The generating of holographic figures by computer frees this type of decoration from the tradition imitative of natural materials (fake leather, wood...) and brings it closer to a newer form of iconography, that of the three-dimensional, mathematically generated pattern, of complex though ordered geometry.

The plastic film used for the holograms, (**PVC** or **PET**), is joined to the structure of the pieces, also in plastic, by hot stamping.

The possibility of reproducing holograms on paper would allow the application of this type of decoration to conventional laminates.

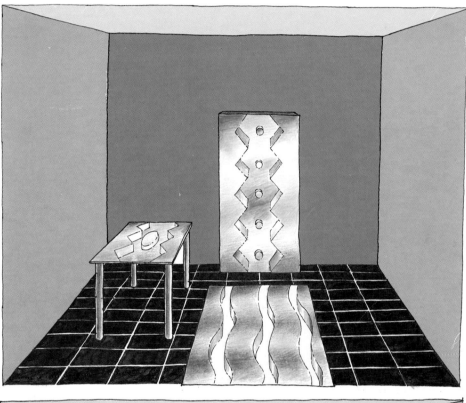

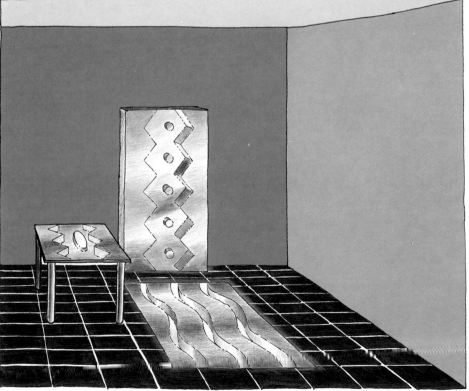

221

Bindings for touring skis must satisfy three fundamental requirements, that is, permit the use of the skis uphill, and guarantee a safe descent, both without adding superfluous weight. ASA 8619 fulfills these objectives by an oscillating walking mechanism, and a separate, integrated safety mechanism. Structurally efficient materials with low specific weights are used. The metal parts are made of die-cast aluminum based alloys; the self-lubricating, no-stick mechanical

elements, of polyamides and acetal resins; and polyester reinforced with carbon fibers is used for the body of the skis.
Separating the functional components allows a considerable weight reduction; the rotating plate and the connecting rods that normally support the mobile heel piece are eliminated. The fact that the heel piece remains fixed also minimizes the wear of the mechanical parts and adjustments to the loaded elements. More-

over, ASA 8619's safety system functions in every accident situation, because it opens in every direction, and is attached very near the ideal axis of the leg.
All of the materials are used in their natural form. This simplifies production, and its esthetically pleasant and aggressively technological impact is characterized by fluid forms suggestive of science fiction.

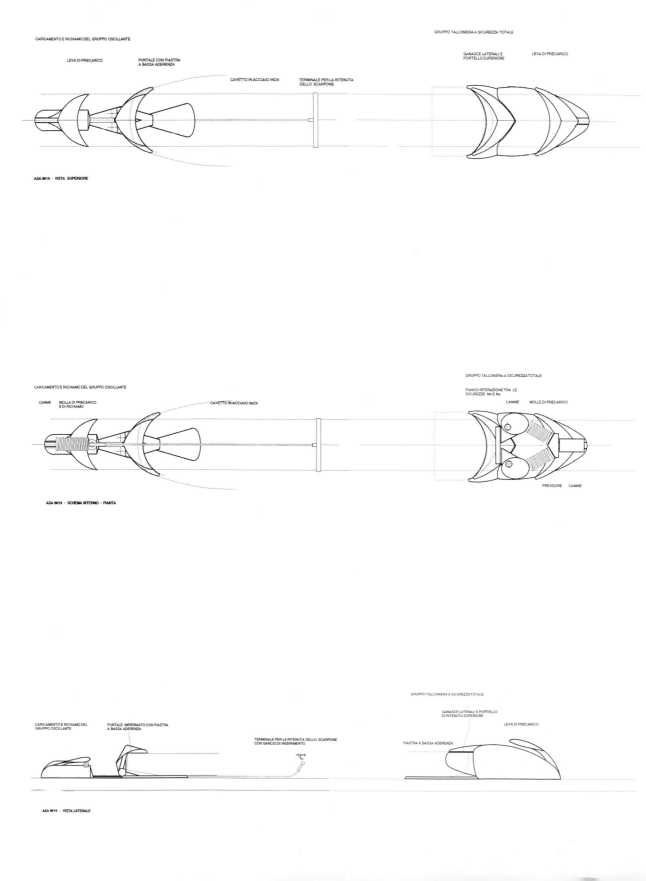

This polyethersulphone lamp is turned on by caressing it. Luminous intensity is regulated by the amount of "stroking". A single touch is all that is required to turn it off.
The lamp contains a bulb, and a touch-activated, switch/phase transformer.
The sensor consists of a copper circuit deposited on an insulating plastic surface, by a photochemical process similar to that used for printed circuits (technique, for deposit on curved surfaces by PCK Technology Div., Melville, N.Y., U.S.A.).

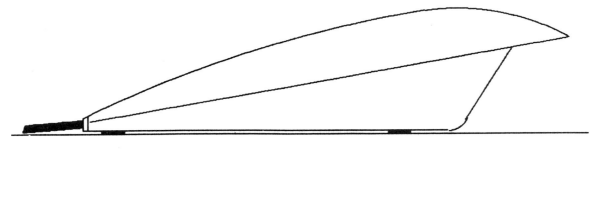

223

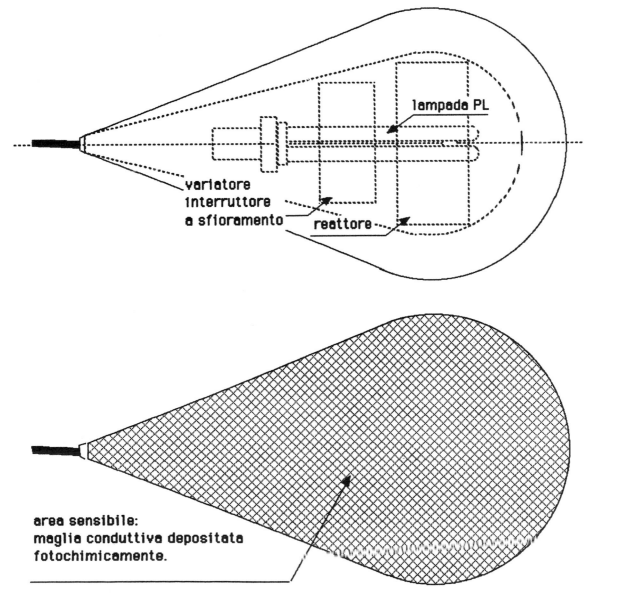

lampada PL

variatore
interruttore
a sfioramento

reattore

area sensibile:
maglia conduttiva depositata
fotochimicamente.

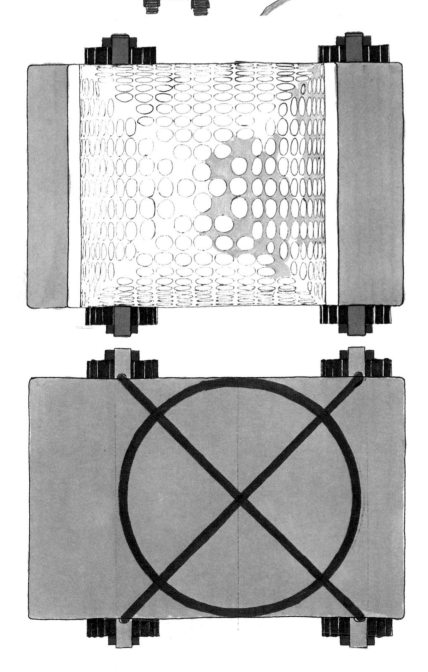

Perhaps we are on the verge of freeing ourselves from the ancient carriage, which has remained unchanged for the last century, even if we have unhitched the horses, and crammed it with mechanisms and electronic signals.

This is also an automobile (in the sense that it moves by itself), that is destined to change the face of the city, which now refuses to digest the long line of boxes that go 200 kilometers per hour; those steel biers we use (when permitted by law) to go "downtown", just to realize that the city is dead and the only problem is getting out of it. We move at a speed close to zero, though statistically proven to be twenty-five kilometers per hour.

This automobile is made of a large, one-piece flexible differentiated-density bumper in polyurethane. Inside, two people can fit comfortably, protected by a transparent polycarbonate shell. Solar cells are housed in a cupola which sits on top of this shell, and contribute to the vehiclés energy supply.

New technology provides this self-propelled shell, which looks like it came out of an antique oriental print, and which can be "worn" like clothing, with exceptional performance features. All of the "mechanical" elements, which are still a part of our 200 km/h car, are left behind.

The cabin rotates on a supporting RTS plate, to which the pivoting wheels are also attached, and which contains the batteries (of the lightest polyacetylene). This rotating cabin eliminates the necessity of moving in reverse, so we can always look ahead while driving.

A flat, electronically controlled motor is connected to every wheel. By turning the rheostat-equipped steering wheel, the difference in velocity transmitted to the two wheels makes the car turn, just as the electronic motor command controls breaking. The wheels are tracked in order to put the vehicle in gear and facilitate stopping on difficult surfaces.

Our car, whose cabin measures 1.10 by 1.10 meters, will then really be mobile. Single lane parking and large asphalt lots will be done away with, and we can then park in little scattered groups, in fields, on hillsides, or even on the stairs.

All of these technological advances are achieved without creating a "high tech" image.

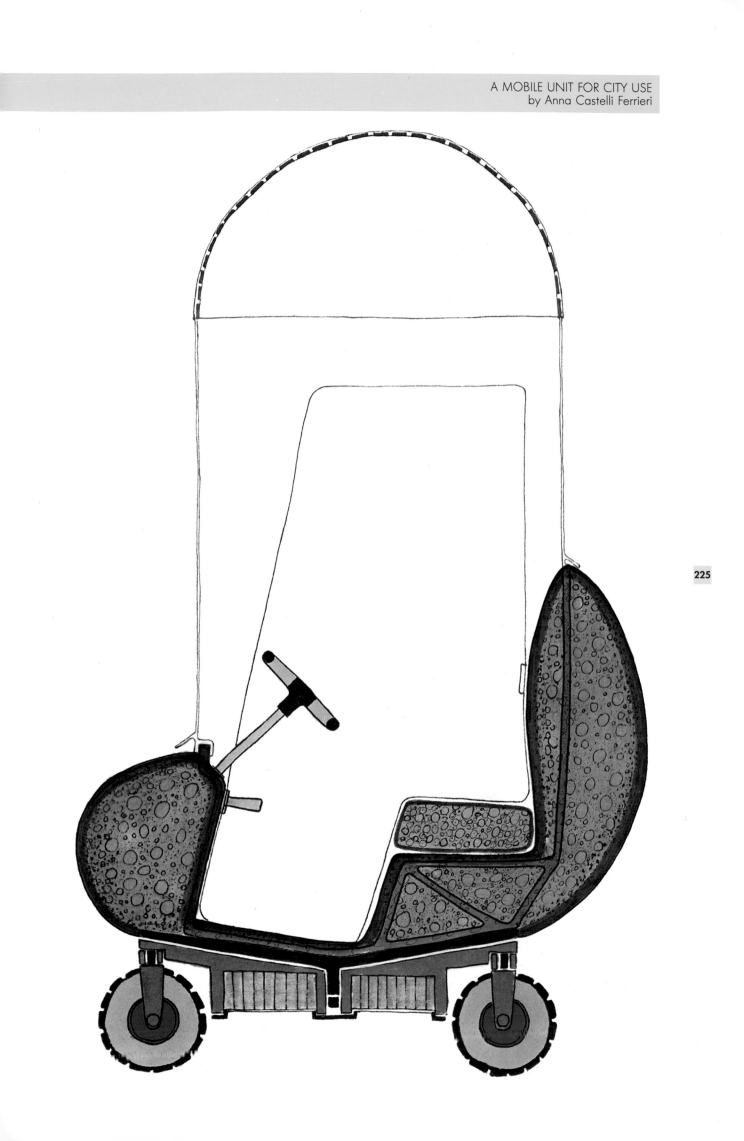

Our objective was to develop a structurally continuous chair without joints, which provides a compromise between rigidity and comfort, two factors normally in opposition.
Therefore, this chair integrates a frame-substituting grid, the structural support (legs, back, seat, etc.) attachments, and an appropriately molded surface that acts as "padding", in one piece.
Polyamide resins or polypropylene are the best materials for this type of application.

226

This helmet provides a 360-degree field of vision, eliminating the necessity of the two rear-view mirrors with which motorcycles are usually equipped.

Rear view is made possible by integrating a system of image transmission within the helmet. This consists of a wide-angle lens, that can be adjusted and focused, on the back of the helmet; optical fibers that run around the crown and transmit the images, and a visor positioned in axis with the driver's forehead.

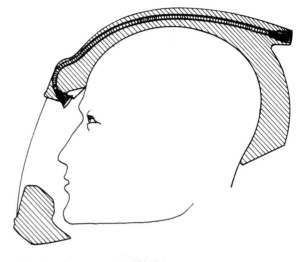

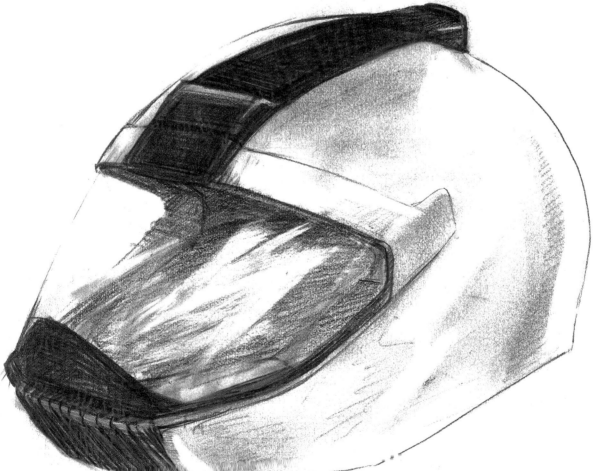

New discoveries in the area of electroluminescence have led to this idea for large, evanescent umbrella-veils, supported by resistant, flexible, slender shafts. Like immense moonlit seagulls, they oscillate when moved by the night breeze.

Here we can escape from dampness, sit down, light a cigarette, enjoy an ice cream, or we can meet our friends in the dead of night on a deserted beach, or in a park, where there are no electrical outlets.

This 3 by 3 meter veil is made of four triangular elements. These in turn consist of two sheets of lightly colored transparent polycarbonate, with a thin polymeric film containing dissolved zinc sulphate particles in between. When solicited by an alternating current, this sandwich emits a faint light.

A polycarbonate fiber shaft supports the veil at its center, and is fixed in a heavy reinforced nylon base filled with water or sand.

228

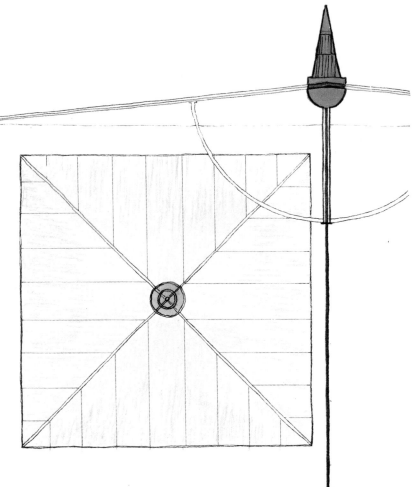

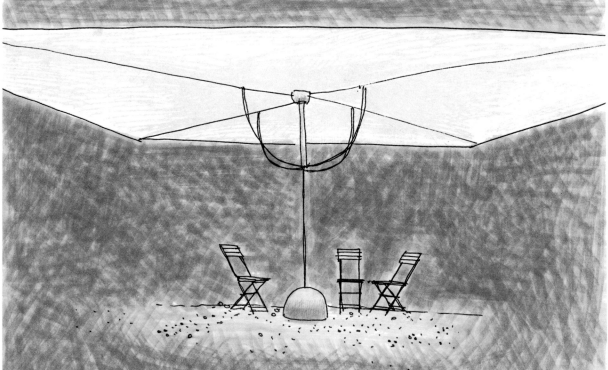

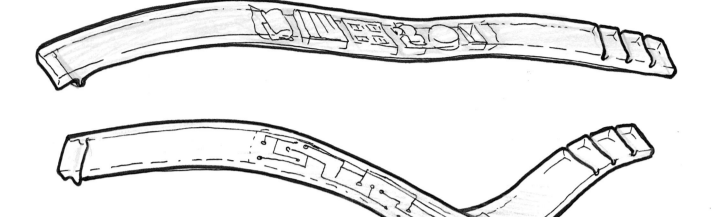

The readout, energy supply, and controls of the **JELLY WATCH** (in addition to possible sonorous and luminous optionals) are encased in a single plastic, transparent, flexible body which has many practical and esthetic advantages.

The feasibility of this design is tied to the two-stage application of a thermoplastic rubber.

This process consists of the following:

A. Injection molding of a support which is accurately designed to house the components. These are insulated and protected by the insertion of a piece of film carrying their integrating circuitry;

B. The completion of the form, including the setting of the watchface (perfectly sealed, functional, and legible), and the notches for its closure, by another injection molding.

This procedure, technically indispensable for the proper insulation of an inserted piece when injection molding is used, provides the following advantages:

- The use of a consistent, perfectly dosed and adjusted mixture in the first, "technological" phase of the

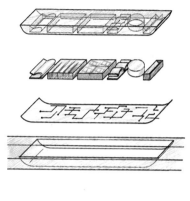

watch's production;

- The possibility of creating a commercially interesting gamut of molded pieces, by varying the quantity and quality of additives.

The design leads to the following considerations and possibilities.

Solar cell batteries can be used, thanks to the semi-transparent housing which protects the mechanism.

The visibility of the liquid crystal readout can be substituted by LEDs. These, in addition to being legible in the dark, can be activated by command, transforming the watch into a purely esthetic object when not consulted.

The LEDs, as well as any eventual sonorous devices, must fuction by solar cell, and this could indicate the advantages of a mixed energy supply, i.e., one that includes dry cell batteries.

Two versions are thus possible; a more sophisticated watch, which would be "disposable" because it includes a conventional battery, and a solar cell model, without LEDs and sonorous devices, which would (theoretically) be eternal.

229

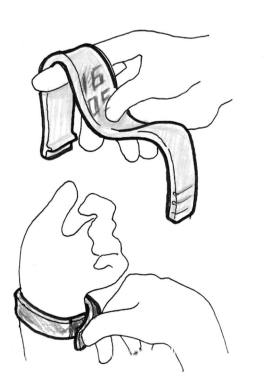

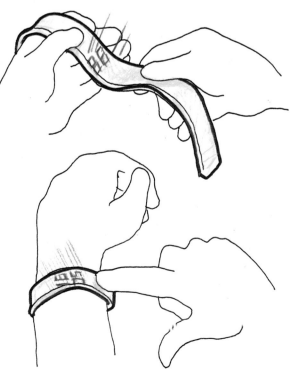

In recent years we have witnessed the development of lightweight architectural coverings that utilize specially made translucent fabrics. They exclude wind, rain, and snow, while allowing the penetration of diffused natural light to the underlying environment.

This project proposes a new, advanced, architectural fabric "skylight", which extends the possibilities of "high tech" tents used for stadiums, exhibition areas, and urban spaces. The incorporation of flat electroluminescent lamps in the fabric construction not only controls the penetration of natural light, but also makes night light or illuminated display possible.

As we look for new qualities within our urban environment, the creation of a covering offering diversity of color, decoration, and graphic signals could help to stimulate new design projects.

These architectural fabrics are based on a woven mesh of fiberglass coated with Teflon PTFE, to guarantee resist-

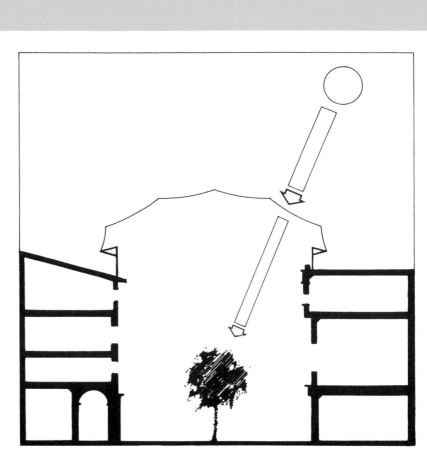

1. "Skylight" fabric
2. "Electroluminescent" lamp
3. Solar cell
4. Sunlight
5. Diffused sunlight
6. Internal reflected light

230

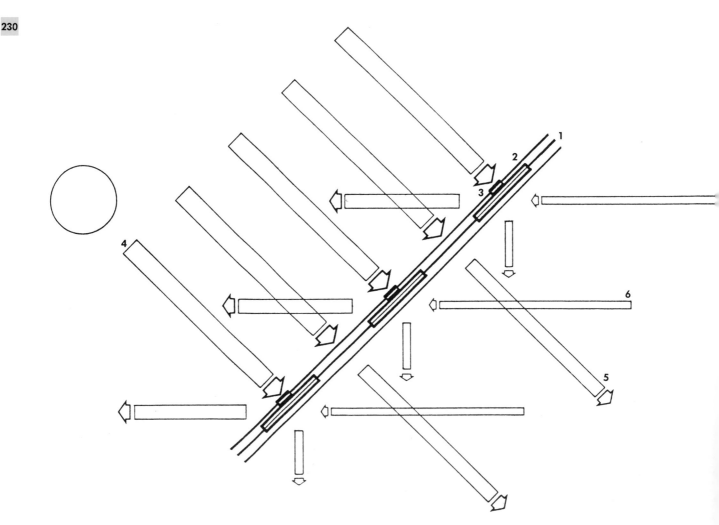

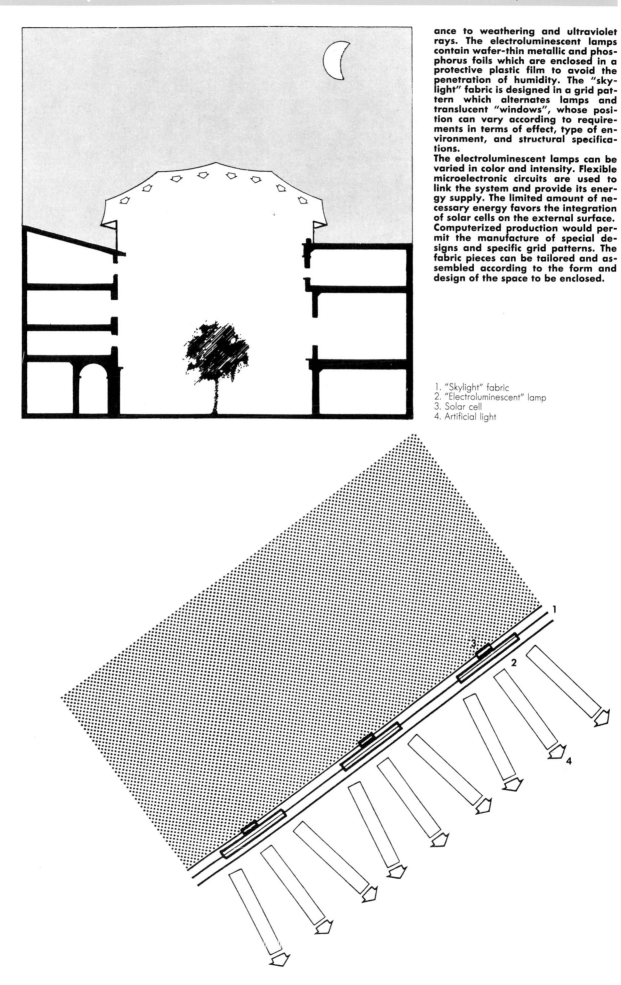

ance to weathering and ultraviolet rays. The electroluminescent lamps contain wafer-thin metallic and phosphorus foils which are enclosed in a protective plastic film to avoid the penetration of humidity. The "skylight" fabric is designed in a grid pattern which alternates lamps and translucent "windows", whose position can vary according to requirements in terms of effect, type of environment, and structural specifications.

The electroluminescent lamps can be varied in color and intensity. Flexible microelectronic circuits are used to link the system and provide its energy supply. The limited amount of necessary energy favors the integration of solar cells on the external surface. Computerized production would permit the manufacture of special designs and specific grid patterns. The fabric pieces can be tailored and assembled according to the form and design of the space to be enclosed.

1. "Skylight" fabric
2. "Electroluminescent" lamp
3. Solar cell
4. Artificial light

231

This is a pyramidal (three or four-sided) table lamp that features the use of the same liquid crystals that are commonly found in pocket video games.

An internal 150-watt Halostar halogen bulb with an aluminum parabolic reflector directs the light onto two (or three) faces of the pyramid.

One of the faces is an electronic panel for controlling the liquid crystal circuits. The others consist of a glass "sandwich", whose interior surface acts as a diffuser, while the external one is transparent. Film containing the liquid crystals with a matrix arrangemen, is located between these two surfaces, and its pattern can be adjusted according to the possibilities provided by the microchip program in the control panel.

The patterns obtained regulate the amount of light transmitted, according to the number of points activated on the matrix. This enables a decorative variation of light intensity. A keyboard located on the lamp's base is used to select the possible combinations.

This lamp can also have some optional features, such as a digital clock, a calendar, or an alarm with screen-displayed or sonorous messages communicated at any time of the day.

A 12-volt electronic transformer attached to the electrical outlet is all that is required to operate the display.

232

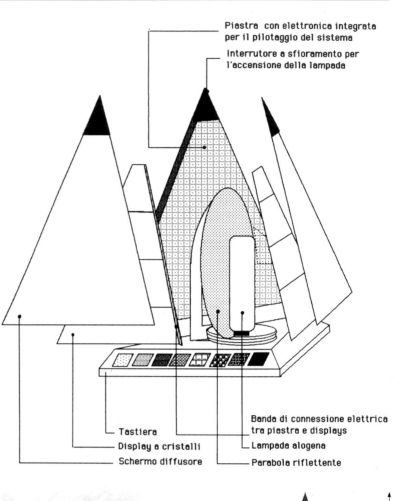

Piastra con elettronica integrata
per il pilotaggio del sistema

Interrutore a sfioramento per
l'accensione della lampada

Tastiera

Display a cristalli

Schermo diffusore

Banda di connessione elettrica
tra piastra e displays

Lampada alogena

Parabola riflettente

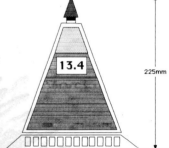

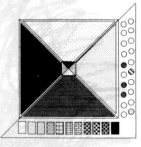

13.4

225mm

199mm

There is another accessory, in addition to the pocket TV, Walkman, and solar cell calculator, which will soon become indispensable to the neo-nomad; it is the roll-up travel scale.

Flexible and "intelligent" materials substitute the mechanisms of the traditional scale. A sheet of piezoresistive elastomer takes the place of the lever system, altering an electric signal in proportion with the pressure exerted; a flexible display, which can also indicate weight variations, replaces the dial.

The material's embossed surface makes it easier to roll up and secure the scale by itself.

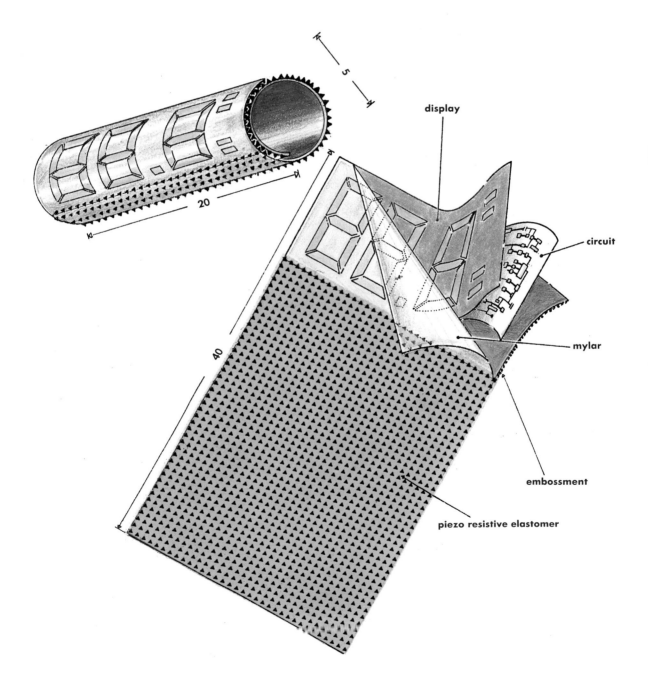

display

circuit

mylar

embossment

piezo resistive elastomer

This extruded plastic wire, bunched together to make a spherical form, can accomodate the body in different positions.

Its name combines the initials of the three members (Gatti, Paolini, Teodoro) of the design studio that I once belonged to. In a certain sense, this project is the result of some ideas that emerged during the design of the "Sacco" (bean bag) chair, and is an attempt to improve some of its features (perhaps worsening others?!).

The most interesting aspects of this piece include its unique material (which goes beyond structure, content, and container-covering inter-relationships); its lightness, elasticity, flexibility of configuration (its volume can also be reduced for packing and shipping), and absence of any "formalism" a priori.

The starting date of this project refers to the initial "Sacco" design. Today, the development of new plastic materials and relative production technologies make it possible to realize the intentions we had back then. So I dedicate this project to Cesare Paolini, who died prematurely in 1983, and Franco Teodoro, who has been happily "exiled" in the Maremma for some years; its design would not have been possible if not for the lively and heated discussions on design that the three of us shared together.

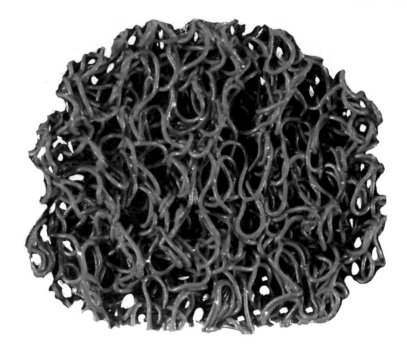

234

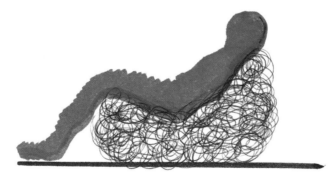

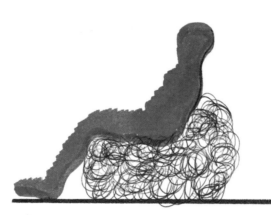

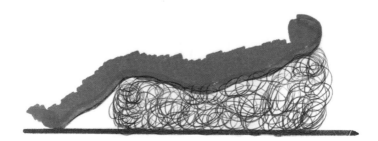

MYDOG is a *Cyborg* (*Cybernetic organism*), that is, a living organism in which some parts are substituted by artificial equivalents, made of various materials.
This term was coined in 1960 by Dr. Clynes and Dr. Kline of New York's Rockland hospital to help describe their work, directed toward the possibility of man's "artificialization", which would enable him to live under special conditions, e.g., on other planets. But this type of being has already been described in the science fiction of the twenties, and comprise the last link of the chain of artificial creatures that range from Archita's pigeon to Erone's self-propelled machines, eighteenth century robots, and, through cabalist tradition (Golem), anthropomorphic androids.
Cyborg is also relevant to the latest experiments in genetic manipulation and the frontiers of artificial intelligence. DNA modification and intervention techniques, and research on organic chips together create a series of possibilities of which MYDOG has a full share (see Antonio Caronia, *Il cyborg. Saggio sull'uomo artificiale*, Theoria, Rome-Naples 1985).

1. MYDOG is a Scottish terrier with "real fake fur", hydroponically grown. His ears and tail are of India rubber, and his collar, liquid crystals.

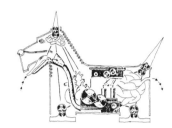

2. MYDOG; section showing functional mechanism.

3. Standard MOBILE (self-propelled) BAR function. Back flap opens to provide wood counter. Works mechanically.

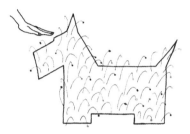

4. Standard PETTING function. Optical fibers which are illuminated in response to caresses by the owner/user are hidden among surface hairs.

235

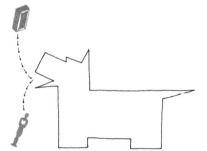

5. Optional ARTIST function. Permits MYDOG to transform an appropriate raw material into an artistic object, both by request on the part of the user, as well as autonomously, as an expression of particular emotions.

6. Standard SMELL DISPENSER function. The dispensing of perfumes, synthesized by MYDOG, using his chemical equipment, can be effected in response to determinate user moods.

7. Standard SELF-ILLUMINATING function. Nose combines the advantages of a light source for MYDOG's night time excursions, as well as for the user, in the event of a blackout.

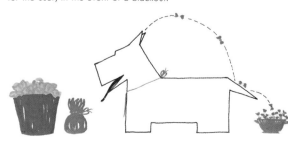

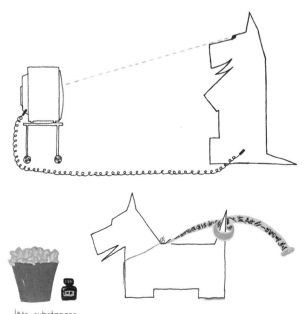

9. and 10. Standard REMNANTS TRANSFORMER function. By adding a selected ingredient, MYDOG transforms rejected material (for example, contents of office wastepaper baskets) into useful, and useless, substances.
9. + sugar candy
10. + ink strips of paper for printing, etc.

A lake is a source of reflection. The hills rise gradually, like an amphitheatre. A sharp architectural image rises from the jet-black water, reflected as in a mirror.

Entrance pavilions, corridors, passages. Three central bodies, each with eleven corridors leading to eleven rectangular halls.

There could be a moon as well, reflected in the water; or only the transient light of this translucent architecture, and the colors, voices, and other sounds that escape this not perfectly transparent, not perfectly opaque structure.

From this (imperfect) panopticon of happiness, shouts, lightning, laughter, and words search for possible meaning. What complicity ties the chaste monk to his cloister, and the libertine to his castle? He who reflects by a lake follows a path, designs his own course. Once upon a time rocks, earth, trees, and bushes were the materials available to the architect; now he fashions the artificial. The path at nature's threshold could then be occasionally (or in unison?) gay, thoughtful, disquieting, light-hearted.

In a large, electronic amusement park, rites of passage between the physical body that walks, sees, touches, and the emotional mind that flies and dreams can be played with. In the translucent architecture on the water, there is a park full of emotional attractions, ready to spark psychic individual or group performances on the narrow confines between the body and the mind. In the Entrance Pavilions, people meet, greet, or ignore one another. Each anticipates his own course. Perhaps it's necessary to wait patiently in line (even dreams are sometimes crowded in the artificial world).

Alone, in couples, in groups; they are met with smiles. In the Menu Pavilion the trip is selected. A rapid exchange of electronic money, and here's the intelligent magnetic card used to open the door that leads to the course.

The only necessary device is the console-glove which must be worn in order to interface the body (the hand) with the external, electronic world.

The corridor — twenty-eight meters to start with — is sensitive to the passing of that particular and expected body (precisely *that* voice, *that* gesture), because it has been programmed by the magnetic card, catalyzed by the console-glove. A shout is enough to trigger the sensitivity of the panels that, with an inaudible swish along the twenty-eight meter length, become red — or violet, or yellow, or crimson — the precise color of *that* voice.

The performance takes place in the hall at the end of the corridor. There are those who want to follow the winding alleys and squares of a deserted Venice; others want to play in a world championship sports match, live a thrilling experience among zombies and replicas, or see what it is like to fly. Directors of imagination, dreams, eroticism, spiritual and pornographic practices, meditation, and unadulterated fun skip through this place where every interactive adventure becomes possible. This is no downtown Disneyland; if anything, it is Hollywood in Quarto Oggiaro.

The halls' reactive panels are the wings of the electronic stage. It is possible that I meet my own image — reflected, multiplied, deformed, transformed — in a voyage beyond the mirror. Actions could be delayed, or accelerated; there is the risk of meeting your future self.

The designer thus sketches experimentally, escaping any requirements that are not of his own invention. It is precisely for this that he isn't subjected to, but rather determines, the materials specifications necessary for this undertaking. For this impossible lakeside architecture which comes to life only under the starry sky, the designer lauches (hurling nothingness into the field of possibility) a new plastic material which is neutral, sensitive (remember celluloid, the material that proved to be excellent for a hundred years?), interactive, translucent, reflective, video-receptive, and can be industrially produced in standard 1.125 by 1.500 mm sheets. Thickness: 3mm. Name: As yet unknown.

Four moral tales

I

Patrizia Nightingale, disappointed by love, is a little bit pale, but not completely unhappy. She dreams of Thomas Mann's Venice, though with music by Liszt.

She has no plans for this Saturday night. She gets out of the bathtub, looks at herself in the mirror, and puts on some perfume. An hour later, when she parks her car in the large, green esplanade, the lights are all lit. At the end of the walk that leads to the entrance to the massive structure reflected in the lake, an electronic barker invites her to enter. Patrizia Nightingale walks into the already crowded hall. She buys her "smart card" with programable memory, at the cash register. A quick glance at the screens in the Menu Pavilion. Next, in the Memory Pavilion, she sits in front of file terminal. She programs her smart card, personalizing it. Slipping on her console-glove, she makes her way toward the appropriate corridor.

She inserts her card at the entrance. It is accepted. She enters. With a gesture, the console-glove activates the panels. The corridor is transformed into a sunny, lonely Venice. It has been restored. There are no Japanese in sight. At the end of the alley, the "calle dei Marrani", at San Geremia in Ghetto, a quartet is playing Liszt. On a bridge, the "Ponte delle Maravegie", some cats watch the green water of the canal.

At the end of the walk, some polaroid shots await her, souvenirs of her visit. A pale signorina in front of ancient and splendid palazzos. The photos are enclosed in an envelope with "airmail" written across it, in colored letters.

Is it possible that a little act of revenge has crossed the mind of Patrizia Nightingale, disappointed in love, pale, but not completely unhappy?

II

Paolo Sorsi bought a leather football for his son Jacopo. Today, Saturday, is his seventh birthday. A few clumsy kicks in the esplanade, and they head for the entrance. Paolo Sorsi smiles at the hostess. He buys a smart card. Jacopo is spellbound by the hundred screens in the Menu Pavilion, but his father is not distracted. At the file terminal in the Memory Pavilion, he quickly programs his smart card. Jacopo, excited, runs in circles clapping his hands. Once in the assigned corridor, his father speaks into the microphone contained in the console-glove. His voice resonates along the corridor, up to the hall at its end. The sensitive panels become electronic mirrors with hidden TV cameras. In that panel on the right, there are two short, chubby figures. In this one, they can see two slim and trim ones. And down there at the end – how weird... the little child, tall and muscular, stands next to a small, insignificant adult.

Paolo Sorsi presses a button on the glove. Now his index finger, pointed towards the panels, can partially erase the reflections. Jacopo laughs happily. That football was really a great gift. But he's waiting for the high spot of the evening. He takes off his shirt in front of one of the electronic mirrors. There appears a light blue T-shirt with a tricolor emblem. Having walked the last few meters of the corridor leading to the hall, father and son enter the sizzling bowl of the Aztec stadium in Mexico City.

A whistle and the game begins. Attending a world cup championship isn't something that happens every day. Nobody seems to notice that there are two footballs on the field.

Passing is frequent and accurate; Jacopo is happy. That football was really a great gift; at least judging by his father's joy. Leaving with a smile on his face, Jacopo has *almost* forgotten about the toy soldiers he asked for, and which he will probably never receive.

III

Tristano Calvero lazily receives his smart card from the hands of a smiling hostess. Pavilion 3. Corridor 7. In the Memory Pavilion he programs his console-glove, creating a perfect interface between his body and the sensitive environment. The automatic door closes behind him. Tristano Calvero looks down the corridor, and sees the hall down at the other end.

Some insignificant thoughts pass slowly across his mind, from right to left. Then nothing. I wonder what color my voice is? He brings the glove near his mouth and shouts. A dark red band flecked with ultramarine immediately appears with a swish, and in a few fractions of a second reaches the end of the corridor.

He brings the glove near his mouth once again, this time whispering. A gentle yellow stretches across the red.

Tristano Calvero presses a little button on the console-glove. He moves his index finger toward the sensitive panels, and over its smooth surface, forming sounds and words with his voice. A large painting, created by voice, touch, and body, begins to take shape.

With his index finger, he traces a graffito, "God is dead". Signed, "Nietzsche". Then with a wave of his hand he now reads, "Nietzsche is dead". Signed, "God".

In the hall at the end of the corridor Tristano finds, as was programmed by his smart card, a gallery of famous paintings. The most important works in the history of art are collected on high-definition panels; it is the "impossible museum". Calvero throws one last glance at his painting, on the corridor panels, and then walks toward the exceptional, imaginary collection. He raises a finger of the console-glove, and begins *correcting* line and color.

IV

Giacomo Morgani parks his small, fiery red convertible next to a graceful elm. Gina Floppi, a shapely twenty-year old, gets out, giving a quick shake to her auburn-black hair.

They enter together. In the Memory Hall, they each program a smart card. This allows them free access to the Great Visual Archives.

They prepare for a battle of images. Still in the corridor, Morgani whispers into his console-glove, and a huge, heated hurricane appears on the sensitive panels. It knocks the two of them down. She immediately responds with an endless and deserted savannah.

He looses a Sahara sandstorm.

She evokes the icy peace of an aurora borealis.

He sets a massive avalanche of the whitest snow in motion.

She slams a heavy gate in front of a spotless villa.

He...

And the enchanted tournament continues, blow for blow. Until time seems to stop.

An hour later, Tristano Calvero offers a ride to a pale girl, not entirely unhappy, who has perhaps been betrayed by a faulty ignition coil. Nearby, a new leather football hits (and breaks) the tail-light of a small, fiery red convertible, parked next to a graceful elm. Calvero is formed to alarm by the braking and resistance a child who suddenly appears from behind a car, chasing the ball. Next to the driver's seat, a girl raises her arm behind the windshield, letting out a little yell. A slight blush briefly passes over her pallid cheeks, as the surrounding lights begin to go out.
Gianni Barbacetto

APPENDICES

Designing Matter

Polymers and Composites

by Leonardo Fiore and Giuseppe Gianotti, Istituto "Guido Donegani," Novara

The systematic exploration of the relationships between property and structure in plastic materials has progressed so greatly that it is now possible to design a material with specific characteristics at the drawing board. It is then only necessary to do quantitative testing of individual parameters for which a theoretical formulation has not yet been reached.

This chapter intends to provide the reader with a rapid description of the principles that govern the relationships between property and structure in plastic materials. For the sake of clarity, the influences deriving from specific structural characteristics and from molecular organization have been examined separately from other macroscopic influences tied to engineering formulations of materials. Among the former influences, aside from the general influence of molecular mass (a characteristic peculiar to this class of materials) we shall consider crystallinity, molecular chemical structure, and cross-linking. Among the influences of engineering formulation, we shall deal only with the most important - blends and advanced composites.

5.1.1

MOLECULAR MASSES

The peculiar characteristics of plastic materials derive from their molecular structure. That structure is based on long chains, or macromolecules, created through the addition or condensation of simple molecular elements (monomers), through special chemical processes (polymerization). Their properties (physical, physical/mechanical, etc.) obviously depend on the number of primary units that form the polymer chain (degree of polymerization), that is, on the molecular weight of the macromolecule ($\overline{M}$). One should note that this parameter, as far as the statistical mechanisms that govern polymerization processes, does not reveal - as it does for micromolecular substances - a single value for each substance, but an average value. This depends on the distribution function, which mathematically represents the law governing the frequency of molecular species present (Molecular Weight Distribution, MWD).

Since the different average molecular weights (by number of monomers, by weight, and so on) depend on the distribution function, it is evident that, at a second glance, this too influences the properties of the material.

Average molecular weight

All the data heretofore acquired on polymer materials indicate that properties in general and mechanical (tensile) properties in particular depend on molecular weight. There is in fact a threshold value (Mc) beneath which the material is inconsistent. Of course, the value varies from polymer to polymer, depending on the nature (structure, polarity, and so on) of the monomer unit. At any rate, it tends to remain at fairly low levels: ($< 4000 \div 5000$).

After a zone of transition, in which the properties depend sharply on the variation of molecular weight, one can register an asymptotic tendency toward a limit condition, which however halts all further processing of the material.

We can therefore determine a useful interval of molecular weight, which constitutes the best compromise among the material's characteristics and processability. The determination of this interval becomes the focus in the design of a new material.

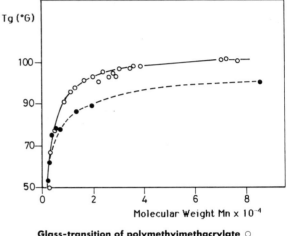

Glass-transition of polymethyimethacrylate ○ and or polystyrene ● as a function of temperature or molecular weight.

The behavior of the curve indicated in fig. 1 can be expressed in a purely empirical fashion by the equation:

$$A = A_\infty \left(1 - \frac{Mc}{M}\right) \qquad [1]$$

in which A indicates the properties considered, A_∞ indicates the asymptotic value, M indicates the molecular mass of the material being examined, and Mc its threshold value. Clearly, the equation correctly interprets only experimental results where $M > Mc$. Below that value, we encounter a physical absurdity.

The first approximation value provided by this equation is certainly important in determining beforehand a material's intrinsic characteristics. A precise theoretical formulation requires fundamental knowledge about relations between specific structural aspects of a macromolecule and each individual property. We, unfortunately, do not yet fully possess this knowledge.

Distribution of molecular weights

As has been pointed out amply in other sections of this volume, it is not always easy to discern the distinction between the product/material from the technology used to transform it into a finished product. It is therefore logical that different typologies or grades of the same material should be on the market, corresponding to special uses or transformation techniques (injection, extrusion, blowing, etc.). In most cases, this range of products corresponds to molecular characteristics of the polymer. Furthermore, aside from the specific average value of molecular weight, diversification often involves its distribution function, which may be narrowed or broadened: for instance, the viscosity of the melt and its rheological behavior depend heavily on this parameter, which has little influence on the characteristics of the finished product, but which is decisive in terms of transformation technology.

Thus injection molding of small complex items, where the

technological factor of speed of production is predominant, is best done with a low molecular weight and a narrow distribution function, while the extrusion of a fairly large-diameter tube (which must support its own weight while in the forming) requires a material with greater molecular weight and a broader distribution function.

It is therefore the task of the macromolecular chemist to isolate synthesis conditions (catalyzers, solvents, temperatures, etc.) that permit custom production of materials for each individual application.

5.1.2

CRYSTALLINITY

The capacity to crystallize is an important structural parameter, and can affect a material's characteristics quite markedly, especially those of a polymer material.

Even though the degree of three-dimensional organization in polymers is far lower than the degree attained by other organic or inorganic micromolecular substances, it is nevertheless sufficient to trigger a dramatic alteration in certain properties. Aside from a few characteristics that are proper to the state itself (melting point, high density, etc.) the advantages of crystallinity are noted also, and chiefly, in the mechanical properties (breaking load, modulus of elasticity, etc.), and in properties of preventing diffusion, solvent-resistance, and their maintenance over a wide range of temperatures.

Therefore, whatever interpretation we use for a partially three-dimensional model such as the one established experimentally for polymers, it is nevertheless essential to examine more closely the structure and composition of the polymer chain at its foundation.

Regularity of structure

If crystallinity, in a polymer material, derives from the establishment of three-dimensional order, the possibility of lateral organization of different polymer chains (or substantial parts of the chain itself) into a crystalline lattice is dependent on the degree of order found in that chain. In other words, the macromolecule must possess a repetitive arrangement along the chain itself. Linear polyethylene, for instance, possesses a planar zig-zag configuration of "trans" bonds that is capable of meeting this condition.

Another example is that of isotactic polyethylene. In the Fifties, Giulio Natta showed that, in the case of the polyolefins, the orderly steric arrangement of groups on the principal polymer chain, or on substantial portions of it, permit these materials to cystallize. When all the substituents on the asymmetrical carbon atoms show the same configuration, they are called "isotactic," while if there are regularly alternating configurations, then they are referred to as "syndiotactic." Deviations from these two models or hybrid states over short-term periods indicate an "atactic" polymer, i.e., an amorphous structure.

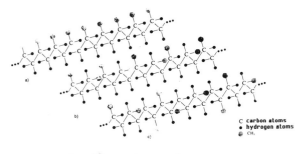

Stearic isomerism in polypropylene
a) isotactic; b) syndiotactic; c) atactic.

The spectacular effect of these structural regularities upon crystallization and, in turn, of crystallization upon many properties - including thermal and mechanical properties - has been demonstrated by much research done on classes of polymers other than polyolefins, and today constitutes a fundamental principle in the design of new structures.

An equally substantial effect on the final properties of materials is exerted by the "cis-trans" isomerism of the double bonds in the chain, the best-known examples of which are offered by polymers with 1-4 disposition of butadiene and isoprene.

Similarly to the "cis" and "trans" isomers with polyisoprene structure that are found in nature (natural rubber and guttapercha), in the correct conditions it has been possible to synthesize practically pure structures of the two "cis" and "trans" isomers of polybutadiene 1-4. They differ sharply one from another - "trans" polybutadiene has characteristics typical of a crystal plastomer with a melting point at arund 140 °C, while the "cis" isomer is an excellent elastomer, which crystallizes under stretching only at temperatures below room temperature.

It is therefore evident that the chain order is a fundamental parameter governing crystallization, which in turn, affects the properties of the material. This rule applies even when the macromolecule is made up of two or more monomer units, such as with copolymers. Indeed, alternating structures of the ABABABAB type can generate crystallinity (with the resulting consequences), while structures with the same relationship between co-monomers but with statistical distribution (for instance, -ABBABABBBAABAA-) are generally amorphous.

There is material for a separate examination of the copolymers in which the chemical species (A and B) can be organized in a long sequence of one species (let's say A) connected to a successive series of the other species (B) and so on, if one should desire materials with several sequences. We shall discuss these materials at greater length later, when examining heterophase systems.

Intermolecular attraction

When flexible macromolecules associate in multimolecular structures, with well-defined side order, the stability of this state of aggregation depends on the sort of forces involved. The presence within the polymer of specific groups capable of establishing powerful intermolecular links can enhance crystallization. This action will be particularly effective if the groups in question are arranged at regular intervals along the axis of the polymer chain, so that they can interact reciprocally without greatly disturbing the remaining bonds of the individual macromolecules.

For instance, in linear polyethylene - whose chain is made up of sequences of groups ($-CH_2-$) and which possesses no specific polar sites - the attraction that holds together chains or portions of chains derives entirely from very weak forces, known as "Van der Waals forces." If, on alternate carbon atoms in the polyethylene chain, one substitutes a hydrogen atom with a fluorine atom, one attains a new structure, known in macromolecular chemistry as polyvinyl fluoride ($-CH_2-CHF^-)_n$. In this structure the *dipolar link* C-F increases the system's cohesive energy, generating a material with great rigidity, high melting point, and resistance to solvents high that its hydrogenated homolog (polyethylene).

Another case in which polarizable groups in the chain exert their beneficial effect on crystallizing materials involves polyesters with chains containing a C = O group. These polymers then possess a very stable and rigid crystal structure.

A far stronger and more polarized link than the foregoing involves the *hydrogen bond*. In synthetic polymers it is present in the polyamides (Nylon). When it is spread evenly along the chain, it can easily generate rigid, insoluble, high-temperature crystal materials. These groups can be distributed along the chain at previously established intervals, by selecting the correct monomers, that is, by spacing the NH-CO groups, which are responsible for the hydrogen bonds, with paraffin sequences of a certain length ($-CH_2)_n$ (where n = 2, 4, 6, and so on). It is therefore possible to design the characteristics of the material, and, if it proves necessary to interrupt this regular sequence of interactions, one can use monomer blends.

Lastly, by using paraffin sequences to space the groups capable of creating interactions, or by interrupting the regularity of their distribution in the chain, one can obtain less and less rigid polymers with lower melting points, until one has crossed over into the territory of what should properly be called elastomer structures.

Polyamides provide an instance of correlation between properties and structure upon which to base the molecular design of several characteristics of the material.

Chain flexibility

The flexibility of a chain is another molecular parameter that wields considerable influence over the end properties of polymer materials. Flexibility is determined by the development of vibrational and rotational motions that affect the various bonds of the macromolecule; these motions can generate different configurations.

The energy barriers that discriminate between the individual configurations have been thoroughly studied in compounds with low molecular weight. The knowledge acquired was transferred, with the appropriate precautions, to macromolecular composites. On these bases it has been possible to establish that the linear polymers that contain only or principally C-C, C-O, or C-N bonds possess fairly low energy barriers to free rotation (approx. 3 Kcal/mole); if they are regular and/or generate sufficiently powerful intermolecular interaction, they can be used to make rigid, high-temperature, relatively insoluble crystal materials.

The ethereal or imine C-O and C-N links and the C = C links in "cis" form, since they sharply lower energy barriers that prevent the rotation of the adjacent bonds (1 Kcal/mole), can generate flexible, easily soluble polymers with typically elastomeric characteristics. This occurs quite markedly when these links are distributed irregularly along the chain, so as to inhibit crystallization.

The insertion of ring structures in the skeleton of the principal chain procures the opposite effect. By reducing the number of possible configurations, it renders the chain more rigid, until, in the end, it inhibits crystallization. The materials that prove crystalline despite all this, are extremely high-temperature melting (Tm > 2500 °C) or even infusible (because they reach their decomposition point before their melting point), rigid, and insoluble. They are clearly very difficult to process. In those cases in which (for various reasons) they maintain an amorphous structure, they are materials endowed with excellent mechanical characteristics, at least at temperatures below that of glass transition (Tg) which tends to be fairly high ($\geq 150 \div 200$ °C).

After indicating several of the molecular aspects peculiar to the crystal state and the corresponding qualities, it would be worth our while, for the sake of an example, to express in a quantity one of these properties (melting point), examining how the possibilities of selectively altering several of the parameters in question affect this chemical-physical quantity.

From a purely thermodynamic viewpoint, the melting point of a substance (macromolecular or not) is determined by the ratio between enthalpy and entropy in the system, i.e.:

$$T = \frac{\Delta H}{\Delta S} \qquad [2]$$

Specifically, the melting point of a polymer is determined by the regularity and interactions of the sites along the chain that generate molecular attraction, which can be expressed through the value of ΔH and by the rigidity of the chain, which in turn affects ΔS. As we remarked earlier, linear polyethylene crystallizes in a planar zig-zag form, with extremely weak, "Van der Waals" interactions among the various chains, and presents a melting point of 135 °C. By replacing a hydrogen atom - on alternate carbon atoms - with a fluorine atom, capable of creating dipolar links with a corresponding increment in ΔH, one causes a rise in the melting point to 200 °C (polyvinyl fluoride).

In the case of polyamides (which can be considered as hydrocarbon chains similar to linear polyethylene with NH-CO groups inserted at regular intervals, capable of providing hydrogen bonds), the melting point reaches 260 °C (Nylon 6,6).

In these examples, the rise in melting point is principally a result of the increase in the upper term of the equation (2), i.e., an increase of the ΔH, but is equally possible to consid-

er cases in which a rise in the melting point can be caused by a reduction in the lower term of the equation ΔS. The classic case is that of aliphatic and aromatic polyesters, in which the aromatic ring drastically reduces the number of possible configurations. Polyethylene adipate, for example, with its completely aliphatic structure

$$[-CO-(CH_2)_4-CO-O(CH_2)_2-O-]_n$$

melts at approximately 50 °C, a lower melting point even than that of linear polyethylene, because of the flexibility produced by the C-O bond, while the corresponding aromatic polymer, polyethylene terephthalate

$$[-CO-\bigcirc-CO-O-(CH_2)_2-O-]_n$$

melts at 260 °C.

A similar operation can clearly be performed with polyamides; but in this case the rise in melting point would bring beyond the decomposition temperature. This material therefore cannot be processed with traditional melting technology, but only with solution techniques (Kevlar).

Melting point is certainly, among the various properties of a crystalline polymer material, the easiest feature to examine, in theoretical as well as in practical terms. It is also the example that best allows us to illustrate the variety of the parameters available to macromolecular chemistry for drawing board design, at a molecular level, of the end properties of a material.

5.1.3

MOLECULAR STRUCTURE

Certain properties of polymers are clearly tied to intrinsic characteristics of the base unit (or of the units) that are repeated in polymer structures. This is particularly true of thermal properties. We have said that, through the selection of the appropriate monomer units, it is possible to obtain crystal-structure polymers with a well-defined melting point. It is easy to grasp how important this is in determining the temperature interval within which the material may be used. Equally important is the glass transition temperature (Tg), which for amorphous polymers indicates the transition from a rigid vitreous state (with excellent mechanical properties) to a fluid viscous state.

Let us say then that the temperatures of melting point and glass transition indicate the temperature field over which the material can be used without undergoing noticable chemical or chemical-physical variations. Another, far more important parameter, however, is provided by thermal stability, determined by the polymer's initial breakdown temperature (TD). The expression "thermal stability" indicates the highest temperature that a polymer can withstand without any changes taking place in its chemical structure. Above this temperature, breaking and rearrangements of bonds in the polymer chain occur, often along with unacceptable decay in the polymer's characteristics.

The thermal stability of a polymer largely depends on the strength of the bonds between the atoms that make up the principal chain of the macromolecule, a force that can be expressed in terms of the dissociation energy of the atoms in free radicals. In table 1, the dissociation energy of the bonds in a few organic substances that may serve as possible models for polymer chains are shown.

Although we must recognize that the skeleton of the principal chain of most macromolecules is largely made up of –C-C bonds, it is important to note that the energy of this bond is rather high (83 Kcal/mole). Nevertheless, even polymer chains formed of different elements (Si, P, O, and so on) possess high bonding energy between atoms. A significant example is that of silicones, in which the energy of the Si-O bond is quite high (106 Kcal/mole). In these cases, one should keep in mind that too high a difference in electro-negativity in the atoms that form the polymer chain leads to excessive bond polarity, with a consequent sharp decline in the force as the temperature rises.

The bonding force between the atoms in the principal chain and the lateral atoms or groups is equally important in determining a high degree of heat stability in polymers. For example, the replacement of H atoms in a linear polyethylene chain with fluorine F atoms (keeping in mind that the energy in C-F links is greater than that in C-H links) explains the greater heat stability of polytetrafluoroethylene (temperature of incipient decomposition is 500 °C) over polyethylene (320 °C).

Working with the data in table 1, it is possible to predict the heat stability of polymer systems, beyond practical feasability.

TABLE 1 - DISSOCIATION ENTHALPIES OF SOME ORGANIC COMPOSITES

Type of bond	Dissociation energy of the bond (Kcal/mole, 0°C)
CH_3-CH_2-H	97
C_6H_5-H	104
$CH\equiv C-H$	114
CH_3-CH_3	83
$C_6H_5-C_6H_5$	118
$N\equiv C-C\equiv C$	112
$C-C$ (benzene)	124
$HC\equiv C$	230
$\overset{O}{\underset{\|\|}{CH_3C}}-OCH_3$	97
$\overset{O}{\underset{\|\|}{C_6H_5C}}-OCH_3$	90
$C_6H_5-OCH_3$	101

Indeed, if we examine the considerable difference in the dissociation energy of the C-C bond of ethane (83 Kcal/mole) and diphenyl (118 Kcal/mole), which derives from the different delocalization of electrons in the two compounds, one can, on this basis alone, conclude that poly-(p-phenylene), a polymer made up of aromatic rings bonded one to another, is certainly more stable (TD ⩾ 480 °C) than polyethylene (TD ≅ 320 °C) with its almost entirely aliphatic chain.

CH₃-CH₃ ⬡-⬡   CH₃-(CH₂)ₙ-CH₃ ⬡-(-⬡-)ₙ-⬡
Ethane   Diphenyl   Polyethylene   Poly-(p-phenylene)

Ring systems, whether they are aromatic or heterocyclical, generally possess high dissociation energies, and so they are of special interest to macromolecular chemists, who tend to use them in synthesizing polymer structures that must withstand, in continual use, elevated temperatures. Many structures have been synthesized and many are being developed. Often, however, substantial improvements in heat resistance induced in a polymer is accompanied by greater difficulties in processing, and can heavily restrict the polymer's use.

Other advantages (that may be more important than heat resistance), which make the materials derived from these polymer structures particularly attractive, are resistance to oxidation, radiation, and chemical agents.

From the above, one can deduce that thermal degradation is a process of homolytic breaking of the weaker bonds in the polymer chain. This problem can be avoided in part through the synthesis of macromolecular structures made up of several closely connected chains (fig. 3), known as ladder polymers, in which it is necessary, in order to break the skeleton of the principal chain, to break not one but two or more covalent bonds, situated in well-defined places, at the same time. For statistical reasons, this is quite difficult to do. Indeed, the radicals formed by the homolytic breaking of a C-C bond, are forced by the specific structure of the macromolecule to remain in adjacent positions, with a very high probability of recombining. The design in fig. 3 clearly illustrates this situation.

Normally, the thermal stability of these polymers goes above 500 °C, and in a few cases even to 600 °C. Their greatest flaw is shared by totally aromatic and heterocyclical structures - difficulty in synthesizing and in transforming them into finished products.

Drawing board design of increasingly heat-resistant polymer structures and the discovery of a practical method for

SINGLE CHAIN POLYMERS

splitting and separation

'LADDER POLYMER'

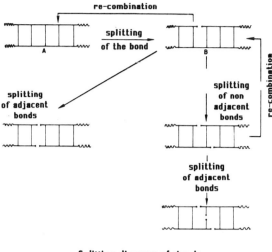

re-combination

splitting of the bond

A   B

splitting of adjacent bonds

splitting of non adjacent bonds

re-combination

splitting of adjacent bonds

Splitting diagram of simple bonds and complex structures.

synthesizing them is one of the most sought-after goals in the sector of advanced materials today.

5.1.4

CROSS-LINKING

Up till now we have considered polymer structure with basically linear chains, that as a consequence of their molecular architecture (i.e., for instance, their capacity to form crystal structures, ladders, and so on) are able to develop fairly high mechanical and thermal properties for organic materials.

It is well known however, that combinations properties similar to the above, or completely original, can be obtained through cross-linking. Let us consider, for example, thermosetting resins and elastomers. In both cases, there are special structures in which cross-links are established between linear portions of the macromolecule, theoretically transforming the material, in microscopic terms, into a single giant macromolecule. The physical, mechanical, and thermal characteristics of these materials, naturally, depends chiefly - aside from the molecular structural parameters that we have already cosidered (chain flexibility, chemical structure, etc.) on the number and type of cross-links present in the materials.

The most common example is that of natural rubber. In the nonvulcanized state, this material possesses good properties of solubility and chain flexibility (Tg -70 °C). By gradually increasing the degree of cross-linking, one obtains an insoluble material, with spectacular elastic properties (elongation ⩾ 300%, with a capacity for instant and total recovery from the deformation); by further increasing the degree of cross-linking, the material stiffens progressively until it becomes a very rigid, hard, insoluble, infusible substance (ebonite).

It is therefore well to distinguish between the two cases - thermosetting resins and cross-linked elastomers.

Thermosetting resins

These are polymer materials that, when heated, can establish cross-links between the various polymer chains, as mentioned above, creating insoluble and infusible materials.

Although, in terms of end results, with a view to the attainment of certain properties, crystallizing and cross-linking

243

may seem like alternative approaches, one should keep in mind that certain differences can have dramatic repercussions on applicative choices. Crystallizing is, in effect, a physical phenomenon in which the bonds of the various macromolecules, including the hydrogen bond ($\leqslant$ 7 Kcal/mole), are fairly weak and - above all - completely reversible by heat action (thermoplastic materials); cross-linking instead is an irreversible chemical phenomenon in which the links between various molecules are of a covalent nature, with dissociation energy levels on the order of those shown in Table 1 (80 Kcal/mole).

The better-known thermosetting resins, both in terms of historical and current applications, are phenolic, melamine, unsaturated polyester, urethane, and epoxy resins. The latter resins are encountering new applications as matrices for advanced composite materials, employed increasingly for their lightness and resistance in the aeronautics and aerospace industries.

Though these materials differ, their advantages are generally heat resistance, dimensional stability, good mechanical and electrical properties, surface hardness, and so on. Among their defects, the most important one (at least for sophisticated applications) is the difficulty of the chemical procedures involved in forming the end product, not always well received by the final user.

Cross-linked elastomers

Elastomers constitute an important class of polymer materials, and possess a peculiar set of properties that no other material can match. They can undergo, under the action of an applied force, remarkable levels of deformation and then instantaneously recover their original shape when that force is removed. It has been shown that this behavior (which is relatively well understood in theoretical terms) is closely linked to the intimate structure of the material.

An ideal elastomer, that will provide optimum performance, must be made up of flexible macromolecules with great molecular weight, connected one to another by cross-links at correct intervals. It would also be well that the macromolecule possess an orderly structure with fairly weak molecular interactions, so as to permit partial and reversible crystallizing of the chain fragments between the cross-links only under special stretching conditions. The frequency of the cross-links, as well, is essential to attaining specific elastic characteristics required of an elastomer. The force needed to obtain a given elongation is a direct function of the degree of cross-linking, i.e., inversely proportional to the average statistical length of the segments of macromolecule between adjacent cross-links.

Without delving into the details of the advanced theories that explain the elastic behavior of rubber, it is nonetheless interesting, for their specific design, to examine their fundamental phenomenology.

The thermodynamic treatment is based on the concept that the segments that constitute the lattice are arranged in statistical bundles, i.e., they are in a state of elevated probability or entropy, and that this entropy diminishes when the chain is extended by an outside force. In these terms, the rubber's elasticity can be considered as a solely entropic phenomenon, unless other molecular interactions were to intervene, inducing further energy variations during stretching and relaxation. This latter aspect, in reality, is not only present by happenstance in a few systems, but is intentionally sought out in formulations of elastomer systems, when necessary, by various artifices.

In the stress/deformation curve of fig. 4, one can see, in the zone of elevated deformation, a sharp increase in the rigidity of the system, which cannot be explained by a mechanism based solely on variations in entropy. It is at this point that intermolecular interactions come into play, with the consequential appearance of crystallinity in the material. This explanation, confirmed by various spectroscopic techniques (XRD, IR, etc.) presupposes that, in extreme elongations, larger and larger portions of the segments of the various chains are parallelized and, therefore, put in conditions in which they can crystallize. Obviously, these crystalline microdomains are inextensible, and cause a further sharp rise in the stress/deformation curve. In other words, the

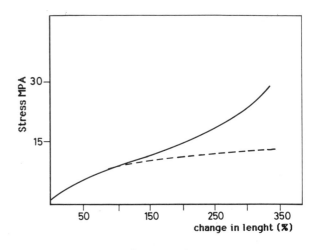

Typical stress strain curve of an elastomer.

elastomer is capable, by means of stretching, of inducing its own self-reinforcing system. Since formation by stretching of crystalline microdomains involves various segments of the molecule, these segments, acting as distributors of stress among various polymer chains, take on a fundamental role in enhancing the breaking and ripping resistance of the material.

All this should be taken as an integrative contribution to the theory of entropy, in the context of an overall understanding of the rubber's elasticity. The theory's validity is confirmed by another type of elastomer behavior, anomalous at first glance - the retraction of stretched rubber in response to a temperature increase.

Based on the above, natural rubber, polybutadiene 1-4 cis, polyisoprene cis, polyisobutene, and so on, which all possess considerable regularity of molecular structure, also display excellent elastomer characteristics.

A further class of elastomers has been developed, with enhanced resistance to oxidation and heat: silicone, fluorinated, and fluorine/silicon rubbers, etc., which constitute quite a vast range of materials that are fundamentally differentiated according to their cost/performance ratio.

5.1.5

POLYMER BLENDS

We have already seen how it is possible, by working with the molecular structure, to provide materials with the characteristics needed. It is not always possible to follow this route. On the one hand, in fact, the use of polymer materials requires specific combinations of properties depending on the different sectors of use. On the other hand, economic considerations limit the potential number of commercial polymers. Therefore, only a finite number of combinations of properties becomes possible without further outside intervention.

Polymer blends make it possible to attain this two-fold objective - that is, to satisfy the individual applicative needs with a "made-to-order" product, and, at the same time, drastically reduce the cost of the material. From this point of view, therefore, a blend may be defined as the physical combination of two or more structurally different polymers, in which each of the two components performs a well-defined action.

By far, most polymer blends are heterophase systems; there are, however, individual cases, of considerable applicative interest, in which the components are reciprocally soluble, and therefore display what seems to be a single homogeneous phase. Intermediate positions between these two extreme cases are offered by block or graft copolymers and interpenetrated networks.

Heterophase systems

The blending of two polymers usually leads, for thermodynamic reasons that are implicit in the very macromolecular

244

structure, to diphasic systems. In effect, the thermodynamic conditions for blending presuppose a drop in free energy (ΔG).

$$\Delta G = \Delta H - T\Delta S \leqslant 0$$

This condition is difficult to attain in a polymer system due to the low contribution of the entropic term (ΔS), and due to the elevated value of the enthalpic term (ΔH), which is usually positive.

Nevertheless, the phenomenon of incompatibility, which may seem to limit heavily polymer systems, may be transformed into a strong point, once it becomes possible to control microstructural phenomena. An evident example is that of heterophase systems designed to enhance the impact resistance of plastic materials. It is nevertheless necessary to point out that heterogeneity of phase cannot *per se* be considered a necessary and sufficient condition for the creation or enhancement of this peculiar characteristic of a material unless it is associated with a few individual properties of the constituent materials, such as morphology and adhesion between phases.

The most appropriate example involves acrylonitrile-butadiene-styrene resins (ABS). The material in this case is made up of a continuous phase, due to the acrylonitrile-styrene copolymer, and a dispersed, slightly cross-linked elastomer phase, upon which acrylonitrile-styrene-based polymer has been chemically grafted. This latter step is necessary to create around the elastomer particle a layer that is compatible with the continous phase (poly-acrylonitrile-styrene) which gives continuity to the matieral, and hence allows it to transfer stress.

Nonetheless, the excellent impact resistance is only attained by giving the appropriate dimension to the particles of rubber present. These gummy microphases have a remarkable capacity to trigger plastic deformations and provoke micro-cracking of the matrix with a substantial absorption of energy.

The preparation of ABS resins is therefore a clear instance of characteristics design of a material with the synergistic assistance of intervention both at the level of molecular structure and at that of superstructures (composition and morphology of phases). The example that we have provided, compared with a simple physical blend, emphasizes the role played by the connection (adhesion) between phases, a fundamental parameter in determining the end characteristics of the blend. Here, an important role is played by block or graft copolymers, both because of their intrinsic properties, and as compatibilizing interphases.

Without dwelling at length on the functions of interphase, which these copolymers can perform with a similar mechanism to that described previously, it is worth while to examine some structural aspects of these materials, which offer, in the macromolecule itself, conditions that could permit the creation of heterophase zones within the system (fig. 5).

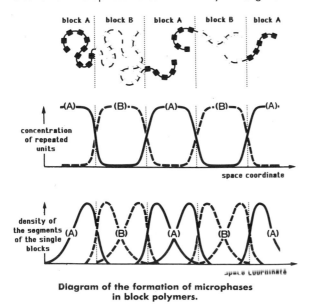

block A   block B   block A   block B   block A

concentration of repeated units

-(A)-   -(B)-   -(A)-   -(B)-   -(A)-

space coordinate

density of the segments of the single blocks   (A)   (B)   (A)   (B)   (A)

space coordinate

Diagram of the formation of microphases in block polymers.

It is due to this structural peculiarity (especially in block copolymers) that the continuous phase and the corresponding morphology are affected so critically by the distribution of length of the blocks. Consequently, with variations in size of the blocks (which, in the final analysis, reflect the constituent ratio of the two components) in a polymer made up of rigid blocks and elastomer blocks, the material's characteristics can vary from those typical of a plastomer to those of an elastomer. This behavior may be further enhanced by blending with corresponding omogopolymers.

In this respect, it is clear that block copolymers that present, a continuous elastomer phase (polybutadiene) and a dispersed phase formed of plastomer microdomains (polystyrene) with a more or less spherical form have the characteristic behavior of a cross-linked elastomer system. Therefore, one of the most important characteristics of these elastomer-block copolymers is their capacity to behave like elastomers while maintaining all the ease of processing typical of thermoplastic materials (injection molding, extrusion, etc.).

These materials are endowed with properties that are typical of elastomers due to a physical cross-linking, brought about by association of the rigid blocks into microdomains that behave like points of chemical cross-linking. Unlike those points, however, the microdomains are thermally labile and, when exposed to temperature, (T > Tg) the material can behave like a normal thermoplastic material (thermoplastic elastomers) with respect to transformation techniques.

Even in a brief examination of the importance of polyphase systems in the design of the superstructures of materials with specific properties, one should certainly not overlook interpenetrated networks (IPN). In these systems, developed uder special polymerization conditions, each polymer forms its own network that physically interpenetrates the network of the other polymer.

From this point of view, IPNs can be considered as more or less intimate blends of two cross-linked polymers, in which the separation of phase may be kinetically inhibited by the tangling of the various chains, as a result of cross-linking. In other words, the de-mixing into separate phases can only take place through breakage of covalent bonds that constitute the molecule.

Therefore, IPNs are considered the transition point between heterophase systems and homogeneous systems. In applicative terms, IPNs possess characteristics and applications that are quite similar to those of blends. IPNs, as a result of their specific topology, offer total control of morphology that is synonymous, as we have seen, with excellent applicative properties.

Homogeneous systems

The development of a polymer blend justifies its existence, as we said above, in the set of properties that the system can provide in comparison to the individual components.

Systems characterized by immiscibility of the constituent phases have been examined, and it is no accident that properties that increased the material's resistance to impact were studied. Despite the unfavorable thermodynamics of polymer blending, in a few cases it is possible to encounter instances of total or partial miscibility, even in polymer systems.

The main feature that provides clues to the existence of an individual phase in a multicomponent system, aside from complicated thermodynamic criteria that are always difficult to detect experimentally, is the temperature of glass transition (Tg). A homogeneous system, in fact, shows a single Tg with a value that is generally midway between the Tg of the components, while heterophase systems possess a Tg number that corresponds to that of the components, which may have the same value (total immiscibility) or slightly shifted with respect to the components in a pure state (partial miscibility).

In a multicomponent polymer system, the Tg is not the only property that is a function of the composition and homogeneity or heterogeneity of the blends: the same is true of the modulus of elasticity, impact resistance, and compliance. It is therefore clearly possible, through blending, to broaden the range of polymer materials in terms of the characteristics desired.

A significant example (in terms of commercial success, as well) is the polystyrene-polyphenylenoxide (PS-PPO). The resulting material is homogeneous (since there is solubility between the two components over the entire range of compositions) and the characteristics of the blends are for the most part determined directly by the ratio of the components. It is possible, in fact, to increase the heat distortion temperature (HDT) of polystyrene (approx. 90 °C), to meet specific applicative requirements (e.g., in materials for the automobile industry), up to (T ≥ 150 °C by increasing the amount of PPO (tg ≅ 210 °C). The use of high-impact polystyrene (HIPS) makes it possible to give the blend this specific resistance as well, when so desired.

A further example of modifications in the properties of blended polymers can be found when one or both of the components are crystalline. For an immiscible system, one should expect no variations in the degree of crystallinity, melting point, and so on (in general, absence of interphases has a negative effect on mechanical properties), while if the system is miscible in the molten state, all these parameters undergo relatively sharp variations, similar to what we have described with respect to the Tg.

Instances of isomorphism that allow two materials to crystallize in a single crystalline phase are, unfortunately, quite rare in polymer systems. This clearly constitutes a serious handicap in the area of design and production of new materials through manipulation on the supermolecular level, such as with crystal structures.

5.1.6

COMPOSITE MATERIALS

The denomination of composite is generally applied to any material made up of several components. Though this definition is correct, it is too broad. It covers such a variety of materials that it is impossible to consider them in a coherent fashion.

For our purposes, the meaning of the term shall be limited to those materials formed of continuous filaments organized in a pre-established fashion in a polymer matrix that serves as a binder. Therefore, the so-called reinforced and filled plastic materials are not included in the category of composites.

In design terms, advanced composites lend themselves to an extremely broad variety of approaches, since it is possible to attain the same objective at each of the three possible levels of materials structure:
- molecular (selection of the type of fiber, matrix, and interface, etc.);
- microscopic (volumetric composition of the reinforcement, geometric characteristics of same and of components);
- macroscopic (arrangement of laminae in the design phase, determination of their typology, sequence, etc.).

It is evident that the predominant factor in differentiating composite materials from traditional homogeneous materials is their complexity, which fundamentally derives from the anisotropic and nonhomogeneous nature of the basic element - the lamina. Design systems used traditionally for isotropic materials, therefore, are no longer adequate and should be adapted to the specific characteristics of the material.

These innovative factors and, as we shall see, manufacturing techniques, are at the heart of competition between advanced composites and traditional structural materials.

The role of components

The primary task of fibers is to give the composite resistance and rigidity; the material must therefore contain a percentage of appropriately arranged fibers, sufficient to withstand the stresses applied. Several specific tensile - i.e., that take into account the material's specific weight - characteristics are shown in Table 2.

The role played by the matrix is more complex - it has the task of protecting the surface and each fiber from abrasion

TABLE 2 - COMPARISON BETWEEN THE CHARACTERISTICS OF FIBERS AND MONODIRECTIONAL COMPOSITES

Fiber/composite	Density g/c.cm	Elastic modulus GPa	Limit stress GPa	Specific stiffness MJ/kg	Specific strenght MJ/kg
Glass-fiber E	2.54	72	2.4	28	0.95
Epoxy composite	2.10	45	1.1	21	0.52
Glass-fiber S	2.49	85	4.5	34	1.80
Epoxy composite	2.00	55	2.0	27	1.00
Boron fiber	2.45	400	3.5	163	1.43
Epoxy composite	2.10	207	1.6	99	0.76
Carbon fiber (high resistance)	1.80	253	4.5	140	2.50
Epoxy composite	1.60	145	2.3	90	1.42
Carbon fiber (hight modulus)	1.85	520	2.4	281	1.30
Epoxy composite	1.63	290	1.0	178	0.61
Kevlar fiber	1.44	124	3.6	86	2.50
Epoxy composite	1.38	80	2.0	58	1.45

and contact with the outside ambient, while keeping the various fibers separate and appropriately spaced, in order to distribute as well as possible the stresses applied to the surface.

To allow the material to perform this function successfully, there must be good adhesion between the fiber and the matrix. This parameter, unfortunately, often leaves much to be desired, given the different natures of the components. In order to overcome this hurdle, the surfaces of the fibers must be treated so as to create artificial interphases between fibers and matrix.

Micromechanics

Micromechanics is based on knowledge of the engineering properties of fibers and matrix. Micromechanics, therefore, provides a link between engineering analysis and molecular theory.

The simplest way of representing an advanced composite is the uni-directional lamina formed of filaments oriented in a parallel sense, intimately bonded by a resin. When the properties of this basic structural element are known, it is possible to calculate the properties of a laminate, with the desired number and orientation of these laminae.

By virtue of its structure, the lamina proves to be microscopically nonhomogeneous and anisotropic, since it is made up of single-directional fibers bonded by a matrix, as we have said. If, nonetheless, the volume used in experimentation is very large in relation to the diameter of the fibers and the thickness of matrix applied, its nonhomogeneity has no influence on the properties of the laminae, which are therefore affected only by the anisotropy of the structure.

Even with considerable simplificatory assumptions, a complete mechanical characterization would require extremely costly, complex, and time-consuming experimentation. Therefore methods have been developed for computing the properties and predictable behavior of the lamina. These equations are indispensable in the later design of any product with the properties required.

Macromechanics

Macromechanical analysis, on the other hand, pays no attention to the microstructure of the layer and considers it as homogeneous but possessing different properties in the direction that corresponds to the orientation of the fibers and at a right angle to that direction. The entire structural element is therefore conceived as a sequence of sheets oriented in different directions. Once the limit conditions of the structural element needed have been established, one can use lamination theory to determine the distribution of stress over individual layers, and, consequently, the orientation of the individual laminae in relation to the conditions of stress to which the structure will be exposed.

Evidently the presence of defects in the basic element (lamina) - e.g., imperfect alignment or fragmentation of fibers, the presence of bubbles, or nonhomogeneous cross-linking in the matrix, can cause considerable deviations in the conditions predicted by the design of the structure, and cause it to collapse when in use.

It is therefore clear that the study of microstructural characteristics of the materials utilized in the production of a com-

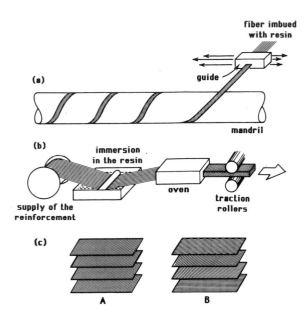

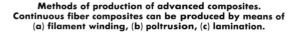

**Methods of production of advanced composites.
Continuous fiber composites can be produced by means of
(a) filament winding, (b) poltrusion, (c) lamination.**

posite (lamina) structure is at least as important as its design. The success of composite material in applications will therefore be largely determined by close cooperation between the designer and experts in the various disciplines involved in the production of such an unusual structure - materials science, stress analysis, quality control, etc.

Properties and techniques

Composites, as structural materials, are required to possess three fundamental properties: resistance, rigidity, and resilience. Other thermal and physical properties are also important, but usually it is in the first three areas that composites must compete with conventional structural materials.

As we have seen, several of the compositès properties (including rigidity and resistance) can be predicted according to the properties of the components, using the rules of micro- and macromechanics. Other properties, such as resilience, are less simple to deal with. We know that this property depends on the tenacity of the components, their structure, and the interface bond. Nevertheless, it is quite difficult to predict its value with any degree of precision, since most of the energy dissipated involves mechanisms of fiber/matrix interaction that are not easy to express in numbers.

These dissipatory mechanisms, based on structural heterogeneity, constitute one of the most significant differences between advanced composites and conventional structural materials.

The differences between designing metals and designing composite materials become particularly clear if we consider manufacturing techniques. In the case of composites, the designer and the technologist must work together closely, since the characteristics of the final product are produced "on site" during the manufacturing phase. The designer must be familiar, through contact with the technologist, all the limits of the technique chosen, and take them into account in his design.

The principal techniques used today (see fig. 6) are lamination, filament winding, and pultrusion. While lamination is purely manual, the others are automated, though there are intrinsic limits of the form of the final products. The common limitation, however, which keeps these techniques from being applied in larger industrial areas, is the slow manufacturing speed. Only with thermoplastic resins will it be possible to overcome this handicap and make composites (costs allowing) widely used materials in many applicative areas.

Glossary

A

Advanced composite
High-performance composite material, in terms of the ratio of mechanical properties to weight and temperature resistance. It is generally formed of fibers of various sorts (fiberglass, aramid, carbon, boron, aluminum, carbonate, or silicon carbide fibers) oriented according to the expected behavior of stresses, and integrated in a matrix. There are also various sorts of matrices (epoxy, polyester, or polyamide resins or even ceramic or metal resins). There are also homogeneous composites, such as carbon fibers in a carbon matrix.

Alloy or Blend
Material containing two or more substances as components. There are metal alloys and polymer blends. Alloys and blends generally have different properties and characteristics from the substances that compose them.

Amorphous polymers
Polymers in which the arrangement of the macromolecules presents no order whatsoever.

Amorphous solids
Non-crystalline, solid materials, devoid of large-scale lattice order.

B

Blend (see Alloy)

Blow molding
Process for forming a material by molding, which utilizes the introduction of compressed air into a block of melted glass or melted plastic contained within a mold.

Brittleness
Characteristic of materials, opposite of tenacity. A brittle material breaks without absorbing much energy, and without apparent plastic deformation.

C

Ceramic materials
Materials in which there are metal and non-metal elements. This family of materials includes both the constituents of traditional ceramic materials, such as clays, and the constituents of new products with special electric, electronic, or technical performances (heat resistance and mechanical resistance).

Cold drawing
Deformation that takes place in polymers, above the temperature of glass transition, subjecting them to a stress, after which the arrangement of the macromolecules develops toward more highly crystalline structure. The result is an increase of the mechanical properties of the material.

Composite
A material that combines substances with differing structures, but that are compatible, in order to create a stable complex with performances superior to those of the constituent parts when taken separately.

Copolymer
Polymer containing more than one type of monomer.

Creep
Phenomenon that cause a slow, but continually increasing deformation in the materials under the stress of constant loads, even if they are below the yielding load. The rate of deformation increases when temperature or load increase. In general, with the same external conditions, the speed of creep varies over time. The phenomenon is particularly pronounced with polymeric metals.

Crystal
A structurally uniform, three-dimensional solid, with an atomic conformation that is repetitive over the long range. A crystal is formed by the repetition of many single cells, in each of which the atoms and molecules and atoms occupy precise positions. In some cases, large crystals form (single-crystal solids). More frequently, poly-crystal solids appear, made up of a great number of small regular crystals closely linked one to another.

D

Diffusion
Migration of atoms or molecules through a material by virtue of a concentration gradient. The effect is enhanced by thermal energy.

Dopant
Substance added in a controlled fashion to a material in order to modify certain of its properties; for example, to increase its conductivity.

Ductility
Property of materials which indicates their capacity to deform before breaking. It is expressed in terms of elongation or reduction of cross-section.

E

Elastic deformation
Reversible deformation, i.e., a deformation that occurs without a permanent shifting of the atoms (or molecules) from their initial reciprocal positions. The deformation proves proportionate to the load applied, as shown by the Law of Hooke, according to a constant represented by the modulus of elasticity of the material under observation.

Elastomer
Polymer which can withstand considerable dimensional variations without permanently deforming. This property is produced by a special conformation of the constituent macromolecules. The ratio between stress and deformation does not follow the Law of Hooke (see **Elastic deformation**).

Energy analysis
An analysis of the amount of energy used both in manufacturing a given product, and in the materials and components integrated in said product. The result of this analysis is also known as a product's energy cost.
This analysis can be extended to the entire life cycle of the product. In that case, alongside its energy cost, one evaluates the energy consumption involved in its use during its life span, and the energy needed for its disposal. Contrariwise, one can consider the energy that can be obtained by recycling (if the product presents a recoverable energy content).

Extrusion
A forming operation that makes it possible to compress the material, thus forcing it to pass through the hole of a spinnerette. The extruded material takes on the shape of the spinnerette through which it was forced.

Fatigue
Phenomenon that leads materials to break after repeated strains caused by dynamic – even low-intensity – loads.

Fiber
Special form in which a material may present itself. Through manufacturing processes, it is possible to orient its molecules so as to acquire, in a given material, resistance that approaches theoretical resistance – which is what one finds if one considers the entire set of atomic bonds.

Filament winding
Process for the manufacture of composites with great mechanical properties, in which a resin-preimpregnated continuous filament is arranged appropriately by winding it continuously around a central form (generally of a cylindrical shape).

Filler
Additive mixed with a polymer in order to reinforce it and/or increase its volume.

Foamed materials
Materials with a cellular structure. The cells may be open or closed, and the material may be rigid or flexible.

Glass-transition temperature
This is the temperature of transition from the solid state to the viscous state. For amorphous polymers, this is the softening temperature; for semicrystalline polymers, this is the softening temperature of the amorphous part.

Generative metaphors
Transposing to an unfamiliar field a repertory of situations and problems stored in one's memory, in search of an appropriate representative model for the problem raised by a new situation.
Generative metaphors provide an image of the problem, such that complex mental processes can lead to the determination of an appropriate solution.

Hardness
Property of solid materials, linked to the strength of interatomic or intermolecular bonds. It is expressed in terms of the material's resistance to penetration.

Hyperselection of materials
Condition of the user when there is no longer just one material that he is almost obliged to choose, but several different materials competing. In this case, the selection can be made only by carefully analyzing the entire manufacturing process or, even, the entire life of the product itself.

Industrial Revolution
The set of technological and cultural transformations that led to the transition from societies based on agricultural activities to those based on manufacturing. The place and time in which it occurs are conventionally agreed to be England during the eighteenth century.
A more attent historical analysis shows that the explosive phenomenon that occurred during that period was the result of a long-term accumulation of social, cultural, and technological transformations.

Injection molding
Forming a material under pressure in a closed mold. For thermoplastic materials, the mold is cooled, while for thermosets, it is maintained at the temperature required for polymerization.

Integral foams/Structural foams
Foamed materials that, by virtue of a special process, possess a compact outer surface. They can be either flexible or rigid. If rigid, and if the "skin" is sufficiently resistant, they are also known as "structural foams."

Integrated circuit
A circuit made up of many electronic components (condensors, diodes, transistors) linked by conductors and grouped on a single board.

Integration of functions
Design and manufacturing orientation which leads to the production of complex components. In manufacturing terms, it means reducing the total number of components and the processing phases required (in general, reduction in number of assemblies).
From the point of view of the end user, this may mean the availability of an object with multiple performances (combining performances that once were provided by different objects).

Liquid crystals
There are liquids whose molecules (general elongated in form) can be arranged spatially in a fairly regular fashion. They therefore present an intermediate structure between that of a solid crystal (maximum level of order) and that of an ordinary liquid (quite disorderly arrangement). This particular conformation can be achieved with different materials made up of reasonably large organic molecules, enhancing properties one quite different from another, ranging from a tendency to orientation if subjected to an electric field (such as in liquid-crystal displays), all the way to the manufacture of polymer materials with high mechanical and thermal performance.

Luminescence
Light emitted, which corresponds to a release of energy, occuring when electrons fill empty orbitals.

Macromolecules
Molecules made up of hundreds or thousands of atoms; their molecular weight may reach very high values.
The constituents of natural substances, such as cellulose, are just as much macromolecules as are the constituents of thermoplastic resins and thermosetting resins.

Materials made to order
Materials whose properties are designed according to given specifications. They can be generated by working on the microstructure (for instance, through the selection of one or more polymers and inclusion of the appropriate fillers and additives) or on the microstructure (by creating composite materials).

Mechanical properties
Characteristics of a material with respect to application of a system of loads. The principal characteristics are hardness, tensile strength, compressive strength, flexural strength, shear strength, torsional strength, hot creep strength, fatigue strength, impact strength.

Melting temperature
In general, this is the temperature at which the transition from the solid to the liquid phase occurs. In semicrystalline polymers it is the melting temperature of the crystallites, that is, of the crystal zones within their structure.

Metals
Materials made up essentially of elements capable of freeing part of their valence electrons; they are characterized by high electric conductivity, which drops at high temperatures. The valence band of metals is not entirely occupied and coincide with the conduction band.

Modernity, Modern thought
Set of values and models for the interpretation of reality which have proved dominant in Western culture over the past 2/3 centuries.
It determines the way in which we see space, time, our relationship with nature, social organization, the role of technology, and the idea of progress. The perception of its current crisis has been defined as the post-modern condition.

Modulus of elasticity
Constant of the proportion between stress and strain, when a material is deformed elastically; it is also known as Young's modulus. It is an index of the rigidity of interatomic or intermolecular links.

Molecular conformation
Spatial arrangement of the atoms of a molecule. In organic molecules, there can be several conformations, produced by the capacity of carbon atoms to rotate around a simple bond – each different conformation has its own stability and chemical-physical behavior.

Molecular weight
Sum of the atomic wieghts of all the atoms which composed a molecule.

Monomer

Elementary unit whose repetition forms a polymer. The union of many monomers generates a polymer macromolecule. The monomer molecule undergoes a modification when it joins other molecules to form a polymer macromolecule, either with the opening of one or more double bonds (polyaddition) or by elimination of several of the atoms that constitute it (polycondensation).

N

Neolithic

Age during which the transition from hunting and gathering cultures to sedentary cultures took place. During the Neolithic, the first animals were domesticated, agriculture and the formation of villages begon. The name comes from Greek *neos*, new, and *lithos*, stone.

Neolithic revolution

The set of technological and cultural transformations that led to the transition from hunting and gathering to that of sedentary agrarian societies. (see **Neolithic**)

Neotechnics

An expression that sums up a set of characteristics of the current phase of technological developments, the common elements of which is a search solutions that require less energy and less matter and that integrate more information.
The previous phase may be defined as Paleotechnics.

O

Organic-inorganic

The original meaning of the term "organic" in the language of chemistry had to do with the classification of substances derived from plants or animals, as opposed to the term "inorganic," used for substances derived from inanimate matter. Later, it was shown that composites defined as organic could be produced artificially from inorganic materials.
Materials produced with carbon chemistry are know as organic.

P

Paleolithic

Prehistoric phase that begins with the first manifestations of the technological capacities of man (chipped rocks, over a million years ago) and ends (approx. 10,000 years ago) when agriculture and herding begin to develop. It is subdivided into three periods – lower (the most ancient), middle, and upper. In the Upper Paleolithic, Neanderthal man disappears and Homo sapiens appears.

Paleotechnics

A expression to describe the phase of technological development previous to the current phase (see **Neotechnics**).

Percolation

In the narrow sense, this is the way in which phase transition occurs in many physical phenomena. Given a system of different elements with a certain number of bonds joining them, the "percolation threshold" is exceeded when the number of bonds and their arrangement are such that the elements are all connected one to another by at least one bond.
This model is also used to describe the propagation of new techniques within a manufacturing system. A new material enters production in a complex object, replacing a traditional material in certain areas, which therefore require redesign. After a certain threshold in terms of number of parts replaced, it is possible to begin thinking about redesigning the object completely, as a function of the new material that has prevailed. This could be the way in which the transition from metal cars to plastic cars will take place.

Piezoelectric material

Dielectric ceramic material with an asymmetrical structure, inasmuch as In its crystal structure the center of gravity of the positive charges does not correspond to that of the negative charges. The material therefore contains many permanent electric dipoles that are sensitive to mechanical deformations or to a state of deformation caused by an electric field imposed upon the material.

Pigment

Colored organic or inorganic, natural or artificial substance. It can be used to color a solid surface over which it is placed.

Plastic deformation

Permanent deformation caused by shifting of atoms (or molecules) to reciprocal positions that differ from their original positions. This occurs when materials are subjected to loads greater than the yielding load, and the deformation is no longer proportionate to the load applied. Plastic deformation takes place under different conditions and according to different mechanisms in metals and in plastic materials.

Plasticizer

Substance that, when applied to a plastic material, increases its deformability and flexibility. This effect is caused by the molecules of the plasticizer which, slipping between the plastic macromolecules, increase their mobility.

Polymer orientation

Process by which polymer molecules are arranged in a preferential direction.

Polymers

Compounds with high molecular weight, whose macromolecule is a product of the combination of simple structural units, known as monomers, that are repeated in a modular fashion. Depending on the type of monomers, polymers can develop in one or more directions.

Problem setting

The phase in design in which the theme is defined and structured. This phase, which orients and delimits all further phases, is typified by the fact that it takes place in dialogue/discussion setting between all the actors involved in the process and in forms that are other than formal and analytic rationality (see **Generative metaphors**).

Problem solving

The phase in design in which solutions are sought to the problem posed in the problem setting phase.

Process

In a broad sense, the set of operations that are used to control or give the appropriate qualities to a material, ranging from the microscopic level to the macroscopic level, maintaining a pre-established balance between the costs that can be faced and acceptable levels of performance.

Productive sector

Subsystem in a manufacturing system where there are special relations between manufacturers of raw materials, semi finished materials, and finished product. (e.g., the steel industry with the automobile industry; or else, the brick and cement industry with the construction industry).

R

Refining

The addition of materials to plastics as fillers, stabilizers, plasticizers, colors, etc.

Refraction

Deflection of a ray of light at the surface separating two different transparent materials. The index of refraction is inversely proportional to the speed of light through the material.

Retroaction loop (feed back)

This occurs whenever there is a bilateral relationship between the parts in a dynamic system, such that, if A influences B, the variations in B in turn influence A.
One says that there is positive feedback when the outcome is an intensification of the phenomenon; and negative when it leads either to the reduction or to the elimination of the phenomenon.

Residual tensions

Tensions that can be found within a material, generated by the existence of differences in temperature within the material during the manufacturing process.

S

Semicrystalline polymers

Polymers containing both crystal regions and amorphous regions.

Sinterizing

Process that allows the manufacture of a product beginning with small granules of material, compressing them, and releasing them at the appropriate temperature. Under these conditions, there is a "diffusion" of the atoms, which leads to a

compact product.
Sinterizing is the only process that can be used for technical ceramics, and one of the processes recently proposed for metals.

Solidification shrinkage
Variation in volume that takes place when a cooling material passes from the melted state to a solid state.

Superalloys
Heat-resistant alloys for high-temperature uses; in general they are alloys of Ni or Co, or of refractory metals such as Nb, Mo, Ta, W, and Zr.

T

Technological revolution
Change of the overall technological systems and its integrations with the social and cultural systems. According to B. Gille, there is a "greater mutation" of this sort when the four fundamental pillars of the technological system are involved, i.e.: information, energy, materials, and techniques having to do with the living world.

Technological transference
Transition of a technological solution (a material or a transformation process) from the manufacturing sectors in which it was developed toward other sectors. The process can be observed both in an entire manufacturing system or in a percolation phenomenon (see **Percolation**). The term is also used, with a similar meaning, in the passage of technological solutions from one country to another at a different level of development.

Tenacity
Property of materials that indicates the mechanical energy needed to break it.

Thermal agitation
Vibration of atoms or molecules from their equilibrium condition. The higher the temperature, the greater the agitation.

Thermal conductivity
Coefficient of thermal flow and temperature gap at the extremities of the material under observation.

Thermal expansion
Expansion caused by an increase in the agitation of atoms due to an increase of thermal energy.

Thermal expansion coefficient
A coefficient with which one can express the dimensional variation that occurs in a material, corresponding to a unit variation in temperature. One can consider both variations in volume or variations in length.

Thermoforming
Forming of a sheet of thermoplastic material through a heat process.

Thermoplastic polymers
Polymers that soften when heated, while they become rigid when cooled. The ri-
gid/soft cycle can be repeated many times.

Thermoset polymers
Polymers that present side bonds in their molecular structure (lattice structure). Therefore, unlike thermoplastic polymers, once they have passed polymerization and attained a certain rigidity, they can no longer be softened or melted.
Semi-finished materials made of thermoset materials can no longer be processed with heat processes, and scraps cannot be recycled.

V

Vacuum forming
Forming a sheet of plastic material through adhesion to a mold by removing the air through the mold itself.

Viscoelasticity
With reference to polymers subjected to a deforming action, this indicates according to which the molecule settle, tending to align with the direction of the stress caused by the deformation itself. This behavior is partially elastic and partially plastic creep, and leads to relaxation of stresses. It is enhanced by heat.

Viscosity
Property that indicates the behavior of a material under stress such that it causes reciprocal creep of its molecules. The coefficient of viscosity represents shear stress and gradient of velocity of creep.

Vulcanization
Treatment necessary to create side bonds between molecular chains of elastomers and give them the required mechanical energies.

Bibliography

Every new book makes its contribution by starting with the reorganization of existing knowledge. In this instance I have used two channels of information and of stimulus. The first is the experience of the people I have come into contact with, and a great quantity of printed paper in a dispersed form: articles in specialized journals, advertisements, working documents. Such sources cannot enter into a bibliography, even though they constitute the principle reference for the knowledge and the technical sensibility on which this book is based.

The second is a group of conceptual instruments that have furnished the key for the interpretation of current technological, social, and cultural transformations. But even here it is impossible to compile an exhaustive bibliography: in the case of a book like *The Material of Invention*, which crosses so many different disciplinary fields, the aim of completeness would result in the citation of an endless number of bibliographic references.

I have chosen, therefore, to renounce the idea of an exhaustive bibliography, proposing instead to present a bibliographical picture of the most important references, the intellectual framework in which I have moved. The bibliography that follows thus does not offer an organic panorama, but rather indicates a route, with all the digressions that every real route brings.

The titles are organized around the major themes that constitute the material or the basis of the subjects treated in this book. Some of the references, because of their content, could be placed in more than one category. I have chosen to include them only once, in reference to the theme to which they have made the greatest contribution.

Finally, I have placed an asterisk next to some titles to indicate that, in these cases, I have a particularly strong cultural debt.

Images of the present

Barthes, Roland. *Mythologies*. Paris: Editions du Seuil, 1957.

Bartolucci, Giuseppe, Marcello Fabbri, Mario Pisani, and Giulio Spinucci, eds. *Paesaggio metropolitano*. Milan: Feltrinelli, 1982.

Baudrillard, Jean. *Pour une critique de l'économie politique du signe*. Paris: Gallimard, 1968.

Baudrillard, Jean. *Le système des objets*. Paris: Denoël/Gonthier, 1968.

Bell, Daniel. *The Coming of the Post Industrial Age*. New York: Basic Books, 1973.

"Informatique matin, midi... et soir!" *Autrement* 37 (February 1982).

Informatique, télématique et vie quotidienne. Proceedings of the international symposium "Informatique et société, 3 vols. Paris: La Documentation Française, 1980.

* Lyotard, Jean-François. *La condition postmoderne*. Paris: Les Editions de Minuit, 1979.

McLuhan, Marshall. *Understanding Media*. New York: McGraw-Hill, 1964.

* Naisbitt, John. *Megatrends*. New York: Warner Books, 1982.

Perec, Georges. *Espèce d'espaces*. Paris: Galilée, 1974.

* Théofilakis, Elie, ed. *Modernes, et après? "Les Immatériaux"*. Paris: Autrement, 1985.

Toffler, Alvin. *Future shock*. London: The Bodley Head, 1970.

Toffler, Alvin. *The Third Wave*. London: Collins, 1980.

Virilio, Paul. *L'Espace critique*. Paris: Christian Bourgois, 1984.

Virilio, Paul. *Vitesse et politique*. Paris: Galilée, 1977.

Tools for interpretation

Bateson, Gregory. *Mind and Nature. A Necessary Unity*. New York: Dutton, 1979.

* Bateson, Gregory. *Steps to an Ecology of Mind*. Novato, Cal.: Chandler and Sharps, 1972.

Chomsky, Noam. *Reflections on Language*. New York: Pantheon, 1975.

Dagognet, François. *Le catalogue de la vie*. Paris: P.U.F., 1970.

* Dagognet, François. *Rématerialiser*. Paris: Librairie philosophique J. Vrin, 1985.

Dagognet, François. *Tableaux et langages de la chimie*. Paris: Editions du Seuil, 1969.

Detienne, Marcel, and Jean-Pierre Vernant. *Les ruses de l'intelligence. La mètis des Grecs*. Paris: Flammarion, 1974.

* Eco, Umberto. *Opera aperta*. Milan: Bompiani, 1962.

Eco, Umberto. *Il segno*. Milan: Mondadori, 1980.

Eco, Umberto. *La struttura assente*. Milan: Bompiani, 1968.

* Mandelbrot, Benoît. *Les objets fractales. Formes, hasard et dimension*. Paris: Flammarion, 1984.

Piaget, Jean. *Six études de psychologie*. Geneva: Gonthier, 1964.

* Prigogine, Ilya, and Isabelle Stengers. *La Nouvelle Alliance. Métamorphose de la science*. Paris: Gallimard, 1979.

Romano, Ruggiero, ed. *Le frontiere del tempo*. Milan: Il Saggiatore, 1981.

* Serres, Michel. *Hermès V. Le passage du Nord-Ouest*. Paris: Les Editions de Minuit, 1980.

Serres, Michel. *La naissance de la physique dans le texte de Lucrèce*. Paris: Les Editions de Minuit, 1977.

Styles of thought

Alexander, Christopher W. *Notes on the Synthesis of the Form*. Cambridge: Harvard University Press, 1964.

Alexander, Christopher W. "Una città non è un albero." In *L'organizzazione della complessità*. Milan: Il Saggiatore, 1977.

* Bocchi, Gianluca, and Mauro Ceruti, eds. *La sfida della complessità*. Milan: Feltrinelli, 1985.

Capra, Fritjof. *The Turning Point. Science, Society and the Rising Culture*. New York: Simon and Schuster, 1982.

* Crozier, Michel, and Erhard Friedberg. *L'acteur et le système*. Paris: Editions du Seuil, 1977.

Elster, Jon. *Ulysses and the Syrens*. New York: Cambridge University Press, 1977.

Gargani, Aldo. *Il sapere senza fondamenti*. Turin: Einaudi, 1975.

Habermas, Jürgen. *Theorie und Praxis*. Neuwied: Luchterhand, 1963.

Habermas, Jürgen and Niklas Luhmann. *Theorie der Gesellschast oder Sozialtechnologie*. Frankfurt: Suhrkamp, 1971.

Hofstadter, Douglas R. *Gödel, Escher, Bach. An Eternal Golden Braid*. New York: Basic Books, 1979.

* Morin, Edgar. *Le methode I. La nature de la nature*. Paris: Editions du Seuil, 1977.

Morin, Edgar. *Pour sortir du Vingtième siècle*. Paris: Nathan, 1981.

* Pardi, Francesco, and Giovan Francesco Lanzara. *L'interpretazione della complessità*. Naples: Guida, 1980.

Pizzorno, Alessandro. "L'incompletezza dei sistemi." In *Razionalità sociale e tecnologie della informazione*, ed. F. Rositi, vol. I, 178. Milan: Edizioni di Comunità, 1973.

Rapoport, Anatol. "General Systems Theory: A Bridge Between Two Cultures." *Behavioral Science Journal of the Society for General Systems Research* 21, no. 4 (July 1976): 234.

Il sapere come rete di modelli. Proceedings of the conference. Modena: Panini, 1981.

* Schön, Donald A. "Generative Metaphor: A Perspective on Problem-Setting in Social Policy." In *Metaphor and Thought*,

ed. A. Ortony, 254-283. New York: Cambridge University Press, 1977.

Searle, John R. *Speech Acts*. New York: Cambridge University Press, 1969.

Simon, Herbert A. *The Science of the Artificial*. Cambridge: MIT Press, 1969.

Simon, Herbert A. "Rational Choice and the Structure of the Environment." *Psychological Review* 63 (1956): 129-138.

Vattimo, Gianni, and Pier Aldo Rovatti, eds. *Il pensiero debole*. Milan: Feltrinelli, 1983.

Models of development

Braudel, Fernand. *Civilisation matérielle et capitalisme, XVe - XVIIIe siècle*. Paris: A. Colin, 1967.

* Braudel, Fernand. *Ecrits sur l'histoire*. Paris: Flammarion, 1969.

Derry, Thomas K, and Trevor I. Williams. *A Short History of Technology*. Oxford: The Clarendon Press, 1960.

Gould, Stephen Jay. *Ever Since Darwin*. New York: Norton and Company, 1977.

* Jacob, François. *Le Jeu des possibles*. Paris: Fayard, 1981.

* Kubler, George. *The Shape of Time*. New Haven: Yale University Press, 1972.

* Kuhn, Thomas S. *The Structure of Scientific Revolutions*. Chicago: The University of Chicago, 1970.

Lazlo, Ervin. *Evolution*. Club of Rome Information Series, no. 3, 1985.

Piaget, Jean, and Rolando Garcia. *Psychogénèse et histoire des sciences*. Paris: Flammarion, 1985.

* Thom, René. *Modèles mathématiques de la morphogénèse*. Paris: 10/18, 1974.

Thoughts on technology

Attali, Jacques. *La parole et l'outil*. Paris: P.U.F., 1975.

Ellul, Jacques. *Le Système technicien*. Paris: Calmann/Léuy, 1977.

Forbes, Robert J. *Man the Maker*. New York: Henry Schuman, 1956.

Gaudin, Thierry. *A l'écoute des silences*. Paris: Gallimard, 1979.

Gaudin, Thierry. *Pouvoirs du rêve*. Neuilly-sur-Seine: Centre de Recherche sur la Culture Technique, 1984.

Giarini, Orio, and Henri Loubergé. *La delusione tecnologica*. Milan: Mondadori, 1978.

Gille, Bertrand. *Les ingénieurs de la Renaissance*. Paris: Editions du Seuil, 1978.

Gille, Bertrand. "Prolégomènes à une histoire des techniques." In *Histoire des Techniques*. Paris: Gallimard, 1978.

Heidegger, Martin. *Vorträge und Aufsätze*. Pfullingen: Verlag Günther Nesker, 1954.

Hottois, Gilbert. *Le signe et la technique*. Paris: Aubier Montaigne, 1984.

* Leroi-Gourhan, André. *Le geste et la parole. Technique et langage*. Paris: Albin Michel, 1964.

* Leroi-Gourhan, André. *L'homme et la matière*. Paris: Albin Michel, 1971.

* Leroi-Gourhan, André. *Milieu et technique*. Paris: Albin Michel, 1973.

* Roqueplo, Philippe. *Penser la technique*. Paris: Editions du Seuil, 1983.

Technology and culture in design

Banham, Reyner. *The Architecture of the Well-Tempered Environment*. London: Architectural Press, 1969.

Banham, Reyner. *Theory and Design in the First Machine Age*. London: Architectural Press, 1960.

* Ban.... André... .. .. Milan: Idea Books, 1981.

* Ciborra, Claudio, and Giovan Francesco Lanzara, eds. *Progettazione delle nuove tecnologie e qualità del lavoro*. Milan: Franco Angeli, 1984.

Ciribini, Giuseppe. *Introduzione alla tecnologia del design*. Milan: Franco Angeli, 1979.

* Ciribini, Giuseppe. *Tecnologia e progetto*. Turin: C.E.L.I.D., 1984.

* Dupire, Alain, Bernard Hamburger, Jean-Claude Paul, Jean-Michel Savignat, and Alain Thiebaut. *Deux essais sur la construction*. Bruxelles-Liège: Pierre Mardaga, 1981.

* Giedion, Siegfried. *Mechanization Takes Command*. New York: Oxford University Press, 1948.

Hamburger, Bernard, and Alain Thiebaut. *Ornement, architecture & industrie*. Bruxelles-Liège: Pierre Mardaga, 1983.
Katz, Sylvia. *Classic Plastics*. London: Thames and Hudson, 1984.

Katz, Sylvia. *Plastics. Design and Materials*. London: Studio Vista, 1978.

Le Corbusier. *Vers une architecture*. Paris: Crès, 1924.

Maldonado, Tomás. *La speranza progettuale*. Turin: Einaudi, 1971.

Maldonado, Tomás, ed. *Tecnica e cultura*. Milan: Feltrinelli, 1979.

Santachiara, Denis, ed. *Le neomerce*. Milan: Electa/Triennale di Milano, 1985.

Trini Castelli, Clino. *Il lingotto primario*. Milan: Arcadia, 1985.

* Venturi, Robert. *Complexity and Contradiction in Architecture*. New York: The Museum of Modern Art, 1977.

The development of materials and manufacturing processes

* Ancori, Bernard. "Vers une chimie de la fonction?" Séminaire F.A.S.T. Strasbourg, April 1981. Doc. no. 7.

Associazione italiana di scienza e tecnologia delle macromolecole. *Fondamenti della trasformazione dei materiali polimerici/Polymer Processing. Proceedings of the conference at Gargano, 23-27 May 1983*. Associazione italiana di scienza e tecnologia delle macromolecole, 1983.

Astarita, Giovanni, and L. Nicolais. *Polymer Processing and Properties*. New York: Plenum, 1984.

Beck, Ronald D. *Plastic Product Design*. New York: Van Nostrand Reinhold, 1980.

Budworth, D. W. *An Introduction to Ceramic Science*. Oxford: Pergamon Press, 1975.

Chandler, M. *Ceramics in the Modern World*. Garden City, N.Y.: Doubleday, 1968.

Clauser, Henry R. *Industrial and Engineering Materials*. Tokyo: McGraw-Hill Kogakusha, 1975.

* Cohendet, Patrick. *"Genie des matériaux et transformation des processus de production."* In *Prospective 2005, Colloque national, Paris, 27-28 novembre 1985; Sept explorations de l'avenir. Rapports des missions de prospective*. Report No. 2. Vol. 1. Commissariat général du plan. Paris: Centre national de la recherche scientifique, n.d.

Colombo, Roberto L. *Le caratteristiche meccaniche dei materiali*. Florence: Sansoni, 1975.

* Colombo, Umberto. *"A View Point on Innovation and the Chemical Industry."* Research Policy 9, no. 3 (1980): 204.

Colombo, Umberto, and Giuseppe Lanzavecchia. *Scienza dei materiali. I materiali nella società moderna*. Florence: Sansoni, 1974.

Dent, Roger. *Principles of Pneumatic Architecture*. London: Architectural Press, 1971.

Flinn, Richard A., and Paul K. Trojan. *Engineering Materials and Their Applications*. Boston: Houghton-Mifflin, 1975.

Gordon, James E., ed. *Structures: or Why Things Don't Fall Down*. New York City: Plenum, 1978.

Grandou, Pierre, and Paul Pastour, eds. *Peintures et vernis*. Paris: Hermann, 1969.

Guinier, André. *La structure de la matière: du ciel bleu à la matière plastique*. Paris: Hachett, 1980.

Hayden, H.W., ed. "Mechanical Behaviour." In *The Structure .... Properties of Materials*, ed. J. Wulff, vol. III. New York: Wiley, 1964-66.

* Larue de Tournemine, Régis, ed. *L'innovation*. Paris: La Documentation Française, 1983.

Levy, Sidney, and John Harry Dubois. *Plastics Products Design Engineering Handbook*. 2nd ed. New York-London: Chapman and Hall, 1984.

Majowiecki, Massimo. *Tensostrutture: progetto e verifica*. Milan: CISIA, 1985.

Malone, F. J. T. *Glass in the Modern World*. Garden City, N.Y.: Doubleday, 1968.

Miles, Lawrence D. *Techniques of Value Analysis and Engineering*. 2nd ed. New York: McGraw-Hill, 1972.

Mohr, J. Gilbert. *SPI Handbook of Technology and Engineering of Reinforced Plastic/Composites*. New York: Van Nostrand Reinhold, 1973.

Moore, G. R., and Kline, D. E. *Properties and Processing of Polymers for Engineers*. Englewood Cliffs, N.J.: Prentice Hall, 1984.

Mott, N. F., and H. Jones. *The Theory of the Properties of Metals and Alloys*. New York: Dover, 1958.

Natta, Giulio, and Mario Farina. *Stereochimica: molecule in 3D*. Milan: Mondadori, 1968.

Nicodemi, Walter, and Raffaello Zoia. *Metallurgia applicata*. Milan: Tamburini, 1985.

Norton, Frederick. *Fine Ceramics*. 2nd ed. Reading, Mass.: Addison-Wesley, 1974.

The Open University. *An Introduction to Materials*. Philadelphia: The Open University Press, 1973.

Papon, Pierre. *Pour une prospective de la science*. Paris: Seghers, 1983.

Parratt, N. S. *Fibre-Reinforced Technology*. London: Van Nostrand Reinhold, 1972.

Pearson. J.R.A. *Mechanics of Polymer Processing*. New York: Elsevier Science Publishing Co., 1985.

* "La révolution de l'intelligence." *Sciences & Techniques*, special issue (March 1985).

Reyne, Maurice. *La recherche de l'économie dans la conception technique*. Paris: Dunod, 1970.

Rogers, B. *The Story of Metals*. 2nd ed. Cambridge: MIT Press, 1965.

Seferis, J. C., and P. S. Theocaris. *Interrelations between Processing, Structure and Properties of Polymeric Material. Proceedings of the IUPAC International Symposium, Athens, August 29-September 2, 1982*. New York: Elsevier Science Publishing Co., 1984.

* SEST. *Table ronde sur les matériaux*. Paris, 13 December 1984. Euroconsult, n.p., n.d.

Thomas, John A. G., ed. *Energy Analysis*. Boulder: IPC Science and Technology Press, Guildford/Westview Press, 1977.

Van Vlack, Lawrence H. *Materials Technology*. Reading, Mass.: Addison Wesley, 1973.

Wai-Chung Chow, William. *Cost Reduction in Product Design*. New York: Van Nostrand Reinhold, 1978.

Photographic credits: page 28 (a), IBM Italia, Milan; page 28 (b), Santi Caleca, Milan; page 30 (b), Mauro Panzeri, Milan; page 33, John Ahearn (*We Are Family*, 1982-83); page 34, Walt Disney Prod.; page 38, Claes Oldenburg (*Soft Typewriter*, 1963); page 50, Giulio Einaudi Publishers, Turin; page 62, Richard Long (*England*, 1967); page 63, Walt Disney Prod.; page 66, Armando Testa (*Plast 22*); page 79 (c,d,e), IBM Italia, Milan; page 84 (a), CWP; pages 92 and 93 (b), Institut für Leichte Flächentragwerke, Stuttgart; page 93 (a), Aux temps de l'Espace; page 96 (a), *Modo* 64, November 1983; page 96 (b), *Ornement Architecture Industrie*; page 99, ICI; page 101 (a, b), Girella; pages 108 and 109, *Architecture d'Aujourd'hui*, October 1982; pages 110-111 (a), Editorial Gustavo Gili; page 111 (b), SD 1981; pages 112-113 (a,b), *Architecture d'Aujourd'hui*, February 1985; page 113 (c), *Modo* 59, May 1983; page 114 (a) and 115 (b), *ID*, March 1985; page 115 (c), *Form* 107, 1984; page 132, Cambridge University Press; page 134 (b), Electa, Milan; page 140 (b), *Industrial Design Magazine*; page 154 (d), Dilmos, Milan; page 203 (b,c), CWP; page 205, Brian Griffin (*Rocket Man*).

The Barbareschi studio was responsible for part of the Montedison documentation.

255

Photosetting: Bassoli Spa, Milano
Separator: Bassoli Spa, Milano
Printed by Arti Grafiche Varesine, Casciago (Varese): January 1989